Paul and Judaism at the End of History

The apostle Paul was a Jew. He was born, lived, undertook his apostolic work, and died within the milieu of ancient Judaism. And yet, many readers have found, and continue to find, Paul's thought so radical, so Christian, even so anti-Jewish – despite the fact that it, too, is Jewish through and through. This paradox, and the question how we are to explain it, are the foci of Matthew Novenson's groundbreaking book. The solution, says the author, lies in Paul's particular understanding of time. This too is altogether Jewish, with the twist that Paul sees the end of history as present, not future. In the wake of Christ's resurrection, Jews are perfected in righteousness and – like the angels – enabled to live forever, in fulfilment of God's ancient promises to the patriarchs. What is more, gentiles are included in the same pneumatic existence promised to the Jews. This peculiar combination of ethnicity and eschatology yields something that looks not quite like Judaism or Christianity as we are used to thinking of them.

MATTHEW V. NOVENSON is Helen H. P. Manson Professor of New Testament at Princeton Theological Seminary. He is the author of, among other works, *Christ among the Messiahs* (2012), *The Grammar of Messianism* (2017), and *Paul, Then and Now* (2022).

Paul and Judaism at the End of History

MATTHEW V. NOVENSON
Princeton Theological Seminary

Shaftesbury Road, Cambridge CB2 8EA, United Kingdom

One Liberty Plaza, 20th Floor, New York, NY 10006, USA

477 Williamstown Road, Port Melbourne, VIC 3207, Australia

314–321, 3rd Floor, Plot 3, Splendor Forum, Jasola District Centre, New Delhi – 110025, India

103 Penang Road, #05-06/07, Visioncrest Commercial, Singapore 238467

Cambridge University Press is part of Cambridge University Press & Assessment, a department of the University of Cambridge.

We share the University's mission to contribute to society through the pursuit of education, learning and research at the highest international levels of excellence.

www.cambridge.org
Information on this title: www.cambridge.org/9781316519844

DOI: 10.1017/9781009019354

© Cambridge University Press & Assessment 2024

This publication is in copyright. Subject to statutory exception and to the provisions of relevant collective licensing agreements, no reproduction of any part may take place without the written permission of Cambridge University Press & Assessment.

When citing this work, please include a reference to the DOI 10.1017/9781009019354

First published 2024

A catalogue record for this publication is available from the British Library

Library of Congress Cataloging-in-Publication Data
Names: Novenson, Matthew V., author.
Title: Paul and Judaism at the end of history / Matthew V. Novenson, Princeton Theological Seminary.
Description: Cambridge, United Kingdom : Cambridge University Press, 2024. | Includes bibliographical references and index.
Identifiers: LCCN 2023058132 (print) | LCCN 2023058133 (ebook) | ISBN 9781316519844 (hardback) | ISBN 9781009011228 (paperback) | ISBN 9781009019354 (epub)
Subjects: LCSH: Bible. Epistles of Paul–Theology. | Eschatology–Biblical teaching. | Paul, the Apostle, Saint–Relations with Jews.
Classification: LCC BS2655.E7 N68 2024 (print) | LCC BS2655.E7 (ebook) | DDC 227/.06–dc23/eng/20240426
LC record available at https://lccn.loc.gov/2023058132
LC ebook record available at https://lccn.loc.gov/2023058133

ISBN 978-1-316-51984-4 Hardback

Cambridge University Press & Assessment has no responsibility for the persistence or accuracy of URLs for external or third-party internet websites referred to in this publication and does not guarantee that any content on such websites is, or will remain, accurate or appropriate.

For Hans, Levi, and Ben
Ὦ παῖ, ζήτει σεαυτῷ βασιλείαν ἴσην· Μακεδονία γάρ σε οὐ χωρεῖ.
–Plutarch, *Alexander* 6

You say the whole world's ending; honey, it already did.
—Bo Burnham

Contents

Acknowledgments		*page* viii
List of Abbreviations		x
1	The Christian Problem of Paul and Judaism	1
2	Paul's Former Occupation in *Ioudaismos*	29
3	Who Says Justification from Works of the Law?	50
4	Paul versus the Gentiles	77
5	The Legalism of Paul	111
6	The Ethnic Chauvinism of Paul	135
7	Carnal Israel	160
8	Liberty and Justice for All	187
9	The End of the Law and the Last Man	209
Bibliography		244
Index of Subjects		285
Index of Ancient Sources		289
Index of Modern Authors		299

Acknowledgments

Had it not been for Mark Elliott's kind invitation to give a plenary address to the 2012 St Andrews conference on Galatians and Christian theology, I might never have conceived the idea for this book. But my paper for that conference, included below in revised form as Chapter 2 "Paul's Former Occupation in *Ioudaismos*," launched my thinking in the direction of the argument here advanced. (Thanks to Baker Academic for permission to re-use and expand my essay from that conference volume: Excerpt from *Galatians and Christian Theology* by Mark W. Elliott, Scott J. Hafemann, N. T. Wright, and John Frederick, eds., copyright © 2015. Used by permission of Baker Academic, a division of Baker Publishing Group.)

The other chapters contained herein were developed in the intervening years, most of them initially as trial balloons at a number of seminars and conferences. In particular, the University of Edinburgh funded me for two research trips – one to the New York metro area in early 2017 and another to the Chicago metro area in early 2020 – which were the occasions for most of the writing of the book. I am very grateful to then-Head of School Helen Bond for her support in this, and to the good colleagues at Yale, Columbia, Princeton, Princeton Theological Seminary, University of Chicago, Loyola University Chicago, and Notre Dame for helping me workshop these ideas. Back home in Europe, I further honed the argument in very congenial seminars in Edinburgh, Glasgow, Aberdeen, Durham, Oxford, Cambridge, Sheffield, Exeter, Vienna, Bern, and Lund. Finally, several topical conferences afforded me opportunity to work out particular pieces of this research: Frantisek Abel's Slovakian government-funded research project on "Paul within Judaism: New Perspectives" at Comenius University Bratislava; a Swedish Research Council-funded project on "Negotiating Identities" based at Lund University and headed by Anders Runesson, Cecilia Wassen, Karin Zetterholm, and Magnus Zetterholm; and the Pauline Epistles, Pauline Theology, and

Acknowledgments ix

Paul within Judaism program units of the Society of Biblical Literature. My Edinburgh graduate students have debated me over most of my arguments in our regular cohort meetings. Ed Kessler and Esther-Miriam Wagner invited me to do a stint as visiting fellow at the Woolf Institute, University of Cambridge, providing me time and space to get the book over the finish line. Beatrice Rehl of Cambridge University Press expertly shepherded the project through from beginning to end. Content manager Bethany Johnson, project manager Vinithan Sethumadhavan, and copyeditor Angela Roberts ensured that the whole thing came together according to plan. James Carleton Paget, Paula Fredriksen, Matthew Thiessen, and the anonymous reviewers at the Press all did me the great kindness of reading through the whole manuscript with critical red pens in hand. Sage feedback from colleagues in all of these settings has yielded a far better book than would have otherwise been the case. How good a book is of course for the reader to decide.

I am a little bit proud of this book, but I am enormously, extravagantly proud of my children. I dedicate the book with love to Hans, Levi, and Ben.

Abbreviations

Abbreviations – including those frequently occurring ones in the list below – follow the systems used in *The SBL Handbook of Style*, 2nd ed. and *Oxford Classical Dictionary*, 4th ed.

AB	Anchor Bible
AGJU	Arbeiten zur Geschichte des antiken Judentums und des Urchristentums
AJEC	Ancient Judaism and Early Christianity
AJR	*Ancient Jew Review*
ANTC	Abingdon New Testament Commentaries
ANF	*Ante-Nicene Fathers*
APhR	Ancient Philosophy and Religion
AYB	Anchor Yale Bible
AYBRL	Anchor Yale Bible Reference Library
BBR	*Bulletin of Biblical Research*
BDAG	Danker, Frederick W., Walter Bauer, William F. Arndt, and F. Wilbur Gingrich. *Greek-English Lexicon of the New Testament and Other Early Christian Literature*. 3rd ed. Chicago: University of Chicago Press, 2000.
BETL	Bibliotheca Ephemeridum Theologicarum Lovaniensium
Bib	*Biblica*
BibInt	*Biblical Interpretation*
BNTC	Black's New Testament Commentaries
BRLJ	Brill Reference Library of Judaism
BTB	*Biblical Theology Bulletin*
BZNW	Beihefte zur Zeitschrift für die neutestamentliche Wissenschaft

CBR	*Currents in Biblical Research*
CBQ	*Catholic Biblical Quarterly*
CEJL	Commentaries on Early Jewish Literature
CMG	Corpus Medicorum Graecorum
ConBibNT	Coniecteana Biblica New Testament Series
CRBR	*Critical Review of Books in Religion*
CRINT	Compendium Rerum Iudaicarum ad Novum Testamentum
DJD	Discoveries in the Judaean Desert
DSD	*Dead Sea Discoveries*
EC	*Early Christianity*
ESCJ	Études sur le christianisme et le judaïsme
ESRA	Edinburgh Studies in Religion in Antiquity
EstBib	*Estudios bíblicos*
EvQ	*Evangelical Quarterly*
ExpTim	*Expository Times*
HBT	*Horizons in Biblical Theology*
HR	*History of Religions*
HTR	*Harvard Theological Review*
HTS	Harvard Theological Studies
ICC	International Critical Commentary
IJO	Inscriptiones Judaicae Orientis
IJST	*International Journal of Systematic Theology*
JAJ	*Journal of Ancient Judaism*
JAJSup	Journal of Ancient Judaism Supplements
JBL	*Journal of Biblical Literature*
JCP	Jewish and Christian Perspectives
JDT	*Jahrbücher für deutsche Theologie*
JECS	*Journal of Early Christian Studies*
JES	*Journal of Ecumenical Studies*
JIWE	Jewish Inscriptions of Western Europe
JJMJS	*Journal of the Jesus Movement in Its Jewish Setting*
JJS	*Journal of Jewish Studies*
JQR	*Jewish Quarterly Review*
JR	*Journal of Religion*

JSJ	*Journal for the Study of Judaism*
JSJSup	Journal for the Study of Judaism Supplements
JSNT	*Journal for the Study of the New Testament*
JSNTSup	Journal for the Study of the New Testament Supplements
JSP	*Journal for the Study of the Pseudepigrapha*
JSPL	*Journal for the Study of Paul and His Letters*
JSQ	*Jewish Studies Quarterly*
JTS	*Journal of Theological Studies*
KD	*Kerygma und Dogma*
KJV	King James Version
LARB	*Los Angeles Review of Books*
LCL	Loeb Classical Library
LHBOTS	Library of Hebrew Bible/Old Testament Studies
LNTS	Library of New Testament Studies
LSJ	Liddell, Henry George, Robert Scott, and Henry Stuart Jones. *A Greek-English Lexicon*. 9th ed. with revised supplement. Oxford: Clarendon, 1996.
LSTS	Library of Second Temple Studies
LXX	Septuagint
MTSR	*Method and Theory in the Study of Religion*
MTSRSup	Method and Theory in the Study of Religion Supplements
NA28	Nestle-Aland. *Novum Testamentum Graece*. 28th ed. Stuttgart: Deutsche Bibelgesellschaft, 2012.
NASB	New American Standard Bible
Neot	*Neotestamentica*
NETS	New English Translation of the Septuagint
NIV	New International Version
NovT	*Novum Testamentum*
NovTSup	Novum Testamentum Supplements
NRSV	New Revised Standard Version
NTOA	Novum Testamentum et Orbis Antiquus
NTS	*New Testament Studies*

List of Abbreviations

OCDSS	Oxford Commentary on the Dead Sea Scrolls
OCM	Oxford Classical Monographs
OECS	Oxford Early Christian Studies
OED	*Oxford English Dictionary*
OECT	Oxford Early Christian Texts
OG	Old Greek
OTP	Charlesworth, James H., ed. *Old Testament Pseudepigrapha*. 2 vols. New York: Doubleday, 1983–1985.
RBL	*Review of Biblical Literature*
RevBib	*Revue Biblique*
RevQ	*Revue de Qumran*
RSR	*Religious Studies Review*
RSV	Revised Standard Version
SacPag	Sacra Pagina
SBL	Society of Biblical Literature
SBLDS	Society of Biblical Literature Dissertation Series
SBLSS	Society of Biblical Literature Semeia Studies
SCE	*Studies in Christian Ethics*
SD	Studies and Documents
SJLA	Studies in Judaism in Late Antiquity
SJT	*Scottish Journal of Theology*
SNTSMS	Society for New Testament Studies Monograph Series
SPhA	*Studia Philonica Annual*
SR	*Studies in Religion/Sciences Religieuses*
STDJ	Studies on the Texts of the Desert of Judah
TBN	Themes in Biblical Narrative
TJT	*Toronto Journal of Theology*
TSAJ	Texts and Studies in Ancient Judaism
TSMEMJ	Texts and Studies in Medieval and Early Modern Judaism
TynBul	*Tyndale Bulletin*
TZTh	*Tübinger Zeitschrift für Theologie*
VC	*Vigiliae Christianae*
WTJ	*Westminster Theological Journal*

WUNT	Wissenschaftliche Untersuchungen zum Neuen Testament
YJS	Yale Judaica Series
ZNW	*Zeitschrift für die neutestamentliche Wissenschaft*
ZPE	*Zeitschrift für Papyrologie und Epigraphik*

1 | The Christian Problem of Paul and Judaism

One often hears it said that the apostle Paul's discourse about the Jewish law – "Paul and the law" or "Paul and Judaism," in industry-standard shorthand – is one of those classically intractable problems, like the problem of evil in philosophical theology or cold fusion in nuclear physics. In fact, however, it is very simple. Simple, but not easy, because the solution, although it is historically clear and compelling (as I shall argue in this book), has proved existentially intolerable to many of Paul's readers. This is a shame, since it has effectively rendered unthinkable to us moderns what is, for its part, a very interesting, important idea, namely: that the world itself came to an end in the first century of the Roman Empire.

According to one Jewish writer from this period, when God sends his son the messiah in the fullness of time, the messiah's job is: to die, so that all his people can participate in his death, and then to effect the resurrection of the dead and the new creation. The Jewish writer I mean is the anonymous author of the apocalypse 4 Ezra (7:28–32),[1] although every word of that summary is also true of his near-contemporary Paul. Both 4 Ezra and Paul think that the messiah must come and die to put an end to the present age and bring about the new creation. Unlike 4 Ezra, however, Paul thinks that the messiah has just now – within his, Paul's, own lifetime – come and died. Hence, Paul reasons, the end of the age has come, and the new creation is here. This idea is not just implied but expressly stated all over Paul's

---

[1] "My son the messiah shall be revealed with those who are with him, and those who remain shall rejoice 400 years. And after these years my son the messiah shall die, and all who draw human breath. And the world shall be turned back to primeval silence for seven days, as it was at the first beginnings, so that no one shall be left. And after seven days the world, which is not yet awake, shall be roused, and that which is corruptible shall perish. And the earth shall give up those who are asleep in it." (4 Ezra 7:28–32; Latin version trans. Metzger in Charlesworth, *OTP*)

letters. The ends of the ages have come (1 Cor 10:11). The form of the cosmos is passing away (1 Cor 7:31). Christ himself was the last man (ὁ ἔσχατος Ἀδάμ, 1 Cor 15:45), the last mere mortal. His resurrection during the reign of Tiberius triggered the resurrection of all the righteous, so that from the 30s CE onward all God's people will enjoy the life everlasting promised to the patriarchs. Everything Paul says about the Jewish law follows from this premise.

So I shall argue in this book. To get there, we shall have to look closely at Paul's letters (and a number of other ancient Jewish texts) on the themes of Jewishness, gentileness, and time – or, in other words, ethnicity and eschatology. In relation to the long, fraught history of research, my goal is to explain why Paul's thought, which in its main lines is so conventionally Jewish (one God, his temple in Jerusalem, the promise to father Abraham, the giving of the Torah to Moses, the coming messiah, etc.), has also struck so many readers as so radical, so Christian, even so anti-Jewish. The answer lies in Paul's particular understanding of time, which is also quite conventionally Jewish (the present age, the end of the age, the day of the lord, etc.), except that Paul perceives the end of the age as present, not future.[2] If understood in a sufficiently vague way, this claim is perhaps relatively uncontroversial. But in the precise way that I mean it, it is quite different from any interpretation of Paul currently on offer. Hence this book.

Ethnicity and Eschatology

In the refrain of his 1889 poem "The Ballad of East and West,"[3] Rudyard Kipling, literary lion of the late British Empire, wrote what would become one of his best-known lines:

Oh, East is East, and West is West, and never the twain shall meet,

---

[2] We now have several recent, thoughtful reconsiderations of Paul's understanding of time, in particular Jamie Davies, "Why Paul Doesn't Mention the Age to Come," *SJT* 74 (2021): 199–208; and, differently, L. Ann Jervis, *Paul and Time: Life in the Temporality of Christ* (Grand Rapids, MI: Baker, 2024). My quarrel with both of these otherwise excellent treatments is their evasion of the *skandalon* of imminent eschatology in Paul's letters.

[3] First published in the *Pioneer* (2 December 1889), then anthologized in Kipling's *Barrack-Room Ballads and Other Verses* (London: Methuen, 1892).

Which is followed immediately by a lesser known but equally significant line:

Till Earth and Sky stand presently at God's great Judgment Seat.

Commenting on this poem, Kingsley Amis once wrote that Kipling was indeed a racist, but less of a racist than any other English writer of his age.[4] I am not competent to judge Amis's defense of Kipling.[5] But I do find "The Ballad of East and West" a helpful starting point for considering the racial attitudes not of Kipling, but of the apostle Paul.

Or, perhaps better, "ethnic attitudes." "Racial" is arguably not quite right for an ancient such as Paul, suggesting, as I think it does nowadays, both a sheen of scientism and a preoccupation with skin color that are part of our modern inheritance.[6] But "ethnic" (from Greek *ethnos*, a word Paul uses some forty-five times in his small

---

[4] Kingsley Amis, *Rudyard Kipling and His World* (London: Thames & Hudson, 1975), 53–54: "Kipling was a racialist, or racist. The White Man's Burden is indeed a burden, an arduous duty, not the inheritance of a natural privilege, and the white men must carry it not because they are white but because they are qualified... Most of the ignorant castigation of Kipling as a racialist in the full aggressive sense comes from a single famous line of verse quoted out of context: *Oh, East is East and West is West and never the twain shall meet*, which is followed by the qualification: *Till Earth and Sky stand presently at God's great Judgment Seat*; which in turn leads to the antithesis: *But there is neither East nor West, Border, nor Breed, nor Birth, When two strong men stand face to face, though they come from the ends of the Earth!* This, however, is not a complete antithesis. What about more than two men, or not-so-strong men, or men just standing about instead of face to face? The twain shall meet only under exceptional conditions. Yet meet they shall. Ifs and buts are bound to clog any treatment of this matter. All that is clear is that Kipling understood and honoured men of other races more deeply than any other English writer, as a reading of *Kim* will suggest."

[5] Though Edward Said, Harish Trivedi, and Bart Moore-Gilbert are. See Edward W. Said, "Introduction," in Rudyard Kipling, *Kim* (London: Penguin, 1987), 7–46; Harish Trivedi, "Reading Kipling in India," in *The Cambridge Companion to Rudyard Kipling*, ed. Howard J. Booth (Cambridge: Cambridge University Press, 2011), 187–199; Bart Moore-Gilbert, "Kipling and Postcolonial Literature," in *Cambridge Companion to Kipling*, 155–168.

[6] A modern inheritance detailed by Robert Wald Sussman, *The Myth of Race: The Troubling Persistence of an Unscientific Idea* (Cambridge, MA: Harvard University Press, 2014). Admittedly, a case can be made for (suitably disciplined) talk of "race" and "racism" in antiquity, as in Benjamin Isaac, *The Invention of Racism in Classical Antiquity* (Princeton: Princeton University Press, 2004); and Denise Kimber Buell, *Why This New Race: Ethnic Reasoning in Early Christianity* (New York: Columbia University Press, 2005). But I prefer to follow Buell's subtitle in speaking instead of "*ethnic* reasoning."

corpus of letters) is just right.[7] Following recent, creative theoretical work by Denise Kimber Buell, Caroline Johnson Hodge, Cavan Concannon, Adi Ophir, and Ishay Rosen-Zvi, among others, I am interested in the way Paul thinks ethnicity – in particular Jewishness and gentileness – in light of his belief in the imminent end of the world as he knows it.[8]

I use the term "Jewishness" advisedly here. Part of the argument of this book is that Paul does not isolate and reify "Judaism" as a thing outside himself on which he could render judgment. (Hence the fatal flaw in the many studies of what interpreters have called "Paul's critique of Judaism.") Judaism is the air Paul breathes, so to speak, the water he swims in. He does not stand in a subject-object relation to it.[9] Most later Christians *did* and *do* stand in a subject-object relation to Judaism; hence their mistaken reading of the apostle as if he did too. But if we think, instead, of "Jewishness" in the sense Shaye Cohen sketches in his *Beginnings of Jewishness*, then we can get better historical purchase on a number of difficult texts in Paul's letters. Cohen summarizes:

The Jews (Judaeans) of antiquity constituted an *ethnos*, an ethnic group. They were a named group, attached to a specific territory, whose members shared a sense of common origins, claimed a common and distinctive history and destiny, possessed one or more distinctive characteristics, and felt a sense of collective uniqueness and solidarity... The most distinctive of the distinctive characteristics of the Jews was the manner in which they worshiped their God, what we today would call their religion... [But] for ancient Greeks and

---

[7] Ethnicity is no less complicated a concept than race – see in particular Rogers Brubaker, *Ethnicity without Groups* (Cambridge, MA: Harvard University Press, 2004); Rogers Brubaker, *Grounds for Difference* (Cambridge, MA: Harvard University Press, 2015) – but for my particular purposes it is less prone to mislead.

[8] Caroline Johnson Hodge, *If Sons Then Heirs: A Study of Kinship and Ethnicity in the Letters of Paul* (Oxford: Oxford University Press, 2007); Cavan W. Concannon, *When You Were Gentiles: Specters of Ethnicity in Roman Corinth and Paul's Corinthian Correspondence* (New Haven: Yale University Press, 2014); Adi Ophir and Ishay Rosen-Zvi, *Goy: Israel's Multiple Others and the Birth of the Gentile* (Oxford: Oxford University Press, 2018). Also very helpful here are the essays in *Ethnicity, Race, Religion: Identities and Ideologies in Early Jewish and Christian Texts and in Modern Biblical Interpretation*, ed. Katherine M. Hockey and David G. Horrell (London: T&T Clark, 2018).

[9] On this essential point, see in particular Matthew Thiessen, *A Jewish Paul: The Messiah's Herald to the Gentiles* (Grand Rapids, MI: Baker, 2023).

Ethnicity and Eschatology

contemporary social scientists, "religion" is only one of many items that make a culture or a group distinctive. Perhaps, then, we should translate *Ioudaismos* not "Judaism" but "Jewishness."[10]

I actually do not think that the Greek word Ἰουδαϊσμός (*Ioudaismos*) itself means either "Judaism" or "Jewishness"; so I argue in Chapter 2. But Cohen's larger point that we should think of ancient Jews as sharing a sense of Jewishness (including ancestry, homeland, god, cult, etc.), as Romans did Romanness or Gauls Gaulishness, is well made in its own right and helpful for thinking the case of Paul.

Many, many books have been written on the subject of Paul and *Judaism*, but as I argue below, most of these books are predicated on a category mistake, or several category mistakes, in fact.[11] Recent research, better attuned to Paul's own ethnic reasoning, has tended to focus on gentiles and gentileness in the letters[12] – and rightly so, since Paul styles himself apostle to the gentiles and addresses his letters to gentiles. This recent research is all for the good, but it effectively leaves Jewishness in Paul unexplored (often, one suspects, in a spirit of polite avoidance).[13] A few studies have wanted to correct the recent

---

[10] Shaye J. D. Cohen, *The Beginnings of Jewishness: Boundaries, Varieties, Uncertainties* (Berkeley: University of California Press, 2001), 7–8.

[11] To footnote them all would be overkill. But see, e.g., Henry St. John Thackeray, *The Relation of St. Paul to Contemporary Jewish Thought* (New York: Macmillan, 1900); W. D. Davies, *Paul and Rabbinic Judaism: Some Rabbinic Elements in Pauline Theology* (London: SPCK, 1948); E. P. Sanders, *Paul and Palestinian Judaism: A Comparison of Patterns of Religion* (Philadelphia: Fortress, 1977); Gerd Lüdemann, *Paulus und das Judentum* (Munich: Kaiser, 1983); Timo Laato, *Paul and Judaism: An Anthropological Approach* (Atlanta: Scholars Press, 1995); Preston M. Sprinkle, *Paul and Judaism Revisited: A Study of Divine and Human Agency in Salvation* (Downers Grove, IL: InterVarsity, 2013).

[12] E.g., Terence L. Donaldson, *Paul and the Gentiles: Remapping the Apostle's Convictional World* (Minneapolis: Fortress, 1997); Matthew Thiessen, *Paul and the Gentile Problem* (Oxford: Oxford University Press, 2016); Paula Fredriksen, *Paul: The Pagans' Apostle* (New Haven: Yale University Press, 2017). On the ancient Jewish concept of gentileness (e.g., *giyut goyim*, "the gentileness of gentiles," in *Sifre Numbers* 158 on Num 31:23), see Vered Noam, "The Gentileness of Gentiles: Two Approaches to the Impurity of Non-Jews," in *Halakhah in Light of Epigraphy*, ed. Albert I. Baumgarten et al., JAJSup 3 (Göttingen: Vandenhoeck & Ruprecht, 2011), 27–41.

[13] E.g., John G. Gager, *Reinventing Paul* (Oxford: Oxford University Press, 2000), 147: "Whatever Paul understood by Peter's gospel to the circumcised (Gal 2.7), Paul preached his own gospel to the uncircumcised... [Regarding the former,] we do not know." Gager is quite right about Paul's gentile audience, but we *can*,

preoccupation with gentiles in Paul by pleading for the more theologically useful category of the *human*.[14] There is something to this impulse, but in my view, it too hastily skips over Paul's demonstrable concern with Jewishness and gentileness, which were theologically significant to him in a way they simply have not been to (gentile) Christian thinkers from the second century to the present. So we need an account of Jewishness in Paul. Not of "Paul and the Jews," since, unlike most Christian thinkers through the centuries, Paul did not perceive "the Jews" as a problem, or even as an entity outside himself.[15] And not of "Paul and Judaism," since, unlike most Christian thinkers through the centuries, Paul did not perceive "Judaism" as a rival religion, or even as a discrete thing. I am not aware of any account quite like what I am describing, so I have tried to give one in this book.

Thus far ethnicity; now to comment briefly on eschatology. My claim is that what interpreters have mistakenly called "Paul's critique of Judaism" is actually just a feature of Paul's imminent eschatology, which is to say, his very particular understanding of time. There has, of course, been more than ample research on Paul's eschatology, much of which I find very helpful and discuss, *passim*, in the chapters that follow.[16] But a common (which is not to say ubiquitous)

I think, say more about what Paul understood by "the gospel for the circumcision" if we are willing to consider the question.

[14] See especially Jonathan A. Linebaugh, "Announcing the Human: Rethinking the Relationship between Wisdom of Solomon 13–15 and Romans 1:18–2:11," NTS 37 (2011): 214–237; Jonathan A. Linebaugh, *God, Grace, and Righteousness in Wisdom of Solomon and Paul's Letter to the Romans*, NovTSup 152 (Leiden: Brill, 2013); and, differently, Susan Grove Eastman, *Paul and the Person: Reframing Paul's Anthropology* (Grand Rapids, MI: Eerdmans, 2017).

[15] Cf. the classic cases explored by Robert L. Wilken, *John Chrysostom and the Jews: Rhetoric and Reality in the Late 4th Century* (Berkeley: University of California Press, 1983); and Paula Fredriksen, *Augustine and the Jews: A Christian Defense of Jews and Judaism* (New Haven: Yale University Press, 2008).

[16] E.g., Richard Kabisch, *Die Eschatologie des Paulus* (Göttingen: Vandenhoeck & Ruprecht, 1893); Geerhardus Vos, *The Pauline Eschatology* (Grand Rapids, MI: Baker, 1930); John S. Mbiti, *New Testament Eschatology in an African Background* (Oxford: Oxford University Press, 1971); L. Joseph Kreitzer, *Jesus and God in Paul's Eschatology*, JSNTSup 19 (Sheffield: Sheffield Academic, 1987); Joseph Plevnik, "Paul's Eschatology," *TJT* 6 (1990): 86–99; Joost Holleman, *Resurrection and Parousia: A Traditio-Historical Study of Paul's Eschatology in 1 Corinthians 15*, NovTSup 84 (Leiden: Brill, 1996); Yon-Gyong Kwon, *Eschatology in Galatians*, WUNT 2/183 (Tübingen: Mohr Siebeck,

problem in this research is a tendency – characteristic of what Stanley Stowers calls "academic Christian theological modernism"[17] – to assume that Paul stands in the same relation to eschatology that his modern (mostly Christian) interpreters do, as if both Paul and, say, Geerhardus Vos were reflecting theologically on the same far-off subject matter. In fact, I argue in this book, that is emphatically not the case. The end of all things lay in the immediate future for Paul in a way it simply has not done for most people down through the ages, and certainly not for the modern, bourgeois guild of professional Bible critics (of which the present writer, alas, is a member).

A number of interpreters before me – Albert Schweitzer, late-career Krister Stendahl, Dale Allison, and Paula Fredriksen, among others – have argued along these lines, but they have often been dismissed with criticisms that are not really to the point. For instance: It is true that, because Paul does not expressly set a date for the coming of the kingdom,[18] his expectation is not, strictly speaking, falsified. But neither is it vindicated.[19] Paul's "very soon" is not as specific or as vulnerable as "in the year x," but it is far, far more specific and vulnerable than "God only knows" (cf. Mark 13:32). It is this "very soon," not the red herring of a set date, that needs accounting for. Or again, it is true that the so-called delay of the parousia (*Parusieverzögerung*) does not arise as a problem in the letters of Paul as it does in 2 Peter or Porphyry. But by no means does it follow that questions of imminent eschatology are therefore irrelevant to the

---

2004); David Luckensmeyer, *The Eschatology of First Thessalonians*, NTOA 71 (Göttingen: Vandenhoeck & Ruprecht, 2009); Sydney Tooth, *The Eschatologies of 1 and 2 Thessalonians* (Tübingen: Mohr Siebeck, forthcoming); Daniel Oudshoorn, *Pauline Eschatology: The Apocalyptic Rupture of Eternal Imperialism* (Eugene, OR: Cascade, 2020); T. J. Lang, "Cosmology and Eschatology," in *The Oxford Handbook of Pauline Studies*, ed. Matthew V. Novenson and R. Barry Matlock (Oxford: Oxford University Press, 2022).

[17] Stanley K. Stowers, "Kinds of Myth, Meals, and Power: Paul and the Corinthians," in *Redescribing Paul and the Corinthians*, ed. Ron Cameron and Merrill P. Miller (Atlanta: SBL Press, 2011), 105–150 at 106–107.

[18] In contrast, e.g., to the *Epistula Apostolorum*'s bold gamble on 150 years.

[19] This is my quarrel with Brad East, "Enter Paul," *Los Angeles Review of Books* (23 June 2019): "The logical distinction here is between the claim that Jesus *may* return *at any time* and the claim that Jesus *will* return within a specific, known time frame. [Paula] Fredriksen infers the latter position from Paul's letters (and, possibly, from other New Testament texts). I believe she is mistaken. Paul's language of 'soon,' 'at hand,' 'nearer now than when we first believed,' and so on, while patient of such a reading, admits of an alternative."

case of Paul.[20] Quite the contrary, in fact. Paul's letters are our only extant sources from the first generation of the Jesus movement, from that brief window before the delay of the kingdom became a fact of life for all Christians ever after. For purposes of history, we should want to understand how things looked to Paul and his contemporaries, not rush to elide their perspective on time with their successors' – let alone our own – perspectives. But popular rubrics like "inaugurated eschatology" (à la Vos, Oscar Cullmann, G. E. Ladd, N. T. Wright, and many others) do precisely this; they make it quick and easy for moderns to imagine Paul's perspective on time as identical with their own. One might argue that this makes for good theology – although whether it does so is debatable – but it certainly makes for bad history.[21] The goal of this book, therefore, is to undo this elision, to show how Paul thought ethnicity and eschatology differently from how his successors' have thought them.

Paul Within or Without Judaism

I make my argument in the context of the recently minted and currently flourishing "Paul within Judaism" movement. Just as to write a book on Paul in the 1980s or 1990s was to reckon with E. P. Sanders's bombshell *Paul and Palestinian Judaism* and the various "new perspective" proposals then current, so to write a book on Paul now is to reckon with a cluster of strong readings now emerging from Israel,

---

[20] This is my quarrel with N. T. Wright, "Hope Deferred? Against the Dogma of Delay," *EC* 9 (2018): 37–82. Modern scholarship has fixated on the delay of the parousia in particular, entranced, I suspect, by the fascinating 2 Pet 3:4 (see James Carleton Paget, "Some Observations on the Problem of the Delay of the Parousia in the Historiography of Its Discussion," *EC* 9 [2018]: 9–36). But imminent eschatology is a much bigger issue. Hence the absence of *Parusieverzögerung* anxiety, in particular, in the letters of Paul is another red herring, not a counterargument.

[21] Thus rightly Dale C. Allison Jr., *Constructing Jesus: Memory, Imagination, and History* (Grand Rapids: Baker, 2010), 31–164; Paula Fredriksen, "*Al Tirah* ('Fear Not!'): Jewish Apocalyptic Eschatology, from Schweitzer to Allison, and After," in *"To Recover What Has Been Lost": Essays on Eschatology, Intertextuality, and Reception History in Honor of Dale C. Allison Jr.*, ed. Tucker S. Ferda et al., NovTSup 183 (Leiden: Brill, 2021), 15–38. The problem with the notion of "inaugurated eschatology" is that it is almost infinitely extensible through time. Of course, that is the very feature that makes it so theological useful! But it also makes it virtually impossible to think the peculiar case of a person (like, say, Paul) from the generation of Jesus himself.

Scandinavia, and North America, from the pens of revisionist interpreters such as Pamela Eisenbaum, Paula Fredriksen, Mark Nanos, Matthew Thiessen, and Magnus Zetterholm.[22] The present book makes its argument in the context of that movement, but it does not toe any party line. It is not a tract either for or against the Paul within Judaism *Schule*. It is just my own interpretation, which, I hope, does not make it "idiosyncratic" in the sense that one uses that word with scorn. On this issue, at least, I think it is best not to think in terms of party lines or *Schulen*, but just of so many interpretations of the relevant texts.[23] The more idiosyncrasy, the better. Not "the new perspective," but James Dunn's reading, or N. T. Wright's reading, or what have you. Not "the Paul within Judaism view," but Pamela Eisenbaum's reading, or Matthew Thiessen's reading, or what have you. We will of course recognize some family resemblances between certain scholars' readings, but boiling down these family resemblances into a single, easily labelled view is sloppy and confusion-making.

Here is an example: My 2012 book *Christ among the Messiahs*,[24] in which I argued, contrary to a longstanding critical orthodoxy, that the apostle Paul thinks of Jesus as the messiah, met with a mixed reception among Paul-within-Judaism interpreters. For some of them, my sketch of Paul as a Jewish messianist comparable to the Qumran covenanters or the Bar Kokhba partisans was a success, a marquee demonstration of the apostle's situatedness within Judaism. For others, however, my argument raised the troubling possibility that Paul imagined Jesus, as

---

[22] The best record of this cluster of strong readings is Mark D. Nanos and Magnus Zetterholm, eds., *Paul within Judaism: Restoring the First-Century Context to the Apostle* (Minneapolis: Fortress, 2015), the proceedings of the eponymous SBL research group. Earlier intimations include the essays collected in *BibInt* 13.3 (2005) and the history of research in Magnus Zetterholm, *Approaches to Paul: A Student's Guide to Recent Scholarship* (Minneapolis: Fortress, 2009). My own biopsy on the movement is Matthew V. Novenson, "Whither the Paul within Judaism *Schule*?" *JJMJS* 5 (2018): 79–88.

[23] With Steve Mason, "Paul without Judaism," in *Paul and Matthew among Jews and Gentiles: Essays in Honour of Terence L. Donaldson*, ed. Ronald Charles, LNTS 628 (London: T&T Clark, 2021), 11: "Inquiry is [history's] only requirement – *not* accuracy in relation to pre-conceived images. If we knew the past in advance, after all, we would not need to investigate it. Whatever prestige history has comes from its relentlessly truth-seeking, ever-questioning nature. If we give that up and descend into camps, we forsake history's aegis."

[24] Matthew V. Novenson, *Christ among the Messiahs: Christ Language in Paul and Messiah Language in Ancient Judaism* (Oxford: Oxford University Press, 2012).

messiah, somehow effecting redemption for Israel, a bridge too far for those interpreters committed to a so-called *Sonderweg* or two-covenant view.[25] How to interpret this mixed reception? Is my interpretation of "Christ" in Paul a Paul-within-Judaism interpretation, or is it not? I like to think yes, but the fact that other people in a position to answer this question thought no just goes to illustrate the conceptual problem.

As is often the case in discussions like this, the nub of the matter lies in the implied contrast term. Fifty or a hundred years ago, to talk about "Paul within Judaism" would have been to imply a contrast with *Hellenism*, as, for instance, in Albert Schweitzer's classic *Mysticism of Paul the Apostle*, whose second chapter is entitled "Hellenistic or Judaic?": "When any attempt is made to explain the Pauline doctrine [of Christ-mysticism] as Hellenistic, it finds itself confronted with the greatest difficulties."[26] Or, a generation later, in W. D. Davies's *Paul and Rabbinic Judaism*: "We shall not seek to deny all Hellenistic influence upon him; we shall merely attempt to prove that Paul belonged to the main stream of first-century Judaism, and that elements in his thought, which are often labelled as Hellenistic, might well be derived from Judaism."[27] Schweitzer and Davies framed their arguments in this way because, for much of the twentieth century, interpretation of the letters of Paul was locked in a strange, zero-sum debate over the relative degree of influence on the apostle of these two supposed cultural streams. Nowadays, happily, we seem mostly to have gotten over this strange habit of thought,[28] and we argue about other things.

---

[25] E.g., Lloyd Gaston, *Paul and the Torah* (Vancouver: University of British Columbia Press, 1987); Gager, *Reinventing Paul*.

[26] Albert Schweitzer, *The Mysticism of Paul the Apostle*, trans. William Montgomery (New York: Seabury, 1968 [1931]), 26.

[27] Davies, *Paul and Rabbinic Judaism*, 1.

[28] Thanks in large part to Martin Hengel, *Judaism and Hellenism: Studies in Their Encounter in Palestine During the Early Hellenistic Period*, 2 vols., trans. John Bowden (Philadelphia: Fortress, 1974), although even Hengel remains beholden in some respects to the dichotomy he tries to undo. A more thoroughgoing criticism is Troels Engberg-Pedersen, ed., *Paul beyond the Judaism/Hellenism Divide* (Louisville, KY: Westminster John Knox, 2001), especially Engberg-Pedersen's introduction (1–16) and Dale Martin's essay "Paul and the Judaism/Hellenism Dichotomy: Toward a Social History of the Question" (29–62). I say "we seem mostly to have gotten over" the Judaism/Hellenism dichotomy, but for discussion of its lingering effects in one important subfield see the essays in

In the twenty-first century, to talk about "Paul within Judaism" is to imply a contrast not with Hellenism but with *Christianity*. This is clearest of all in the title of Pamela Eisenbaum's important 2009 book *Paul Was Not a Christian*,[29] but it is also a leitmotif in numerous works of the Paul-within-Judaism *Schule*. Paula Fredriksen, for instance, characterizes her *Paul: The Pagans' Apostle* as a counterpart to certain "works arguing that Paul is a Christian theologian who repudiates Judaism."[30] Fredriksen's rhetoric here is by no means tilting at windmills. The view to which she is reacting is evident not just in the unconscious habit whereby exegetes refer to Paul and his auditors as "Christians" but also in major efforts such as N. T. Wright's *Paul and the Faithfulness of God*: "My proposal is that Paul actually invents something we may call 'Christian theology.'"[31] Whereas Wright, here representing the majority, views Paul in continuity with a tradition that came after him ("the inventor of Christian theology"), Paul-within-Judaism interpreters have wanted to view the apostle strictly with reference to categories available to him. And "Christian," which word is earliest attested around the turn of the second century, was not such a category.[32] For my part, I have no problem with calling Paul a Christian in a redescriptive sense for certain heuristic purposes, as Daniel Ullucci, for instance, has done quite fruitfully.[33] For the purposes of this study, however, such usage would confuse rather than clarify, because one main effect of reading Paul as Christian is to elide

---

Matthew V. Novenson, ed., *Monotheism and Christology in Greco-Roman Antiquity*, NovTSup 180 (Leiden: Brill, 2020).

[29] Pamela Eisenbaum, *Paul Was Not a Christian: The Original Message of a Misunderstood Apostle* (San Francisco: HarperCollins, 2009).

[30] Fredriksen, *Pagans' Apostle*, 230n43.

[31] N. T. Wright, *Paul and the Faithfulness of God*, 2 vols. (London: SPCK, 2013), 1: xvi.

[32] On this point, see especially Anders Runesson, "The Question of Terminology: The Architecture of Contemporary Discussion on Paul," in Nanos and Zetterholm, *Paul within Judaism*, 53–78.

[33] Daniel C. Ullucci, *The Christian Rejection of Animal Sacrifice* (Oxford: Oxford University Press, 2012), 177: "I define [*Christian*] as a subset of religion. Religion (and religious positions) posits the existence of superhuman agents. I define *Christian positions* as those positing that Jesus was/is a superhuman agent. Thus, Paul clearly displays Christian positions, regardless of what he would call himself."

the very phenomenon that we are here concerned to examine: his thoroughgoing eschatology.[34]

A main contribution of the present book is to give attention to some key Pauline texts that have gone largely neglected in recent Paul-within-Judaism research. The movement has been around long enough now that critics have begun to suggest that neglect of certain texts is significant, possibly intentional, and in any case incriminating. For instance, James Dunn, reviewing Nanos and Zetterholm's *Paul within Judaism*, complains as follows:

> One of the most curious features of the volume is that two key Pauline texts, key for the whole discussion, are never really discussed. One is Gal. 2:16, which was the focus of the original "New Perspective" essay [i.e., Dunn's 1983 "The New Perspective on Paul"]... Still more surprising from my perspective is that Paul's use of the key phrase "in/within Judaism," which occurs only in Gal. 1:13–14 (twice) is never really discussed... It is very disappointing, then, that a collection of essays entitled "Paul within Judaism" never really discusses what presumably should be regarded as the key text.[35]

To Gal 2:16 ("a person is not put right from works of the law except through trust of Jesus Christ") and Gal 1:13 ("you heard of my former occupation in *Ioudaismos*"), we may add at least Gal 2:19 ("through the law I died to the law"), 2 Cor 3:6 ("we are attendants of a new covenant, not of letter but of spirit"), and Rom 10:4 ("Christ is the end of the law unto righteousness for everyone who trusts") to the list of texts brandished by recent critics of the Paul-within-Judaism hypothesis.[36] It is fair to ask for a discussion of these texts but wrong to assume that they could not admit of new, alternative interpretations. In this book, I will offer a number of such interpretations. I do so in the rather pollyannish belief that, although it is impossible to convince everyone, it is nevertheless possible and desirable to argue one's case to the widest range of colleagues in the field. If taking this approach

---

[34] To borrow William Montgomery's memorable English gloss for Albert Schweitzer's *konsequente Eschatologie*.

[35] James D. G. Dunn, review of Mark D. Nanos and Magnus Zetterholm, *Paul within Judaism*, in *JTS* 66 (2015): 782–784.

[36] E.g., Joshua D. Garroway, "Paul: Within Judaism, Without Law," in *Law and Lawlessness in Early Judaism and Early Christianity*, ed. David Lincicum et al., WUNT 420 (Tübingen: Mohr Siebeck, 2019), 49–66; Mason, "Paul without Judaism."

means that no particular school is likely to rally around the account I offer here, well, I can live with that.

Comparing Things

The predominant way, by far, that interpreters have tried to think of Paul and Judaism has been to *compare* the former with the latter.[37] But the glaring flaw at the heart of this entire tradition is the assumption that one can profitably compare a single person (Paul) with an entire ethno-religion (Judaism)[38] – where, to skew the comparison even further, the person in question is himself a member of that ethno-religion. It is not that such a comparison is *impossible*; we can, of course, compare anything we like – apples with oranges, Paul with Judaism, Shakespeare with bioluminescence, etc. – because comparison is a mental operation performed by a thinking subject. Things do not compare themselves; thinkers compare things.[39] But comparisons can be more or less profitable, more or less interesting, more or less instructive depending on the choice of comparanda and the particular questions posed about them.[40] And it is here that the myriad scholarly comparisons of Paul and Judaism betray their conceptual deficiency. Every such study *has* to conclude with a claim about how, exactly, Paul differs from Judaism; the form of the conclusion is required by the set-up. But any claim of this form, no matter how well-researched or perceptive, is predicated on a gross generalization about (whatever

---

[37] This trend is documented and diagnosed by Beverly Roberts Gaventa, "Comparing Paul and Judaism: Rethinking Our Methods," *BTB* 10 (1980): 37–44. And now see also William S. Campbell, "Reading Paul in Relation to Judaism: Comparison or Contrast?" in *Earliest Christianity within the Boundaries of Judaism: Essays in Honor of Bruce Chilton*, ed. Alan J. Avery-Peck et al., BRLJ 49 (Leiden: Brill, 2016), 120–150.

[38] "Ethno-religion" is Shaye Cohen's term in his *Beginnings of Jewishness*. On the question of the aptness of the term, cf. David Goodblatt, *Elements of Ancient Jewish Nationalism* (Cambridge: Cambridge University Press, 2006); and the discussion of both Cohen and Goodblatt by Martha Himmelfarb, "Judaism in Antiquity: Ethno-Religion or National Identity," *JQR* 99 (2009): 65–73.

[39] Jonathan Z. Smith, "In Comparison a Magic Dwells," in *Imagining Religion: From Babylon to Jonestown* (Chicago: University of Chicago Press, 1982), 19–35.

[40] See Jeffrey Stout, "What Is the Meaning of a Text?" *New Literary History* 14 (1982): 1–12; and for application of this rule to comparative projects, Oliver Freiberger, *Considering Comparison: A Method for Religious Studies* (Oxford: Oxford University Press, 2019).

the writer in question includes under the heading) "Judaism." Comparisons of this type cannot do otherwise than find Paul to be unique or anomalous; they are purpose-built to find that. In fact, the supposed uniqueness or anomaly is not a discovery but a presupposition, not a conclusion but an unacknowledged premise. As Brent Nongbri has aptly put it:

> If we go looking for differences between the writings of Paul on the one hand and all other Jewish writings on the other, we shall surely find them... If one were to carry out a similar exercise by isolating another Jewish document and comparing it with all other Jewish literature from the Second Temple period, it would not be surprising to find that the isolated Jewish document had "unique" elements. Would we then conclude on this basis that the document was not Jewish? Unlikely. Yet, such a conclusion is exactly what one finds when Paul is compared with "Judaism" in this way.[41]

Regarding Nongbri's counterfactual "If one were to carry out a similar exercise by isolating another Jewish document and comparing it with all other Jewish literature...," in bibliographical fact this is almost never done. (It has occasionally been done with Jesus, but this is the exception that proves the rule. What is more, because Jesus left no writings, his is a quite different case, more like Socrates than Paul in this respect.) None of the great studies of Ben Sira, Salome Alexandra, Philo, Josephus, Babatha, or Rabbi Judah the Patriarch – let alone the many anonymous and pseudonymous Jewish texts from antiquity – is framed as a comparison of the lone figure on the one hand with all of ancient Judaism on the other. Because, in most cases, we recognize intuitively that that is an ill-formed kind of comparison, like comparing Jane Austen with all of English literature, or Gerald Ford with all of America. We can think those comparisons, but there is little to be gained by doing so. Much more profitable to compare Jane Austen with Walter Scott, or Louisa May Alcott, or Zadie Smith; or to compare Gerald Ford with Spiro Agnew, or Abraham Lincoln, or Phyllis Schlafly. In this connection, one recent, salutary trend has been a vogue of studies comparing Paul with just one other ancient figure on a topic of common interest. Examples include Bruce Longenecker's study of Paul and 4 Ezra on covenant, John Barclay's study of Paul and Philo on circumcision, Jonathan Linebaugh's study of Wisdom of

---

[41] Brent Nongbri, "The Concept of Religion and the Study of the Apostle Paul," *JJMJS* 2 (2015): 1–26 at 17 and n60.

Solomon and Paul on grace, George Carras's study of Paul and Josephus on diaspora, Niko Huttunen's study of Paul and Epictetus on law, and Alexander Muir's study of Paul and Seneca on consolation.[42] One might reasonably complain that, at a disciplinary level, the enormous volume of attention devoted to Paul in contrast to other ancient figures is itself a corrupting influence on historical understanding.[43] But at least the form of these recent comparative studies is a great improvement.

The one comparison of Paul and Judaism that towers over all others is E. P. Sanders's 1977 *Paul and Palestinian Judaism: A Comparison of Patterns of Religion*.[44] Sanders is so brilliant an exegete that, when he gets down to the work of reading primary texts, he manages to be right much, even most of the time. But in the architecture of the project, Sanders goes astray in precisely the way detailed above. To give him due credit, he does not attempt to compare Paul with *all of Judaism*, but with all of Palestinian Judaism ca. 200 BCE to 200 CE (including the Mishnah, Tosefta, tannaitic midrashim, all the Dead Sea Scrolls, Ben Sira, 1 Enoch, Jubilees, Psalms of Solomon, and 4 Ezra), which is still more than enough to yield an absurd asymmetry.[45] Another problem is Sanders's notion of a "pattern of religion," which turns out to mean roughly "soteriology,"[46] of which he finds one Pauline

---

[42] Bruce W. Longenecker, *Eschatology and the Covenant: A Comparison of 4 Ezra and Romans 1–11*, JSNTSup 57 (Sheffield: JSOT Press, 1991); John M. G. Barclay, "Paul and Philo on Circumcision: Rom 2:25–9 in Social and Cultural Context," *NTS* 44 (1998): 536–556; Linebaugh, *God, Grace, and Righteousness*; George P. Carras, *Two Diaspora Jews: Josephus and Paul – A Historical, Social, and Theological Comparison of Hellenistic Jewry* (Leiden: Brill, forthcoming); Niko Huttunen, *Paul and Epictetus on Law: A Comparison*, LNTS 405 (London: T&T Clark, 2009); Alexander Muir, "Paul and Seneca on Consolation" (PhD diss., University of Edinburgh, 2022).

[43] A point well made by Melanie Johnson-DeBaufre and Laura S. Nasrallah, "Beyond the Heroic Paul: Toward a Feminist and Decolonizing Approach to the Letters of Paul," in *The Colonized Apostle: Paul through Postcolonial Eyes*, ed. Christopher D. Stanley (Minneapolis: Fortress, 2011), 161–174.

[44] On the influence of the book, see the retrospective essays by Anders Runesson, Matthew Thiessen, Neil Elliott, Adele Reinhartz, and Gregory Tatum in *JJMJS* 5 (2018).

[45] As Jacob Neusner rightly points out, if Paul is allowed a pattern of religion all his own, then the Ben Sira should be allowed his own, 1 Enoch its own, the Mishnah its own, and so on ("Comparing Judaisms," *HR* 18 [1978]: 117–191).

[46] See Nils A. Dahl, review of E. P. Sanders, *Paul and Palestinian Judaism*, in *RSR* 4 (1978): 155: "'Pattern of religion' for Sanders means much the same as 'soteriology,' but the latter term has connotations which he wants to avoid...

type (viz. participationist eschatology) and a different, pan-Jewish type (viz. covenantal nomism).

Sanders sets up his comparison as follows: "What is clearly desirable, then, is to compare an entire religion, parts and all, with an entire religion, parts and all; to use the analogy of a building, to compare two buildings, not leaving out of accounts their individual bricks. The problem is how to discover two wholes, both of which are considered and defined on their own merits and in their own terms, to be compared with each other."[47] Writing at the time, Jonathan Z. Smith subjected this plan to stern but warranted criticism:

> Allowing, for the moment, the language of "entire" and "wholes" to stand unquestioned, and setting aside the difficulty, indeed the impossibility, of comparing two different objects, each "considered" and "defined in their own terms" – a statement which he cannot mean literally, but which he gives no indication as to how he would modify – Sanders compounds confusion by further defining the notion of pattern... I am baffled by what "entire religion, parts and all" could possibly mean for Sanders. I find no methodological hints on how such entities are to be discovered, let alone compared.[48]

Notwithstanding the enormous and almost entirely positive influence of *Paul and Palestinian Judaism* on the field of Pauline studies,[49] Smith is quite right about the conceptual problems. If not even Sanders's *magnum opus* could successfully compare Paul with Judaism, how much more is this true of the many lesser attempts at that ill-advised project.

A more recent trend in this research area speaks not of "Paul and Judaism" but rather of "Paul the Jew." Instances of this trend begin by granting (!) that Paul was a Jew but then add a descriptor qualifying what kind of Jew he was: "Paul, an [x] Jew." There is some precedent for this rubric in older scholarship. Kaufmann Kohler classed Paul as an archetypal *self-hating* Jew, one who had internalized Greco-Roman anti-Judaism and thus wrote with contempt for his own ancestral

> The concentration on (soteriological) patterns makes it possible for Sanders to compare the religion of one individual, Paul, with centuries of Palestinian Judaism. The approach leaves room for variations but, on the whole, is ahistorical."

[47] Sanders, *Paul and Palestinian Judaism*, 16.
[48] Smith, "In Comparison a Magic Dwells," 33–34.
[49] On which see Matthew Thiessen, "Conjuring Paul and Judaism Forty Years after *Paul and Palestinian Judaism*," *JJMJS* 5 (2018): 7–20.

Comparing Things   17

traditions.⁵⁰ Markus Barth, in a provocation to his mainline Protestant interlocutors, classed Paul as a *good* Jew: "His was the life of a good Jew: a struggle for the rights of the neighbor."⁵¹ But studies of the form "Paul, an [x] Jew" have only really come in vogue since the 1990s. Daniel Boyarin classes Paul as a *radical* Jew: "I read Paul as a Jewish cultural critic, and I ask what it was in Jewish culture that led him to produce a discourse of radical reform of that culture... My fundamental idea... is that what motivated Paul ultimately was a profound concern for the one-ness of humanity."⁵² Calvin Roetzel classes Paul as a Jew *on the margins*, a member of his tribe but not of its orthodox, orthoprax center.⁵³ Going further than Roetzel, Love Sechrest classes Paul as a *former* Jew, one who has dissociated from his Jewish identity in order to associate with the *tertium genus*, the third race, of the Christ-believers.⁵⁴ Contrariwise, Mark Nanos classes Paul as a *Torah-observant* Jew, one who keeps the commandments that pertain to him and teaches gentiles-in-Christ to keep the (far fewer) commandments that pertain to them.⁵⁵ Similarly but less specifically, Gabriele Boccaccini classes Paul as a *Second-Temple* Jew, full stop. "Paul should be regarded as nothing other than a Second Temple Jew. What else should he have been? Paul was born a Jew, of Jewish parents, was circumcised, and nothing in his work supports (or even suggests) the idea that he became (or regarded himself as) an apostate."⁵⁶ But Boccaccini's "nothing other than" is overstatement; he himself also regards Paul as a Pharisee and an apostle, among other categories. Most recently, Brant Pitre, Michael Barber, and John

---

⁵⁰ Kaufmann Kohler, "Saul of Tarsus," *Jewish Encyclopedia* (New York: Funk & Wagnalls, 1906), 11:79–87, on which see further Daniel R. Langton, *The Apostle Paul in the Jewish Imagination: A Study in Modern Jewish-Christian Relations* (Cambridge: Cambridge University Press, 2010), 57–96.
⁵¹ Markus Barth, "St. Paul – A Good Jew," *HBT* 1 (1979): 7–45, here 37.
⁵² Daniel Boyarin, *A Radical Jew: Paul and the Politics of Identity* (Berkeley: University of California Press, 1994), 52.
⁵³ Calvin J. Roetzel, *Paul, a Jew on the Margins* (Louisville, KY: Westminster John Knox, 2003).
⁵⁴ Love L. Sechrest, *A Former Jew: Paul and the Dialectics of Race*, LNTS 410 (London: T&T Clark, 2009).
⁵⁵ Mark D. Nanos, *Reading Paul within Judaism* (Eugene, OR: Cascade, 2017), 1–60, subtitled "Paul as a Torah-observant Jew."
⁵⁶ Gabriele Boccaccini, "The Three Paths to Salvation of Paul the Jew," in *Paul the Jew: Rereading the Apostle as a Figure of Second Temple Judaism*, ed. Gabriele Boccaccini and Carlos A. Segovia (Minneapolis: Fortress, 2016), 2.

Kincaid have classed Paul as a *new covenant* Jew: "We follow Paul's lead and refer to him as a 'minister of a new covenant' (2 Cor 3:6) – that is, as a *new covenant Jew*... [This label can] account for elements of both continuity ('covenant') and discontinuity ('new') with Judaism in Paul's theology."[57] Other critics have tried to explain Paul by classing him as a proselyte Jew, a Hellenistic Jew, a Palestinian Jew, a Pharisaic Jew, an apocalyptic Jew, an eschatological Jew, and other categories beside.

Perhaps the most interesting and most influential of these proposals is John Barclay's mid-1990s classification of Paul as an *anomalous diaspora* Jew.[58] Barclay rightly questions why his predecessors (e.g., W. D. Davies, E. P. Sanders, Alan Segal) had compared Paul with *Palestinian* Jewish sources if Paul's social context was so obviously the diaspora. He writes, "Paul can properly be regarded as a Diaspora Jew and compared with other Jews living in this social environment... By observing him in this, his primary social context, we can plot his social and cultural location amongst other Diaspora Jews. As we shall see, his position there is distinctly anomalous."[59] There are two key moves here. Historiographically, Barclay situates Paul among other Greek-speaking diaspora Jewish writers, yielding real heuristic gains. But analytically, then, he argues that Paul is an anomaly relative to all of them. The first of these moves is a great advance on older scholarship, but the second, as Ronald Charles has pointed out, actually reproduces the conclusions of that older scholarship.[60] Barclay

---

[57] Brant Pitre, Michael P. Barber, and John Kincaid, *Paul, a New Covenant Jew: Rethinking Pauline Theology* (Grand Rapids, MI: Eerdmans, 2019), 62.

[58] John M. G. Barclay, "Paul among Diaspora Jews: Anomaly or Apostate?" *JSNT* 18 (1996): 89–119; John M. G. Barclay, *Jews in the Mediterranean Diaspora: From Alexander to Trajan (323 BCE – 117 CE)* (Edinburgh: T&T Clark, 1996), 381–396; and now also John M. G. Barclay, *Pauline Churches and Diaspora Jews* (Grand Rapids, MI: Eerdmans, 2016). The "anomalous Jew" rubric has been adopted by, e.g., F. Gerald Downing, *Cynics, Paul, and the Pauline Churches* (London: Routledge, 1998), 250–266; Carl R. Holladay, "Paul and His Predecessors in the Diaspora: Some Reflections on Ethnic Identity in the Fragmentary Hellenistic Jewish Authors," in *Early Christianity and Classical Culture: Comparative Studies in Honor of Abraham J. Malherbe*, ed. John T. Fitzgerald et al., NovTSup 110 (Leiden: Brill, 2003), 429–460; and most recently and programmatically Michael F. Bird, *An Anomalous Jew: Paul among Jews, Greeks, and Romans* (Grand Rapids, MI: Eerdmans, 2016).

[59] Barclay, *Jews in the Mediterranean Diaspora*, 381.

[60] Ronald Charles, *Paul and the Politics of Diaspora* (Minneapolis: Fortress, 2014), 87–124, especially 104–107.

explicates the Pauline anomaly thusly: "In his conceptuality Paul is most at home among the particularistic and least accommodated segments of the Diaspora; yet in his utilization of these concepts, and in his social practice, he shatters the ethnic mould in which that ideology was formed… By an extraordinary transference of ideology, Paul deracinates the most culturally conservative forms of Judaism in the Diaspora and uses them in the service of his largely Gentile communities."[61] Barclay is too careful a thinker to call Paul *unique*, but nevertheless, in the respect that Barclay cares about, Paul stands on one side of a dividing line, all other diaspora Jews on the other. Only Paul "shatters the ethnic mould" and "deracinates" the tradition via an "extraordinary transference of ideology." One wonders whether, as Charles suggests, this kind of anomaly is just uniqueness by another name.[62]

Some of the "Paul, an [x] Jew" proposals are simply false. I am virtually certain, contra Hyam Maccoby, that Paul was not a Greek who turned proselyte in order to marry a Jewish woman.[63] I am not certain but relatively confident, contra Michael Satlow, that Paul was not a born and raised Jerusalemite Jew.[64] Many "Paul, an [x] Jew"

---

[61] Barclay, *Jews in the Mediterranean Diaspora*, 393.

[62] Charles, *Paul and the Politics of Diaspora*, 104: "*Anomalous* is, admittedly, not synonymous with *unique*, and Barclay may have carefully chosen this term to sidestep some of the issues that Jonathan Z. Smith raises with regard to the positions holding up Christianity as sui generis. But Barclay's position as it relates to Paul in the Diaspora is very close to a position of placing Paul in a unique place." Barclay neither cites Smith nor comments on the problem of uniqueness anywhere in the book, so I think it unlikely that he is responding to Smith, even implicitly. But Barclay has now engaged with Smith in his "'O wad some Pow'r the giftie gie us, To see oursels as others see us!': Method and Purpose in Comparing the New Testament," in *The New Testament in Comparison: Validity, Method, and Purpose in Comparing Traditions*, ed. John M. G. Barclay and B. G. White (London: T&T Clark, 2020), 9–22. Further on Barclay's Paul the anomalous Jew, see Thiessen, "Conjuring Paul and Judaism."

[63] Hyam Maccoby, *The Mythmaker: Paul and the Invention of Christianity* (New York: Barnes & Noble, 1986), on which see John Gager's review in *JQR* 79 (1988): 248–250.

[64] Michael L. Satlow, *How the Bible Became Holy* (New Haven: Yale University Press, 2014), 210–223; Michael L. Satlow, "Paul, a Jew from Jerusalem," *Bible and Interpretation* (September 2014); Michael L. Satlow, "Paul's Scriptures," in *Strength to Strength: Essays in Honor of Shaye J. D. Cohen*, ed. Michael Satlow (Providence, RI: Brown University Press, 2018), 257–274. I consider and respond to Satlow's proposal in my "*Ioudaios*, Pharisee, Zealot," in *Paul, Then and Now* (Grand Rapids, MI: Eerdmans, 2022) 24–45.

proposals, however, are technically accurate, depending what point is being made; but the crucial question is what we actually gain from them. It is true – and most critics would agree that it is true – that Paul was a Second-Temple, diaspora, Pharisaic, apocalyptic, nonconformist (etc., etc.) Jew. But the fact that most critics would agree to this litany is proof that the application of the labels tells us relatively little, because they can mask huge differences of interpretation. Regarding Pitre, Barber, and Kincaid's "new covenant Jew" proposal, I have argued elsewherethat it is *both* a welcome hedge against the imposition of ill-suited categories *and* a barrier to taxonomy, because neither ancient nor modern writers ever use "new covenant" to denominate a certain subset of ancient Jews.[65] To identify Paul as a Hellenistic Jew is to say that he is like, for example, Philo of Alexandria in some relevant respect.[66] Likewise, to identify Paul as an apocalyptic Jew is to say that he is like, for example, the Qumran covenanters in some relevant respect.[67] But what does it mean to identify Paul as a new covenant Jew? Who are the other members of that set? Indeed, are there any? Paul only uses the label "attendants of a new covenant" of himself (and perhaps also Timothy, 2 Cor 1:1), not of the other apostles or other Christ-believers, let alone any other Jews outside the Christ sect. So perhaps to identify Paul as a new covenant Jew is simply to say that he is a Paulinist. But that is a tautology, or very close to one. Simply to label is not yet to understand. Thus my goal in this book is not, for instance, to prove that Paul was an eschatological Jew, as if proving that could tell us very much. I do think that Paul was an eschatological Jew, and a Second-Temple Jew, and a diaspora Jew, and a great many other things – all suitably defined and qualified, of course. But I do not think that just to apply any of those labels is yet to understand him. My goal in this book is to explore how Paul (who was of course an x, y, and z Jew) thinks ethnicity and eschatology. That is a different and, I think, much more productive project.

---

[65] Matthew V. Novenson, review of Brant Pitre, Michael P. Barber, and John A. Kincaid, *Paul: A New Covenant Jew*, in *SJT* 74 (2021): 93–94.

[66] As explored, e.g., in the essays in *Paul in His Hellenistic Context*, ed. Troels Engberg-Pedersen (Edinburgh: T&T Clark, 1994).

[67] As explored, e.g., in the essays in *The Dead Sea Scrolls and Pauline Literature*, ed. Jean-Sebastien Rey, STDJ 102 (Leiden: Brill, 2014).

Speaking of Paul

For the purposes of this study, I mostly use "Paul" as a shorthand for the author of the seven (almost) undisputedly authentic letters: 1 Thessalonians, Galatians, 1–2 Corinthians, Romans, Philippians, and Philemon. Of course, this shorthand masks numerous problems. Not even these seven letters are really undisputed; even today, a few interpreters would defend only F. C. Baur's list of four, or Bruno Bauer's list of zero, or other permutations besides.[68] With the majority, however, I think that we can attribute these seven letters to Paul, or better: to Paul and his colleagues. As Laura Nasrallah has rightly emphasized, all but one (viz. Romans) of the seven letters are expressly co-authored:[69] Paul, Silvanus, and Timothy in 1 Thessalonians (1:1); Paul and Sosthenes in 1 Corinthians (1:1); Paul and Timothy in 2 Corinthians (1:1), Philippians (1:1), and Philemon (1); Paul and "all the brothers" in Galatians (1:1–2). And even Romans comes from the hand of Tertius the scribe (Rom 16:22), not Paul the author.[70] What is more, not only are the letters products of Paul's network; the letters *as we have them* are products of the third-, fourth-, and fifth-century tradents of our best manuscripts. We are necessarily ignorant, for the most part, about the text of the letters for the roughly two centuries between their composition and the earliest extant witnesses.[71] At least one of the letters – 2 Corinthians – was very probably not written in the form we

---

[68] On the moving target of an ostensibly undisputed canon of authentically Pauline letters, see Benjamin L. White, *Remembering Paul: Ancient and Modern Contests over the Image of the Apostle* (Oxford: Oxford University Press, 2014); Patrick Hart, *A Prolegomenon to the Study of Paul*, MTSRSup 15 (Leiden: Brill, 2020); Benjamin Petroelje, *The Pauline Book and the Dilemma of Ephesians*, LNTS 665 (London: T&T Clark, 2022).

[69] Laura Salah Nasrallah, *Archaeology and the Letters of Paul* (Oxford: Oxford University Press, 2019), 1–4.

[70] On Tertius, and the possibility that he was enslaved to Paul or to another Christ-believer in Corinth or Cenchreae, see Candida R. Moss, "The Secretary: Enslaved Workers, Stenography, and the Production of Early Christian Literature," *JTS* 74 (2023): 20–56.

[71] Thus rightly Brent Nongbri, "To See Paul as Paul Saw Himself," *Syndicate* (2 June 2020): "Even if we grant (as all of us effectively do) that the textual critics have been basically successful at obtaining the earliest recoverable text of Paul's letters, it bears recalling that this is essentially the text of Paul's letters as it existed in the fourth century... We have no good way of knowing what the text of Paul's letters looked like in the second century, never mind the middle of the first century."

now have it but is a composite of two or more shorter communications. And while we have good reason to trust that our critical text of Paul is mostly free of later interpolations,[72] the case of the doxology at Rom 16:25–27 should keep us on our toes.[73] All of which is to say that even the so-called undisputed letters cannot transport us directly to the apostle himself.

That being the case, one might be tempted to abandon the authentic/ pseudonymous distinction altogether and simply let "Paul" mean the whole late ancient *corpus Paulinum*, including at least 2 Thessalonians, Colossians, Ephesians, 1–2 Timothy, and Titus. Luke Timothy Johnson, to cite one eminent example, has recently proposed something along these lines.[74] And for reception-historical and theological purposes, such an approach has much to commend it. But it has significant liabilities, too. Most importantly, there is no such thing as *the* late ancient *corpus Paulinum*; rather, there are several of them, at least.[75] Do we include Hebrews, which counted as "Paul" in the Greek East but not the Latin West, and in modern Bibles sits awkwardly between the Pauline letters and the Catholic letters? Or 3 Corinthians, accepted among the Syrian and Armenian churches but not elsewhere? Or the Pastoral Epistles, absent from the early ten-letter corpus of church letters attested in P46? It is *not* a simple choice between a seven-letter critical corpus and a thirteen-letter ecclesiastical corpus. What we actually have are some twenty-odd ancient letters attributed to Paul, preserved in several partly overlapping ancient editions (a ten-letter corpus, a thirteen-letter corpus, a fourteen-letter corpus, and so on), *none* of which includes *all* of those twenty-plus extant letters. So there is just no getting around the obstinate historical questions about the relative proximity of each of these texts to the apostle, even if we must abandon the naïve hope of access to the mind of the man himself. In this study, therefore, I appeal to the seven letters, minus some textually dubious passages, as first-order evidence for Paul (in the

---

[72] Contra William O. Walker, *Interpolations in the Pauline Letters*, JSNTSup 213 (Sheffield: Sheffield Academic, 2001).

[73] Harry Gamble, *The Textual History of the Letter to the Romans*, SD 42 (Grand Rapids, MI: Eerdmans, 1977).

[74] Luke Timothy Johnson, *Constructing Paul* (Grand Rapids, MI: Eerdmans, 2020), volume 1 of his tellingly titled *The Canonical Paul*.

[75] See Harry Y. Gamble, "The Formation of the Pauline Corpus," in *Oxford Handbook of Pauline Studies*, 338–354.

sense stipulated above), while in the footnotes I also comment selectively on relevant passages from 2 Thessalonians, Colossians, Ephesians, 1–2 Timothy, and Titus, as well as Hebrews, 3 Corinthians, Laodiceans, Paul and Seneca, Apocalypse of Paul, Prayer of Paul, Acts of the Apostles, Acts of Paul, and more. These are sources of a different order, much less proximate to the apostle, but they are sources nonetheless, part of the "Pauline archive" with which we have to work.[76]

Even setting aside the problem of the sources, which is not easily set aside, there is an equally thorny problem with the word "author" in my breezy "shorthand for the author of the seven authentic letters." Margaret Mitchell helpfully distinguishes between what she calls *the historical Paul* – "the actual flesh-and-blood human person in his finite and complicated life, as best as we can reconstruct him" – and *the historical-epistolary Paul* – "the mini-corpus of the seven scholarly homologoumena, which has itself had many lives since."[77] We would, of course, be delighted to have straightforward access to the historical Paul (and likewise the historical Socrates, the historical Cleopatra, and so on), but in fact we only know him by way of the historical-epistolary Paul, which is not the same thing, because, as Mitchell puts it, "no person is equivalent to or reducible to a selective body of his or her rhetorically forceful and occasional writings."[78] The two are related, because there is good reason to think that at least the seven letters do come, via whatever slings and arrows of composition and transmission, from the historical figure himself. But not even an (ostensibly) undisputed passage in an (ostensibly) undisputed letter is a transparent deliverance of the mind of Paul. As Mitchell rightly notes, our author "was strategic and canny, often deliberate and acting aforethought, but also inclined to antithetical reasoning, combativeness, and hyperbole, often followed by or associated with, forms of

---

[76] "Pauline archive" is the preferred term of Hart, *Prolegomenon*; and Cavan W. Concannon, *Profaning Paul* (Chicago: University of Chicago Press, 2021). See also Gregory Fewster, "Archiving Paul: Manuscripts, Religion, and the Editorial Shaping of Ancient Letter Collections," *Archivaria* 81 (2016): 101–128.
[77] Margaret M. Mitchell, "Paul and Judaism now, Quo vadimus?" *JJMJS* 5 (2018): 61–62. For further application of this distinction, see Margaret M. Mitchell, *Paul and the Emergence of Christian Textuality: Early Christian Literary Culture in Context*, WUNT 393 (Tübingen: Mohr Siebeck, 2017).
[78] Mitchell, "Paul and Judaism," 62.

conciliation, whether tonal pauses, shifts from categorical to temporal arguments, and types of diction."[79] As will become clear in the argument below, I am more optimistic than Mitchell is about the possibility of synthesizing at least some of Paul's main ideas. She is absolutely right that "Paul's letters never did and still do not have a single, unequivocal meaning."[80] In fact, I would go further still and do without talk of meaning(s), whether singular or plural, altogether.[81] I do not claim to pronounce on *the* meaning of the letters, only to offer one reading that I think makes good historical-contextual sense.[82]

The Past and Its Uses

I come to interpret Paul, not to praise him. I have no interest in perpetuating the Great Man approach to the letters, a hermeneutical stance that assumes that Paul is the upright party in all his disputes, the hero of the story of which he is part. Melanie Johnson-DeBaufre and Laura Nasrallah have perceptively identified and criticized this commonplace in their excellent essay "Beyond the Heroic Paul." Over against such a hermeneutical stance, Johnson-DeBaufre and Nasrallah urge, "There is much to gain from reading the letters of Paul – in their writing, reception, and afterlives – as sites of debate, contestation, and resistance rather than as articulations of one individual's vision and heroic community-building efforts."[83] That is, we can read Paul's letters in order to understand not just his ideas and goals, but also the (different, sometimes contrary) ideas and goals of Cephas, Apollos, Phoebe, Euodia, Syntyche, the Corinthian women prophets, and others. Following Johnson-DeBaufre and Nasrallah, I try in what

---

[79] Mitchell, "Paul and Judaism," 63.
[80] Mitchell, "Paul and Judaism," 62. She develops this point in detail in her *Paul, the Corinthians, and the Birth of Christian Hermeneutics* (Cambridge: Cambridge University Press, 2010).
[81] Following Stout, "What Is the Meaning of a Text?"
[82] That is, I do precisely what Mitchell elsewhere describes as follows: "Pauline interpretation is fundamentally an artistic exercise in conjuring up and depicting a dead man from his ghostly images in the ancient text, as projected on a background composed from a selection of existing sources. All these portraits are based upon a new configuration of the surviving evidence, set into a particular, chosen framework" (Margaret M. Mitchell, *The Heavenly Trumpet: John Chrysostom and the Art of Pauline Interpretation* [Louisville, KY: Westminster John Knox, 2002], 428).
[83] Johnson-DeBaufre and Nasrallah, "Beyond the Heroic Paul."

follows "to turn away from the question of whether the ancient Paul was a hero or a villain and instead to imagine him and his interpreters as fully engaged in the messier political subjectivities of the diverse communities to which he wrote."[84] Now, inasmuch as the present study does focus on Paul's own ideas and goals, rather than those of Apollos or Phoebe, it runs the risk of appearing to be another drop in the sea of "heroic Paul" readings. But I consider that a risk worth taking, for I think that we have not yet understood Paul on ethnicity and eschatology precisely because we have cast him as a hero. Only by allowing ourselves to imagine Paul *otherwise* than as heroic or villainous, perhaps even as tragic, can we think our way to the end of this particular problem.

Cavan Concannon has argued still further along the lines sketched by Johnson-DeBaufre and Nasrallah. In a bracing manifesto entitled "Paul Is Dead. Long Live Paulinism!" Concannon pleads, "We have to kill Paul... I am calling for an overthrowing of Paul as the representative of the Platonic One in favor of the creation of a vibrant, polyvalent Pauline archive... In other words, and to paraphrase Marx, let's stop interpreting Paul and start creating Paulinisms that can change the world."[85] Concannon is understandably weary of the modern project of historicizing the apostle and rightly suspicious of the many claims of Pauline warrant for various theological and ethical visions. He proposes, therefore, that we abandon the quest for the historical Paul and mine the whole, vast Pauline tradition ("authentic," pseudo-, deutero-, trito-, apocryphal, and otherwise) for anything we find ethically useful. "Let's not start with the presumption that the Pauline archive will provide us with answers once we have revealed the real Paul; rather, we should allow our work to ask if anything from the Pauline archive (or any early Christian text for that matter) might yet become weaponizable in the struggle for a more just future."[86] My reading of Paul in the present book is more old-fashioned than what Concannon proposes in one respect and more radical in another. It is more old-fashioned in that I do not abandon the (hermeneutically chastened) quest for a historical Paul. I think that there is still much to be gained from Spinoza's (and Albert Schweitzer's, and Paula

---

[84] Johnson-DeBaufre and Nasrallah, "Beyond the Heroic Paul," 173.
[85] Cavan W. Concannon, "Paul Is Dead. Long Live Paulinism!" *AJR*, (1 November 2016).
[86] Concannon, "Paul Is Dead."

Fredriksen's) historicizing project.[87] But my reading is more radical in that, while I am a comrade in Concannon's "struggle for a more just future," I am even more willing than he is to leave Paul (and Paulinism) out of that struggle. After all, it is our struggle, not Paul's. Christians will of course have good reason to invoke Paul as an authority and a resource. But others will not, and I see no reason why students of religion in antiquity, in their capacity as such, should do. Like Concannon, but even more so, I am happy to let Paul be *useless* for our modern projects, and I think that by doing so we stand to understand him better. In contrast to the dominant approach to Paul, which Stanley Stowers rightly diagnoses as "academic Christian theological modernism,"[88] the historical reading offered in this book reckons with the fact that Paul is irremediably different from us in certain fundamental respects.[89]

With those methodological parameters in place, the argument of this book unfolds as follows. Chapter 2 considers the only passage in any of the books comprising the New Testament that contains the word Ἰουδαϊσμός, *Ioudaismos*, often transliterated "Judaism": Gal 1:13–14. I show that that word does not actually mean (what we mean by) "Judaism" and explain how exactly Paul positions himself in relation to it. Chapter 3 examines that Pauline bugbear "justification from

---

[87] I cite Spinoza here because Concannon cites him disapprovingly, Schweitzer because Concannon cites him approvingly, and Fredriksen (whom Concannon does not cite) because she is, in my view, the most incisive current theorist of history, theology, and ethics in the study of Paul, e.g., in her "*Al Tirah!*" and "Historical Integrity, Interpretive Freedom: The Philosopher's Paul and the Problem of Anachronism," in *St. Paul among the Philosophers*, ed. John D. Caputo and Linda Martin Alcoff (Bloomington, IN: Indiana University Press, 2009), 61–73.

[88] Stowers, "Kinds of Myth, Meals, and Power," 106–107: "The dominant approach to Paul and the Corinthian letters I characterize as academic Christian theological modernism... The tradition is thoroughly grounded in the situation developing from the aftermath of the Protestant Reformation, but took form as part of the crystallization of European modernity in the nineteenth century and the institutionalization of confessional faculties in the universities... [It assumes that] with regard to science and cosmology, the ancients and the early Christians are other in a rather absolute sense, but with regard to religion, morals, sociality, and subjectivity, the early Christians are the same as us. They are the same people in different clothes, with a different 'science.'" Mason, "Paul without Judaism" gives a similar diagnosis of and warning to modern studies of Paul.

[89] I develop this programmatic claim further in my *Paul, Then and Now*, in particular chapter 1 "Our Apostles, Ourselves," in dialogue with Concannon, *Profaning Paul*.

works of the law" and asks who in antiquity actually argued *for* such a thing. Chapter 4 mines the letters for evidence regarding the ethnicity(s) of Paul's opponents. I show that the centuries-old and still-popular image of Paul versus "Jewish Christianity" is not tenable. Chapter 5 starts from the traditional picture of Paul as an anti-legalist and proceeds to show a mass of evidence for (what anywhere else we would call) legalism in Paul's own letters. Chapter 6, similarly, starts from the traditional picture of Paul as an anti-ethnocentrist and proceeds to show a mass of evidence for (what anywhere else we would call) ethnic chauvinism in Paul's own letters. Chapter 7 considers all those passages where interpreters have thought that Paul redefines Israel to mean Christ-believers, demonstrating that he never does so. Chapter 8 explores why Paul sometimes says that Christ effects righteousness for *gentiles*, other times for *all people*, giving a summary account of what Paul thinks Christ does for gentiles and Jews, respectively. The concluding Chapter 9 explains the logic of Paul's controversial claim that Christ is the end of the law, proving its relation to ancient Jewish and Christian speculation about the physics of immortality.

Conclusion

Let us return, briefly and finally, to Rudyard Kipling. I suggested above *that*, but did not explain *how*, the opening lines of Kipling's "Ballad of East and West" help to illustrate Paul's way of thinking Jewishness and time.

> Oh, East is East, and West is West, and never the twain shall meet,
> Till Earth and Sky stand presently at God's great Judgment Seat.

Some ancients did, like Kipling, perceive the peoples of the world in terms of east and west, ἀνατολή and δύσις, *oriens* and *occidens*. "The eastern group are more masculine, vigorous of soul, and frank in all things... Those to the west are more feminine, softer of soul, and secretive" (Ptolemy, *Tetrabiblos* 2.2.9 LCL). "Many shall come from east and west and recline with Abraham, Isaac, and Jacob in the kingdom of heaven" (Matt 8:11). And so on. Paul does not classify peoples in this way, but he does presuppose another binary just as fundamental: Jews and gentiles, or, in the singular, Jew and Greek. Although in actual social practice, Jews and gentiles did meet all the time and everywhere in the ancient Mediterranean world,[90] Paul, like some other Jewish thinkers of his day, thought of the two as deeply, even ontologically different – *Jews are Jews, and gentiles gentiles* – in a way not bridgeable otherwise than by the re-creation of the universe itself.

But – and here Kipling's second line comes in – Paul also believed in the re-creation of the universe itself, not in the distant future as an article of faith, but in his immediate present as an empirical fact. Whereas Kipling, like most Christians down through the centuries[91] (and, *mutatis mutandis*, most Jews, too), imagines God's great judgment seat as a feature of the dim and distant future, Paul perceives it as a reckoning about to happen right now. The end of the ages has come. East and west, Jew and Greek, finally meet in the presence of the one God who is over all. In fact, not coincidentally, Kipling's phrase "God's great Judgment Seat" is itself a Paulinism: "We shall all stand before the judgment seat of God" (Rom 14:10); "We must all be revealed in front of the judgment seat of Christ" (2 Cor 5:10). In the dawning new creation, Jews are perfected in righteousness and made to live forever, like the angels, in fulfilment of God's long-ago promises to the patriarchs; meanwhile, gentiles are transformed from their natural state of debauchery into the same pneumatic existence promised to the Jews. Because of this peculiar combination of ethnicity and eschatology, the religion of Paul is neither what we normally think of as Judaism, nor what we normally think of as Christianity. And that fact is the cause of most of the confusion in the long history of Paul-and-Judaism debates. That is to put the thesis of this book. Now it only remains to prove it.

---

[90] See Louis H. Feldman, *Jew and Gentile in the Ancient World: Attitudes and Interactions from Alexander to Justinian* (Princeton: Princeton University Press, 1993); Paula Fredriksen, "What 'Parting of the Ways?' Jews, Gentiles, and the Ancient Mediterranean City," in Adam H. Becker and Anette Yoshiko Reed, eds., *The Ways That Never Parted: Jews and Christians in Late Antiquity and the Early Middle Ages*, TSAJ 95 (Tübingen: Mohr Siebeck, 2003), 35–64.

[91] Kipling's own religion is a famous puzzle. In a 1908 letter to Lady Edward Cecil, he identifies himself as "a God-fearing Christian atheist."

2 | *Paul's Former Occupation* in Ioudaismos

Modern New Testament studies is absolutely littered with discussions of the topic "Paul and Judaism." Arguably the most important book in Pauline studies in the last half-century was one titled *Paul and Palestinian Judaism*, which was itself in part a response to another influential volume titled *Paul and Rabbinic Judaism*.[1] Just since 2010, we have seen the release of Thomas G. Casey and Justin Taylor's *Paul's Jewish Matrix*, Reimund Bieringer and Didier Pollefeyt's *Paul and Judaism*, Mark Nanos and Magnus Zetterholm's *Paul within Judaism*, and Preston Sprinkle's *Paul and Judaism Revisited*.[2] And lest one think that this is merely a preoccupation of Anglophone scholarship, from the European continent we have, for instance, Gerd Lüdemann's *Paulus und das Judentum*;[3] Timo Laato's *Paulus und das Judentum*;[4] and Martin Hengel and Ulrich Heckel's edited volume *Paulus und das antike Judentum*.[5] Full disclosure: Even the present writer has a book whose subtitle, at least, takes the form "x in Paul and y in ancient Judaism."[6]

For all that, however, the word "Judaism" itself (or rather, its supposed Greek equivalency Ἰουδαϊσμός, *Ioudaismos*) occurs only twice in the Pauline corpus – the only two instances, in fact, in the entire New

---

[1] Sanders, *Paul and Palestinian Judaism*; Davies, *Paul and Rabbinic Judaism*.
[2] Thomas G. Casey and Justin Taylor, eds., *Paul's Jewish Matrix* (Rome: Gregorian & Biblical Press, 2011); Reimund Bieringer and Didier Pollefeyt, eds., *Paul and Judaism: Crosscurrents in Pauline Exegesis and the Study of Jewish-Christian Relations*, LNTS 463 (London: T&T Clark, 2012); Nanos and Zetterholm, *Paul within Judaism*; Sprinkle, *Paul and Judaism Revisited*.
[3] Lüdemann, *Paulus und das Judentum*.
[4] Timo Laato, *Paulus und das Judentum: Anthropologische Erwagungen* (Åbo: Åbo Academy Press, 1991).
[5] Martin Hengel and Ulrich Heckel, eds., *Paulus und das antike Judentum*, WUNT 58 (Tübingen: Mohr Siebeck, 1991).
[6] Novenson, *Christ among the Messiahs*.

Testament. Paul refers to Ἰουδαϊσμός (which I leave untranslated for now so as not to beg the question) twice in a single sentence in Galatians 1 in which he relates a brief bit of autobiography. The pertinent passage reads as follows:

Ἠκούσατε γὰρ τὴν ἐμὴν ἀναστροφήν ποτε ἐν τῷ Ἰουδαϊσμῷ, ὅτι καθ' ὑπερβολὴν ἐδίωκον τὴν ἐκκλησίαν τοῦ θεοῦ καὶ ἐπόρθουν αὐτήν, καὶ προέκοπτον ἐν τῷ Ἰουδαϊσμῷ ὑπὲρ πολλοὺς συνηλικιώτας ἐν τῷ γένει μου, περισσοτέρως ζηλωτὴς ὑπάρχων τῶν πατρικῶν μου παραδόσεων.

For you heard of my former occupation in Ἰουδαϊσμός, that I was prosecuting the assembly of God aggressively, and was destroying it, and was excelling in Ἰουδαϊσμός beyond many of my peers among my people, being exceedingly zealous for my ancestral traditions. (Gal 1:13–14)[7]

In this passage, Paul uses the term Ἰουδαϊσμός to signify an aspect of his own pattern of activity (ἀναστροφή, "occupation") in the time before the divine revelation that he mentions elliptically in Gal 1:16: εὐδόκησεν... ἀποκαλύψαι τὸν υἱὸν αὐτοῦ ἐν ἐμοί, ἵνα εὐαγγελίζωμαι αὐτὸν ἐν τοῖς ἔθνεσιν, "He [God] was pleased to reveal his son in me so that I might preach him among the gentiles."[8] But what is Ἰουδαϊσμός? From the plain etymological analogy, most modern English versions render it with "Judaism" (so RSV, NRSV, NASB, NIV; cf. KJV: "the Jews' religion"; and cf. Luther Bibel: *Judentum*).[9] This identification of Paul's word Ἰουδαϊσμός with our word for the religion of Jewish people, together with the polemical program of an epistle in which Paul opposes those who would "compel gentiles to judaize" (Gal 2:14), has given us the traditional trope of Galatians as a manifesto against Judaism.[10] Many modern exegetes, however, have questioned whether

---

[7] On the choice of "assembly" rather than "church" for ἐκκλησία here and throughout, I am especially influenced by Jennifer Eyl, "Semantic Voids, New Testament Translation, and Anachronism: The Case of Paul's Use of *Ekklesia*," *MTSR* 26 (2014): 315–339.

[8] On this event, see in particular Alan F. Segal, *Paul the Convert: The Apostolate and Apostasy of Paul the Pharisee* (New Haven: Yale University Press, 1990), 58–71.

[9] Similarly Hengel, *Judaism and Hellenism*, 1:2: "The word [Ἰουδαϊσμός] means both political and genetic association with the Jewish nation and exclusive belief in the one God of Israel, together with observance of the Torah given by him."

[10] On which see John Riches, *Galatians through the Centuries* (Oxford: Blackwell, 2008), 84–87; and Michael Bachmann, *Anti-Judaism in Galatians? Exegetical Studies on a Polemical Letter and on Paul's Theology*, trans. Robert L. Brawley (Grand Rapids, MI: Eerdmans, 2008 [German original 1999]).

Paul actually addresses Judaism as a religion in Galatians, and very recently, some have raised the question whether the word Ἰουδαϊσμός even means "Judaism." It is this latter question, as it pertains to Galatians, that is the burden of this chapter.

Ioudaismos from Ignatius of Antioch to Steve Mason

There has been diversity in the particulars of the interpretation of Ἰουδαϊσμός in Gal 1, but a leitmotif in most interpretation since late antiquity is the notion that Ἰουδαϊσμός signifies Judaism, the religion of Jewish people, and that this epistle comprises in part Paul's criticism of that religion. It is not Paul himself but Ignatius of Antioch who introduces the terminological distinction between Ἰουδαϊσμός and Χριστιανισμός, the latter word possibly an Ignatian coinage.[11] Infamously, Marcion of Sinope also reads Galatians as the story of a conflict between two opposing religions, but he takes the further step of inferring a conflict between two opposing gods.[12] Tertullian, anticipating the emerging catholic position, rejects Marcion's ditheism but concedes his exegetical point: "The epistle which we also allow to be the most decisive against Judaism [*Iudaismus*] is that wherein the

---

[11] See Ignatius, *Magn.* 10.3: Ἄτοπόν ἐστιν, Ἰησοῦν Χριστὸν λαλεῖν καὶ ἰουδαΐζειν. Ὁ γὰρ Χριστιανισμὸς οὐκ εἰς Ἰουδαϊσμὸν ἐπίστευσεν, ἀλλ' Ἰουδαϊσμὸς εἰς Χριστιανισμόν, εἰς ὃν πᾶσα γλῶσσα πιστεύσασα εἰς θεὸν συνήχθη, "It is absurd to profess Jesus Christ and to judaize. For Christianity did not trust in Judaism, but Judaism in Christianity, in which every tongue that trusts in God has been gathered together"; Ignatius, *Phld.* 6.1: Ἐὰν δέ τις Ἰουδαϊσμὸν ἑρμηνεύῃ ὑμῖν, μὴ ἀκούετε αὐτοῦ. Ἄμεινον γάρ ἐστιν παρὰ ἀνδρὸς περιτομὴν ἔχοντος Χριστιανισμὸν ἀκούειν, ἢ παρὰ ἀκροβύστου Ἰουδαϊσμόν, "If someone interprets Judaism to you, do not listen to him. For it is better to listen to Christianity from a circumcised person than Judaism from someone with a foreskin" (Greek text ed. P. T. Camelot, *Ignace d'Antioche. Polycarpe de Smyrne. Lettres. Martyre de Polycarpe*, 4th ed., Sources chrétiennes 10 [Paris: Éditions du Cerf, 1969]). On these passages, see Shaye J. D. Cohen, "Judaism without Circumcision and 'Judaism' without 'Circumcision' in Ignatius," *HTR* 95 (2002): 395–415; Daniel Boyarin, "Why Ignatius Invented Judaism," in *The Ways That Often Parted: Essays in Honor of Joel Marcus*, ed. Lori Baron et al. (Atlanta: SBL Press, 2018), 309–324.

[12] See Marcion, *Antitheses*, as reconstructed by Adolf von Harnack, *Marcion: The Gospel of the Alien God*, trans. John E. Steely and Lyle D. Bierma (Durham, NC: Labyrinth, 1990), 53–63; and cf. the fragments in Tertullian, *Against Marcion* book 4. See further Sebastian Moll, *The Arch-heretic Marcion*, WUNT 250 (Tübingen: Mohr Siebeck, 2010), 84–89, 107–115.

apostle instructs the Galatians" (Tertullian, *Marc.* 5.2).[13] Augustine's reading of our passage is similar to Tertullian's, albeit subtler in certain respects. He writes, "If by persecuting the church of God and trying to destroy it Paul advanced in Judaism [*Iudaismus*], it is clear that Judaism is opposed to the church of God, not because of the spiritual law that the Jews [*Iudaei*] received but because of their own carnal and slavish way of life" (Augustine, *Exp. Gal.* 7.2).[14]

This interpretive tradition, according to which Galatians is Paul's own treatise *adversus Iudaeos*, only gains steam in the modern period. Martin Luther reads Paul's "former occupation in Judaism" as a cipher for the vain religious hopes of "the pope, the Turks, the Jews, and all such as trust in their own merits."[15] In this Lutheran vein, Rudolf Bultmann comments that in Gal 1:13–14 Paul realizes "God's judgment upon his [Paul's] self-understanding up to that time – i.e. God's condemnation of his Jewish striving after righteousness [*jüdischen Strebens nach der Gerechtigkeit*] by fulfilling the works of the law."[16] Karl Barth's comment on our passage in *Church Dogmatics* IV.3 does not impugn Jewish religiousness as Bultmann's does, but Barth, too, sees in Galatians a criticism of Judaism as such. "There can be no doubt that his attitude and conduct (ἀναστροφή, Gal 1:13) accorded with the mode of Jewish life [*jüdischer Art*] (ἐν Ἰουδαϊσμῷ) as then expected... What he did not know was the necessity of radical conversion thus laid upon Israel, its obligation to accept the divine decision which actually precludes all seeking of its own righteousness."[17] Among the most recent generation of interpreters, Hans Dieter Betz writes, "According to Galatians, Judaism is excluded from

---

[13] Trans. Peter Holmes in *ANF*, vol. 3, ed. Alexander Roberts and James Donaldson (Grand Rapids, MI: Eerdmans, 1986). See further John M. G. Barclay, "Tertullian, Paul, and the Nation of Israel: A Response to Geoffrey D. Dunn," in *Tertullian and Paul*, ed. Todd D. Still and David E. Wilhite (London: T&T Clark, 2013), 98–103.

[14] Augustine, *Commentary on Galatians*, trans. Eric Plumer, OECS (Oxford: Oxford University Press, 2003). See further Fredriksen, *Augustine and the Jews*, esp. 213–234.

[15] Martin Luther, *Commentary on St. Paul's Epistle to the Galatians* (Philadelphia: Smith, English & Co., 1860), 151.

[16] Rudolf Bultmann, *Theology of the New Testament*, 2 vols., trans. Kendrick Grobel (New York: Scribner, 1951–1955), 1:187.

[17] Karl Barth, *Church Dogmatics*, ed. and trans. G. W. Bromiley and T. F. Torrance (London: T&T Clark, 2004 [1961]), IV.3:199–200.

salvation altogether."[18] And, playing Barth to Betz's Bultmann, J. Louis Martyn cautions, "The ruling polarity [in Galatians] is not that of Christianity versus Judaism, church versus synagogue... [but] rather the cosmic antinomy of God's apocalyptic act in Christ versus religion." [19] Like Barth, however, Martyn reckons that, by the logic of Galatians, Judaism must finally fall on the "religion" side of this antinomy.[20]

This whole interpretive tradition, of course, is predicated on the notion that Paul refers to or at least assumes the existence of something called "Judaism." But is that the case? In an ingenious and provocative 2007 journal article, Steve Mason proposed a radical revision of the prevailing understanding of Ἰουδαϊσμός and its cognates.[21] Mason argues that "there was no category of 'Judaism' in the Graeco-Roman world, no 'religion' too, and that the *Ioudaioi* were understood until late antiquity as an ethnic group comparable to other ethnic groups."[22] This article has attracted a great deal of attention in the years since, especially to do with Mason's claim that the substantive adjective Ἰουδαῖος always has the ethnic-regional sense "Judean," never the religious sense "Jew."[23] For the purposes of this chapter, I am concerned only with the much rarer term Ἰουδαϊσμός, so I set aside the Judean-versus-Jew debate altogether. In what follows, I render Ἰουδαῖος

---

[18] Hans Dieter Betz, *Galatians: A Commentary on Paul's Letter to the Churches in Galatia*, Hermeneia (Philadelphia: Fortress, 1979), 251.
[19] J. Louis Martyn, *Galatians: A New Translation with Introduction and Commentary*, AB 33A (New York: Doubleday, 1997), 37.
[20] Martyn, *Galatians*, 38.
[21] Steve Mason, "Jews, Judaeans, Judaizing, Judaism: Problems of Categorization in Ancient History," *JSJ* 38 (2007): 457–512.
[22] Mason, "Jews, Judaeans, Judaizing," 457.
[23] Among the numerous responses to Mason, see in particular Daniel Boyarin, "Rethinking Jewish Christianity: An Argument for Dismantling a Dubious Category," *JQR* 99 (2009): 7–36; David M. Miller, "The Meaning of *Ioudaios* and Its Relationship to Other Group Labels in Ancient 'Judaism,'" *CBR* 9 (2010): 98–126; David M. Miller, "Ethnicity Comes of Age: An Overview of Twentieth-Century Terms for *Ioudaios*," *CBR* 10 (2012): 293–311; Seth Schwartz, "How Many Judaisms Were There?" *JAJ* 2 (2011): 208–238; Beth A. Berkowitz, *Defining Jewish Difference: From Antiquity to the Present* (Cambridge: Cambridge University Press, 2012), 112–115; Adiel Schremer, "Thinking about Belonging in Early Rabbinic Literature: Proselytes, Apostates, and 'Children of Israel,'" *JSJ* 43 (2012): 249–275.

with "Jew" throughout, since doing so is conventional and will not distract from my central point.[24]

One of the main points of Mason's article is the morphological observation that the abstract noun Ἰουδαϊσμός is directly related to the verb ἰουδαΐζω, "to judaize," which means "to act like a Jew" or "to adopt Jewish customs" (see LSJ, BDAG, Lampe, s.v. ἰουδαΐζω).[25] Of course, all the various Ἰουδαι- cognates derive finally from the geographic root Ἰουδαία, the Greek name for the region of the southern Levant. But, Mason points out, the word Ἰουδαϊσμός does not signify just the religion practiced in Ἰουδαία or by Ἰουδαῖοι. Rather, it is a nominal form of the verb "to judaize," and – this is the crucial point – judaizing is something that only non-Jews can do. The verb ἰουδαΐζω, like virtually all Greek -ιζω verbs built on ethnic roots (ἀττικίζω, λακωνίζω, μηδίζω, ἑλληνίζω, and so on), signifies the adoption of native practices by non-native persons.[26] As Shaye Cohen puts it, "*Medizein* means neither 'to be a Mede' nor 'to become a Mede,' but 'to act like a Mede.'"[27] And again, "Jews do not judaize, any more than Medes medize or Greeks hellenize."[28]

If so, then Ἰουδαϊσμός ought to mean not "the customs of the Jewish people," as we generally use it to mean, but rather "the adoption of Jewish customs by non-Jewish people." Perhaps, then, Ἰουδαϊσμός should not be translated as "Judaism" at all, but rather something like "judaizing" or "judaization," and this is precisely what Mason proposes.[29] On his account, Ἰουδαϊσμός emphatically does not correspond to our word "Judaism." In fact, Mason reckons, no ancient word

---

[24] With Schwartz, "How Many Judaisms," I think that there are good reasons for retaining the translation "Jew," but I will not make that argument here (see my essay "*Ioudaios*, Pharisee, Zealot"). On the Jew-versus-Judean debate, see the excellent roundtable discussion "Jew and Judean," in *Marginalia* (August 2014), with essays by Adele Reinhartz, Steve Mason, Daniel Schwartz, Annette Yoshiko Reed, Joan Taylor, Malcolm Lowe, Jonathan Klawans, Ruth Sheridan, and James Crossley; and also Cynthia M. Baker, *Jew* (New Brunswick, NJ: Rutgers University Press, 2016).

[25] Mason, "Jews, Judaeans, Judaizing," 460–470.

[26] Similar to what we nowadays call cultural appropriation, and with similar attendant ethical concerns, on which see James O. Young and Conrad G. Brunk, eds., *The Ethics of Cultural Appropriation* (Oxford: Wiley-Blackwell, 2012).

[27] Cohen, *Beginnings of Jewishness*, 178.

[28] Cohen, "Judaism without Circumcision," 398.

[29] Mason, "Jews, Judaeans, Judaizing," 463–464.

corresponds to our word "Judaism."³⁰ Ancient writers, for their part, had the concept "indigenous ancestral traditions" which pertained to any given ethnic group (the πάτρια or ἔθη or νόμοι of the Medes or the Greeks or the Jews), but they did not have *ethnos*-specific words for these traditions. They also had the word Ἰουδαϊσμός (and its counterparts Μηδισμός, Ἑλληνισμός, and so on), but these words referred to the act of trans-ethnic sympathization or imitation, not to the indigenous traditions themselves.³¹

When Mason, therefore, reads Paul speaking of his own former occupation in Ἰουδαϊσμός, he takes this to be a reference not to a religion, Judaism, but to a kind of extreme (but unspecified) judaizing activity: "It is not as though the Judaizers [i.e., Paul's opponents in Galatians] are doing something he [Paul] has neglected, for the same mindset was part of his background."³² Not that Paul was a judaizer himself, of course, because that would be impossible by definition – Paul is a Jew, and only non-Jews can judaize. Perhaps, however, Paul means that before his apostolic call he was involved in efforts to encourage non-Jews to judaize in some way. Mason rightly concedes that Paul tells us little about the details of his pre-apostolic work,³³ but on his revisionist account of Ἰουδαϊσμός some such reading of Gal 1:13–14 would seem to follow.³⁴ If so, this would materially affect both our understanding of Paul's biography – perhaps he was a Jewish missionary to gentiles before his apostolic call³⁵ – and our understanding of the situation in the Galatian Christ-assemblies – perhaps Paul opposes not the religion Judaism but the *ethnos*-bending practice of

---

[30] Mason, "Jews, Judaeans, Judaizing," 460–480.
[31] Mason further claims that ancient writers had no such concept as "religion" ("Jews, Judaeans, Judaizing," 480–488), but this is a much more ambitious claim that does not necessarily follow from his lexical observations.
[32] Mason, "Jews, Judaeans, Judaizing," 469.
[33] Mason, "Jews, Judaeans, Judaizing," 469: "We do not know whether Paul ever 'compelled gentiles to judaize' in his pre-Christian life, as he now charges Peter with doing."
[34] In personal correspondence, Mason tells me that he is simply agnostic on the question which of Paul's own former activities Paul means by the term Ἰουδαϊσμός.
[35] As suggested, in different forms, by Hans Hübner, "Gal 3,10 und die Herkunft des Paulus," *KD* 19 (1973): 215–231; Martin Hengel, *The Pre-Christian Paul*, trans. John Bowden (London: SCM, 1991), 57–61; and Donaldson, *Paul and the Gentiles*, 273–284; among others.

judaization.³⁶ But is this proposal correct? Is there really no such thing as Judaism in Galatians, or indeed anywhere in antiquity?³⁷

A Modest Proposal

I propose that Mason's incisive proposal is partly right and partly wrong (or partly incomplete, at least),³⁸ that the verbal noun Ἰουδαϊσμός does indeed designate a sectarian activity rather than a whole religious system, but that, contrary to etymology, it is an activity undertaken by Jews. So, first of all, it is indeed the case that the verb "to judaize" means for a non-Jew to adopt Jewish customs. To put the same point differently, the grammatical subject of the verb "to judaize" is always a gentile, never a Jew. So in Gal 2, when Paul rebukes Peter for withdrawing from table fellowship with the gentile believers at Antioch, he says, εἰ σὺ Ἰουδαῖος ὑπάρχων ἐθνικῶς καὶ οὐχὶ Ἰουδαϊκῶς ζῇς, πῶς τὰ ἔθνη ἀναγκάζεις ἰουδαΐζειν, "If you, being a Jew, live gentilishly and not Jewishly, how can you compel the gentiles to judaize?" (Gal 2:14) Here, significantly, Peter himself is not judaizing; rather, he is compelling gentiles to judaize. The scholarly convention that calls Paul's opponents "judaizers" is therefore exactly the wrong way around. "Judaizing" is not what Paul's opponents are doing; it is what the Galatian believers are contemplating doing.³⁹ In grammatical

---

³⁶ As suggested by Stanley K. Stowers, *A Rereading of Romans: Justice, Jews, and Gentiles* (New Haven: Yale University Press, 1994), whose argument is related to but distinguishable from the treatments of Gaston, *Paul and the Torah*; Gager, *Reinventing Paul*; and Eisenbaum, *Paul Was Not a Christian*.

³⁷ In the years since Mason's article, others have taken this provocative idea further still. Daniel Boyarin, in particular, has lately argued that there was neither Judaism (Daniel Boyarin, *Judaism* [New Brunswick, NJ: Rutgers University Press, 2019]) nor religion (Carlin A. Barton and Daniel Boyarin, *Imagine No Religion: How Modern Abstractions Hide Ancient Realities* [New York: Fordham University Press, 2016]) anywhere in antiquity. Regarding the latter, see also Brent Nongbri, *Before Religion: A History of a Modern Concept* (New Haven: Yale University Press, 2013). But in critical response to Nongbri, David Frankfurter (review in *JECS* 23 [2015]: 632–634) rightly insists on the prerogative of modern scholars to use our own redescriptive terms for ancient phenomena.

³⁸ In personal correspondence, Mason tells me that he does not actually take his account to disagree with the account I offer here, which comes as happy news to me.

³⁹ A point well made by John M. G. Barclay, *Obeying the Truth: A Study of Paul's Ethics in Galatians* (Edinburgh: T&T Clark, 1988), 36n1.

terms, ἰουδαΐζω is an intransitive, not a transitive verb.⁴⁰ Paul's usage reflects the standard sense of the word. At the end of the Greek version of Esther, when the Jews arm themselves against their would-be executioners, the narrator reports that πολλοὶ τῶν ἐθνῶν περιετέμοντο καὶ ἰουδάιζον διὰ τὸν φόβον τῶν Ἰουδαίων, "Many of the gentiles underwent circumcision and judaized for fear of the Jews" (Esth 8:17 OG).⁴¹ Likewise in classical usage: Plutarch relates the story of Cicero's prosecuting a former praetor named Verres, one of whose accusers was a freedman named Caecilius, who himself had been "accused of judaizing" (ἔνοχος τῷ ἰουδαΐζειν), that is, of improperly following Jewish customs rather than his own (Plutarch, *Cicero*. 7.6).⁴² In short, when Jews follow their own ancestral customs, there is no special word for that, but when gentiles follow Jews' ancestral customs, it is called "judaizing."⁴³

Second, again in agreement with Mason, it is the case that the form Ἰουδαϊσμός is the nominalization of the verb ἰουδαΐζω, so that by the normal rules of etymology Ἰουδαϊσμός ought to mean "the observance of Jewish customs by non-Jewish persons."⁴⁴ This is the normal pattern for verbs ending in -ιζω and their respective nominalized forms ending in -ισμός.⁴⁵ So βαπτίζω means to perform a water ritual, and a βαπτισμός is the ritual washing itself. Καθαρίζω means to purify, and a

---

⁴⁰ As are all ethnic -ιζω verbs in the vast majority of instances. There are a few exceptions, e.g., the late (fourth c. C.E.) use of ἑλληνίζω in Libanius, *Or*. 11.103: καὶ ὅλως οὐδένα τόπον ἐπιτήδειον δέξασθαιπόλιν ἀφῆκε γυμνόν, ἀλλ' ἑλληνίζων διετέλεσε τὴν βάρβαρον, "In sum, no place that was suitable for receiving a city did he [Seleucus] leave bare, but in his hellenizing he finished the barbarian world." Unlike Mason, I do think that the transitive/intransitive distinction is important for understanding ancient usage of ἰουδαΐζω and Ἰουδαϊσμός.

⁴¹ For the text of Greek Esther, I follow A. Rahlfs, *Septuaginta*, vol. 1, 9th ed. (Stuttgart: Württemberg Bible Society, 1935). On this episode, see Cohen, *Beginnings of Jewishness*, 181–182.

⁴² On this episode, see Feldman, *Jew and Gentile in the Ancient World*, 345; and Brian A. Krostenko, *Cicero, Catullus, and the Language of Social Performance* (Chicago: University of Chicago Press, 2001), 160–161.

⁴³ This usage is also attested in Josephus, *War* 2.454, 463; Ignatius, *Magn*. 10.3; Alexander Polyhistor (citing Theodotus, *On the Jews*) apud Eusebius, *Praep. ev.* 9.22.5.

⁴⁴ In a different context, Cohen recommends glossing Ἰουδαϊσμός with "Jewishness" (Cohen, *Beginnings of Jewishness*, 1–10). Relative to the particular issues with which Cohen is there concerned (in particular, the modern categories of ethnicity and religion), his translation is apt, but it does not account for the features of ancient usage with which we are concerned here.

⁴⁵ So rightly Mason, "Jews, Judaeans, Judaizing," 461–462.

καθαρισμός is a purification or cleansing. Θερίζω means to reap or harvest, and a θερισμός is a reaping or a harvest. The same is true, albeit with some variation, of ethnic -ισμός nouns. The verb ἑλληνίζω means "for a non-Greek to adopt Greek ways";[46] and the noun Ἑλληνισμός means "the adoption by non-Greeks of Greek ways."[47] Since Ἰουδαϊσμός is the nominalization of the verb ἰουδαΐζω, "to behave like a Jew," then it should simply mean "the act of behaving like a Jew," and like its parent verb it should signify something that only non-Jews can do.

Third and finally, however – and here I go beyond Mason – that is *not* what Ἰουδαϊσμός means in actual use. In all of the (admittedly few) pre-Christian instances of the word up to and including Paul, the noun Ἰουδαϊσμός is something that Jews do, even though sometimes in the very same texts, including Galatians, the verb ἰουδαΐζω is something that non-Jews do.[48] In this instance, as happens all too often in natural languages, use belies etymology. If we consider Mason's reading of Gal 1:13–14 ("my former judaizing activity"), the fly in the ointment is that there is no mention of gentiles in the passage. Paul does not say that he used to compel gentiles to judaize, as he accuses Peter of doing in Gal 2:14.[49] Rather, Paul identifies his own former activity as Ἰουδαϊσμός; he himself is the implied subject of the verbal idea.

In this respect, Paul's usage actually conforms entirely to convention. In 2 Maccabees and its literary imitator 4 Maccabees, Ἰουδαϊσμός is the name of the cause championed by Judah Maccabee and his Jewish

---

[46] Or a more specific variation on this meaning, especially "to speak the Greek language" (e.g., Sextus Empiricus, *Math.* 1.246, where it is a contrast term for βαρβαρίζω). Cf. the old political use of μηδίζω in the sense "to take the side of the Medes" in, e.g., Herodotus, *Hist.* 4.144; Thucydides 3.62.

[47] So LSJ, s.v. Ἑλληνισμός: "imitation of the Greeks," as in 2 Macc. 4:13: ἦν δ' οὕτως ἀκμή τις Ἑλληνισμοῦ καὶ πρόσβασις ἀλλοφυλισμοῦ διὰ τὴν τοῦ ἀσεβοῦς καὶ οὐκ ἀρχιερέως Ἰάσωνος ὑπερβάλλουσαν ἀναγνείαν, "Thus there was such an extreme of hellenization and increase of foreignization on account of the exceeding impurity of Jason, who was impious and no high priest" (Greek text ed. Rahlfs, *Septuaginta*). Well into late antiquity, Ἑλληνισμός sometimes signifies "paganism" in contrast to Christianity (as in Julian, *Ep.* 84), but this usage is a world away from Paul's social context in the Julio-Claudian period.

[48] I say "pre-Christian" because in patristic usage from Ignatius onward, Ἰουδαϊσμός takes on a new, stereotyped sense which is beyond the scope of this chapter. On this development, see Cohen, *Beginnings of Jewishness*, 185–192; Mason, "Jews, Judaeans, Judaizing," 470–476; Boyarin, "Rethinking Jewish Christianity," 8–12.

[49] As Mason himself concedes ("Jews, Judaeans, Judaizing," 469).

partisans (2 Macc 2:21; 8:1; 14:38; 4 Macc 4:26), on which I will have more to say below.⁵⁰ In the Roman period, the word Ἰουδαϊσμός is attested twice in the epigraphic record, once in a third- or fourth-century CE funerary inscription for a woman from Porto near Rome, and once in a third-century CE synagogue benefaction inscription from Stobi in Macedonia. The relevant bit of the epitaph of Cattia Ammias (CIJ 537 = JIWE 2.584) reads as follows:⁵¹

Καττία Ἀμμιὰς θυγάτηρ Μηνοφίλου πατ(ρὸς) συναγωγῆς τῶν Καρκαρησίων καλῶς βιώσασα ἐν τῶ ἰουδαϊσμῶ ἔτη ζήσασα τριάκοντα καὶ τέσσαρα μετὰ τοῦ συμβίου.

Cattia Ammias, daughter of Menophilus the father of the synagogue of the Karkaresians, lived virtuously in Ἰουδαϊσμός, having dwelt thirty-four years with her spouse.

And the relevant bit of the Stobi synagogue inscription (CIJ 694 = IJO 1 Mac. 1) reads as follows:

[Κλ.] Τιβέριος Πολύχαρμος ὁ καὶ Ἀχύριος, ὁ πατὴρ τῆς ἐν Στόβοις συναγωγῆς ὃς πολειτευσάμενος πᾶσαν πολειτείαν κατὰ τὸν ἰουδαϊσμὸν εὐχῆς ἕνεκεν τοὺς μὲν οἴκους τῷ ἁγίῳ τόπῳ.

Claudius Tiberius Polycharmus, also called Achyrius, father of the synagogue at Stobi, who, having administered every policy in accordance with Ἰουδαϊσμός, has in fulfillment of a vow [given] the buildings for the holy place.

Scholars have generally taken Ἰουδαϊσμός in both inscriptions to mean simply "Judaism" in the sense of the religion practiced by the presumably Jewish honorees.⁵² In favor of this majority opinion, there is no

---

⁵⁰ On this usage, see Jan Willem van Henten, *The Maccabean Martyrs as Saviours of the Jewish People: A Study of 2 and 4 Maccabees*, JSJSup 57 (Leiden: Brill, 1997), 201–204. Mason, "Jews, Judaeans, Judaizing," 469 rightly connects Paul's idiom directly with that of 2 Maccabees.
⁵¹ For the Greek text of both inscriptions, I follow the edition of Jean-Baptiste Frey, ed., *Corpus inscriptioum iudaicarum*, 2 vols (Rome: Pontifical Institute of Christian Archaeology, 1936–1952).
⁵² Thus, e.g., A. Marmorstein, "The Synagogue of Claudius Tiberius Polycharmus at Stobi," *JQR* 27 (1937): 373–384; Martin Hengel, "Die Synagogeninschrift von Stobi," *ZNW* 57 (1966): 145–183; Yehoshua Amir, "The Term *Ioudaismos*: A Study in Jewish-Hellenistic Self Identification," *Immanuel* 14 (1982): 34–41 (in Hebrew); Margaret H. Williams, "The Meaning and Function of *Ioudaios* in Graeco-Roman Inscriptions," *ZPE* 116 (1997): 249–262; Lee I. Levine, *The Ancient Synagogue: The First Thousand Years* (New Haven: Yale University Press, 2005), 270–273.

positive evidence that either Cattia Ammias or Polycharmus was a gentile proselyte unless we allow the word Ἰουδαϊσμός itself to count as evidence to that effect, as Mason cautiously does.[53] There is more to say about this, but for now it is enough to note that both inscriptions make very good sense if we take them to use the word Ἰουδαϊσμός (as 2 Maccabees, 4 Maccabees, and Galatians certainly use it) to signify something that Jews themselves do.

To summarize the argument to this point: the verb ἰουδαΐζω means for non-Jews to observe Jewish customs, whereas the cognate noun Ἰουδαϊσμός means the defense and promotion of Jewish customs by Jewish people. This phenomenon runs contrary to the rules of etymology, but it is the case. In this instance, as sometimes happens, etymology is not a trustworthy guide. The vicissitudes of language use yield an anomaly, and that anomaly becomes fixed as a new pattern of speech.

How did this particular anomaly emerge? The answer, I propose, lies in the second-century BCE Maccabean revolt, and especially in the literary account of the revolt related in 2 Maccabees. It is a well-known fact that the word Ἰουδαϊσμός is first attested in and was perhaps coined by 2 Maccabees, either by Jason of Cyrene or by the anonymous redactor whose condensed version of Jason's account has come down to us.[54] More to the point, 2 Maccabees introduces the word Ἰουδαϊσμός as a contrast term for Ἑλληνισμός, the adoption of Greek customs by non-Greeks. In a programmatic statement, the author laments how, in the period just prior to the revolt, ἦν δ' οὕτως ἀκμή τις Ἑλληνισμοῦ καὶ πρόσβασις ἀλλοφυλισμοῦ διὰ τὴν τοῦ ἀσεβοῦς καὶ οὐκ ἀρχιερέως Ἰάσωνος ὑπερβάλλουσαν ἀναγνείαν, "there was such an extreme of hellenization and increase of foreignization on account of the exceeding impurity of Jason, who was impious and no high priest" (2 Macc 4:13).

---

[53] Mason, "Jews, Judaeans, Judaizing," 479: "A scenario in which Polycharmus was either a wealthy gentile sympathizer or a convert, who donated his private property for the sacred use of the *Ioudaioi*, seems at least as good an explanation... as the assumption that he was a *Ioudaios* born and raised." Hans Lietzmann made the same suggestion about Polycharmus of Stobi already in 1933 (Hans Lietzmann, "Die Synagogeninschrift in Stobi/Ausgrabungen in Doura-Europos," *ZNW* 32 [1933]: 93–95).

[54] See Amir, "The Term *Ioudaismos*"; Cohen, *Beginnings of Jewishness*, 105–106; Van Henten, *Maccabean Martyrs*, 201–204; Mason, "Jews, Judaeans, Judaizing," 460, 464.

The heroes of the book, by contrast, are those stout-hearted Jews who reject the siren song of Ἑλληνισμός and devote themselves to the cause that 2 Maccabees names Ἰουδαϊσμός. The author tells of the heavenly visions that were given to τοῖς ὑπὲρ τοῦ Ἰουδαϊσμοῦ φιλοτίμως ἀνδραγαθήσασιν, "those who with honor acted manfully for the sake of Ἰουδαϊσμός" (2 Macc 2:21). During the persecutions under Antiochus IV, Judah Maccabee and his band secretly canvas the villages of Judea, προσεκαλοῦντο τοὺς συγγενεῖς καὶ τοὺς μεμενηκότας ἐν τῷ Ἰουδαϊσμῷ προσλαμβανόμενοι, "summoning their kinfolk and enlisting those who had persevered in Ἰουδαϊσμός" (2 Macc 8:1). The martyr Razis, called an elder of Jerusalem and a patriarch of the Jews, κρίσιν εἰσενηνεγμένος Ἰουδαϊσμοῦ, καὶ σῶμα καὶ ψυχὴν ὑπὲρ τοῦ Ἰουδαϊσμοῦ παραβεβλημένος, "was indicted for Ἰουδαϊσμός and risked life and limb for the sake of Ἰουδαϊσμός" (2 Macc 14:38).[55]

In all these instances, the neologism Ἰουδαϊσμός signifies the defense under duress of Jewish ancestral traditions by a certain subset of Jews. Unlike our word "Judaism," Ἰουδαϊσμός in 2 Maccabees does not simply mean "what Jews do." It means, rather, "what Jews *who reject hellenization* do," "what *zealous* Jews do," or – in 2 Maccabees's gendered idiom – "what *manly* Jews do."[56] In 2 Maccabees – and this is very important – not all Jews practice Ἰουδαϊσμός, because Ἰουδαϊσμός is the name not of an ancestral religion but of a cause, a political movement, a program of activism. It is not the ancestral religion itself; it is one party's program for defending the ancestral religion.[57] To put it another way: Before the persecutions under Antiochus IV, there was no such thing as Ἰουδαϊσμός. There was a set of Jewish ancestral traditions, of course, but those traditions did not have a name because they did not have to be chosen, maintained, or defended. Before the Antiochene persecutions, they were just "what we Jews do." In the course of the Antiochene persecutions, however, the decision to persevere publicly in certain ancestral traditions (abstaining from pork, circumcising male infants, and so on) became an incendiary political

---

[55] On these passages, see Martha Himmelfarb, "Judaism and Hellenism in 2 Maccabees," *Poetics Today* 19 (1998): 19–40.

[56] On the theme of manfulness in 2 Maccabees, see Himmelfarb, "Judaism and Hellenism," 34–37.

[57] On this point, see the famously provocative treatment of Elias Bickerman, *The God of the Maccabees: Studies on the Origin and Meaning of the Maccabean Revolt*, SJLA 32 (Leiden: Brill, 1979).

statement. To reappropriate a famous phrase from the sociologist Peter Berger, Jewish religion in the Hellenistic period came under "the heretical imperative."[58] To practice it at all meant to choose it, which had not been the case for Jews before, and this choice warranted a name.[59] Of course, there was already a name for gentiles choosing to observe Jewish customs, namely, the verb ἰουδαΐζω, "judaizing." The neologism Ἰουδαϊσμός, "judaization," is a morphological twist on that existing term, a new word used to signify the suddenly radical choice by Jews to follow their own ancestral ways.

Galatians before Judaism

Let us find our way back to Paul's Letter to the Galatians. The extant literary and documentary evidence suggests that even after the tumultuous events that gave rise to the term, this activist connotation remained part of the sense of the noun Ἰουδαϊσμός. As in the Hellenistic period, so also in the Roman period, when ancient writers refer to Jewish religion and culture, they use the standard terms νόμοι ("laws"), ἔθη ("customs"), παραδόσεις ("traditions"), πάτρια ("ancestral ways"), and so on.[60] When they very infrequently use the word Ἰουδαϊσμός, they mean not the ancestral customs themselves but a sectarian program for the defense and promotion of those customs. This proposal makes good sense of the two late ancient Ἰουδαϊσμός

---

[58] See Peter L. Berger, *The Heretical Imperative: Contemporary Possibilities of Religious Affirmation* (New York: Doubleday, 1979). For Berger, the heretical imperative refers to the characteristic situation of religions in modernity, whereas my concern here is Judaism in the Hellenistic period. In both historical contexts, as distant as they are from one another, it is the encounter with religious pluralism that brings about the necessity of choice.

[59] Mason, "Jews, Judaeans, Judaizing," 468 aptly suggests that 2 Maccabees "seems to coin the word [Ἰουδαϊσμός] as an *ironic* counter-measure to Ἑλληνισμός" (emphasis mine). Ironic because, 2 Maccabees reckons, it is absurd that one should have to go to extraordinary lengths simply to observe one's own ancestral traditions.

[60] Examples of this convention are myriad. To cite just a few by way of illustration: ἀλλάξει τὰ ἔθη ἃ παρέδωκεν ἡμῖν Μωϋσῆς, "he will change the customs which Moses handed down to us" (Acts 6:14); οὐδὲν ἐναντίον ποιήσας τῷ λαῷ ἢ τοῖς ἔθεσι τοῖς πατρῴοις, "I did nothing hostile to the people or the ancestral customs" (Acts 28:17); παρέβησαν τὰ πάτρια... ἐπὶ τοὐναντίον οἷς ὁ νόμος αὐτῶν ἐκέλευε ποιοῦντες, "They transgressed the ancestral ways... doing contrary to what their law commanded" (Josephus, *Ant.* 4.139 [Greek text ed. Benedict Niese, *Flavii Iosephi opera* (4 vols; Berlin: Weidmann, 1887–1890)]).

inscriptions discussed earlier. On my reading, Cattia Ammias and Polycharmus were not just good Jews (*pace* Hengel and Levine) nor proselytes (*pace* Lietzmann and Mason) but rather Jewish activists, advocates for the cause of Ἰουδαϊσμός in their respective diaspora contexts. As Mason rightly points out, the Stobi inscription says of Polycharmus that he πολειτευσάμενος πᾶσαν πολειτείαν κατὰ τὸν ἰουδαϊσμὸν, "administered every policy in accordance with Ἰουδαϊσμός."[61] This πολειτεία language becomes much more intelligible if Ἰουδαϊσμός signifies a party platform rather than just an ancestral religion. Indeed, I suspect that the word Ἰουδαϊσμός is as rare as it is, in inscriptions as in literary texts, precisely because it pertains not to Jews in general but to a certain subset of activist Jews in particular.

Which brings us back to Gal 1. Interpreters ancient and modern have noted, of course, that Paul portrays himself in Gal 1:13–14 as an exceptionally zealous Jew: περισσοτέρως ζηλωτὴς ὑπάρχων τῶν πατρικῶν μου παραδόσεων, "being exceedingly zealous for my ancestral traditions." Most have thought, however, that the word Ἰουδαϊσμός in these verses refers to Jewish religion in general and that Paul's zeal was something added to it, so to speak.[62] On this conventional reading, all ancient Jews practice Ἰουδαϊσμός, but Paul practiced it more earnestly than most. But this is wrong. Paul writes about Jewish religious practice, both his own and others', in a number of passages. He speaks, for instance, of infant circumcision, the people Israel, the Hebrew race, tribal ancestry, halakhic schools of thought, ritual purity, the covenants, the law of Moses, the temple service, the divine promises, and the ancestors (Rom 9:4–5; Phil 3:5–6). In none of these contexts, however, does Paul ever use the word Ἰουδαϊσμός.[63]

Galatians 1:13–14 is different, however, because the subject at hand is not Jewish religion as such but Paul's own past involvement in anti-Christ-group agitation. The point of the passage is not that Paul used to be a Jew but is now a Christian.[64] The point is that Paul's gospel can

---

[61] See Mason, "Jews, Judaeans, Judaizing," 478.
[62] See, e.g., Arland J. Hultgren, "On Translating and Interpreting Galatians 1:13," *Bible Translator* 26 (1975): 146–148; Arland J. Hultgren, "Paul's Pre-Christian Persecutions of the Church: Their Purpose, Locale, and Nature," *JBL* 95 (1976): 97–111.
[63] A point well made by Mason, "Jews, Judaeans, Judaizing," 469–470.
[64] So rightly and famously Krister Stendahl, "Paul among Jews and Gentiles," in *Paul among Jews and Gentiles* (Philadelphia: Fortress, 1976), 7–23.

only have come from God himself, because up to the time of his revelation Paul had been a leader in a party under whose auspices he opposed the Christ groups. The point becomes clearer if we gloss Ἰουδαϊσμός not with "Judaism" but with something like "the judaization movement": "For you heard of my former occupation in the judaization movement, that I was prosecuting the assembly of God aggressively, advancing in the movement on account of my exceeding zeal," and so on. For Paul as for 2 Maccabees, not all Jews practice Ἰουδαϊσμός. Virtually all Jews follow the ancestral traditions, but only a subset fight for the cause of judaization, defending the traditions even to the point of harassing other Jews whom they suspect of endangering those traditions, as both Judah Maccabee and Paul did. It is this kind of political activism that goes by the name Ἰουδαϊσμός in ancient sources.[65]

There is one other passage later in the Letter to the Galatians that interpreters have tried to coordinate with Paul's "former occupation in Ἰουδαϊσμός," namely Gal 5:11: Ἐγὼ δέ, ἀδελφοί, εἰ περιτομὴν ἔτι κηρύσσω, τί ἔτι διώκομαι; ἄρα κατήργηται τὸ σκάνδαλον τοῦ σταυροῦ.[66] The RSV translates, "But if I, brethren, still preach circumcision, why am I still persecuted? In that case the stumbling block of the cross has been removed." A respectable rendering. It makes the possible but not necessary decision to take both instances of the adverb ἔτι as temporal – "still" – making the verse say that Paul previously preached circumcision (whatever that means) but does so no longer.[67] Interpreters who go this way then dispute *when*, exactly, Paul preached circumcision

---

[65] Robert Jewett, "The Agitators and the Galatian Congregation," *NTS* 17 (1971): 198–212 draws a different, more indirect connection between Galatians 1 and Jewish zeal: "My hypothesis therefore is that Jewish Christians in Judea were stimulated by Zealotic pressure into a nomistic campaign among their fellow Christians in the late forties and early fifties... The Judean Christians convinced themselves that circumcision of Gentile Christians would thwart Zealot reprisals." But I take a very different position on the identity of the agitators in Galatians, on which see Chapter 4.

[66] Some manuscripts of the so-called Western type (D, F, and G, to cite the earliest) omit the ἔτι in the first clause but not the second, thus: "If I preach circumcision, why am I still persecuted." This is intriguing, but the reading is likely secondary, perhaps an ancient attempt to solve the very problem with which we are concerned here.

[67] Martyn, *Galatians*, 475–477 rightly points out that ἔτι can mark not only time but also space and degree. Standard glosses include, in addition to "still," "yet," "another," "besides," "further," and "more" (see LSJ, *ad loc.*).

and, relatedly, *what* this "preaching circumcision" was. A few have suggested that Paul preached gentile circumcision *together with* Christ-faith earlier in his apostolate – Douglas Campbell: because he had not yet learned to acculturate his message to gentiles;[68] Joshua Garroway: because he had not yet received a second revelation of the circumcision-free gospel[69] – exactly as the rival teachers are doing when Paul writes Galatians.[70] But a distinguished majority take Gal 5:11 to mean that Paul preached circumcision *before* his revelation of Christ and commission to be an apostle. And if so, they reason, then perhaps "preaching circumcision" – understood as urging proselyte circumcision upon gentiles – is (at least part of) what Paul means by his "former occupation in Ἰουδαϊσμός" in Gal 1:13.[71]

Maybe. I am not certain that this view is wrong, but neither do I have much confidence that it is right.[72] *If* we take ἔτι here as temporal, and *if* we take the whole verse as straightforwardly autobiographical – neither of which is strictly necessary – then the Donaldson-Thiessen hypothesis is probably more persuasive than any of the commonly-cited alternatives (Watson, Campbell, Garroway, et al.). But urging gentiles to undergo proselyte circumcision is never called Ἰουδαϊσμός in any of our sources. If you squint a little bit, then you could perhaps think of the Hasmoneans' circumcising uncircumcised boys in Israel

---

[68] Douglas A. Campbell, "Galatians 5:11: Evidence of an Early Law-observant Mission by Paul?" *NTS* 57 (2011): 325–347. But see the incisive criticisms raised by Justin K. Hardin, "'If I Still Proclaim Circumcision' (Gal 5:11a): Paul, the Law, and Gentile Circumcision," *JSPL* 3 (2013): 145–164.

[69] Joshua D. Garroway, *The Beginning of the Gospel: Paul, Philippi, and the Origins of Christianity* (London: Palgrave Macmillan, 2018), 19–89. But see the incisive criticisms raised by Paula Fredriksen, review in *RBL* (June 2020).

[70] Francis Watson, in the first edition of his *Paul, Judaism, and the Gentiles* (Cambridge: Cambridge University Press, 1986), but not the second (Grand Rapids, MI: Eerdmans, 2007), takes the verse to mean that the newly minted apostle Paul preached Christ *to the* circumcision, i.e., to Jews (aligning, perhaps, with a certain construal of Paul's career in Acts). This is ingenious, but it is not what Gal 5:11 says, since there circumcision is the direct object, not the indirect object, of the verb.

[71] The strongest iterations of this reading, in my view, are Donaldson, *Paul and the Gentiles*, 273–284; and Thiessen, *Paul and the Gentile Problem*, 37–41.

[72] See the masterful discussion of all the proposals on offer in Ryan D. Collman, *The Apostle to the Foreskin: Circumcision in the Letters of Paul*, BZNW 259 (Berlin: De Gruyter, 2023).

(1 Macc 2:46) as analogous.[73] But 1 Maccabees does not call this, or indeed anything, Ἰουδαϊσμός; and neither 2 Maccabees nor 4 Maccabees, which do have the word, connect it with the circumcision of gentiles. Ryan Collman has recently argued that Paul "formerly preached circumcision" in the sense that he formerly insisted that eighth-day circumcision (i.e., genealogical Jewishness) alone could confer Abrahamic sonship, but since his revelation and commission he now knows that gentiles, too, can receive the pneuma of Christ and become seed and sons of Abraham.[74] Collman's interpretation is entirely new, as far as I know, but it is as good as or better than any of the other autobiographical interpretations of Gal 5:11.

But all autobiographical interpretations of the verse have to reckon with one objection to which I have not yet seen a satisfactory answer. Namely: "If I *still* preach circumcision" (assuming it is counterfactual) suggests that Paul has ceased preaching circumcision. But "I am *still* persecuted" (which is presented as empirically true) suggests that Paul has continuously been, and still is, persecuted. But the latter claim contradicts Paul's autobiography in Galatians and elsewhere: that in his previous life he emphatically was *not* persecuted, but was himself a *persecutor* (Gal 1:13, 23; Phil 3:6). It is only since he started preaching the cross that he finds himself on the receiving end of persecution. In short, the majority reading of the first clause makes nonsense of the second clause. Perhaps that is a price worth paying, since there is no reading of this verse that solves all the problems effortlessly. But I, for one, demur. After all, we do not *have* to read the verse as autobiography. J. Louis Martyn suggested that Gal 5:11 is a report not of autobiography but of an accusation levelled at Paul by his rivals: that he sometimes, inconsistently, disingenuously urges circumcision upon gentiles-in-Christ (cf. 1 Cor 9:19–23; Acts 16:3).[75] There are problems with this hypothesis, too,[76] but no more or worse problems than there are with the several autobiographical interpretations. Perhaps Gal 5:11 is not autobiographical but rhetorical, even prosopopoetic. We have

---

[73] Thiessen, *Paul and the Gentile Problem*, 40 makes precisely this argument. I disagree with it for the reasons noted above, but there is also the issue recently raised by Isaac Soon ("'In Strength' Not 'By Force': Rereading the Circumcision of the Uncircumcised ἐν ἰσχύι in 1 Macc 2:46," *JSP* 29 [2020]: 149–167) that 1 Macc 2:46 does not actually say, as most have taken it to say, that the Hasmoneans had a policy of *forcible* circumcision.

[74] Collman, *Apostle to the Foreskin*.   [75] Martyn, *Galatians*, 475–477.

[76] See the criticisms raised by Campbell, "Galatians 5:11."

Galatians before Judaism

many, many examples of Paul speaking rhetorically, even (or *especially*) in the first person: "I belong to Paul, I belong to Apollos" (1 Cor 3:4); "Why am I still condemned as a sinner?" (Rom 3:7); "Branches were broken off so that I might be grafted in" (Rom 11:19); and so on.[77] And Gal 5:7–12 is otherwise not about Paul at all, but entirely about his anonymous rivals: "Who hindered you?" (Gal 5:7). "He will bear the judgment, whoever he may be" (Gal 5:10). "Would that those who are agitating you would cut themselves off" (Gal 5:12). In light of all this, a single clause in Gal 5:11 is a very thin thread on which to hang a theory of an early Pauline circumcising mission. In sum, I am not sure what "preaching circumcision" in Gal 5:11 means, but I am pretty confident that it is not Ἰουδαϊσμός (Gal 1:13). And in any case, to return to our main point, Ἰουδαϊσμός is not (what we moderns call) Judaism.

What, finally, *does* Galatians say about "Judaism" in our sense, that is, the religion of Paul's non-Christ-believing Jewish contemporaries? In truth, very little. Galatians certainly does not portray Jewish religion as such as a rival means of justification.[78] Indeed, Gal 2:15–16 suggests exactly the opposite: Ἡμεῖς φύσει Ἰουδαῖοι καὶ οὐκ ἐξ ἐθνῶν ἁμαρτωλοί εἰδότες ὅτι οὐ δικαιοῦται ἄνθρωπος ἐξ ἔργων νόμου ἐὰν μὴ διὰ πίστεως Ἰησοῦ Χριστοῦ, καὶ ἡμεῖς εἰς Χριστὸν Ἰησοῦν ἐπιστεύσαμεν, "We who are Jews by nature (not sinners from among the gentiles), because we know that a person is not justified from works of the law except through the faith of Jesus Christ, we have also trusted in Christ Jesus."[79] In other words, gentile sinners (like the gentiles in the Galatian Christ-assemblies) might mistakenly think that the law is a mechanism for getting oneself justified, but Jews know better than to make that category mistake.[80] In Galatians, Paul's expectation concerning his Jewish kinfolk is that Peter's apostolate to the circumcision (Gal 2:8) will bring them into the messianic fold in due course. Their religion as such is not in view in

---

[77] In my view, the discussion of this phenomenon by Stowers, *Rereading of Romans*, remains unsurpassed.

[78] See further Chapter 3.

[79] The adverbial participle εἰδότες is frequently taken as a concession (e.g., RSV: "yet who know...") on the assumption that Paul expects his fellow Jews to aspire to be justified by the law, but this assumption is by no means obvious, and it is arguably exactly wrong.

[80] Indeed, this might further suggest that the agitators themselves are judaizing gentiles-in-Christ rather than Jews-in-Christ, which, if true, would resolve some of the difficulties surrounding Paul's description of them in Gal 6:12–13. See further Chapter 4.

Galatians, because it does not present a problem. It will eventually present a problem in Romans 9–11, because there Paul reckons with the realization that Peter's apostolate to the circumcision has been less than entirely successful. In Galatians, however, Paul seems to expect that the messianic ingathering of Israel will take care of itself.

Which suggests an interpretation of the curious benediction upon "the Israel of God" in Gal 6:16: ὅσοι τῷ κανόνι τούτῳ στοιχήσουσιν, εἰρήνη ἐπ' αὐτοὺς καὶ ἔλεος καὶ ἐπὶ τὸν Ἰσραὴλ τοῦ θεοῦ, "As many as follow this rule, peace be upon them, and mercy also upon the Israel of God."[81] "This rule" is the notion that new creation has rendered obsolete both circumcision and foreskin (Gal 6:15), and "those who follow it" are the receptive among Paul's Galatian audience, those who take his view over against his opponents' view (cf. Gal 5:10). In the immediate context, this pertains to the circumcision controversy in the letter, which is of course a matter of concern for the gentile Christ-assemblies in Galatia. As for "the Israel of God," everywhere else that Paul uses the word Ἰσραήλ and cognates (Rom 9:6, 27, 31; 10:19, 21; 11:2, 7, 25, 26; 1 Cor 10:18; 2 Cor 3:7, 13; Phil 3:5), the word refers to the Jewish *ethnos*.[82] As Susan Eastman has shown, there is very good reason to think that the same is true here.[83] This second clause wishes mercy upon God's people Israel (cf. "mercy" and "Israel" in Rom 9:14–29; 11:25–32), who Paul expects will soon trust the messiah through Peter's apostolate to the circumcision (Gal 2:7–8). It parallels the first clause, which wishes peace upon all who heed Paul's plea to be rightwised not by judaizing but by trusting Christ.[84]

---

[81] The syntax of the benediction is difficult but not impenetrable. An excellent recent treatment is Susan Grove Eastman, "Israel and the Mercy of God: A Rereading of Galatians 6:16 and Romans 9–11," *NTS* 56 (2010): 367–395, with whom my argument here has close affinities.

[82] So rightly E. P. Sanders, *Paul, the Law, and the Jewish People* (Philadelphia: Fortress, 1983), 176, who unnecessarily concludes that Gal 6:16 is an exception to this rule. See my discussion of all the relevant passages in Chapter 7.

[83] See Eastman, "Israel and the Mercy of God," 385–390, against the tide of majority opinion. The main alternatives are that Paul uses "the Israel of God" to signify Jewish Christ-believers (thus classically Gottlob Schrenk, "Was bedeutet 'Israel Gottes'?" *Judaica* 5 [1949]: 81–94) or all Christ-believers (thus classically Nils A. Dahl, "Der Name Israel," *Judaica* 6 [1950]: 161–170).

[84] Paula Fredriksen, "Judaizing the Nations: The Ritual Demands of Paul's Gospel," *NTS* 56 (2010): 232–252, rightly notes that technically Paul *does* expect his gentiles to judaize inasmuch as they must reject their own ancestral gods and worship the Jewish god (e.g., 1 Thess 1:9). In this respect Paul's gospel is not "law-free." Judaizing comes in degrees, however, and in comparison to his rival teachers in Galatia Paul demands very little in the way of judaizing, so little that, as Paul himself sees it, he does not demand judaizing at all (Gal 2:14).

Conclusion

To summarize: In Galatians Paul is simply not concerned with (what we call) Judaism, that is, the religion of majority, non-Christ-following Jews. He is incensed at the prospect of gentile Christ-believers judaizing (Gal 2:14; 5:2–12), but that is an altogether different thing: a particular kind of *ethnos*-bending activity. He recalls his own former advocacy for "judaization" (Gal 1:13–14), but that too is an altogether different thing: a particular political cause. It is true, of course, that Paul was very much involved in his ancestral religion before his apostolic call, but then, Paul was very much involved in his ancestral religion *after* his apostolic call, as well, indeed, to the very end of his life.[85] But that is not what he is talking about in Gal 1:13–14. He is talking about his former occupation in a movement for the defense of Jewish ancestral ways, a sectarian political program that Paul, like other Hellenistic- and Roman-period writers, calls Ἰουδαϊσμός. For Paul's reflections on what we call Judaism – that is, the observance of Jewish customs by Jewish people – one must look to his Letter to the Romans: "Israel have pursued a law of righteousness as if by works" (Rom 9:31–32), "Israel undertook to establish a righteousness of their own" (Rom 10:3), and so on. And ultimately, not even Romans can provide all that the Christian tradition needs for a theological account of Judaism, because even at the end of his epistolary career Paul did not yet imagine Judaism as we know it.[86]

---

[85] See further Matthew V. Novenson, "Did Paul Abandon Either Judaism or Monotheism?" in *Paul, Then and Now*.

[86] So rightly Sanders, *Paul, the Law, and the Jewish People*, 197. This recognition is the starting point for any serious Christian theological account of Judaism, such as, e.g., Krister Stendahl, *Final Account: Paul's Letter to the Romans* (Minneapolis: Fortress, 1995); R. Kendall Soulen, *The God of Israel and Christian Theology* (Minneapolis: Fortress, 1996), building on the work of Michael Wyschogrod, especially the essays now collected in Wyschogrod, *Abraham's Promise: Judaism and Jewish-Christian Relations* (Grand Rapids, MI: Eerdmans, 2004).

3 | Who Says Justification from Works of the Law?

Voltaire deserves credit for pointing out that some of our most important philosophical and theological ideas are, or at least started out as, terms of abuse. In the entry on "Idolatry" in his *Philosophical Dictionary*, he writes, "It appears that that there has never been any people on the earth who took for themselves the name of idolater. This word is an insult that the Gentiles, the Polytheists seemed to deserve; but it is certain that if one had asked at the Senate of Rome, at the Areopagus of Athens, at the court of the kings of Persia, 'Are you idolaters?' they would hardly have understood the question."[1] Indeed, idolatry is one of those big, important ideas in the history of religions that have come down to us almost exclusively from the pens of their naysayers, ideas for which, once we take the time to look, we are hard-pressed to identify any actual proponents anywhere in the historical record.[2] My purpose in this chapter is to explore another such idea – namely, justification from works of the law – and to press the question who, if anyone, was ever a proponent of this idea. Who actually says justification from works of the law?

---

[1] Voltaire, "Idol, Idolator, Idolatry," *Encyclopedia of Diderot & d'Alembert Collaborative Translation Project*, trans. Erik Liddell (Ann Arbor: University of Michigan Library, 2006); French original *Encyclopédie ou Dictionnaire raisonné des sciences, des arts et des métiers* (Paris, 1765), 8:500–504. In an interesting instance of reception history, Voltaire's point about idolatry here becomes important for Wilfred Cantwell Smith's account of religion in *The Meaning and End of Religion* (Minneapolis: Fortress, 1991 [1962]).

[2] See further Alexi Chantziantoniou, "Paul and the Politics of Idolatry: Ancient Mediterranean Cult Images and Iconic Ritual in the Letters of Paul" (PhD diss., University of Cambridge, 2023).

An Idea in Search of a Proponent

An ocean of ink has been spilled in the centuries-long effort to ferret out what the apostle Paul means when he speaks of being justified from works of the law (Gal 2:16; Rom 3:20, 28; cf. also Gal 2:21; 3:11, 21, 24; 5:4; Phil 3:9).[3] Does that troublesome phrase mean earning God's goodwill by means of one's moral achievements?[4] Hoarding God's goodwill for one's in-group while denying it to outsiders?[5] Putting one's confidence in human religion rather than divine revelation?[6] Undertaking a religious path from which one is excluded on account of one's ethnicity?[7] Rather than start with yet another explication of this much-contested phrase, I want to start by posing this second-order question: Who ever thought that a person *is* justified from works of the law? And, relatedly, who did Paul think thought such a thing? Posing this more oblique question is a worthwhile exercise in its own right and also stands to yield some otherwise unavailable insight into what justification from works of the law actually means.

Some classic discussions of the issue bypass this second-order question entirely. They only care about the useful theological idea, not the question who might have actually subscribed to it. Other classic discussions recognize the importance of our question but presuppose their (oftentimes predictable) answers. Martin Luther had some strongly held opinions about what kinds of people think that one is justified from works of the law, and he was happy to name names. "As many as are in the world that hold not this doctrine [of justification by faith], are either Turks, Jews, papists, or heretics. For between 'the righteousness of the law' and 'Christian righteousness,' there is no mean. He then that strayeth from this 'Christian righteousness' must

---

[3] Alister E. McGrath, *Iustitia Dei: A History of the Christian Doctrine of Justification*, 4th ed. (Cambridge: Cambridge University Press, 2020) provides a thorough history of this centuries-long effort.

[4] Thus, classically, Luther, *Epistle to the Galatians*; and, in a more modern form, Bultmann, *Theology of the New Testament*.

[5] Thus the so-called New Perspective on Paul, in particular James D. G. Dunn, *The New Perspective on Paul*, rev. ed. (Grand Rapids, MI: Eerdmans, 2008); and N. T. Wright, *What Saint Paul Really Said: Was Paul of Tarsus the Real Founder of Christianity?* (Grand Rapids, MI: Eerdmans, 1997).

[6] Thus Karl Barth, *The Epistle to the Romans*, trans. Edwyn C. Hoskyns (Oxford: Oxford University Press, 1968 [1933]).

[7] Thus Eisenbaum, *Paul Was Not a Christian*.

needs fall into 'the righteousness of the law.'"[8] Whereas Luther worried about Turks, Jews, papists, and heretics, modern historical critics have attributed the idea of justification from works of the law almost exclusively to Jews. For instance, James Dunn, architect of the so-called New Perspective on Paul,[9] writes, "It was his [Paul's] fellow Jews in particular who needed to hear that no one is justified by works of the law."[10] Simon Gathercole, Dunn's student and critic, agrees with Dunn on who it is who affirms what Paul denies: "When he [Paul] talks of justification apart from works of the Law, he is opposing a Jewish position whereby obedience to the Law in a comprehensive sense results in final vindication by God."[11] And so on.[12] Ironically – and we will come back to this – many recent "radical" interpreters actually agree with Luther, Dunn, and Gathercole that the official ancient Jewish position is that Jews, at least, are indeed justified from works of the law. (And this unusual pattern of agreement in the secondary literature ought to make us stop and think.)

But who actually thought that a person is justified from works of the law? It turns out that the evidence for any ancient person claiming that view for him- or herself is virtually nil. Significantly, Paul does not take over the phrase from the Jewish scriptures. The three relevant terms (δικαιοσύνη, ἔργα, and νόμος, and their cognates) never cluster together in any of Paul's chief source texts (Genesis, Deuteronomy, Psalms, Isaiah), nor in any other books later numbered among the Tanakh.[13] In short, "justification from works of the law" is not a thing – good, bad, or indifferent – anywhere in the Jewish scriptures.

---

[8] Martin Luther, "The Argument of the Epistle of St. Paul to the Galatians," in Martin Luther, *Epistle to the Galatians*, lxxviii.
[9] Dunn, "The New Perspective on Paul," in *New Perspective on Paul*, 99–120.
[10] Dunn, "The New Perspective on Paul: Whence, What and Whither," in *New Perspective on Paul*, 44–45.
[11] Simon Gathercole, "Justified by Faith, Justified by His Blood: The Evidence of Rom 3:21–4:25," in *Justification and Variegated Nomism, Volume 2*, ed. D. A. Carson et al. (Tübingen: Mohr Siebeck, 2004), 148.
[12] On this very telling point of agreement between Old and New Perspectives, see Thiessen, "Conjuring Paul and Judaism."
[13] Once in the Jewish Greek text Wisdom of Solomon all three roots do cluster together, though not at all in the way that Paul combines them. Wis 2:12: "[The wicked say:] Let us lie in wait for the righteous man [τὸν δίκαιον], because he is inconvenient to us, and he opposes our actions [τοῖς ἔργοις ἡμῶν] and reproaches us for sins against the law [ἁμαρτήματα νόμου] and ascribes to us sins against our training" (trans. NETS).

An Idea in Search of a Proponent 53

Paul does not take over the phrase from scripture, but he does explain it with reference to scripture. In Romans 3, Paul cites an oracle from the psalms as establishing the principle that justification is *not* from works of the law. He writes, διότι ἐξ ἔργων νόμου οὐ δικαιωθήσεται πᾶσα σάρξ ἐνώπιον αὐτοῦ, διὰ γὰρ νόμου ἐπίγνωσις ἁμαρτίας, "Because from works of the law *all flesh shall not be justified before him* [Ps 142:2 OG], for through the law comes knowledge of sin" (Rom 3:20). Admittedly, Paul does not mark this as a citation, and he reads πᾶσα σάρξ, "all flesh," where our Old Greek Psalms manuscripts read πᾶς ζῶν (for Hebrew כל־חי), "everyone living,"[14] but it is nevertheless right to see here a citation rather than an accident. The striking thing is that the psalm says nothing at all about works or law. In its own context, it is simply a plea for divine mercy: "Do not enter into judgment with your slave, for everyone living shall not be justified before you [οὐ δικαιωθήσεται ἐνώπιόν σου πᾶς ζῶν]." Paul *adds* the crucial qualifier ἐξ ἔργων νόμου, "from works of the law" to the psalmist's denial of the possibility of justification before God. Paul brings the idea to the psalm rather than finding it there. And he takes the psalm to agree with him,[15] not to attest the view that he opposes.

Elsewhere Paul cites a different oracle in support of the same claim. In Gal 3:11 he states as an axiom that ὅτι δὲ ἐν νόμῳ οὐδεὶς δικαιοῦται παρὰ τῷ θεῷ δῆλον, "It is clear that by the law no one is justified with God," citing as warrant the Old Greek text of Hab 2:4: ὅτι ὁ δίκαιος ἐκ πίστεως ζήσεται, "for *The person who is righteous from trust shall live.*"[16] This oracle, like Old Greek Psalm 142 in Romans 3, says nothing at all about either works or law, nor does it even have Paul's characteristic verb δικαιόω, "rightwise" or "justify." But it does have the adjective δίκαιος and, crucially, the prepositional phrase that Paul

---

[14] It is quite possible that Paul may have deliberately modified his source text (on which phenomenon see Christopher D. Stanley, *Paul and the Language of Scripture: Citation Technique in the Pauline Epistles and Contemporary Literature*, SNTSMS 74 [Cambridge: Cambridge University Press, 1992]) in order to keep *flesh* on the side of that which cannot be justified and *life* on the side of that which can be and is. My thanks to Matthew Thiessen for suggesting this possibility to me in conversation.

[15] As rightly seen by Richard B. Hays, "Psalm 143 and the Logic of Romans 3," *JBL* 99 (1980): 107–115.

[16] On the logic of the citation, see Timothy H. Lim, "Why did Paul cite Habakkuk 2:4b?" *ExpTim* 133 (2022): 225–232.

sets up opposite "from works of the law": ἐκ πίστεως, "from trust."[17] (Equally important, I think, is the prophet's use of ζῆν, "to live,"[18] which makes some sense out of Paul's rather idiosyncratic use of "righteousness"; more on this below.) In Romans 1, too, Paul cites the same oracle of Habakkuk, this time in support of his positive claim that the righteousness of God now revealed is ἐκ πίστεως.[19] He writes, δικαιοσύνη γὰρ θεοῦ ἐν αὐτῷ ἀποκαλύπτεται ἐκ πίστεως εἰς πίστιν, καθὼς γέγραπται· ὁ δὲ δίκαιος ἐκ πίστεως ζήσεται, "In it [the good announcement] the righteousness of God is revealed from trust to trust, as it is written, *The person who is righteous from trust shall live* [Hab 2:4 OG]" (Rom 1:17). Here again, the oracle of the prophet is taken to attest Paul's own view, not the view that he denies.

Because Paul appeals to Hab 2:4 in both Galatians and Romans, and because he can produce no source text that has even the phrase "from works of the law," much less "righteousness from works of the law," I think Francis Watson is surely right in proposing that Paul actually coined the phrase "righteousness from works of the law" based on (what he sees as) its opposite in Hab 2:4: "righteous[ness] from trust." Watson writes, "The phrase, 'by works of law' (*ex ergōn nomou*) has apparently been constructed on the model of Habakkuk's 'by faith' (*ek pisteōs*).... If, as the prophet teaches, we are righteous by faith, then the logical corollary is that we are not righteous by the law. The negation is derived from the scriptural assertion; it belongs to the interpretation of the scriptural text."[20] Just so. If, as E. P. Sanders pointed out, Paul reasons from solution to plight,[21] Paul also reasons from solution to counter-solution: He knows that there is such a thing

---

[17] The significance of which is not lost on Sanders, *Paul, the Law, and the Jewish People*, 21: "We should consider how Paul chooses the quotations in Galatians 3. The argument is terminological. It depends on finding prooftexts for the view that *Gentiles* are *righteoused* by *faith*. Those three words are crucial... Paul cites the only two passages in the Septuagint (LXX) in which the *dik-* root is connected with *pistis* (Gen 15:6; Hab 2:4)."

[18] Thus rightly Andrew K. Boakye, *Death and Life: Resurrection, Restoration, and Rectification in Paul's Letter to the Galatians* (Eugene, OR: Pickwick, 2017), 120–139 on this passage.

[19] On which see Benjamin Schliesser, "Christ-Faith as an Eschatological Event (Galatians 3.23–26): A Third View on *Pistis Christou*," *JSNT* 38 (2016): 277–300.

[20] Francis Watson, *Paul and the Hermeneutics of Faith* (London: T&T Clark, 2004), 56–57.

[21] Sanders, *Paul and Palestinian Judaism*, 442–447.

as righteousness from Christ-faith; he encounters certain people disagreeing with him about it; and he attributes to them a view that he calls righteousness from works of the law.

There is, however, precisely one passage in the Torah that Paul reads as describing what he calls "righteousness from the law": "Moses writes about the righteousness from the law that *The person who does these things shall live in them* [Lev 18:5]" (Rom 10:5). Elsewhere, Paul cites this same lemma from Leviticus as confirming a related point, namely, that whereas the sending of the messiah is from trust, the law is not. Paul writes, "The law is not from trust, but rather: *The one who does these things shall live in them* [Lev 18:5]" (Gal 3:12). Paul does *not* say here – and indeed elsewhere he strenuously denies the notion – that the law as such teaches justification from works of the law. (See, in particular, Gal 4:21: "You who want to be under the law, do you not heed the law?" where Paul goes on to argue, yet again, that the law actually teaches... justification from trust!) As Watson notes, what Paul does here is to read one part of the law *against* another part.[22] The conclusion Paul draws from this divinatory exegesis is not a contradiction, however, but rather scriptural testimony to two kinds of righteousness (from the law and from trust, respectively) for two kinds of life (mortal and immortal, respectively).[23] This important idea appears in a nutshell in Rom 10:5–8: "Moses writes about the righteousness from the law that *The person who does these things shall live in them* [Lev 18:5]. But the righteousness from trust says... *The word is near you, in your mouth and in your heart* [Deut 30:14]." The contrast here is not law versus gospel, but rather (one part of the) law versus (another part of the) law. All of it is Torah, but Paul finds in Torah both a righteousness from the law and a righteousness from trust. Which is to say that we cannot simply lay "justification from works of the law" at the feet of Moses, either, since Paul does not do so.[24]

---

[22] Watson, *Paul and the Hermeneutics of Faith*, 48–69. I disagree with Watson on how, exactly, this counter-reading works, in particular his idea of "the law's failed project." Paul's point is not that the law tried and failed, but that the law succeeded at its own task while also testifying to a new state of affairs to arrive with the messiah.

[23] On which see further Chapter 9.

[24] *Pace* Simon Gathercole, "Torah, Life, and Salvation: Leviticus 18:5 in Early Judaism and the New Testament," in *From Prophecy to Testament: The Function of the Old Testament in the New*, ed. Craig A. Evans (Peabody, MA:

Rather embarrassingly for Paul's modern interpreters, the first person in antiquity expressly to attest the motif of "justification from works of the law" turns out to be... Paul himself. Its earliest appearance is in Paul's own rhetoric, not anywhere "in the wild" in Jewish sources prior to Paul. And what is more, the elusive claim for which we are searching – that a person is justified from works of the law – is precisely as well attested in *post*-Pauline Jewish texts as it is in *pre*-Pauline Jewish texts, which is to say, almost not at all.[25] Philo does not claim it,[26] nor does Josephus, nor R. Yohanan ben Zakkai, nor R. Akiba, nor R. Judah the Patriarch. We do not find it in the Mishnah, Tosefta, Talmud Yerushalmi, Talmud Bavli, or any of the classical midrashim.[27] Nor, again, in any of the targumim.[28] This is striking (not to say damning) if, *ex hypothesi*, justification from works of the law is supposed to be a defining characteristic of ancient Jewish piety.

Paul versus the Qumran Covenanters?

Having searched in vain, literally for centuries, for any evidence at all of any ancient Jewish writer saying, in so many words, that he or she would be justified from works of the law, interpreters of Paul were elated when, after an decades-long delay, the text of six fragments from Qumran cave 4 – 4Q394, 4Q395, 4Q396, 4Q397, 4Q398, 4Q399, which together comprise 4QMMT, *Miqsat Ma'aseh ha-Torah*

Hendrickson, 2004), 131–150 at 142: "Rom 10:5, where Paul contrasts the righteousness described by Moses with the righteousness that comes by faith." In Rom 10:5, in fact, Paul contrast two kinds of righteousness *both* described by Moses, one from the law and the other from trust.

[25] The post-Pauline Epistle of James claims that a person is justified *from works*, though not *from works of the law*. "From works a person is justified, and not from trust alone" (James 2:24). But while James may here be responding to (his understanding of) Paul, Paul is certainly not responding to James. And in any case, James, like Paul, comes from Christ-partisan Jewish circles, not from majority (non-Christ-partisan) Jewish circles. So if there is a debate between them, it is an in-house debate.

[26] See discussion below under "Paul versus Philo of Alexandria?"

[27] See Philip S. Alexander, "Torah and Salvation in Tannaitic Literature," in *Justification and Variegated Nomism, Volume 1*, ed. D. A. Carson et al. (Tübingen: Mohr Siebeck, 2001), 261–302.

[28] See Martin McNamara, "Some Targum Themes," in *Justification and Variegated Nomism, Volume 1*, 303–356.

(also called 4QHalakhicLetter) – was finally published in 1994.²⁹ The red meat was right there in the title assigned to the text by Elisha Qimron and John Strugnell: *miqsat maʿaseh ha-Torah*, "some works of the law."³⁰ The fragmentary text begins *in medias res* with a discussion of the authors' sectarian calendar and proceeds to give legal rulings on numerous points: offerings from gentiles, the slaughter of sacrificial animals, intermarriage between priests and laypeople, the purity of poured liquids, purification for skin diseases, and other such.

Finally, a concluding exhortation provides a bit of context for the assemblage of all these legal opinions.³¹ The author or authors (the voice is first-person plural) explain to their audience:³²

We have also written to you concerning some of the observances of the Law, which we think are beneficial to you and your people. For [we have noticed] that prudence and knowledge of the Law are with you. Understand all these (matters) and ask Him to straighten your counsel and put you far away from thoughts of evil and the counsel of Belial. Consequently, you will rejoice at the end of time when you discover that some of our sayings are true. *And it will be reckoned for you as righteousness* [Gen 15:6] when you perform what is right and good before Him, for your own good and for that of Israel. (4Q398 14–17 ii)³³

---

²⁹ Elisha Qimron and John Strugnell, eds., *Qumran Cave 4 V: Miqsat Maʿaseh ha-Torah*, DJD 10 (Oxford: Clarendon, 1994). Prior to the publication of the DJD edition, Qimron and Strugnell had issued some short preliminary publications, and Hershel Shanks published a leaked version of the text, exposing himself to legal jeopardy.

³⁰ And red meat it is. The work itself bears no title in the manuscripts. Qimron and Strugnell's choice of those few words to title the work as a whole was guaranteed (calculated?) to make New Testament scholars come running.

³¹ On the text as a whole, see John Kampen and Moshe J. Bernstein, eds., *Reading 4QMMT: New Perspectives on Qumran Law and History* (Atlanta: Scholars Press, 1996); Hanne von Weissenberg, *4QMMT: Reevaluating the Text, the Function, and the Meaning of the Epilogue*, STDJ 82 (Leiden: Brill, 2008); and now Vered Noam, *4QMMT*, Oxford Commentary on the Dead Sea Scrolls (Oxford: Oxford University Press, forthcoming).

³² Whoever that audience may be. Earlier scholarship on 4QMMT generally took it to be a genuine letter to some second party, whereas recent research has tended toward taking it as a treatise in artificial epistolary form; see Steven D. Fraade, "To Whom It May Concern: 4QMMT and Its Addressees," *RevQ* 19 (2000): 507–526.

³³ Trans. Geza Vermes, *The Complete Dead Sea Scrolls in English*, 7th ed. (London: Penguin, 2012).

The authors call what they are commending מעשי התורה, *ma'aseh ha-Torah*, which in Greek could plausibly be rendered ἔργα νόμου, "works of the law."[34] And not only so, but they say that those who heed their instruction about these works will find, as father Abraham found in Gen 15:6, "it reckoned to them for righteousness." Interpreters of Paul could not help but hear an echo of the apostle's citation of the same verse – but including a crucial preceding clause – in Gal 3:6 and Rom 4:3: "Abraham trusted God, and it was reckoned to him for righteousness."

Here, at last, was the smoking gun! Proof positive that ancient Jews really did think that they would be justified from works of the law, and therefore that the apostle was vindicated in making that accusation.[35] Writing soon after the publication of the manuscript, Martin Abegg commented, "It does not seem unreasonable to suggest that Paul consciously reflected the term 'works of the law' which was used by the author of 4QMMT and – I would suggest – by Paul's opponents as recorded in the book of Galatians. In addition, it appears highly likely that Paul was reacting to a position that was espoused in 4QMMT by the Qumran covenanters, namely, that a person was reckoned righteous by keeping 'works of the law.'"[36] James Dunn took 4QMMT to represent a view held not just at Qumran but among ancient Jews more widely: "The weight of evidence does seem to suggest that MMT preserves a vocabulary and manner of theologising which left its mark on a wider spectrum of Jewish thought and practice, and that it was just this sort of theologising and practice which confronted Paul in Antioch and which he wrote Galatians to counter."[37] Similarly N. T. Wright: "What MMT adds to the discussion, apart from a strong reinforcement of a covenantal and eschatological understanding of

---

[34] Greek ἔργον is the most common, though by no means the only, equivalency for Hebrew מעשה in the LXX/OG. In 4QMMT, as many interpreters have noted, the particular sense is perhaps closest to "observances." On this issue, see further Michael Bachmann, "Was für Praktiken? Zur jüngsten Diskussion um die ἔργα νόμου," *NTS* 55 (2009): 35–54.

[35] On the fascinating history of New Testament scholarship engaging with 4QMMT, see Jörg Frey, "Contextualizing Paul's Works of the Law: MMT in New Testament Scholarship," in *Qumran, Early Judaism, and New Testament Interpretation: Kleine Schriften III*, ed. Jacob N. Cerone, WUNT 424 (Tübingen: Mohr Siebeck, 2019), 743–762.

[36] Martin Abegg, "4QMMT C 27, 31 and 'Works Righteousness,'" *DSD* 6 (1999): 140.

[37] Dunn, "4QMMT and Galatians," in *New Perspective on Paul*, 345.

justification, is the fact that 'justification by works of Torah,' in the broad sense described, was not just a Pharisaic doctrine, nor simply something that the Galatian 'agitators' were urging. It characterized sectarian Judaisms of various sorts, and perhaps mainstream Judaism (insofar as there was such a thing) as well."[38]

Abegg, Dunn, Wright, and others[39] may be forgiven their excitement at the discovery of so close a verbal parallel as this. Upon inspection, however, the evidence does not bear out their very ambitious claims. For one thing, even were we to grant that 4QMMT attests the view that Paul opposes, we have no grounds for generalizing from the lone instance in 4QMMT to "sectarian Judaisms of various sorts," let alone "mainstream Judaism." But more important still, it is not in fact the case that 4QMMT attests the view that Paul opposes. To be sure, there are crucial key words in common (if we make reasonable allowance for possible translation equivalencies) – "works of the law," "reckoned to you for righteousness"[40] – but the words refer to quite different things in their respective contexts. In 4QMMT, the "works of the law" are the particular halakhot that the authors recommend over against competing halakhot (which would of course also be "works of the law"!), for instance, a 364-day calendar as opposed to a 365-day calendar, or a prohibition of priest/laity intermarriage as opposed to a permission for it. And when the authors say that "it will be reckoned to you for righteousness," they mean that those who follow their legal opinion will, in the end, be vindicated.[41]

---

[38] N. T. Wright, "4QMMT and Paul," in *Pauline Perspectives: Essays on Paul, 1978–2013* (Minneapolis: Fortress, 2013), 353.

[39] E.g., David Flusser, "Gesetzeswerke in Qumran und bei Paulus," in *Geschichte – Tradition – Reflexion*, ed. H. Cancik et al., 3 vols. (Tübingen: Mohr Siebeck, 1996), 1:395–403; James D. G. Dunn and James H. Charlesworth, "Qumran's Some Works of Torah and Paul's Galatians," in *The Bible and the Dead Sea Scrolls, Volume 3* (Waco, TX: Baylor University Press, 2006), 187–201; Jacqueline C. R. De Roo, *Works of the Law at Qumran and in Paul* (Sheffield: Sheffield Phoenix, 2007); Yongbom Lee, "Getting in and Staying in: Another Look at 4QMMT and Galatians," *EvQ* 88 (2017): 126–142; Sprinkle, *Paul and Judaism Revisited*.

[40] Otto Betz, "Rechtfertigung in Qumran," in *Jesus, der Messias Israels* (Tübingen: Mohr Siebeck, 1987), 39–58 makes the apt point that there is no equivalency at all in Qumran Hebrew for the Greek verb δικαιόω.

[41] Simon Gathercole (*Where Is Boasting: Early Jewish Soteriology and Paul's Response in Romans 1–5* [Grand Rapids, MI: Eerdmans, 2002], 93–95) is right in saying that the eschaton is in view here, but wrong in concluding that "reckoned for righteousness" therefore means the attainment of salvation.

For Paul, "works of the law" means both more and less than it does in 4QMMT: more because it has in view Torah observance in general and as such – this is a controversial claim, but I think a true one[42] – and less because the only actual presenting issue for Paul is proselyte circumcision.[43] And when he speaks of "it being reckoned to a person for righteousness," Paul means much more than vindication in right opinion; he means the obliteration of all sin and establishment in perfect, pneumatic existence.[44] As Lutz Doering has recently put it in a retrospective assessment, "The expression 'works of (the) law' in MMT and in Paul represent two different ends of a common spectrum of meaning. Paul may draw on a discourse similar to that in MMT, but I am not sure we can say that what Paul attacks in Galatians is precisely the kind of Judaism evident in MMT. In particular, MMT is about disagreement in halakhic opinion, whereas Paul addresses the question whether Gentiles are, in the first place, obliged to observe halakhah or not."[45] I would put this last point differently,[46] but all in all, Doering's assessment is quite right. In the quest for ancient Jews who thought they would be justified from works of the law in the sense Paul means, 4QMMT turns out to be a red herring.[47]

---

[42] With Frey, "Contextualizing Paul's Works of the Law"; see further my argument in Chapter 9.

[43] Gal 4:10 ("You are observing days and months and seasons and years") is no exception, in my view; see Christina Harker, *The Colonizers' Idols: Paul, Galatia, and Empire in New Testament Studies*, WUNT 2/460 (Tübingen: Mohr Siebeck, 2018).

[44] See further Chapter 8.

[45] Lutz Doering, "4QMMT and the Letters of Paul," in Rey, ed., *The Dead Sea Scrolls and Pauline Literature*, 78–79.

[46] There are in fact certain commandments for which Paul holds gentiles responsible, but they are few and well defined (e.g., no idolatry, no *porneia*, love your neighbor); see Fredriksen, "Judaizing the Nations." Paul, like most of his Jewish contemporaries, does not think that gentiles are liable for all the commandments incumbent upon Jews, which is precisely the point of 1 Cor 7:19: "Circumcision is nothing, and foreskin is nothing; only keeping the commandments of God [pertinent to each]." On this crucial point, see further Holger M. Zellentin, *Law beyond Israel: From the Bible to the Quran* (Oxford: Oxford University Press, 2022).

[47] Thus rightly John M. G. Barclay, *Paul and the Gift* (Grand Rapids, MI: Eerdmans, 2015), 375n64: "In any case, it is doubtful that this rare Hebrew expression [*miqsat ma'aseh ha-Torah* in 4QMMT] can determine the meaning of Paul's Greek."

Paul versus Philo of Alexandria?

But perhaps, New Testament scholars reasoned, ancient Jews *thought* that a person is justified from works of the law, even if they did not *say* it. (The increasing desperation of this reasoning should have been a warning...) The task, then, would be to search the primary sources not for the words, but for the underlying idea that Paul supposedly meant by those words. And this is what most modern studies in fact do. Of all the many places where interpreters have claimed to find the putative concept of justification from works of the law in Jewish sources, there is one with enough possible warrant to merit some discussion here, namely: the works of Philo of Alexandria. In a couple of important articles on Philo's program of "ethical circumcision" – as when he writes, τὸ περιτέμνεσθαι ἡδονῆς καὶ παθῶν πάντων ἐκτομὴν... ἐμφαίνει, "Receiving circumcision portrays the excision of pleasure and all passions" (Philo, *Migration* 92) – Peder Borgen proposes that that is the same program advanced by the anonymous "agitators" in Paul's Letter to the Galatians, that what Paul calls "justification from works of the law" is nothing other than moral therapy at the feet of Moses, *à la* Philo.[48] Borgen writes, "Among the Jews of that time circumcision was understood to portray the removal of passions and desires and the evil inclination. In the works of Philo of Alexandria this interpretation of circumcision is very common, and he uses terminology similar to that which Paul uses."[49]

More recently, Ernest Clark has made a related case for Galatians, explicating Philo's account of the divinely appointed harmony between the elements of the universe (στοιχεῖα τοῦ κόσμου) and the law of Moses

---

[48] Peder Borgen, "Observations on the Theme 'Paul and Philo': Paul's Preaching of Circumcision in Galatia (Gal 5:11) and Debates on Circumcision in Philo," in *Die Paulinische Literatur und Theologie*, ed. S. Pedersen (Aarhus: Aros, 1980), 85–102; Peder Borgen, "Paul Preaches Circumcision and Pleases Men," in *Paul and Paulinism: Essays in Honour of C. K. Barrett*, ed. M. D. Hooker and S. G. Wilson (London: SPCK, 1982), 37–46. Both essays are collected in Peder Borgen, *Paul Preaches Circumcision and Pleases Men, and Other Essays on Christian Origins* (Trondheim: Tapir, 1983).

[49] Borgen, "Paul Preaches Circumcision and Pleases Men," 38. Borgen goes further and suggests that the agitators claimed that this was also Paul's own view, taking Paul's question in Gal 3:3 as patient of being read as a positive encouragement: "Having begun with the pneuma, will you now [please] complete with the flesh?" This I think unlikely, but that the agitators themselves held such a view is certainly plausible.

(νόμος) – as when Philo writes, τοῦ νομίμου ἀνδρὸς εὐθὺς ὄντος κοσμοπολίτου, πρὸς τὸ βούλημα τῆς φύσεως τὰς πράξεις ἀπευθύνοντος, "The man who observes the law is at once a citizen of the cosmos, directing his actions in relation to the rational purpose of nature" (Philo, *Creation* 3) – and arguing that precisely such an account underlies the "justification from works of the law" against which Paul rages. Thus Clark:

> Many of the agitators' thoughts and practices which caused Paul such concern correspond to actual propositions in Philo's works. To state the point absurdly, I am not suggesting that Philo received a letter from "the rabbis in Palestine" and left to tour and teach in the Galatian assemblies. I am suggesting, however, that the agitators were influenced by an amalgam of early Jewish thought best articulated by Philo (and now most available to us in his extant works).[50]

More recently still, Andrew Rillera has argued that the rhetorical diatribe in Rom 1–3, which, like Galatians, raises and rejects the idea of justification from works of the law, presupposes a specifically Philonic opponent. Rillera writes, "The teaching of the interlocutor in Rom 1–2 that Paul opposes matches both with broader Philonic views such as the natural knowledge of God and the presence of a natural law, and also with certain details peculiar to his tradition.... The 'character' in question [begins] to come into focus as a distinctively Philonic Teacher."[51] For Rillera, not only Galatians but Romans, too, attests Paul's mighty struggle with Philo, the unheralded architect of "justification from works of the law."

Interestingly, an earlier iteration of hypothesis was entertained and rejected by Samuel Sandmel in his deservedly famous 1962 article "Parallelomania" (which had been his SBL presidential address for 1961). In that article, Sandmel weighs a number of putative parallels between Philo and other ancient Jewish writers (including Paul), raising several methodological objections along the way. One of these methodological objections is a distinction between *apparent* and *real*

---

[50] Ernest P. Clark, "Enslaved under the Elements of the Cosmos" (PhD diss., University of St Andrews, 2018), 156. With his reference to "the rabbis in Palestine," Clark is quoting and dismissing an objection raised by Samuel Sandmel, "Parallelomania," *JBL* 81 (1962): 1–13 at 5, on which more in a moment.

[51] Andrew R. Rillera, "Paul's Philonic Opponent: Unveiling the One Who Calls Himself a Jew in Romans 2:17" (PhD diss., Duke University, 2021), 422.

parallels. Thus Sandmel: "The neophytes and the unwary often rush in, for example, to suppose that Philo's *nomos agraphos* and the rabbinic *torah she-be'al pe* are one and the same thing, for unwritten law and oral torah do sound alike. But... it turns out from detailed study that the two similar terms have no relationship whatsoever. In this case we have not a true parallel, but only an alleged one."[52] And even if a parallel is *real*, Sandmel further argues, it may not be *significant*. He writes, "Since all this literature is Jewish, it should reasonably reflect Judaism. Paul and the rabbis should overlap, and Paul and Philo and the Qumran writings and the rabbis should overlap. Accordingly, even true parallels may be of no great significance in themselves."[53]

As regards "justification from works of the law," as we have noted, the phrase itself does not occur in Philo, so in that sense there is no parallel at all. At a higher level of abstraction, however, I think that we can speak of a real and at least partly significant parallel between Philo's idea that Jewish circumcision is the first step toward virtue (even for gentiles!) and the message preached by Paul's rivals in Galatia (to the limited extent to which we can reconstruct that message).[54] With Sandmel,[55] however, I think it would be too much to reason from that similarity of ideas to a supposed proselyte-circumcising mission exported from Egypt to Asia Minor or Italy. Granted, it is only in Philo that we find these ideas articulated so elaborately, but they could easily have arisen elsewhere and otherwise in the Jewish diaspora, too.[56] Hence it seems to me a bridge too far to identify Paul's

---

[52] Sandmel, "Parallelomania," 2–3.   [53] Sandmel, "Parallelomania," 3.

[54] On how limited an extent, John M. G. Barclay, "Mirror-Reading a Polemical Letter: Galatians as a Test Case," *JSNT* 10 (1987): 73–93 is basically right, although I disagree with a few of his particular judgments; see further Chapter 4.

[55] See Sandmel, "Parallelomania," 5: "I am not prepared to suppose that Philo of Alexandria had to go to his mailbox at regular intervals, learn by letter what the rabbis in Palestine were saying, and then be in a position to transmute the newly received data into philosophical ideas. Again, I am not prepared to believe that there was a bridge for one-way traffic that stretched directly from the caves on the west bank of the Dead Sea to Galilee, or even further into Tarsus, Ephesus, Galatia, and Mars Hill... The various Jewish movements... make sense to me only if I conceive of them as simultaneously reflecting broad areas of overlapping and restricted areas of distinctiveness."

[56] E.g., Josephus writes from Rome, "Moses did not begin the arrangement of the laws with contracts and the rights of people with one another in a manner similar to others, but he led their thoughts up to God and the structure of the

rivals in Galatia – let alone his rhetorical interlocutor in Romans – as Philonists. But even if we could, that would not add up to evidence of the phenomenon with which we are here concerned, namely: "justification from works of the law" as a supposedly native species of Jewish piety. At the very most, it would be an instance of one figure (Philo) saying something that, when another figure ("the agitators") 1,500 miles across the sea says something possibly similar in an entirely different context, a third figure (Paul) calls "justification from works of the law." This is as good as it gets for studies of this type.

The reason that even the best of these studies are liable to this criticism has to do with their form.[57] They begin by positing their (widely varying) accounts of what justification from works of the law means, and then they adduce Jewish texts that they think attest their respective accounts. Thus Billerbeck points to texts that supposedly show ancient Jews earning God's goodwill by their own moral efforts,[58] Dunn to texts that supposedly show them excluding gentiles from salvation,[59] Gathercole to texts that supposedly show them claiming vindication at the last judgment on account of their performance of the law,[60] Barclay to texts that supposedly show them making the law a criterion of human worth,[61] and so on. And all say that what they identify in the sources is what Paul means by justification from works of the law. E. P. Sanders's remarkable *Paul and Palestinian Judaism* is, in a sense, one massive test of this threadbare approach. Sanders replicates Billerbeck's experiment with the primary sources and gets a different, even opposite result. The deep problem is that the approach itself is circular. It presupposes that Paul's "justification from works of the law" denotes some feature x of Jewish piety, and then goes in search of x. But that presupposition lacks any explicit warrant in Paul's letters and, as we shall see, is in fact wrong.

---

cosmos" (*Ant.* 1.21), which Elias Bickerman (*The Jews in the Greek Age* [Cambridge, MA: Harvard University Press, 1988], 114) plausibly attributes to widespread diaspora Jewish speculation.

[57] See Kent L. Yinger, "The Continuing Quest for Jewish Legalism," *BBR* 19 (2009): 375–391.

[58] Hermann L. Strack and Paul Billerbeck, *Kommentar zum Neuen Testament aus Talmud und Midrasch*, 4 vols. (Munich: Beck, 1922–1928), especially the excurses in vol. 4.

[59] Dunn, *New Perspective on Paul.*   [60] Gathercole, *Where Is Boasting.*

[61] Barclay, *Paul and the Gift.*

If You Know, You Know

The reason that scholars have failed to find ancient Jewish texts attesting the view that a person is justified from works of the law is that the phrase is Paul's own. He himself coins it, only in order to deny it. And if so – if justification from works of the law is not a naturally occurring motif in ancient Judaism but a term coined by Paul for a phenomenon identified by himself – then the pertinent question becomes: Where does *Paul* identify it? Who does *he* think holds the view that a person is justified from works of the law? What we should like to see is Paul using the relevant terms (righteousness, works, law, trust) together with verbs of thinking, knowing, perceiving, etc. attributed to certain people or types of people. And we do in fact see this.

The key text here is Gal 2:15–16, which has received ample comment, though not on this particular point. The passage comes in the middle of Paul's famous rebuke to Cephas at Antioch. *You must not pressure these gentiles-in-Christ to judaize*, Paul urges Cephas (Gal 2:14). Because, Paul reasons, Ἡμεῖς φύσει Ἰουδαῖοι καὶ οὐκ ἐξ ἐθνῶν ἁμαρτωλοί· εἰδότες [δὲ] ὅτι οὐ δικαιοῦται ἄνθρωπος ἐξ ἔργων νόμου ἐὰν μὴ διὰ πίστεως Ἰησοῦ Χριστοῦ, καὶ ἡμεῖς εἰς Χριστὸν Ἰησοῦν ἐπιστεύσαμεν, ἵνα δικαιωθῶμεν ἐκ πίστεως Χριστοῦ καὶ οὐκ ἐξ ἔργων νόμου (Gal 2:15–16). Most modern treatments, *presupposing* that Paul thinks that Jews think they can get justified from works of the law,[62] take Paul to be saying how remarkable it is that he and Cephas trusted in Christ, since, being Jews, they might have been expected not to do so, but to put their confidence in works of the law instead. The old RSV, for instance, reads: "We ourselves, who are Jews by birth and not Gentile sinners, *yet who know* that a man is not justified by works of the law but through faith in Jesus Christ, *even we* have believed in Christ Jesus, in order to be justified by faith in Christ." On this expansive translation, Paul and Cephas come to know that righteousness is not from works of the law *despite* being Jews. *Even they,* Jewish though they be, have

---

[62] This assumption is ubiquitous in the secondary literature, but one good example is Timo Eskola, "Paul the Theologian," in *A Narrative Theology of the New Testament*, WUNT 350 (Tübingen: Mohr Siebeck, 2015), 254: "In Paul's letters we see that he assumes that Jews have a positive attitude toward *erga nomou* and that he creates a conflict precisely around this issue. A typical passage linking Jews with a positive attitude toward works of the law and justification without law is Galatians 2."

trusted in Christ!⁶³ Such a reading reinforces the common presupposition, noted above, about what Paul thinks Jews think, but it does not fit easily with the syntax of the passage, which actually suggests the reverse.

Ἡμεῖς φύσει Ἰουδαῖοι καὶ οὐκ ἐξ ἐθνῶν ἁμαρτωλοί· εἰδότες [δὲ] ὅτι οὐ δικαιοῦται ἄνθρωπος ἐξ ἔργων νόμου. Thus NA28 prints it. The editors insert a stop after ἁμαρτωλοί, taking everything up to that point as an independent clause, because they are provisionally (hence the square brackets) reading δέ after εἰδότες. The δέ is not read in P46 or Alexandrinus, but it is read in Sinaiticus, Vaticanus, and Ephraemi Rescriptus.⁶⁴ The verse is intelligible whether the δέ is read or not, and it does not mean vastly differently either way,⁶⁵ but I think it more likely that the δέ is secondary, added in transmission to break a cumbersome sentence into clearer sense units. The syntax of this cumbersome sentence works as follows:

subject	We Jews by nature,
adverbial participle	knowing that a person is not put right from works of the law,
verb	trusted in Christ.

The two "and not" phrases are neatly parallel to one another: We Jews by nature (not gentile sinners), knowing that righteousness comes from trust in the messiah (not works of the law), trusted in the messiah. In other words, natural-born Jews know that righteousness

---

⁶³ Thus, e.g., Ernest De Witt Burton, *A Critical and Exegetical Commentary on the Epistle to the Galatians*, ICC (New York: Scribner's, 1920), 119: "The clause ['Ἡμεῖς φύσει Ἰουδαῖοι καὶ οὐκ ἐξ ἐθνῶν ἁμαρτωλοί] is *concessive* in relation to καὶ ἡμεῖς... ἐπιστεύσαμεν, etc. below."

⁶⁴ Bruce M. Metzger, *A Textual Commentary on the Greek New Testament* (London: United Bible Societies, 1971), makes no comment on this variant. On the text of this letter, see Günther Zuntz, *The Text of the Epistles: A Disquisition upon the Corpus Paulinum* (Oxford: British Academy, 1953); Stephen C. Carlson, *The Text of Galatians and Its History*, WUNT 2/385 (Tübingen: Mohr Siebeck, 2015).

⁶⁵ *Pace* N. T. Wright, *Galatians* (Grand Rapids, MI: Eerdmans, 2021), 134, who rightly perceives the exegetical question whether it is *Jews* or *Christ-believers* who know that a person is not justified (etc.), but wrongly claims that the answer hinges on whether we read the δέ or not. In fact, the answer hinges on Paul's own explicit contrast in this passage: Jews versus gentiles, not Christ-believers versus non-Christ-believers.

comes from Christ-faith, gentile sinners do not.⁶⁶ The emphatic καὶ ἡμεῖς following the participial phrase means not "even we" but "we indeed": "We indeed trusted in Christ in order to be rightwised," but these gentile sinners do not have the good sense to do so; they rely on the example of the apostles, which you, Cephas, have just ruined. Indeed, Paul's whole rebuke is predicated on the presumption of gentile ignorance: these naïve gentiles are going to get the wrong idea, that eschatological righteousness comes from works of the law. A good Jew like Cephas knows better than that, so shame on him for pressuring the hapless Antiochene gentiles to judaize.

Paul's presumption of general gentile ignorance is widely recognized in other contexts in his letters,⁶⁷ but curiously, and unfortunately, not often here (I suspect only because of the modern stereotype about a supposed *Jewish* propensity to justification from works of the law). Paul famously exhorts his male gentiles-in-Christ in Thessaloniki to acquire their vessels (i.e., wives) in holiness, "not in the passion of desire like the gentiles, who do not know God" (1 Thess 4:4).⁶⁸ He reminds his gentiles-in-Christ in Corinth how "when you were gentiles, you were led away after speechless images" (1 Cor 12:2).⁶⁹

---

⁶⁶ On the ethnic stereotypes "Jews by nature" and "gentile sinners," see Matthew V. Novenson, "Gentile Sinners: A Brief History of an Ancient Stereotype," in *Negotiating Identities*, ed. Karin Hedner Zetterholm et al., Minneapolis: Fortress, 2022), 159–179; and my fulsome discussion in Chapter 6. Also R. Barry Matlock, "Jews by Nature: Paul, Ethnicity, and Galatians," in *Far From Minimal: Celebrating the Work and Influence of Philip R. Davies*, ed. Duncan Burns and J. W. Rogerson (London: T&T Clark, 2012), 304–315 at 311, commenting on Gal 2:15–16: "When Paul touches explicitly on what we would regard as matters of 'ethnicity,' he does so in entirely conventional ways… Paul is a 'primordialist,' then – not in any theoretical sense, but in the unreflective or folk-anthropological way that ethnic actors tend to be."
⁶⁷ See, e.g., Stowers, *Rereading of Romans*; Dale B. Martin, "Heterosexism and the Interpretation of Romans 1:18–32," in *Sex and the Single Savior: Gender and Sexuality in Biblical Interpretation* (Louisville, KY: Westminster John Knox, 2006), 51–64; Donaldson, *Paul and the Gentiles*; Sean F. Winter, "Paul's Attitudes to the Gentiles," in *Attitudes to Gentiles in Ancient Judaism and Early Christianity*, ed. David C. Sim and James S. McLaren (London: T&T Clark, 2013), 138–153; Linebaugh, *God, Grace, and Righteousness*.
⁶⁸ See Lone Fatum, "Brotherhood in Christ: A Gender Hermeneutical Reading of 1 Thessalonians," in *Constructing Early Christian Families*, ed. Halvor Moxnes (London: Routledge, 1997), 183–198; Dale B. Martin, "Paul without Passion: On Paul's Rejection of Desire in Sex and Marriage," in *Sex and the Single Savior*, 65–76.
⁶⁹ Concannon, *When You Were Gentiles*.

In Rom 1, he supplies an aetiology for this situation, explaining how, because gentiles in the distant past did not see fit to keep God in knowledge, "God handed them over to an unfit mind" (Rom 1:28).[70] My point here is that Paul assumes that this gentile ignorance extends not just to ethics but also to (what we might call) theology. Because gentiles in their natural state do not know God, when they try to think God, they get it wrong. "Are you ignorant that the kindness of God leads you to repentance?" (Rom 2:4), Paul challenges an imaginary gentile interlocutor in Rom 2. Even Paul's own gentiles-in-Christ not infrequently get it wrong, as he notes with frustration.[71] "Sober up rightly, and do not sin. For some people are ignorant of God, I say to your shame" (1 Cor 15:34). "You senseless Gauls, who bewitched you?" (Gal 3:1) "Are you so senseless, that having begun with the pneuma, now you are finishing with the flesh?" (Gal 3:3) If senseless gentiles are ever to perceive theological truth, such as the truth that a person is not justified from works of the law, it will require an unmaking and a remaking of their unfit minds.[72] As he says elsewhere about gentile minds, "Do not be conformed to this age; rather, be transformed by the renewal of the mind, so that you approve the will of God" (Rom 12:2).

Jews, by contrast, normally think God correctly, according to the apostle.[73] By his lights, this is to be expected, because Jews, unlike gentiles, "were entrusted with the oracles of God" (Rom 3:2). Or, as he says more fulsomely elsewhere, "They are the Israelites, to whom belong the adoption as sons [of God], the divine presence, the covenants, the giving of the law, the temple service, the promises, the ancestors, and from whom comes the messiah, according to the flesh" (Rom 9:4–5). Whereas gentile minds are darkened to the things of

---

[70] Stowers, *Rereading of Romans*, 83–100; Stephen L. Young, "Paul's Eschatological Myth of Jewish Sin," *NTS* (forthcoming).

[71] A phenomenon well explained by Laura Dingeldein, "Gaining Virtue, Gaining Christ: Moral Development in the Letters of Paul" (PhD diss., Brown University, 2014).

[72] Stowers, *Rereading of Romans*, 317–320; Stanley Stowers, "The Dilemma of Paul's Physics: Features Stoic-Platonist or Platonist-Stoic?" in *From Stoicism to Platonism: The Development of Philosophy, 100 BCE–100 CE*, ed. Troels Engberg-Pedersen (Cambridge: Cambridge University Press, 2017), 231–253; Emma Wasserman, *The Death of the Soul in Romans 7: Sin, Death, and the Law in Light of Hellenistic Moral Psychology*, WUNT 2/256 (Tübingen: Mohr Siebeck, 2008).

[73] A point well made by Eisenbaum, *Paul Was Not a Christian*.

God, Jewish minds generally perceive and always have perceived them clearly. There is precisely one exception, one respect in which Paul says that Jewish minds go astray, but it has only happened just now, for the first time in the history of the nation, within Paul's own adult lifetime.[74] The one thing of which Paul says the Jews are ignorant is that the crucified man Jesus is the messiah; that idea is to (most of) them a *skandalon*, a cause of offense (1 Cor 1:23; cf. 2:2). Specifically in regard to Christ, Paul says, "the thoughts of the Israelites are hardened" (2 Cor 3:14), in the sense that, when they read the very scriptures that (Paul thinks) transparently attest the messiah Jesus, they do not see what he sees. "For up to the present day, the same veil [of Moses] remains over the reading of the old covenant, and is not unveiled, because in Christ it is undone. For up to today, whenever Moses is read, a veil lies over their heart" (2 Cor 3:14–15). It is just this that Paul means when he says that Jews "do not recognize the righteousness of God" (Rom 10:3). "They have zeal for God, but not with recognition. For being ignorant of the righteousness of God and seeking to establish their own, they were not subjected to the righteousness of God" (Rom 10:2–3). Just to the extent, that is, that they are not subjected to the messiah Jesus.[75]

On the *principle*, however, that a person is not justified from works of the law, Paul expects all good Jews to agree with him, even if gentile sinners, predictably, do not. That is his point in Gal 2:15–16.[76] Which

---

[74] Paul's occasional references to instances of rebellion in the biblical story of Israel (e.g., the golden calf incident in Exod 32/1 Cor 10, or the apostasy to Baal in 1 Kings 19/Rom 11) are presented as ad hoc correspondences to his, Paul's, present. "These things were examples for us" (1 Cor 10:6). "So too at the present time" (Rom 11:5). They are not – and Paul does not ever say they are – proof of any kind of endemic deviance in the people Israel. Interpreters who take them to be such (e.g., Wright, *Paul and the Faithfulness of God*; Linebaugh, "Announcing the Human"; Jason A. Staples, *Paul and the Resurrection of Israel* [Cambridge: Cambridge University Press, 2023]) are reading their own biblical theologies into the text of Paul's letters. It is no sin to read one's own biblical theology into a scriptural text, but it is a very different reading strategy from the one I am pursuing here.

[75] See further Matthew V. Novenson, "The Self-Styled Jew of Romans 2 and the Actual Jews of Romans 9–11," in Novenson, *Paul, Then and Now*, 91–117; Young, "Eschatological Myth of Jewish Sin."

[76] Thus rightly Richard B. Hays, "Galatians," in *The New Interpreter's Bible*, vol. 11 (Nashville: Abingdon, 2000), 241: "Paul underscores his claim that the gospel of justification/rectification through God's act in Christ is entirely consistent with what those who are 'Jews by birth' already know... [namely,

is why he charges Cephas, Barnabas, and the other Jews in the Antioch Christ-assembly with ὑπόκρισις, hypocrisy or playacting, which is a very different, even opposite charge from ignorance. They know the axiom in question – not, Paul says, because they are *Christ-followers* but because they are *Jews* – but they betray their principles with their behavior. Thus directly contrary to much of the modern history of interpretation, Paul does not portray belief in justification from works of the law as a characteristically Jewish error; quite the opposite. Paul believes – and he expects all good Jews, not just Jews-in-Christ, to agree with him in principle – that eschatological righteousness and life come from trust in the messiah. That is the messiah's job, after all: to appear at the end of the present evil age and to put things right.[77] (That Paul was perhaps overconfident in his estimation of what all good Jews would agree with him about is another matter.)

Just here, there is a fascinating irony in the recent secondary literature. Many Christian theological interpreters (Lutheran, Reformed, New Perspective, "apocalyptic," and other flavors beside) and many "radical" Paul-within-Judaism interpreters actually agree with one another that Paul thinks that Jews think they will be justified from works of the law. For most Christian theological interpreters, Paul thinks that the Jews are *wrong* in their belief, and he tries to reason them out of it. For most Paul-within-Judaism interpreters, Paul thinks that the Jews are *right* in their belief; he just does not want gentiles to imagine that the same rule applies to them.[78] But all parties agree

---

that] we are set in right relationship with God only through God's own act of grace." Elsewhere ("Have We Found Abraham to Be Our Forefather according to the Flesh? A Reconsideration of Rom 4:1," *NovT* 27 [1985]: 76–98 at 85) Hays plausibly connects this to what Paul says in Rom 3:30, which he punctuates (correctly, though unconventionally) as follows: "If God, who will rightwise the circumcision from trust, is one, [then he will] also [rightwise] the foreskin through trust." In other words, Paul takes it to be a Jewish axiom that God will rightwise Israel from trust. In fact, it is even more than this: Paul thinks that all good Jews know that final righteousness comes not just from God's grace in general, but from God sending the messiah, in particular. The *skandalon* is not that theologoumenon, but the much more controversial claim that the messiah is the recently crucified man Jesus.

[77] On this axiom, see Manse Rim, "Messiah and Righteousness in Paul and His Context" (PhD diss., University of Edinburgh, 2023).

[78] Thus Gaston, *Paul and the Torah*; Gager, *Reinventing Paul*; Eisenbaum, *Paul Was Not a Christian*; Runar M. Thorsteinsson, "Not Everyone Will Be Justified Before Him by Works of the Law: A Fresh Reading of Romans 3:20"

(*mirabile dictu*!) that Paul thinks that Jews think they will be justified from works of the law.

But Paul does not think this, and he says as much in so many words. What Paul actually says is that *no one* will be justified from works of the law,[79] and that Jews know this fact, while gentiles do not know it. Whether Jews should *do* the works of the law, and enjoy peaceful, quotidian relationship with God by doing so – which I think is what most Paul-within-Judaism interpreters actually want to affirm – is another matter entirely. Paul says that Jews should do that, and do in fact do that (most of them, most of the time) (Rom 9:31), as many other ancient Jewish sources also say. But that is not justification.[80] Justification – which, remember, is Paul's own technical term, not an already-current general-purpose word for good religion! – is how one gets transferred out of the present age of sin and death and into the undying life of the kingdom of God. No one gets *that* otherwise then by the messiah. Paul thinks Jews know this, because they know the law and prophets. But gentiles do not know it, because they do not know the law and prophets. That is why they keep on circumcising themselves, mistakenly thinking that that will somehow effect their justification. Silly gentiles, circumcision is for Jewish mortals.[81]

Once More, What Is Justification?

This brings us back around to the question what justification, whether from works of the law or from Christ-faith, actually is. This particular research niche does not often see new proposals, but in the last few years we have had one ingenious new proposal from Paula Fredriksen. In a 2014 journal article and then further in her 2017 book, Fredriksen

---

(forthcoming); Runar M. Thorsteinsson, *Commentary on Romans* (forthcoming).

[79] *Pace* Gabriele Boccaccini, *Paul's Three Paths to Salvation* (Grand Rapids, MI: Eerdmans, 2020), who takes the idiosyncratic view that, for Paul, righteous Jews are justified from works of the Mosaic law, righteous gentiles from works of the natural law, and only sinners (whether Jewish or gentile) from Christ-faith. Boccaccini is right to take seriously Paul's claim in Rom 2 that people will be judged according to their deeds, but wrong to think this means that only a minority are sinners in need of Christ-faith.

[80] *Pace* Eisenbaum, *Paul Was Not a Christian*, 244: "What the Torah does for Jews, Jesus does for Gentiles."

[81] See Thiessen, *Paul and the Gentile Problem*.

argues that δικαιοσύνη for Paul, as for Josephus,[82] signifies the duties prescribed in the second table of the Decalogue, justice toward one's neighbors, which is the counterpart to εὐσέβεια, piety toward God, prescribed in the first table of the Decalogue. Paul's notion of "pagan justification by faith," Fredriksen argues, is that "[gentiles'] πίστις in Christ (confidence that he had died, had been raised, and was soon coming back) righteoused them (through the giving of the πνεῦμα, which also effected adoption) so that they could 'fulfill the law,' specifically, the Law's Second Table, δικαιοσύνη."[83] Now, this summary of what Paul thinks happens to gentiles-in-Christ is basically right. But it is not what Paul means by the word δικαιοσύνη. For Paul, who, unlike Josephus, never uses the term εὐσέβεια (!),[84] δικαιοσύνη actually subsumes *all* of the duties prescribed in the Decalogue,[85] and equally or more importantly, signifies the performing of all those duties maximally, effortlessly, and forever (what Christine Hayes has called "robo-righteousness").[86] So Paul's δικαιοσύνη is something rather more than what Fredriksen suggests it is. But it certainly is, as Fredriksen rightly insists, an eschatological state of affairs.

In fact, a besetting problem with much recent discussion (and older discussion, too) is that almost all of it *deflates* what Paul means by δικαιοσύνη. Most interpreters – whether traditional or radical, Jewish or Christian, conservative or liberal, religious or not – take Paul to be

---

[82] Josephus, *Ant.* 18.117: τοῖς Ἰουδαίοις κελεύοντα ἀρετὴν ἐπασκοῦσιν καὶ τὰ πρὸς ἀλλήλους δικαιοσύνῃ καὶ πρὸς τὸν θεὸν εὐσεβείᾳ. In this, Josephus's summary of what John the Baptist preached, the overarching virtue is excellence (ἀρετή), and its two component parts are justice (δικαιοσύνη) toward other people and piety (εὐσέβεια) toward God. Here Josephus does not expressly mention a twofold division in the Decalogue, but he does in *Ant.* 3.101: "the two tablets on which were inscribed the ten words, five on each."

[83] Paula Fredriksen, "Paul's Letter to the Romans, the Ten Commandments, and Pagan Justification by Faith," *JBL* 133 (2014): 801–808 at 808. See further Fredriksen, *Pagans' Apostle*.

[84] A very significant lexical choice, which suggests to me that Paul does not think of what he teaches as a regimen of piety (even if we might reasonably redescribe it as such). T. Christopher Hoklotubbe, *Civilized Piety: The Rhetoric of Pietas in the Pastoral Epistles and the Roman Empire* (Waco, TX: Baylor University Press, 2017) perceptively explains why εὐσέβεια emerges as an arch-virtue in the Pastoral Epistles, whereas it had not been in the authentic letters of Paul.

[85] And not just the Decalogue, but all of the duties prescribed in the entire law (thus Rom 7:12; 9:31).

[86] Christine Hayes, *What's Divine about Divine Law?* (Princeton: Princeton University Press, 2015), 48–51, 148–149.

talking about, well, patterns of religion,[87] ways of getting on with God, or of getting transferred into right relation with God. Most Christian theological interpreters take Paul's talk of righteousness to be (or indeed, *need* it to be) identical with what (they think) Christianity actually offers: forgiveness of sins, or membership in the people of God, or a countercultural way of reckoning human worth, etc. To cite one eminent recent example, "Paul opposes those who think Torah-observance is the essential expression of faith not because 'law' or 'works' are problematic principles of soteriology, but because the Torah – like every other pre-constituted norm – has been dethroned as a criterion of worth by the unconditioned gift of Christ."[88] Where Paul writes "righteousness," Barclay glosses it with "worth," which, not coincidentally, emerges in Barclay's conclusion as a matter of pressing contemporary concern in the churches.[89]

But in an analogous way, ironically, many recent "radical" interpreters take Paul's talk of righteousness to signify just what (they think) Judaism actually offers, only now for gentiles: access to right relation to God, membership in the seed of Abraham, and so on. Thus, for instance, Stanley Stowers: "The reading for which I have been arguing requires that [Rom] 3:20 ['All flesh will not be put right before him from works of the law'] be primarily about gentiles and that *dikaioō* ('to justify,' 'to make righteous,' 'to show mercy') be a transfer term. It ['justification' in Rom 3:20] has reference only to those who are outside of a positive relationship with God. As such, it could only refer to gentiles or perhaps to extremely wicked and unrepentant Jews. God 'makes righteous' when he provides a way for people who have no positive relation to have a relation."[90] Now, Paul's gentiles-in-Christ do of course gain "a positive relationship with God" where there was none before, but then, so do godfearers and proselytes, as they had done for centuries by the time Paul came preaching Christ.[91]

---

[87] As in the subtitle to Sanders, *Paul and Palestinian Judaism*: "a comparison of patterns of religion."

[88] Barclay, *Paul and the Gift*, 568.

[89] As it surely is. As a coreligionist with Barclay, I welcome his theological/ethical reading of Paul as a mostly helpful one for Christian use. As a historian and exegete, however, I disagree with Barclay about the meaning of Paul's words in their first-century context.

[90] Stowers, *Rereading of Romans*, 190.

[91] See Arthur Darby Nock, *Conversion: The Old and the New in Religion from Alexander the Great to Augustine of Hippo* (Oxford: Oxford University Press,

So is that really all Paul means by δικαιοσύνη? I think it cannot be. All such interpretations – from Barclay to Stowers, and almost everything in between – miss what seems to me the crucial point, namely, that Paul's talk of righteousness does not match up with what any quotidian lived religion, Judaism, Christianity, or otherwise, actually offers. It could not possibly do, because Paul's talk of righteousness is so impracticably utopian and eschatological. I suppose it is right to say, with Sanders, that for Paul δικαιοσύνη is a transfer term,[92] but it means transfer not into polite, pious relationship with God but rather into the age to come, into pneumatic immortality.

Here, as on so many points of interpretation, Albert Schweitzer had it very nearly right almost a century ago. About Paul's use of δικαιοσύνη, Schweitzer wrote, "This righteousness is therefore, properly speaking, a condition of the Messianic era, like the 'resurrection state of existence.' As such it can only be considered as already attained as a consequence of the being-in-Christ, by means of which believers possess in advance the state of existence proper to the Messianic Kingdom."[93] In recent research, Matthew Thiessen has provided resources for an even fuller account along these lines, although he does not undertake to explicate δικαιοσύνη in particular. Thiessen shows how Paul's assumption that God promised father Abraham the pneuma (Gal 3:14), which is not explicit in Genesis (Hebrew, Greek, or otherwise), or any other extant version of the Abraham story, comes from Paul's reading of Gen 15:5, where God tells Abraham to look at the stars and promises him: οὕτως ἔσται τὸ σπέρμα σου, "so shall your seed be" (Gen 15:5, cited in Rom 4:18). Stars, in certain strands of ancient physics, are both pneumatic (that is, made of pneuma) and also divine (that is, superhuman and immortal),[94] which is precisely what

---

1933); Martin Goodman, *Mission and Conversion: Proselytizing in the Religious History of the Roman Empire* (Oxford: Clarendon, 1994); Feldman, *Jew and Gentile in the Ancient World*, 288–382.

[92] Sanders, *Paul and Palestinian Judaism*, 501.   [93] Schweitzer, *Mysticism*, 205.
[94] This idea is especially associated with Stoicism, but not all Stoic sources subscribe to it, and other sources do. See recent discussion in Engberg-Pedersen, ed., *From Stoicism to Platonism*; Abraham P. Bos, *Aristotle on God's Life-Generating Power and on* Pneuma *as Its Vehicle* (Albany, NY: SUNY Press, 2018); Phillip Sidney Horky, ed., *Cosmos in the Ancient World* (Cambridge: Cambridge University Press, 2019); Hynek Bartoš and Colin Guthrie King, eds., *Heat, Pneuma, and Soul in Ancient Philosophy and Science* (Cambridge: Cambridge University Press, 2020); John Granger Cook, "1 Cor 15:40–41: Paul and the Heavenly Bodies," ZNW 113 (2022): 159–179.

Paul says people-in-Christ become. Thiessen writes, "Enabled by Christ's *pneuma* to participate in the pattern of Christ's life, Paul's gentiles can live a moral life that is comparable to the unblemished life of the stars."[95]

That is what Paul means by "righteousness," as, for instance, in Gal 3:21: "Had a law been given that could *make alive*, then *righteousness* would indeed be from the law." To have the kind of righteousness Paul means here is to have undying life. But if so, that is more than Paul thinks even good, pious Jews already have in hand.[96] Jews, Paul reckons, always had the *promise* of the pneuma, but only now at the end of the present evil age and the arrival of the messiah do they have access to the thing itself. The kind of righteousness Paul means here is also more than most (all?) Christian accounts of justification think Christians have in hand. Such accounts define justification down to mean forgiveness of pre-baptismal sins, or forgiveness of all sins, or what have you. They do so because they intuit that whatever Paul means by justification, it must be something they, Christians, currently enjoy. (Or, for recent radical interpreters: something that Jews currently enjoy.) And there's the rub. For if what we want is a good historical understanding of Paul's letters, then modern religious experience, whether Jewish or Christian, is not admissible as evidence.

Conclusion

To conclude with the question with which we began: Who ever thought that a person is justified from works of the law? Well, no ancient writer ever claims that view for him- or herself, so in that sense, no one ever thought it. One tantalizing exception is the anonymous authors of 4QMMT, who recommend "some works of the law which we think are good for you" in the hope that, for those who adopt them, "it will be reckoned to you for righteousness." But 4QMMT does not mean by "righteousness from works of the law" what Paul means by the same phrase. 4QMMT means just that those who adopt their halakhah will be proved right, whereas Paul means by the phrase a program of Torah observance undertaken in defiance of his, Paul's,

---

[95] Thiessen, *Paul and the Gentile Problem*, 150.
[96] And this is the fatal flaw in the hypothesis (e.g., of Gaston, *Paul and the Torah*) that Paul simply endorses the Jewish *status quo ante*.

Christ announcement. Philo of Alexandria – and perhaps other philosophically minded Jews of the diaspora – reasons that tutoring in the law of Moses is the surest path to righteousness for gentiles as well as Jews. Some such notion may lie behind the program of the "agitators" in Galatians, but both the label "justification from works of the law" and its connotations are Paul's, not theirs.

This is why no ancient writer claims the view for himself: because it is Paul's own polemical invention. The only people who think it are those who Paul says think it. (In this respect, it is like idolatry in Voltaire's *Dictionary*.) In most of the relevant passages, the people in question are gentiles-in-Christ who are contemplating certain voluntary acts of Torah observance, in particular, male proselyte circumcision. These are the people to whom Paul thunders that a person is put right from Christ-faith, not from works of the law. Precisely twice, however, Paul also speaks critically of "righteousness from works of the law" in connection with certain Jews, namely: himself in the period when he was bringing indictments against the Christ-assemblies (Phil 3:4–6) and his Jewish contemporaries who consider the crucified messiah an offense while still diligently keeping Torah (Rom 9:30–10:4). What these two cases have in common with judaizing gentiles-in-Christ is just this: They have encountered the apostolic announcement of the risen Christ and rebuffed it (or at least Paul's ideal version of it), opting instead for a more conventional regimen of religious devotion. "Justification from works of the law" in Paul's idiom is not any pre-existing form of piety; it is a strategy for not buying what Paul is selling.

4 | *Paul versus the Gentiles*

We know that Paul fiercely opposed the circumcision of gentiles-in-Christ, and we know that the particular type of circumcision on offer was Jewish proselyte circumcision (i.e., not Egyptian or Arabian or another Mediterranean or West Asian variety). But we do not know precisely *who* was promoting what Paul opposed. From the secondary literature, one would think it was perfectly obvious who, but that impression is only due to naivete or bluster on the part of the modern interpreters. Because it was Jewish proselyte circumcision that was on offer, most have either assumed or insisted that it must have been Jewish people (either majority non-Christ-believing Jews[1] or – what is more often proposed – Christ-believing Jews) who were urging it upon Paul's gentiles-in-Christ. But this is a colossal *non sequitur*. It is of course one possible conclusion, but it would take a great deal more argument to prove it than is usually offered. The reason such argument is not usually offered is that Paul's opposition to "law-observant Jewish Christianity" is an axiom dating back to the birth of modern Pauline criticism in 1830s Tübingen. It is the kind of assumption that, even now, 200 years later, one's contemporaries will let one get away with (to paraphrase Richard Rorty).[2]

The purpose of this chapter is to avoid that *non sequitur*, to stop and consider what positive evidence there is for the ethnic identity of Paul's proselyte-circumcision-preaching opponents. The chapter is, therefore,

---

[1] Thus, e.g., Mark D. Nanos, *The Irony of Galatians: Paul's Letter in First-Century Context* (Minneapolis: Fortress, 2002).

[2] Relatively few critics nowadays expressly defend the Baur hypothesis as such, although see Gerd Lüdemann, *Opposition to Paul in Jewish Christianity*, trans. M. Eugene Boring (Minneapolis: Fortress, 1989 [German original 1983]); and Michael Goulder, *St. Paul versus St. Peter: A Tale of Two Missions* (Louisville, KY: Westminster John Knox, 1994). But Baur's basic schema is assumed in much, even most, research on Paul down to the present, including such leading lights as Boyarin, *Radical Jew*; and Martyn, *Galatians*.

concerned with the old chestnut of "Paul's opponents," but only with one quite particular aspect of that question.³ I argue that the proponents of proselyte circumcision whom Paul opposes in Galatians and Philippians and imagines in Romans are themselves recently circumcised gentile proselytes. Elsewhere, in the Corinthian correspondence, Paul does ferocious rhetorical battle with certain Jewish Christ-apostles, but those opponents have nothing whatsoever to do with the circumcision controversy. If we imagine it as a Venn diagram, the overlap between the set of Paul's *Jewish* opponents and the set of Paul's *circumcision-preaching* opponents is nil. As far as the proselyte circumcision controversy is concerned, it is Paul versus the gentiles.

Paul's Jewish Opponents

One would hope that any account of supposedly "Jewish Christian" opposition to Paul⁴ would start from a critical mass of solid evidence of, well, Jewish Christ-believers opposing Paul. And yet this is not what we find in the secondary literature, one suspects because there is actually very little such evidence in our sources. What there is (1) a smattering of possible primary evidence (on which see below) and (2) a 200-year-old grand unified theory of Christian origins that is still, somehow, given the benefit of the doubt. I refer, of course, to F. C. Baur's Hegelian scheme of Petrine Jewish Christianity, Pauline gentile Christianity, and the eventual synthesis of the two.⁵ We will come back

---

³ On the larger question, see John J. Gunther, *St. Paul's Opponents and Their Background: A Study of Apocalyptic and Jewish Sectarian Teachings*, NovTSup 35 (Leiden: Brill, 1973), immensely learned if a bit prone to parallelomania; Jerry L. Sumney, *Servants of Satan, False Brothers, and Other Opponents of Paul*, JSNTSup 188 (Sheffield: Sheffield Academic, 1999), who rightly highlights the diversity among the numerous persons and groups who take verbal lashings in Paul's letters; and the essays in *Paul and His Opponents*, ed. Stanley E. Porter (Leiden: Brill, 2005), in particular Sumney's essay on the *status quaestionis*.
⁴ E.g., famously, Lüdemann, *Opposition to Paul in Jewish Christianity*.
⁵ First outlined in F. C. Baur, "Die Christuspartei in der korinthischen Gemeinde, der Gegensatz des paulinischen und petrinischen Christentums in der ältesten Kirche, der Apostel Petrus in Rom," *TZTh* 3.4 (1831): 61–206; and applied systematically to the letters of Paul in F. C. Baur, *Paul the Apostle of Jesus Christ*, trans. Eduard Zeller, rev. A. Menzies, 2 vols. (London: Williams & Norgate, 1876 [German original 1845]). For excellent discussion, see the essays in Martin Bauspiess, Christof Landmesser, and David Lincicum, eds., *Ferdinand Christian Baur and the History of Early Christianity*, trans. Robert F. Brown and Peter C. Hodgson (Oxford: Oxford University Press, 2017).

to that theory. But about that possible primary evidence: There are many passages in the letters that mention opponents of unspecified ethnicity whom modern critics have labeled as Jewish. But in most of these passages, as I will argue below, there is no evidence for their Jewishness and actually positive evidence for their gentileness. I leave these aside for the moment. Meanwhile, there are a handful of passages in which Paul mentions his relations with other Jews (especially Jewish apostles) with no express indication of opposition, but modern critics have read opposition into these mentions. And then finally there are a few legitimate instances of opposition between Paul and other Jewish Christ-apostles. Let us consider.

In 1 Thessalonians, there is no evidence whatsoever of opposition from rivals such as we find in Galatians, 1–2 Corinthians, Philippians, and (indirectly) Romans.[6] There is the curious period in 1 Thess 2:14–16 about "the Judeans who killed the lord Jesus and the prophets, who chased us out, who are not pleasing to God but are opposed to all people, who hinder us from speaking to the gentiles." There are some good reasons for thinking that this passage may be a post-Pauline interpolation,[7] although its uniform attestation in the manuscript tradition weighs against this. But if it is authentic, as Markus Bockmuehl has plausibly argued,[8] the target of criticism here is not Peter and James but – ironically for the Baur hypothesis – those non-Christ-believing Judeans who supposedly harassed Peter and James. If we take 2 Thessalonians as authentic and thus relevant to our question,[9] it is conspicuous for attesting a quite specific rival idea ("that the day of the lord has happened") which is not, however, attributed to any rival teachers, only to "a pneuma or a message or a letter as if from us" (2 Thess 2:2). No opposition to Paul here, "Jewish

---

[6] But Sumney, *Servants of Satan*, 214–228 devotes a chapter to 1 Thessalonians because, although he concedes that there is no mention of opponents in the letter, it takes him a chapter to pick through all the modern proposals about supposed opponents.

[7] Ably presented by Birger A. Pearson, "1 Thessalonians 2:13–16: A Deutero-Pauline Interpolation," *HTR* 64 (1971): 79–94.

[8] Markus Bockmuehl, "1 Thessalonians 2:14–16 and the Church in Jerusalem," *TynBul* 52 (2001): 1–31.

[9] About which I still have my doubts. But I am challenged by the incisive discussions of Paul Foster, "Who Wrote 2 Thessalonians? A Fresh Look at an Old Problem," *JSNT* 35 (2012): 150–175; and Tooth, *Eschatologies of 1 and 2 Thessalonians*.

Christian" or otherwise.[10] Nor in Philemon, which is authentic. I take 1 Timothy, 2 Timothy, and Titus all to be pseudonymous and thus not relevant to the question of Paul's mid-first-century opponents (though all three letters share a concern with false teachers in their own, later context).[11] I also take Ephesians to be pseudonymous, which is neither here nor there for present purposes, since it is entirely without polemic.[12]

Colossians is tricky. It has a stronger claim to authenticity than Ephesians or the Pastorals do, though I happen to think it is pseudonymous.[13] What is more, notwithstanding the voluminous modern literature on the so-called Colossian heresy (an unfortunate anachronism), there is no actual polemic in the letter. At most, there is a brief series of warnings about what a hypothetical someone might do or say: "Watch lest anyone take you captive through philosophy" (Col 2:8); "Let not anyone judge you regarding food or drink or a festival or month or sabbath" (Col 2:16); "Let no one deprive you by wanting humility and worship of angels" (Col 2:18). But the author never specifies who might do such a thing, or even speaks of a particular "him" or "them," let alone "agitators," "false brothers," "false apostles," or the like. And as regards the question before us, there is certainly no hint either of specifically Jewish opponents or of proselyte-circumcision-preaching opponents in Colossians. It may even be, as Morna Hooker perceptively argues, that there are no opponents of any kind in Colossians.[14]

Paul mentions numerous coworkers and acquaintances throughout the letters, many of them, like Paul, Jews (e.g., συγγενεῖς, "kinfolk" or "co-ethnics," in Rom 16:7, 11, 21): James, Cephas, John, Barnabas, Andronicus, Junia, Herodion, Lucius, Jason, Sosipater, Apollos, and perhaps some of the other named persons in the letters. Timothy is a curious case: From the letters one might reasonably assume that he was

---

[10] Despite the many modern proposals discussed by Sumney, *Servants of Satan*, 229–252.

[11] On which see Andrew M. Langford, "Diagnosing Deviance: Pathology and Polemic in the Pastoral Epistles" (PhD diss., University of Chicago, 2018).

[12] On this feature of the letter, see Petroelje, *The Pauline Book and the Dilemma of Ephesians*.

[13] With Paul Foster, *Colossians*, BNTC (London: T&T Clark, 2016).

[14] Morna D. Hooker, "Were There False Teachers in Colossae?" in *From Adam to Christ: Essays on Paul* (Cambridge: Cambridge University Press, 1990), 121–136.

a born Jew. But the Acts of the Apostles imagines that he was born to a Jewish mother and a Greek father, and only circumcised as an adult by Paul (Acts 16:1–3). Maybe.[15] The vast majority of Paul's mentions of Jewish apostles are in fact very warm (though see below on Apollos), and Melanie Johnson-DeBaufre and Laura Nasrallah rightly argue that we might better imagine the whole network of gentile Christ-assemblies as *theirs* (and others') rather than *Paul's*, his proprietary rhetoric notwithstanding.[16]

For Baur, however, the thin end of the wedge was Paul's mention of Christ-believers at Corinth saying, variously, "I am of Paul" or "I am of Apollos" or "I am of Cephas" or "I am of Christ" (1 Cor 1:12). Baur took this verse to betray (what he thought was) an actual *twofold* rift between a Paul party and a Cephas party.[17] This reading is implausible in the extreme, as Nils Dahl rightly argued.[18] (We will have more to say below about Apollos, who, unlike Cephas, *was* an important figure in the Christ-assembly in Corinth.) Better – though still insufficient – grist for Baur's mill comes from Galatians 1–2, where Paul does expressly mention tensions with Cephas and (indirectly) with James. Even here, however, there is no disagreement between Paul and Jerusalem on the proselyte circumcision question. Paul withholds flattery from the Jerusalem apostles, only calling them οἱ δοκοῦντες στῦλοι, "those *reputed to be* pillars" (Gal 2:2, 6, 9). He insists upon his independence from them, but he concedes that he did go up to confer with them (Gal 1:18; 2:1) and that both they and he agreed that gentiles-in-Christ should not undergo proselyte circumcision (Gal 2:1–10). *Someone* at Jerusalem argued otherwise, but Paul only calls these someones "false brothers" (Gal 2:4); they are not the pillar

---

[15] If Timothy's ethnicity and circumcision were along the lines of what Luke suggests, his case would be analogous to that of Moses's son in the LXX of Exod 4:24–26, where, because he is a Hebrew, his circumcision must go ahead even if after the eighth day. Thus in the LXX Zipporah says to the destroying angel, "The blood of my child's circumcision stands," and not, as in the MT, to Moses, "You are a bridegroom of blood to me." Thanks to Kelly Holob for this excellent observation.

[16] Johnson-DeBaufre and Nasrallah, "Beyond the Heroic Paul."

[17] Baur, "Christuspartei."

[18] Nils A. Dahl, "Paul and the Church at Corinth according to 1 Corinthians 1:10–4:21," in *Studies in Paul: Theology for the Early Christian Mission* (Minneapolis: Augsburg, 1977), 40–61.

apostles. Are they Jewish? Since they are at Jerusalem, there is a good chance, but it is by no means certain.[19]

Next Paul narrates the story of his clash with Cephas at Antioch, the only secure evidence for any conflict between the two. Crucially, however, nothing in this story says or even suggests that Cephas opposes Paul's position on proselyte circumcision. Quite to the contrary, Paul accuses Cephas of *hypocrisy*, that is, of believing one thing (the right thing, from Paul's perspective) but pretending to believe otherwise when other people are looking. The other people, in this case, are "certain people who came from James" (Gal 2:12), which could suggest a conflict between Paul and *James*, though not between Paul and *Cephas*. These bothersome "people from James," however, do not urge proselyte circumcision upon anyone! What they do, apparently, is shame Cephas and other Jewish apostles like Barnabas into eating separately from the gentiles-in-Christ (Gal 2:12). This is bad, from Paul's perspective. But it is not a proselyte circumcision mission.[20] Paul calls these visitors οἱ ἐκ περιτομῆς, "those from *the circumcision*" (Gal 2:12), meaning "those from among *the Jews*," which is always, without exception, what "the circumcision" means in Paul (Rom 3:1; 4:9; 1 Cor 7:19; Gal 2:7, 8, 9; Phil 3:3). The common mistranslation "the circumcision *party*," which implies that these people were agitating for proselyte circumcision, is an imposition. Paul consistently uses an entirely different set of epithets for people who do that (see below).

---

[19] Acts 15:5 says that it was *Pharisees* in the Jerusalem Christ-assembly who proposed this, which is perplexing in part because Paul the Pharisee staunchly opposes the idea. On Luke's assumptions about Pharisees see Joshua D. Garroway, "The Pharisee Heresy: Circumcision for Gentiles in the Acts of the Apostles," NTS 60 (2014): 20–36; on Paul's, see Novenson, "*Ioudaios*, Pharisee, Zealot." Paul certainly does not claim that the "false brothers" in Gal 2:4 are Pharisees. Indeed, his chosen phrase might mean to suggest that they are (what he considers to be) false Jews, i.e., proselytes. Thanks to Matthew Thiessen for suggesting and discussing with me this possible interpretation.

[20] Very probably, this so-called Antioch incident was a matter of homeland versus diaspora halakhah, as recently explained by Ruben A. Bühner, *Paulus im Kontext des Diasporajudentums: Judenchristliche Lebensweise nach den paulinischen Briefen und die Debatten um 'Paul within Judaism'*, WUNT 511 (Tübingen: Mohr Siebeck, 2023).

In fact, the only secure instance of opposition between Paul and other Jewish apostles is that recounted in 2 Corinthians 10–13.[21] We know that they are *Jewish* apostles from Paul's counter in 2 Cor 11:21–22: "In whatever one might dare [to boast] – I am speaking foolishly – I also dare: Are they Hebrews? So am I! Are they Israelites? So am I! Are they seed of Abraham? So am I!" And we know that they are Jewish *apostles* from the several variations on that title sprinkled throughout: "super-apostles" (2 Cor 11:5; 12:11), "false apostles" (2 Cor 11:13), "apostles of Christ" (2 Cor 11:13), "apostles" (2 Cor 12:12). With Bultmann, I think that we can be certain that Paul's polemic in 2 Corinthians 10–13 is aimed at one group, not two.[22] The "super-apostles" (2 Cor 11:5; 12:11) and the "false apostles" (2 Cor 11:13) are one and the same. The main reason for thinking otherwise (as, e.g., Baur, Käsemann, and Barrett did)[23] is to make room to squeeze the Jerusalem apostles into the conflict in 2 Corinthians, there being otherwise no evidence to place them there. Undeterred by this lack of evidence, interpreters downstream from Baur have wanted to take the "super-apostles" in 2 Corinthians (11:5; 12:11) as identical with the "pillars" in Galatians (Gal 2:9): Cephas, James, and John. On this theory, then, the "false apostles" in Corinth are not these eminent three but their envoys or lackeys, sent from Jerusalem to trouble Paul. But if we reject – as we should – Baur's *idée fixe* that behind every opponent of Paul stands a monolithic Jerusalem establishment, then we are free to follow the simpler, more likely hypothesis that these opponents in 2 Corinthians are just...

---

[21] On which see Dieter Georgi, *The Opponents of Paul in Second Corinthians* (Edinburgh: T&T Clark, 1987 [German original 1964]); Jerry L. Sumney, *Identifying Paul's Opponents: The Question of Method in 2 Corinthians*, JSNTSup 40 (Sheffield: Sheffield Academic, 1990); Thomas R. Blanton IV, *Constructing a New Covenant: Discursive Strategies in the Damascus Document and Second Corinthians*, WUNT 2/233 (Tübingen: Mohr Siebeck, 2007).

[22] Rudolf Bultmann, *Exegetische Probleme des zweiten Korintherbriefes* (Darmstadt: Wissenschaftliche Buchgesellschaft, 1963).

[23] Baur, "Christuspartei"; Baur, *Paul the Apostle*; Ernst Käsemann, "Die Legitimität des Apostels: Eine Untersuchung zu II Korinther 10–13," ZNW 41 (1942): 33–71; C. K. Barrett, "Paul's Opponents in 2 Corinthians," in *Essays on Paul* (London: SPCK, 1982), 60–86.

other Jewish apostles in Corinth. "Super-apostles" is Paul's ironic name for them, "false apostles" his unironic name.[24]

These super-apostles are Jews, but their message – whatever it is – has nothing to do with judaizing. There is not the slightest hint anywhere in our passage that circumcision, dietary customs, holy days, or any other feature of the law of Moses is in view.[25] In fact, there are very few hints of the content of their teaching at all (though there might be some, in particular the phrase "another Jesus, a different pneuma, a different announcement" in 2 Cor 11:4). And this probably suggests that the conflict in 2 Corinthians is not actually about teaching, but simply about jurisdiction, authority, control.[26] As Paul writes in this context, "*We* [first] reached all the way to you with the gospel of Christ; *we* are not boasting out of place in other people's labors" (2 Cor 10:14–15). And again, "I am jealous for you with the jealousy of God" (2 Cor 11:2). Paul expects and demands total loyalty from "his" gentiles-in-Christ,[27] but at least some of them evidently have transferred their loyalty to other apostles, ones who are as Jewish as Paul is and better skilled in philosophy and rhetoric than he (see 2 Cor 11:5–6). *Maybe*, as Dieter Georgi and, differently, Birger Pearson argue – though this is a stretch, in my view – these other apostles teach a version of the Christ announcement ("gospel") that is somehow more Hellenistic or pneumatic or divine-man-ish than Paul's version ("another Jesus, a different pneuma, a different announcement" [2 Cor

---

[24] Thus rightly Christopher Forbes, "Comparison, Self-Praise, and Irony: Paul's Boasting and the Conventions of Hellenistic Rhetoric," *NTS* 32 (1986): 1–30 at 17.

[25] As Wilhelm Lütgert, *Freiheitspredigt und Schwarmgeister im Korinth* (Gütersloh: Bertelsmann, 1908) already perceived! Both Margaret Thrall, *2 Corinthians 8–13*, ICC (London: T&T Clark, 2004) and Blanton, *Constructing a New Covenant* argue ingeniously that these halakhic issues are *implicit* in the polemic of 2 Corinthians 10–13, but their ingenuity is not convincing, to my mind.

[26] It is, in other words, a matter of competition amongst freelance religious experts, on which see Heidi Wendt, *At the Temple Gates: The Religion of Freelance Experts in the Roman Empire* (Oxford: Oxford University Press, 2016).

[27] See Elisabeth Schüssler Fiorenza, "Rhetorical Situation and Rhetorical Reconstruction in 1 Corinthians," *NTS* 33 (1987): 397: "In 1 Corinthians Paul introduces the vertical line of patriarchal subordination not only into the social relationships of the *ekklesia*, but into its symbolic universe as well by arrogating the authority of God, the 'father,' for himself." And more generally on this point Elizabeth A. Castelli, *Imitating Paul: A Discourse of Power* (Louisville, KY: Westminster John Knox, 1991).

11:4]).²⁸ But Paul's version is itself pretty conspicuously Hellenistic, pneumatic, and divine-man-ish, as recent research has tended to bear out.²⁹ So even here, I think that we are hard pressed to find much daylight between the *teaching* of Paul and the *teaching* of the super-apostles.³⁰

It may be that these other Jewish apostles must simply remain anonymous, as Paul's rivals in Galatia must. In the Corinthian correspondence, however, there is at least the possibility of a prosopography, however hypothetical. While it is not and never will be verifiable, there is a good deal of circumstantial evidence pointing to Apollos and his circle. Apollos is not mentioned by name at all in 2 Corinthians, but of course he is frequently in 1 Corinthians, where he sometimes stands alongside Paul and Cephas in prominence (1:12; 3:22) and sometimes alongside Paul alone (3:4, 5, 6; 4:6; 16:12). Regarding the four notorious factions of 1 Cor 1:12 (of Paul, of Apollos, of Cephas, of Christ), Antoinette Clark Wire plausibly reasons, "If the real struggle in Corinth is polarized around the names of Paul and Apollos, with Cephas introduced to defuse the conflict and Christ to stop it, Paul has reason to use a singular form when he speaks of 'another' who is building on the foundation he has laid [1 Cor 3:10]."³¹ Alas, Paul says next to nothing about Apollos's biography. The Acts of Apostles says more, though it is late and hagiographical. Luke introduces him as Ἰουδαῖος δέ τις Ἀπολλῶς ὀνόματι, Ἀλεξανδρεὺς τῷ γένει, ἀνὴρ λόγιος... δυνατὸς ὢν ἐν ταῖς γραφαῖς, "a certain Jew named Apollos, an Alexandrian by clan, a [rhetorically] learned man... capable with the

---

²⁸ Georgi, *Opponents of Paul in Second Corinthians*; Birger A. Pearson, *The Pneumatikos-Psychikos Terminology in 1 Corinthians*, SBLDS 12 (Missoula, MT: SBL, 1973).

²⁹ See Troels Engberg-Pedersen, *Cosmology and Self in the Apostle Paul: The Material Spirit* (Oxford: Oxford University Press, 2010); Fredriksen, *Pagans' Apostle*; Jennifer Eyl, *Signs, Wonders, and Gifts: Divination in the Letters of Paul* (Oxford: Oxford University Press, 2019).

³⁰ Thus rightly, already, John Calvin, *Commentary on the Epistles of Paul the Apostle to the Corinthians* (Grand Rapids, MI: Baker, 1981), 2:102: "During Paul's absence false apostles had crept in, not, in my opinion, to disturb the Church openly with wicked doctrines, or designedly to undermine sound doctrine; but priding themselves in the splendour and magnificence of their address, or rather, being puffed up with an empty loftiness of speech, they looked upon Paul's simplicity, and even the Gospel itself, with contempt."

³¹ Antoinette Clark Wire, *The Corinthian Women Prophets: A Reconstruction through Paul's Rhetoric* (Minneapolis: Fortress, 1995), 42.

scriptures" (Acts 18:24), and places his performance of religious expertise in Corinth (Acts 19:1).

If all of this were true,[32] it would fit both with what Paul says about Apollos in 1 Corinthians and with what Paul says about his Jewish rivals in 2 Corinthians. To be sure, in 1 Corinthians Paul speaks diplomatically (though not warmly) about the former, whereas in 2 Corinthians he speaks angrily about the latter. But if, as Larry Welborn has argued, the conspicuous falling-out that occurred between 1 Corinthians and 2 Corinthians had to do with a defection of one or more prominent Corinthians from Paul's camp to Apollos's,[33] then the change in tone is no objection to the identification of the Apollos camp with the super-apostles. Francis Watson's summary of the situation is exactly right:

> If this identification [of Apollos with the false apostles of 2 Corinthians 10–13] is not correct, then the false apostles show remarkable resemblances to Apollos. Like Apollos, they come to Corinth armed with a letter of recommendation from another church. *Like Apollos, they were Jewish Christians uninterested in imposing circumcision on Gentiles.* Like Apollos, they were more eloquent speakers than Paul was. They visited Corinth at just the time when a visit from Apollos might have been expected. These are unlikely coincidences, and the most plausible and economical explanation is that Apollos did indeed revisit Corinth, that this second visit was still more damaging to Paul's reputation there than the first, and that Paul therefore saw fit to denounce Apollos and his companions as false apostles and as servants of Satan.[34]

I have added the italics just above to bring out the key point for our purposes: The super-apostles in 2 Corinthians 10–13, who could very

---

[32] In his forthcoming book on Christianity in ancient Alexandria, David Litwa argues that Luke is right about all of these details *except* Apollos's Jewishness. On Litwa's account, Apollos was an Egyptian gentile Christian who mastered learning in Jewish scriptures. This is possible but, in my view, less likely than the alternative hypothesis that Luke is right on all essential points: Apollos was Alexandrian, Jewish, learned, and operated at Corinth.

[33] See Larry L. Welborn, *An End to Enmity: Paul and the "Wrongdoer" of Second Corinthians*, BZNW 185 (Berlin: De Gruyter, 2011). Welborn's account – of Gaius's initial allegiance to Paul, defection to Apollos, charge of embezzlement against Paul, and role as the unnamed wrongdoer in 2 Corinthians – is too confident about too many uncertain points to win me over entirely, but it does make very good sense of a remarkable amount of evidence across 1 and 2 Corinthians.

[34] Watson, *Paul, Judaism, and the Gentiles* (2d ed.), 152–156 (emphasis mine).

well be Apollos and his circle, are (1) Jewish and (2) *not* champions of proselyte circumcision. We turn now to Galatians and Philippians, with a brief foray into Romans, where, it turns out, the demographics are exactly the inverse of this.

Paul's Circumcision-Preaching Opponents

One might get the impression from the secondary literature that Paul was always and everywhere doing battle with circumcision-preaching opponents, but in fact the sources are relatively few. Such conflict is certainly a, even *the*, theme of Galatians. It is a less prominent but still important theme in Philippians. Romans, which revisits some material from Galatians,[35] discusses proselyte circumcision as an idea, though not as a clear and present danger. First Corinthians mentions in passing the possibility of either removing or adding a foreskin, but there is no indication in that letter of anyone actually advocating doing so.[36] Philemon, 1 Thessalonians, and 2 Corinthians have nothing whatsoever to say about circumcision. The three letters that do indicate a debate are less than crystal-clear about who, exactly, is on the other side of the debate. That it is Jewish circumcision being urged upon gentiles does not by any means entail that it is Jewish people doing the urging, and in fact there is a critical mass of evidence pointing in a quite different direction.

Even the majority of interpreters who assume the Jewishness of Paul's circumcision-preaching opponents are generally aware of one piece of counterevidence, namely, Gal 6:13: οὐδὲ γὰρ οἱ περιτεμνόμενοι αὐτοὶ νόμον φυλάσσουσιν ἀλλὰ θέλουσιν ὑμᾶς περιτέμνεσθαι, ἵνα ἐν τῇ ὑμετέρᾳ σαρκὶ καυχήσωνται, "Those who undergo circumcision do not guard the law themselves, rather, they want you to undergo circumcision so that they may boast in your flesh." The present participle περιτεμνόμενοι pretty straightforwardly suggests not eighth-day circumcised Jews – as the secondary *varia lectio* περιτετμημένοι (in P46 and Vaticanus) might, although really for that we would expect the noun περιτομή – but rather recently circumcised proselytes.[37] "Those who

---

[35] See Novenson, "Romans and Galatians," in *Paul, Then and Now*, 67–90.
[36] See the discussion in Collman, *Apostle to the Foreskin*.
[37] My point here is not that the present participle marks present time (indeed, on my hypothesis, this instance would actually be pointing to recent past time), just that it suggests imperfective aspect rather than perfective. In Paul's usage, Jews

want you to undergo circumcision" are themselves "those who undergo circumcision." Both the circumcision-preachers and their audience belong to the same demographic. Like the proverbial blind leading the blind, in Gal 6:13 we behold gentiles circumcising gentiles, giving the lie to the dominant Baurian theory of a *Jewish* pro-circumcision faction versus a *gentile* anti-circumcision faction.

This argument from this verse is especially associated with the name of Johannes Munck. Writing in Aarhus in 1954, Munck reasoned, "The present participle with the article οἱ περιτεμνόμενοι is rightly applied by [Hans] Lietzmann to the Gentile Christians who become circumcised under the pressure of Judaistic demands; but, as v. 13b shows, these Gentile Christians are those who are agitating among the Galatians for Judaism."[38] And more succinctly and polemically, "To sum up, we may say that the Judaizing movement does not, as the Tübingen School thought, represent the original Christian conception of the Church in the period from Jesus to Paul, but that it is a Gentile Christian heresy that was possible only in the Pauline churches."[39] This lattermost phrase is an overreach, I think, but the observation that our sources point to a *gentile*, not a Jewish, fetish for proselyte circumcision in the Christ assemblies (a "Gentile Christian heresy" in Munck's idiom) is remarkably perceptive.

Unfortunately, this hypothesis received, and has continued to receive, a cool reception partly due to misgivings about other aspects of Munck's reconstruction. John Gale Hawkins rightly comments, "The theory that the judaizers in Galatia were Gentile Christians is probably connected in most people's minds with the work of Johannes Munck. This is unfortunate for the theory, because the merits of its exegetical foundation are apt to remain unconsidered when people reject Munck's bitter anti-Tübingen polemic as a whole or reject his unique explanation of the way in which the Gentile Christians began to

---

exist in a state of circumcision, whereas proselytes *undergo* circumcision. See further A. E. Harvey, "The Opposition to Paul," *Studia Evangelica*, vol. 4 (Berlin: Akademie Verlag, 1968), 319–332, who reaches the right conclusion but without due attention to verbal aspect; and Thiessen, *Paul and the Gentile Problem*, 95–96, who is right both about the grammar and about the historical reconstruction.

[38] Johannes Munck, *Paul and the Salvation of Mankind*, trans. Frank Clarke (Richmond, VA: John Knox, 1959 [German original 1954]), 87–88.

[39] Munck, *Paul and the Salvation of Mankind*, 134.

judaize without any external stimulus."⁴⁰ In fact, the core idea is much older than Munck, as he himself pointed out, and it has had other proponents both before and after Munck who put the pieces together differently than he.⁴¹ But the hypothesis has also suffered due to a mistaken assumption that Gal 6:13 is the only evidence on offer. John Barclay, for instance, objects, "Certainly it would be precarious to build an important thesis about their Gentile origin on 6.13 alone (as Munck did)."⁴² That would indeed be precarious, but there is no need to build on such a fragile foundation. In fact, Munck adduces several other texts from Galatians, to which we may add still more from Galatians, and from Philippians and Romans, as well.

In addition to Gal 6:13, Munck also points – rightly, in my view – to Gal 5:3: μαρτύρομαι δὲ πάλιν παντὶ ἀνθρώπῳ περιτεμνομένῳ ὅτι ὀφειλέτης ἐστὶν ὅλον τὸν νόμον ποιῆσαι, "I testify again to every person who undergoes circumcision that he is obligated to do the whole law." He comments on this verse, "If... the Gentile Christians thought that part of the Law ought to be kept, but not the whole Law, that is probably an expression of their wish to keep the Law to the best of

---

⁴⁰ John Gale Hawkins, "The Opponents of Paul in Galatia" (PhD diss., Yale University, 1971), 22.

⁴¹ Before Munck: A. Neander, *Geschichte der Pflanzung und Leitung der christlichen Kirche durch die Apostel*, vol. 1, 4th rev. ed. (Hamburg: Friedrich Perthes, 1847), 366–367; H. A. Schott, *Epistolae Pauli ad Thessalonicenses et Galatas* (Leipzig: Barth, 1834), 287, 605; F. Windischmann, *Erklärung des Briefes an die Galater* (Mainz: Schott & Thielmann, 1843); F. Bleek, *Einleitung in das Neue Testament*, ed. W. Mangold, 3rd ed. (Berlin: Reimer, 1875), 488–489; K. H. Weizsäcker, "Paulus und die Gemeinde in Korinth," *JDT* 21 (1876): 608; J. H. Ropes, *The Singular Problem of the Epistle to the Galatians*, HTS 14 (Cambridge, MA: Harvard University Press, 1929), 44–45; E. Hirsch, "Zwei Fragen zu Galater 6," *ZNW* 29 (1930): 192–197; W. Michaelis, "Judaistische Heidenchristen," *ZNW* 30 (1931): 83–89; H. W. Beyer, "Der Brief an die Galater," in *Die kleineren Briefe des Apostels Paulus*, Das Neue Testament Deutsch vol. 8 (Göttingen: Vandenhoeck & Ruprecht, 1933), 2, 32, 42; M. S. Enslin, *Christian Beginnings* (New York: Harper, 1938), 221 222. (On this early history of research, see Hawkins, "Opponents of Paul," 5–85.) After Munck: Harvey, "The Opposition to Paul"; David Flusser, "Die Christenheit nach dem Apostelkonzil," in *Antijudaismus im Neuen Testament?* ed. W. Eckert, N. P. Levinson, and M. Stohr (Munich: Kaiser, 1967), 62–63; Markus Barth, "Was Paul an Anti-Semite?" *JES* 5 (1968): 93; Peter Richardson, *Israel in the Apostolic Church*, SNTSMS 10 (Cambridge: Cambridge University Press, 1969), 84–97; Martin Goodman, "Galatians 6:12 on Circumcision and Persecution," in *Strength to Strength: Essays in Honor of Shaye J. D. Cohen*, ed. Michael L. Satlow (Providence, RI: Brown Judaic Studies, 2018), 275–280.

⁴² Barclay, "Mirror-Reading a Polemical Letter," 86.

their ability. To a former rabbinic pupil that attempt was bound to seem pitifully amateurish."⁴³ Now, there is a further question, which Munck does not consider, whether ὅλον τὸν νόμον here means the whole law of Moses (i.e., all the commandments) or the whole law of circumcision (i.e., all of its component parts). Munck assumes the former, which is indeed possible, though there are also good reasons in favor of the latter sense in this context.⁴⁴ Either way, though, his point that Paul here implies that his rivals are amateurs is well made.⁴⁵

For if Paul implies that in Gal 5:3, he says it in so many words in the first part of Gal 6:13 (cited above): οὐδὲ γὰρ οἱ περιτεμνόμενοι αὐτοὶ νόμον φυλάσσουσιν, "Those who undergo circumcision *do not guard the law themselves.*" The charge here is not that the opponents are egregious wrongdoers, but rather that, despite their good intentions to bring people under the law, they make a hash of interpreting the commandments ("do not guard the law"). Moving beyond Munck, and following Matthew Thiessen,⁴⁶ I think that this is a direct reference to the opponents' attempt to apply Jewish circumcision – which the Torah enjoins upon Jewish infant boys (Gen 17, especially v. 14)⁴⁷ – to grown gentile men. By so doing, they bungle the commandment, "they do not guard the law." The whole situation is, as Munck puts it, "pitifully amateurish." In contrast to all this, Paul presents the other Jewish apostles as being *on his side* in the proselyte circumcision controversy. Like Paul, they are "Jews by nature," not "gentile sinners" (Gal 2:15); hence they know how to guard the law. In Galatians, in other words, *all* of the Jewish apostles, not just Paul, oppose proselyte circumcision for gentiles-in-Christ.⁴⁸ The only people who foolishly agitate for proselyte circumcision are other proselyte-circumcised judaizers, οἱ περιτεμνόμενοι, "those who get themselves circumcised."

---

[43] Munck, *Paul and the Salvation of Mankind*, 92.
[44] On this question see Thiessen, *Paul and the Gentile Problem*, 91–95.
[45] See further my argument in Chapter 5.
[46] Thiessen, *Paul and the Gentile Problem*, 95–96.
[47] On the textual variants attesting an insistence on this issue, see Matthew Thiessen, "The Text of Genesis 17:14," *JBL* 128 (2009): 625–642.
[48] Ironically for the Baur hypothesis, the evidence of Paul's letters is pretty unequivocal on this point. The Acts of the Apostles, by contrast, which Baur thought *moderated* an original Pauline anti-Judaism, actually *introduces* some conflict between Paul and Jewish Christ-believers (though not with the Jerusalem apostles) on proselyte circumcision where there is no such in the letters.

In Philippians, the evidence that Paul's circumcision-preaching opponents are gentile proselytes is even more explicit than in Galatians.[49] How exactly *these* opponents in Macedonia are related to *those* opponents in Asia Minor is not obvious – are they the very same people? different delegates of the same movement? independently like-minded movements? – and I think that we probably must remain agnostic on that question.[50] But that proselyte circumcision for gentiles-in-Christ is the point of dispute is certain. In Galatians that prospect is presented as immediate, whereas in Philippians it appears future and hypothetical, occasioning a warning rather than a desperate intervention. That warning comes in Philippians 3:

Βλέπετε τοὺς κύνας, βλέπετε τοὺς κακοὺς ἐργάτας, βλέπετε τὴν κατατομήν. ἡμεῖς γάρ ἐσμεν ἡ περιτομή, οἱ πνεύματι θεοῦ λατρεύοντες καὶ καυχώμενοι ἐν Χριστῷ Ἰησοῦ καὶ οὐκ ἐν σαρκὶ πεποιθότες, καίπερ ἐγὼ ἔχων πεποίθησιν καὶ ἐν σαρκί. Εἴ τις δοκεῖ ἄλλος πεποιθέναι ἐν σαρκί, ἐγὼ μᾶλλον· περιτομῇ ὀκταήμερος, ἐκ γένους Ἰσραήλ, φυλῆς Βενιαμίν, Ἑβραῖος ἐξ Ἑβραίων, κατὰ νόμον Φαρισαῖος, κατὰ ζῆλος διώκων τὴν ἐκκλησίαν, κατὰ δικαιοσύνην τὴν ἐν νόμῳ γενόμενος ἄμεμπτος. [Ἀλλὰ] ἅτινα ἦν μοι κέρδη, ταῦτα ἥγημαι διὰ τὸν Χριστὸν ζημίαν.

Look at the dogs, look at the bad workers, look at the incision. For *we* are the circumcision, who offer cult by the pneuma of God and boast in Christ Jesus and do not put confidence in the flesh. Though I myself do have confidence in the flesh. If any other person thinks he has confidence in the flesh, much more so I: in regard to circumcision an eighth-dayer, from the race of Israel, from the tribe of Benjamin, a Hebrew from Hebrews, in regard to the law a Pharisee, in regard to zeal indicting the assembly, in regard to righteousness in the law being blameless. But whatever things were a gain to me, these things I regard as loss for the sake of Christ. (Phil 3:2–7)

This passage is thick with interpretive problems, many of which I address at the relevant points in other chapters of this book.[51] The key question for our present purposes is the ethnic identity of "the

---

[49] Another unfortunate aspect of the reception of the Munck hypothesis in subsequent scholarship, since Munck restricted his argument to Galatians.
[50] Contra Lüdemann, *Opposition to Paul in Jewish Christianity*; Douglas A. Campbell, *The Deliverance of God: An Apocalyptic Rereading of Justification in Paul* (Grand Rapids, MI: Eerdmans, 2009); and many others.
[51] Especially, regarding "we are the circumcision" in Phil 3:3, see my argument in Chapter 7 that there is no redefinition or dispossession of Israel here.

dogs, the bad workers, the incision."[52] It is useful to start with a comparison with 2 Corinthians 11, discussed above. There Paul says about the so-called super-apostles, "Are they Hebrews? So am I! Are they Israelites? So am I! Are they seed of Abraham? So am I!" (2 Cor 11:22), insisting that his ethnic *bona fides* are equal to those of his rivals. In Philippians 3, by contrast, he writes, "If any other person thinks he has confidence in the flesh, *much more so I*: in regard to circumcision an eighth-dayer, from the race of Israel, from the tribe of Benjamin, a Hebrew from Hebrews," and so on. Here Paul pleads not his *equality* but his *superiority* on ethnic terms. He is a Hebrew, an Israelite, circumcised on the eighth day. They – whoever they are – are not. Paul has more confidence in the flesh, better ethnic *bona fides*, than they do. The super-apostles in 2 Corinthians are Paul's equals; the "bad workers" in Philippians are his inferiors.

And inferior *as regards Jewishness and circumcision*. Paul is a Hebrew; the bad workers are not. Paul was circumcised on the eighth day; the bad workers were not. But if Paul boasts over against them that he has *eighth-day* circumcision, then they presumably have... not-eighth-day circumcision, which is to say, proselyte circumcision. And this explains why Paul would choose to use the baroque heritage names "Hebrew," "Israelite," and "Benjamin" in this context.[53] His proselyte-circumcised opponents might be able to claim the title *Ioudaios*, "Jew" or "Judean," by virtue of their having so thoroughly adopted Jewish customs. As Cassius Dio writes, the name *Ioudaios* can apply not only to natural-born Jews, "but also to other people who, although they are of other races, affect their customs [τοὺς ἄλλους ἀνθρώπους ὅσοι τὰ νόμιμα αὐτῶν, καίπερ ἀλλοεθνεῖς ὄντες, ζηλοῦσι]" (*Roman History* 37.17.1).[54] (Indeed, as I argue below, Paul speaks to this very onomastic phenomenon in Rom 2.)[55] But even if these "bad

---

[52] Matthew D. C. Larsen, *Early Christians and Incarceration: A Cultural History* (Oxford: Oxford University Press, forthcoming) has recently argued that these terms actually refer to persons associated with Paul's current imprisonment: the "dogs" are prison guards, the "bad workers" criminals, i.e., other detainees. An ingenious proposal, but I am not yet persuaded.

[53] The rhetorical rationale for these terms is expertly explained by Jennifer Eyl, "'I Myself Am an Israelite': Paul, Authenticity, and Authority," *JSNT* 40 (2017): 148–168. And see further my "*Ioudaios*, Pharisee, Zealot."

[54] On this text, see further Cohen, *Beginnings of Jewishness*, 58–62, 149–154.

[55] See further Novenson, "The Self-Styled Jew of Romans 2 and the Actual Jews of Romans 9–11."

workers" can claim to be Jews-by-custom, they cannot claim to be Hebrews or Israelites, for they are not descended from any of the twelve sons of Jacob, as Paul is from Benjamin.[56] That is the logic of Paul's boast here: These workers may come with what seems an impressive pedigree; they are Jews-by-custom, proselytes in good standing. But that pales next to Paul's blue-blooded Israeliteness ("If any other person thinks he has confidence in the flesh, much more so I!").[57] The whole thing works on the premise that Paul has what his rivals *lack*, not, as in 2 Corinthians 11, that Paul has what his rivals *have*. The super-apostles in Corinth are natural-born Jews like Paul. The bad workers, by contrast, are gentile poseurs.

This hypothesis also solves the problem of the epithet "dogs" in v. 2, which has long horrified (or, God help us, thrilled) interpreters who took Paul to be turning on his own people in a fit of race-traitor rage. Thus the majority view: that Paul here takes what was supposedly an ancient Jewish term of abuse for gentiles and turns it back on the Jews. As Mark Nanos has shown, however, the evidence that "dogs" was a Jewish term of abuse for gentiles in antiquity is virtually nil.[58] And such meagre evidence as there is appears, in the earliest instance, on the lips of... Jesus (Mark 7:27; Matt 15:26)! Or perhaps Paul, depending what exactly he is saying in Phil 3:2–7, which is the question before us. In fact, as Matthew Thiessen has shown, evidence for ancient Jews calling gentiles dogs (and other unclean animals, too, for that matter) comes almost entirely from *within* the Jesus movement. It was Christ-following Jews, not ancient Jews generally, who had a habit of calling gentiles dogs.[59] That could be exactly what is happening in Phil 3:2. If Paul's opponents here are gentile proselytes, he may be scorning them, as Jesus does the Canaanite woman, with the ethnic term of

---

[56] See Jason A. Staples, *The Idea of Israel in Second Temple Judaism* (Cambridge: Cambridge University Press, 2021).

[57] As Thiessen, *Paul and the Gentile Problem*, 70 rightly perceives, Paul trades on a value-laded *physis/nomos* distinction which is at least as old as Aristotle. On this distinction, to have a property by *physis* is better than to have it merely by *nomos*.

[58] Mark D. Nanos, "Paul's Reversal of Jews Calling Gentiles 'Dogs' (Philippians 3.2): 1600 Years of an Ideological Tale Wagging an Exegetical Dog," *BibInt* 17 (2009): 448–482.

[59] Matthew Thiessen, "Gentiles as Impure Animals in the Writings of Early Christ Followers," in *Perceiving the Other in Ancient Judaism and Early Christianity*, ed. Michal Bar-Asher Siegal et al., WUNT 394 (Tübingen: Mohr Siebeck, 2017), 19–32.

abuse "dogs." Alternatively – or perhaps in addition – "dogs" here may have to do not with ethnicity but with unmentionable body parts. As Ryan Collman has shown, perhaps the most common ancient slang use of "dog" was for the *membrum virile*, like (another animal word) "cock" in modern English slang. Because the point of dispute in Philippians 3 is proselyte circumcision, a surgical modification of the gentile penis, the most plausible interpretation may be that Paul is here insulting his opponents with crass slang for the male member.[60]

What calls forth such an insult is not just any circumcision, but proselyte circumcision in particular. Eighth-day circumcision for Jewish infant boys Paul regards as a good (Phil 3:5), always giving it its proper, traditional name περιτομή, "circumcision." But in Phil 3:3 he refers to the "bad workers" via metonymy as the κατατομή, "incision" or "mutilation." In Greek it is a wordplay on περιτομή; hence my use of English "incision." (Also, LSJ gives "incision" as a gloss where κατατομή refers to a notch or groove in a rock face or prepared stone.)[61] This wordplay, in this polemical context, can only mean that these workers are urging proselyte circumcision upon gentiles-in-Christ, just like what we find in Galatians. But here Paul does not dignify it with the name "circumcision"; it is only "incision," the gouging of a gentile penis which is *naturally* foreskinned (Paul's idiom, Rom 2:25). And Paul uses that term not just for the act but for the people whose message it is. *They* are the incision, both because they preach incision and because, being gentile proselytes themselves, they bear it on their own bodies. As Karin Neutel and Peter-Ben Smit have argued, proselyte circumcision in the letters of Paul can be helpfully understood as a case of ritual failure.[62] By Paul's lights, to circumcise a gentile at all is to do circumcision wrong. (Other ancient Jews took

---

[60] Ryan D. Collman, "Beware the Dogs! The Phallic Epithet in Phil 3.2," NTS 67 (2021): 105–120.

[61] On the lexical issue see Isaac T. Soon, *A Disabled Apostle: Impairment and Disability in the Letters of Paul* (Oxford: Oxford University Press, 2023).

[62] Karin B. Neutel, "Circumcision Gone Wrong: Paul's Message as a Case of Ritual Disruption," *Neot* 50 (2016): 373–396; Peter-Ben Smit, "In Search of Real Circumcision: Ritual Failure and Circumcision in Paul," *JSNT* 40 (2017): 73–100. My understanding of precisely how, for Paul, proselyte circumcision effects ritual failure differs from both Neutel's and Smit's, but I could only come to my understanding thanks to their articles.

different views on this matter, of course.)⁶³ As he sees it, a proselyte circumcision can never be a circumcision, only ever an incision. Whereas Jewish infant circumcision is pious and decorous, the circumcision of gentile men amounts to a perverse obsession with the penis (thus "dogs").

Which brings us to the latter part of Philippians 3, where there is yet another reference to perverse obsession with the penis. Or so I think there is, following Francis Watson, although other interpreters have not seen it. At Phil 3:18–19, just a paragraph after the warning about the "dogs," Paul writes, πολλοὶ γὰρ περιπατοῦσιν οὓς πολλάκις ἔλεγον ὑμῖν, νῦν δὲ καὶ κλαίων λέγω, τοὺς ἐχθροὺς τοῦ σταυροῦ τοῦ Χριστοῦ, ὧν τὸ τέλος ἀπώλεια, ὧν ὁ θεὸς ἡ κοιλία καὶ ἡ δόξα ἐν τῇ αἰσχύνῃ αὐτῶν, οἱ τὰ ἐπίγεια φρονοῦντες, "For there are many – about whom I often told you and now tell you while weeping – who walk as enemies of the cross of Christ, whose end is destruction, whose god is the *koilia*, whose glory is in their shame, who think on earthly things." The reference I mean is the curious phrase ὧν ὁ θεὸς ἡ κοιλία, "whose god is the *koilia*." I have left the latter noun untranslated here so as not to beg the question. Most English translations give the not-unreasonable gloss "belly" and take it as a reference to gluttony or self-indulgence. Maybe. But that is difficult to square with the immediate context, and even more so with the preceding passage (Phil 3:2–7), where the problem is certainly proselyte circumcision. This has left many interpreters confusedly speculating about two completely different groups of opponents – judaizing circumcisers on the one hand, gluttonous libertines on the other – within a single chapter.⁶⁴

But κοιλία need not mean "belly" as in stomach, appetite. Most basically it means "cavity of the body" (thus LSJ), especially the abdomen. But more specifically, it can signify any of the body parts (and their functions) of that lower region: the stomach (digestion) and intestines (excretion), but also the uterus (gestation) and the penis and testes (insemination). In Jewish Greek, in particular, there is an old biblical usage according to which the male genitalia are politely called

---

⁶³ As decisively shown by Matthew Thiessen, *Contesting Conversion: Genealogy, Circumcision, and Identity in Ancient Judaism and Christianity* (Oxford: Oxford University Press, 2011).
⁶⁴ See the discussion of this history of research in A. F. J. Klijn, "Paul's Opponents in Philippians III," *NovT* 7 (1965): 278–284.

the κοιλία, "loins," as one might say in old-fashioned English.⁶⁵ And if Philippians 3 is already about (what Paul perceives to be) a disordered focus on male genitalia ("dogs" in Phil 3:2), then there is very good reason to take κοιλία here along similar lines. Not "their god is the stomach" but "their god is the male member." This is corroborated by the following clause ἡ δόξα ἐν τῇ αἰσχύνῃ αὐτῶν, "their glory is in their shame." Αἰσχύνη (or its cognate ἀσχημοσύνη), "shame," is a very common euphemism for the genitals, even elsewhere in Paul's letters: "Our shameful parts have greater modesty" (1 Cor 12:23).⁶⁶ These "enemies of the cross of Christ" in Philippians 3 glory in their "shame," their private parts, an accusation that makes good sense in one proximate context: the proselyte circumcision controversy.⁶⁷ Francis Watson suggests such a reading of Phil 3:17–18, noting the language suggestive of cults of male fertility: "It seems here that he alludes to phallic cults such as that of Priapus, which spread to Greece and the great Hellenistic cities after the time of Alexander... If this is correct, Paul here denounces his opponents as worshippers of the phallus. This would again be a reference to the missionaries of circumcision."⁶⁸ Watson does not take the further step of identifying these missionaries as gentile proselytes themselves, but this seems to me the obvious conclusion. What Paul considers a perverse priapic fixation is the circumcision not of Jewish infants, but of gentile men. The people who preach this are not eighth-day-circumcised Hebrews like himself, but "incised" gentile proselytes.

The Letter to the Romans contains far less polemic against circumcision-preaching opponents than Galatians or Philippians does. Where Romans covers some similar ground to those letters, it is generally in a discursive rather than a combative mode. Admittedly, Romans is conspicuous for its chapters-long use of the diatribe form ("But you will say... What then shall we say?... What then?... Is it the case that?... By no means," etc.), but as Stanley Stowers demonstrated over against Rudolf Bultmann, that form is a schoolroom exercise, not

---

[65] See LXX Deut 7:13; 28:4, 11, 18, 53; 30:9; 2 Kdgms 7:12=1 Chron 17:11; OG Ps 131:11.
[66] The same usage occurs in LXX Exod 20:26; Rev 16:15.
[67] Indeed, elsewhere Paul insists on the same antinomy between *proselyte circumcision* on the one hand and *the cross* on the other (Gal 5:11; 6:12).
[68] Watson, *Paul, Judaism, and the Gentiles* (2nd ed.), 145.

a weapon of rhetorical war.⁶⁹ It imagines and answers possible questions and objections; it does not presuppose an enemy behind every question, or any enemies at all, for that matter.

Paul's diatribe in Romans does expressly raise the issue of circumcision at one point: the end of Rom 2, whence it remains a theme through the middle of Rom 4, after which Paul does not mention it again (except Rom 15:8, where "the circumcision" appears as a metonym for the Jews).⁷⁰ Unlike in Galatians, there is no instance of the verb περιτέμνω in Romans, hinting that the prospect of people undertaking the ritual act is neither as real or as imminent. In Rom 2–4, the noun περιτομή appears frequently paired with ἀκροβυστία, "circumcision" and "foreskin": the two kinds of bodies – Paul says – of which Abraham is father and upon which God confers righteousness.⁷¹ (No mention at all of women's bodies, which are neither circumcised nor foreskinned! Paul here assumes a patriarchal schema wherein to speak of the relevant kinds of *men* is, as far as he has thought about it, to speak of the relevant kinds of *people*.⁷² But he undercuts this schema elsewhere in the letter when he speaks of numerous particular women-in-Christ [Rom 16; 1 Cor 1:11; Phil 4:2; and see 1 Cor 7; 11]). "If God, who will rightwise the circumcision from trust, is one, then [he will rightwise] also the foreskin through trust" (Rom 3:30).⁷³ "Abraham is father of all who trust through foreskin... and father of the circumcision" (Rom 4:11–12).

---

⁶⁹ Stanley K. Stowers, *The Diatribe and Paul's Letter to the Romans*, SBLDS 57 (Missoula, MT: Scholars Press, 1981); contra Rudolf Bultmann, *Der Stil der paulinischen Predigt und die kynisch-stoische Diatribe* (Göttingen: Vandenhoeck & Ruprecht, 1910).

⁷⁰ Thus rightly J. Ross Wagner, "The Christ, Servant of Jew and Gentile: A Fresh Approach to Romans 15:8–9," *JBL* 116 (1997): 473–485; contra Joshua D. Garroway, "The Circumcision of Christ: Romans 15:7–13," *JSNT* 34 (2012): 303–322.

⁷¹ Karin B. Neutel, "Restoring Abraham's Foreskin: The Significance of *akrobustia* for Paul's Argument about Circumcision in Romans 4:9–12," *JJMJS* 8 (2021): 53–74.

⁷² On this schema see Shaye J. D. Cohen, *Why Aren't Jewish Women Circumcised? Gender and Covenant in Judaism* (Berkeley: University of California Press, 2005).

⁷³ On the syntax of this sentence, I follow the minority (but correct) view of Hays, "Have We Found Abraham?" building on Nils A. Dahl, "One God of Jews and Gentiles," in *Studies in Paul*, 178–191. Pace Stowers, *Rereading of Romans*, I think the key here is the repetition of πίστις, "trust," not any strong distinction between the prepositions ἐκ and διά.

One could almost read Rom 2–4 as not posing the question of *proselyte* circumcision at all, but simply as assuming circumcised Jews and foreskinned gentiles to comprise the mass of humanity.[74] It is a bit more complicated than this, however, at least in Rom 2. Romans 2:17 raises the notion of a person *calling himself*, or *being called*, a Jew (Ἰουδαῖος ἐπονομάζῃ),[75] which makes the most sense as a (less polemically heated) reference to the same phenomenon as in Gal 5–6 and Phil 3: a male gentile-in-Christ making himself a Jew by proselyte circumcision.[76] This is corroborated, I think, in Rom 2:25 and following, where circumcision comes to the fore of the discourse:

Circumcision confers benefit if you practice the law. But if you are a transgressor of the law, then your circumcision has become a foreskin. If, therefore, the foreskin[ned man] guards the upright things of the law, won't his foreskin be reckoned as a circumcision? And the naturally foreskin[ned man] who completes the law will judge you who through the letter and circumcision are a transgressor of the law. (Rom 2:25–27)

The "you" being addressed here I take to be the hypothetical gentile proselyte who mistakenly imagines that his ersatz circumcision will confer benefit upon him.[77] (But alas, he does not actually practice the law; it is only an ersatz circumcision!) Such a person will ironically, tragically find himself inferior to ("judged by") a naturally foreskinned gentile who, however, has the pneuma of Christ and so completes the

---

[74] See my argument in Chapter 6.

[75] Lionel J. Windsor, "The Named Jew and the Name of God: The Argument of Romans 2:17–29 in Light of Roman Attitudes to Jewish Teachers," *NovT* 63 (2021): 229–248 insists that this can only be a passive, not a reflexive form ("is called," not "calls oneself"). I think Windsor's conclusion here is overdrawn, but even if he were right it would not change the crucial point: that Paul only allows this hypothetical person the *name* Jew, not the thing itself.

[76] Thus – rightly, in my view – Runar M. Thorsteinsson, *Paul's Interlocutor in Romans 2: Function and Identity in the Context of Ancient Epistolography*, ConBibNT 40 (Stockholm: Almqvist & Wiksell, 2003); Matthew Thiessen, "Paul's Argument against Gentile Circumcision in Romans 2:17–29," *NovT* 56 (2014): 373–391; Rafael Rodriguez, *If You Call Yourself a Jew: Reappraising Paul's Letter to the Romans* (Eugene, OR: Cascade, 2014); Rafael Rodriguez and Matthew Thiessen, eds., *The So-Called Jew in Paul's Letter to the Romans* (Minneapolis: Fortress, 2016). But admittedly, this is still a minority view. See the recent critical discussion by Paul T. Sloan, "Paul's Jewish Addressee in Romans 2–4: Revisiting Recent Conversations," *JTS* (2023).

[77] With Thiessen, "Paul's Argument against Gentile Circumcision."

law.⁷⁸ Proselyte circumcision, Paul reasons – rather uncharitably, it must be said – is only a performance for human approval. He continues:

> For it is not the Jew on display, nor the circumcision on display in the flesh, but rather the Jew in secret, and the circumcision of the heart in pneuma, not letter, whose praise comes not from humans but from God. What, then, is the advantage of the Jew? Or what benefit is circumcision? Much in every way! Firstly, they were entrusted with the oracles of God. (Rom 2:28–3:1)

Proselyte circumcision is only for display, in the flesh, to win praise from humans. (By contrast, the non-ostentatious circumcision of the Jewish heart, preached by Moses and Jeremiah [Deut 10:16; Jer 4:4], does win praise from God.)⁷⁹ All this is not to say that Jews and circumcision enjoy no advantage. They do! But only *Jews* and *actual* circumcision (i.e., the people Israel who received the oracles of God from the prophets), not gentile proselytes and their faux circumcisions.

In Rom 2–4, then, Paul discusses the *idea* of proselyte circumcision, but there is no evidence of any real opponents actually preaching it. (Compare Galatians and Philippians, where there demonstrably are such opponents.)⁸⁰ I say no evidence, but at the very end of Romans we do find one brief, enigmatic warning about certain anonymous troublemakers:

> I exhort you, brothers, to watch out for those to cause divisions and offenses contrary to the teaching that you learned, and stay away from them. For such people are slaves not to our lord Christ but to their own *koilia* [οἱ γὰρ τοιοῦτοι τῷ κυρίῳ ἡμῶν Χριστῷ οὐ δουλεύουσιν ἀλλὰ τῇ ἑαυτῶν κοιλίᾳ]; through attractive speech and good speech they deceive the hearts of the innocent. For your obedience has reached everyone. Therefore I rejoice over you, and I want you to be wise to the good, but unfamiliar with the bad. The God of peace will swiftly crush the satan under your feet. The grace of our lord Jesus be with you. (Rom 16:17–20)

---

⁷⁸ See Barclay, *Paul and the Gift*, 461–474 on Rom 2:14, rightly arguing that the gentile who completes the law here is one who has the pneuma of Christ.

⁷⁹ On heart circumcision, of which this is the only mention anywhere in the New Testament (!), see Collman, *Apostle to the Foreskin*.

⁸⁰ Campbell, *Deliverance of God* tries mightily to argue that Romans is every bit as polemical as Galatians, and against the very same false teaching. But this argument seems to me to rest on a great deal of reading between the lines (admittedly excepting Rom 16:17–20). On this issue see Barclay, *Paul and the Gift*, 458.

This is a strange paragraph in context, so much so that a number of interpreters have thought that it must be a later interpolation.[81] This is a tempting hypothesis, but there is no direct manuscript evidence to support it. All those witnesses that read Romans 16 read these verses here. But of course, notoriously, not all witnesses to the text of Romans read Romans 16! Or Romans 15, for that matter. Because the ending of Romans is so rife with textual problems,[82] there is, at the very least, more reason to entertain an interpolation hypothesis here than there would be elsewhere in the Pauline corpus.

Jewett, who takes our passage to be an interpolation, is most bothered by the violent reference to crushing the satan, but this seems to me pretty unexceptional for Paul.[83] Much more perplexing are the many *hapax legomena* in a very short space: ἐκκλίνω (though Paul quotes this word once in a citation of OG Ps 13:3 at Rom 3:12), χρηστολογία, ἄκακος, συντρίβω, ἀφικνέομαι, and ἐν τάχει, none of which Paul uses anywhere else. Equally strange are a couple of words that Paul otherwise consistently uses to signify good things but that here signify bad things: σκάνδαλον, the glorious "offense" of Christ and his cross in Rom 9:33; 11:9; 1 Cor 1:23; Gal 5:11 (but see Rom 14:13 for a partial parallel to Rom 16:17), and εὐλογία, elsewhere "blessing" (Rom 15:29; 1 Cor 10:16; 2 Cor 9:5, 6; Gal 3:14) but here "[deceitfully] good speech." None of these things is proof of an interpolation, but taken together they do make one suspicious. Even assuming that the paragraph is authentic, however, there is little to no evidence that these anonymous opponents teach anything to do with circumcision. The one word κοιλία, "abdomen," is admittedly a point in common with Phil 3; but otherwise "divisions," "offenses," "contrary teaching," "attractive speech," "deceit," and "the satan" do not suggest a circumcision controversy. Romans 16:17–20, then, may have in view

---

[81] Thus, e.g., John Knox, "Romans," in *Interpreter's Bible*, vol. 9 (Nashville: Abingdon, 1954), 664; Walter Schmithals, "The False Teachers of Romans 16:17–20," in *Paul and the Gnostics* (Nashville: Abingdon, 1972), 219–238; Brendan Byrne, *Romans*, SacPag (Collegeville, MN: Liturgical Press, 1996), 446–456; and most recently (to my knowledge) Robert Jewett, *Romans*, Hermeneia (Minneapolis: Fortress, 2006).

[82] See Gamble, *Textual History of the Letter to the Romans*.

[83] On the strong note of theomachy in Paul, see Emma Wasserman, *Apocalypse as Holy War: Divine Politics and Polemics in the Letters of Paul*, AYBRL (New Haven: Yale University Press, 2018); Paula Fredriksen, "Philo, Herod, Paul, and the Many Gods of Ancient Jewish 'Monotheism,'" HTR 115 (2022): 23–45.

opponents who are *neither* Jewish *nor* proponents of proselyte circumcision! But in any case, this passage in no way alters the overall picture we get from the letters: first, that Paul's certainly Jewish opponents did not preach proselyte circumcision and, second, that his circumcision-preaching opponents were born gentiles.

The Ethnic Demographics of "Jewish Christianity"

The evidence from Paul's letters that we have discussed to this point is, to my mind, pretty decisive. My aim in this final section, then, is not to say anything more about Paul but rather to bolster my argument with some corroborating context from ancient sources for and recent research on so-called Jewish Christianity. The big idea is this: contrary to Baur's seductively tidy twofold scheme – Petrine Jewish Christianity on the one hand, Pauline gentile Christianity on the other – the primary sources attest many and various permutations of Jewish and gentile Christ-believers doing Jewish and gentile things.[84] As Joan Taylor aptly summarizes, "The beliefs and practices of Jews within the Church would have varied as much as did Christian Gentiles' beliefs and practices, and there is no reason to doubt that both ethnic groups participated in the full spectrum of possible attitudes."[85] In particular, as regards our argument in this chapter, a great deal of what older scholarship lazily called "Jewish Christianity" is more accurately called *judaizing* Christianity, that is, Christ-devotion involving various Jewish customs (proselyte circumcision, ritual ablutions, food scruples,

---

[84] So much so, in fact, that there are powerful arguments in favor of abandoning the term "Jewish Christianity" entirely, as outlined by Matt Jackson-McCabe, *Jewish-Christianity and the History of Judaism*, AYBRL (New Haven: Yale University Press, 2020). On the other hand, Annette Yoshiko Reed, *Jewish-Christianity and the History of Judaism*, TSAJ 171 (Tübingen: Mohr Siebeck, 2018), xxi, makes a good case for keeping the troublesome term around precisely as a "heuristic irritant."

[85] Joan E. Taylor, "The Phenomenon of Early Jewish-Christianity: Reality or Scholarly Invention?" *VC* 44 (1990): 314. Minority voices in previous generations have made similarly perceptive points, and yet the Baur hypothesis juggernaut rolls on. Older studies that still repay reading include W. Michaelis, "Judaistische Heidenchristen," *ZNW* 30 (1931): 83–89; Helmut Koester, "Gnomai Diaphorai: The Origin and Nature of Diversification in the History of Early Christianity," in *Trajectories through Early Christianity*, ed. James M. Robinson and Helmut Koester (Philadelphia: Fortress, 1971), 114–157; Raymond E. Brown, "Not Jewish Christianity and Gentile Christianity but Types of Jewish/Gentile Christianity," *CBQ* 45 (1983): 74–79.

holy days, etc.) performed by gentiles or proselytes, not born Jews.⁸⁶ And in a great many instances, the impetus for such forms of Christ-devotion came from *other such people*, that is, from other gentiles or proselytes, in precisely the way I have argued above for the case of proselyte circumcision in the Pauline Christ-assemblies. All of this is well documented in the body of research on "Jewish Christianity," but interpreters of Paul have not yet reckoned with the implications for their, our, sources. Let us try to do so briefly here.

In her recent, magisterial *Jewish-Christianity and the History of Judaism*, Annette Yoshiko Reed puts it thusly: "Often, these various categories are presumed to be overlapping, *due to the assumption that Torah observance, low Christology, etc. naturally follow only from Jewish ethnicity*. In effect, then, these [modern] approaches follow Epiphanius in conflating Jewish ethnicity with Jewish practice, reading 'Jewishness' as a mark of deviance from a purported norm of Christian belief, and reifying 'Jewish Christianity' as a form of heresy."⁸⁷ As Reed rightly charges, modern critics often check their critical faculties at the door when reading the heresiologists. They simply take, say, Epiphanius at his word when he says that Nazarene and Ebionite "heresies" follow inevitably from Jewish ethnicity: Τὰ πάντα δέ εἰσιν Ἰουδαῖοι καὶ οὐδὲν ἕτερον, "In all respects they are Jews and nothing else" (*Panarion* 29.7.1; et passim in *Panarion* 29–30).⁸⁸

But why this lapse in critical judgment? In her study of the third-century Syriac *Didascalia Apostolorum*, Charlotte Fonrobert argues persuasively that modern critics have found Epiphanius's logic

---

⁸⁶ Thus rightly Taylor, "Jewish-Christianity," 319: Two centuries [after Ignatius] it is doubtful whether most of the Judaisers were Jewish at all"; ibid., 325: "Jewish influence, Judaistic practices, the use of Jewish or even Jewish-Christian texts all may contribute to the Church Fathers seeing groups as 'Ebionite,' or relating to the Ebionites, or heretical in a 'Jewish' way. Many modern scholars follow suit in labelling them 'Jewish-Christian' even if the groups themselves may have been ethnically Gentile"; ibid, 326: "There is only one group, among all of those described in patristic literature, which appears to have a good case for being a continuation of an early Jewish-Christian church. This was identified by the Church Fathers as the sect of the Nazoraeans... [but] theologically, there is nothing that would have distinguished them as being anything but broadly orthodox."

⁸⁷ Reed, *Jewish-Christianity and the History of Judaism*, 111; emphasis mine.

⁸⁸ For a much more aptly critical approach to Epiphanius, see Andrew S. Jacobs, *Epiphanius of Cyprus: A Cultural Biography of Late Antiquity* (Berkeley: University of California Press, 2021).

appealing because it tidily quarantines the ostensible problem of Jewish-Christian heresy within a small and ever-diminishing ethnic minority of the early church. Citing Georg Strecker's account[89] as an example, Fonrobert writes:

> This identification of "Jewish Christian" heresies with ethnically Jewish converts has been a classic tenet of scholarship on Jewish Christianity. Ultimately, however, it is not sufficient to merely identify and name the *Didascalia*'s opponents "Jewish Christians," as those who converted from Judaism, and then confine the problem of the "Jewish Christian" heresy to those who happen to be Jewish converts, as Georg Strecker has suggested... For Strecker then, confining the problem to Christians who are ethnically Jewish provides a satisfying solution because he has fenced it in.[90]

But conceptual tidiness does not make Strecker's or any other such account true. (Indeed, if anything, an excess of tidiness might suggest the opposite.) In the fascinating case of the *Didascalia*, the "heresy" about which the author complains certainly has to do with certain Jewish customs ("vain obligations, purifications and sprinklings and baptisms and distinction of meats" [*Did. apost.* 26]), but only those included in the "Second Legislation" given to Moses *after* the golden calf episode. What our author calls "the Law" (comprising the commandments given *before* the golden calf episode) abides forever, he insists. So both he and the so-called heretics are "Torah-observant" – to use the familiar but vague modern phrase – but in different respects.[91] As regards ethnicity, sometimes our author singles out Jewish Christians as susceptible to this heresy ("you who have been converted from the People to believe in God our saviour Jesus Christ, do not henceforth continue in your former conversation" [*Did. apost.* 26]), other times he has in view Jewish Christians or gentile Christians or both ("whether from the People or from the gentiles" [*Did. apost.*

---

[89] Georg Strecker, "On the Problem of Jewish Christianity," in Walter Bauer, *Orthodoxy and Heresy in Early Christianity*, trans. Robert A. Kraft et al. (Philadelphia: Fortress, 1971), 241–285.
[90] Charlotte Elisheva Fonrobert, "The *Didascalia Apostolorum*: A Mishnah for the Disciples of Jesus," *JECS* 9 (2001): 500–501.
[91] Thus rightly Fonrobert, "*Didascalia*," 496: "Both the author(s) and his or their opponents share the language of law. Both of their versions of Christianity include or are even based on a body of rules, prohibitions and laws, on the very concept of 'law.' However, the concept of law which the opponents have is belittled as only 'secondary.'"

25]).⁹² And he certainly counts himself as a *Jewish* Christian, his rejection of the Second Legislation notwithstanding ("our savior did not say this to the gentiles, but he said it to *us his disciples from among the Jews*" [*Did. apost.* 26]). The author of the *Didascalia* presents himself, just as Paul presents himself, as a Jewish apostle competent to rule certain observances of the law of Moses out of order.

Michele Murray has perhaps done more than any other recent critic to document how much of so-called Jewish Christianity in antiquity is actually judaizing gentile Christianity. In her *Playing a Jewish Game*, she canvasses a great mass of evidence up to the end of the second century. Some of it does point to Jewish Christ-believers influencing their gentile coreligionists to judaize, although direct evidence of this is far sparser than one might guess. A parade example, conspicuous for its explicitness,⁹³ is Justin, *Dial.* 47.4: "But if, Trypho... some of your [Jewish] race who say they believe in this Christ compel those gentiles who believe in this Christ to live in all respects according to the law given by Moses, or choose not to associate so intimately with them, I in like manner do not approve of them. But I believe that even those who have been persuaded by them to observe the legal dispensation along with their confession of God in Christ shall probably be saved." Justin knows of certain Jewish Christ-believers who urge gentile Christ-believers to judaize. He disapproves of this, but he thinks that even judaizing gentiles-in-Christ will be saved, so long as their law-observance does not tempt them to abandon Christ altogether.

But the lion's share of the evidence covered by Murray suggests, instead, a kind of self-replicating gentile Christian judaizing.⁹⁴ That is,

---

[92] See further Taylor, "Jewish-Christianity," 324: "Some of the 'heretics' described in the third-century Syriac *Didascalia Apostolorum* are, for example, clearly Jewish-Christians (*Didasc.* 23–26), but their opponents in the 'catholic church, holy and perfect' (*Didasc.* 9) know of no neat title under which they could be defined and no founding heresiarch who could be denounced; only that the wrong to observe [certain kinds of] Jewish praxis."

[93] Contrast the much more ambiguous Acts of the Apostles, which attributes to certain Christ-believing (Jewish) Pharisees both the pro- (15:5) and anti- (23:6; 26:5) positions on proselyte circumcision. See Garroway, "Pharisee Heresy."

[94] See her summary comment: "Assuming that judaizing was indeed occurring, there is no substantive evidence that Jews were the instigators of such behavior among Christians. Rather... fellow Gentile Christians more likely were the primary aggressors.... It is unlikely that Jewish Christians followed a policy of aggressive missionizing learned as Jews, for, as discussed earlier, there is no evidence in extant sources from antiquity for a standard missionary policy

contrary to the Baur hypothesis, there is no program of propaganda issuing from Jerusalem or from Jewish Christian communities more broadly. Rather, some gentile Christ-believers – quite unsurprisingly, given the Jewish origins of the Christ movement – take a shine to certain Jewish customs (proselyte circumcision, or sabbath-keeping, or ritual ablutions, or reading practices, or what have you) and promote them in their own circles. One text rightly adduced by Murray in this connection is Ignatius's early second-century Letter to the Philadelphians, in which he warns his audience not to heed gentiles who come to them teaching *Ioudaismos*: "If anyone interprets *Ioudaismos* to you, do not listen to him. For it is better to listen to *Christianismos* from a man who has circumcision than *Ioudaismos* from a foreskin. But both of them, if they do not speak of Jesus Christ, are monuments and graves of the dead, on which are written only names of humans" (Ignatius, *Phld.* 6.1.). What exactly Ignatius (or anyone, for that matter!) means by *Ioudaismos* is a complicated question.[95] With Shaye Cohen and Daniel Boyarin, though, I think it is clear that here it does not simply mean "Judaism" in our customary sense of "Jewish people keeping Jewish traditions."[96] For Ignatius, *Ioudaismos* signifies a certain kind of (deviant) *Christian* practice: the adoption of certain Jewish traditions (but which ones?) by Christians. It is not for them, he says, to listen to *Ioudaismos*, because they have their own counterpart – *Christianismos* – a word that is first attested here and may in fact be Ignatius's own neologism.

The key thing for our purposes, though, is who it is that Ignatius imagines might come teaching *Ioudaismos*: not a Jew but a foreskinned gentile. As Cohen rightly comments on this passage, "There is no indication whatsoever that the foreskinned preacher of 'Judaism' was an ethnic Jew or a member of the Jewish community. It is far more likely that he was a gentile member of the Christian community."[97] Likewise Stephen Wilson on the same passage: "Some (if not all) of the Judaizers were Gentile in origin. That is the plain sense of

---

among Jews" (Michele Murray, *Playing a Jewish Game: Gentile Christian Judaizing in the First and Second Centuries CE*, ESCJ 13 [Waterloo, ON: Wilfrid Laurier University Press, 2004], 118-119).

[95] See my discussion in Chapter 2.
[96] Cohen, "Judaism without Circumcision"; Boyarin, "Why Ignatius Invented Judaism."
[97] Cohen, "Judaism without Circumcision," 414.

Phld. 6.1 – those who expounded Judaism were uncircumcised."[98] Now, it could be, as Cohen goes on to suggest, that the whole thing is a rhetorical hypothetical, that Ignatius simply means to urge his audience to listen always and only to *Christianismos*. Maybe. But even if so, the hypothetical that he imagines is precisely this: a gentile teaching *Ioudaismos*.[99]

The same is probably true of the early second-century *Epistle of Barnabas*, which is notorious for its anti-Jewish rhetoric[100] but whose actual stated anxiety is that its own Christ-believing audience might become proselytes to the law of Moses. The author writes, "The one who is patient anticipated, brothers, that the people he prepared in his beloved would believe, in a state of innocence. And so he revealed all things to us in advance, that we not be dashed against their law as newcomers [or: proselytes] [ἵνα μὴ προσρησσώμεθα ὡς ἐπήλυτοι [or: προσήλυτοι] τῷ ἐκείνων νόμῳ]" (*Barn.* 3:6; text and trans. Ehrman in LCL). There is a text-critical question here, whether to read ἐπήλυτοι or προσήλυτοι, "newcomers" or "proselytes." Either way, the sense is very nearly the same. *Barnabas* works so hard to denigrate Jewish rituals because he worries about his own audience judaizing. But here again, there is no indication of a mission from Jewish people, whether within or without the Christ group.[101] When he raises the issue of circumcision (*Barn.* 9), *Barnabas* says that, whereas Christian

---

[98] Stephen G. Wilson, *Related Strangers: Jews and Christians, 70–170 CE* (Minneapolis: Fortress, 1995), 164.

[99] For more debate on this difficult text, see C. K. Barrett, "Jews and Judaizers in the Epistles of Ignatius," in *Jews, Greeks, and Christians: Religious Cultures in Late Antiquity*, ed. Robert Hamerton-Kelly and Robin Scroggs (Leiden: Brill, 1976), 220–244; Paul J. Donahue, "Jewish Christianity in the Letters of Ignatius of Antioch," VC 32 (1978): 81–93.

[100] Robert A. Kraft, "The Epistle of Barnabas: Its Quotations and Their Sources" (PhD diss., Harvard University, 1961) argues that *Barnabas* is anti-cultic, not anti-Jewish. It is true that many of *Barnabas*'s allegorizing interpretations are entirely possible within a Jewish matrix (cf. Philo), but it seems to me that the particular use to which *Barnabas* puts those interpretations is deservedly called anti-Jewish.

[101] Here I differ with William Horbury, "Jewish-Christian Relations in the Epistle of Barnabas and Justin Martyr," in *Jews and Christians in Contact and Controversy* (Edinburgh: T&T Clark, 1998), 127–161; and James Carleton Paget, "Paul and the Epistle of Barnabas," *NovT* 38 (1996): 359–381. Horbury and Carleton Paget are right, I think, that *Barnabas* knows actual Jews and Judaism, not just gentile judaizers, but wrong to infer from this a hypothetical Jewish proselytizing mission.

circumcision of the heart is a divine good, Jewish circumcision of the flesh was always an error, having been given not by God but by an evil angel (*Barn.* 9:4).[102] Perhaps he fears that his gentile Christian audience might consider proselyte circumcision (although even this is not crystal clear), but there is no evidence in the text of any Jews urging it upon them. More likely, as Clare Rothschild has argued,[103] the *Epistle of Barnabas* is a theater for gentile Christians arguing with other gentile Christians about Jewish things.

Meanwhile, those texts that do plausibly come from ethnic Jewish Christ-believing circles betray, more or less, *no interest whatsoever* in proselyte circumcision for gentile Christ-believers.[104] This fact has occasionally been noted with puzzlement,[105] but it has rarely been juxtaposed with the related phenomenon we have considered here: a fixation with proselyte circumcision in some gentile Christian circles. Q, if indeed there was such a (Galilean, Jewish) text,[106] says nothing at all about proselyte circumcision, or infant circumcision, for that matter. The Gospel of Matthew, which is emphatic about binding future gentile disciples to keep all the commandments given by Jesus (Matt 28:19–20), includes rulings on marriage, adultery, divorce, assault, theft, foods, oaths, almsgiving, prayers, sacrifices, tithes, and much more besides, but not so much as a whisper about circumcision.

---

[102] An outlier of a claim even among the many early Christian criticisms of Jewish circumcision. See discussion in James Carleton Paget, "Barnabas 9:4: A Peculiar Verse on Circumcision," VC 45 (1991): 242–254; and Isaac T. Soon, "Satan and Circumcision: The Devil as the *angelos poneros* in Barnabas 9:4," VC 76 (2021): 60–72.

[103] Clare K. Rothschild, "Soteriology and the Allegorical Construction of Opponents in the Epistle of Barnabas," in *Soteria: Salvation in Early Christianity and Antiquity*, ed. David S. du Toit et al., NovTSup 175 (Leiden: Brill, 2019), 561–576.

[104] An apparent, but not real, exception is Luke's attribution of the proselyte circumcision scheme to "some from the party of the Pharisees" in Acts 15:5, on which dubious literary device see Garroway, "Pharisee Heresy"; and Novenson, "*Ioudaios*, Pharisee, Zealot."

[105] On the assumption that any self-respecting Jewish Christian text *should* fly the flag for proselyte circumcision, which assumption is precisely what we are questioning here on account of the conspicuous lack of actual evidence for it.

[106] Thus, recently, Sarah E. Rollens, *Framing Social Criticism in the Jesus Movement: The Ideological Project in the Sayings Gospel Q*, WUNT 2/374 (Tübingen: Mohr Siebeck, 2014); Giovanni B. Bazzana, *Kingdom of Bureaucracy: The Political Theology of Village Scribes in the Sayings Gospel Q*, BETL 274 (Leuven: Peeters, 2015); Sara Parks, *Gender in the Rhetoric of Jesus: Women in Q* (Minneapolis: Fortress, 2019).

Likewise the Jewish Epistle of James: nothing. The Gospel of John is an interesting case, since it is much disputed whether the author and his audience are Jews or gentiles.[107] John *does* include some brief words of Jesus on circumcision, but only eighth-day Jewish circumcision (John 7:22–23, on the case of a baby boy whose eighth day falls on a Sabbath), not proselyte circumcision, so it is no exception to our rule. The Revelation of John, which I take to be a certainly Jewish text,[108] says nothing about proselyte circumcision, even though, like Matthew, it is explicit about gentile inclusion in the messianic kingdom. Indeed, Revelation might even inveigh *against* proselyte circumcision if his complaints about "those who say they are Jews and are not" (Rev 2:9; 3:9) has proselytes and other judaizers in view, which I think likely.[109] The *Didache*, too, a book of Jewish legal rulings for gentile followers of Jesus – "If you can bear the whole yoke of the lord, you will be perfect, but if you cannot, then do what you can" (Did. 6:2) – includes not a word on proselyte circumcision.[110]

I suppose one could object, speculatively, that Q, Matthew, James, John, Revelation, or *Didache* would have come out in favor of proselyte circumcision had they had more time and space. But even the huge corpus of the Pseudo-Clementines is silent on the matter! The most we find is a mention in *Recognitions* 1.33 of the nations that practice circumcision: "Others settled in Arabia, of whose posterity some also have spread into Egypt. From them some of the Indians and of the Egyptians have learned to be circumcised, and to be of purer observance than others, although in process of time most of them have turned to impiety what was the proof and sign of purity." Circumcision, our author says here, is "the proof and sign of purity."

---

[107] In favor of John's Jewishness, see Wally V. Cirafesi, *John within Judaism: Religion, Ethnicity, and the Shaping of Jesus-Oriented Jewishness in the Fourth Gospel*, AJEC 112 (Leiden: Brill, 2022); against it, Adele Reinhartz, *Cast out of the Covenant: Jews and Anti-Judaism in the Gospel of John* (Minneapolis: Fortress, 2018).

[108] With John W. Marshall, *Parables of War: Reading John's Jewish Apocalypse*, ESCJ 10 (Waterloo, ON: Wilfrid Laurier University Press, 2001).

[109] With David Frankfurter, "Jews or Not? Reconstructing the 'Other' in Rev 2:9 and 3:9," HTR 94 (2001): 403–425.

[110] David Flusser, who was right about so many things, was, in my view, wrong about supposed anti-Paulinism in the *Didache*. See his otherwise excellent "Paul's Jewish-Christian Opponents in the *Didache*," in *The Didache in Modern Research*, ed. Jonathan A. Draper (Leiden: Brill, 1996), 195–211.

But never does he enjoin it on gentile Christ-believers. In fact, another passage in *Recognitions* 5.34 sounds almost Pauline in the way it does *not* do so. "For in God's estimation he is not a Jew who is called a Jew among men, nor is he a gentile who is called a gentile, but he who, believing in God, fulfils his law and does his will, even though he is not circumcised. He is a true worshiper of God." Here circumcision is expressly excluded from what is required of the true worshiper of God. Interpreters have debated whether our author *assumes* that gentile Christ-believers normally should undergo proselyte circumcision,[111] but he certainly does not *say* it. To the various arguments about what the author assumes, however, Annette Reed rightly points out that "perhaps more intriguing... is the text's own lack of explicit concern with the question of whether Gentile followers of Jesus should be circumcised."[112] And we could say the same about *all* the other ethnic Jewish Christian texts we have considered here. Which, not coincidentally, is entirely consistent with the verdict of *non-Christian* Jewish texts on this issue: Jews do not make proselytes; proselytes present themselves.[113] None of this, of course, proves anything about the case of Paul and his opponents in the letters. But the context it provides does point overwhelmingly in the same direction.

---

[111] E.g., Georg Strecker, *Das Judenchristentum in den Pseudoklementinen* (Berlin: Akademie Verlag, 1958), 221–254; F. Stanley Jones, *An Ancient Jewish Christian Source on the History of Christianity: Pseudo-Clementine Recognitions 1.27–71* (Atlanta: Scholars Press, 1995), 157–168.

[112] Reed, *Jewish-Christianity and the History of Judaism*, 101n62. And see further Karin Hedner Zetterholm, "Jewish Teachings for Gentiles in the Pseudo-Clementine Homilies," *JJMJS* 6 (2019): 68–87.

[113] As demonstrated in meticulous detail by Goodman, *Mission and Conversion*. As Goodman also shows, even the very few oft-cited counterexamples are not really counterexamples: The missionizing Pharisees in Matt 23:15 are converting other Jews to Pharisaism, not gentiles to Judaism. The impetus for the proselyte circumcision of Izates of Adiabene (Josephus, *Ant.* 20.34–48) comes from Izates himself, not from the Jew Eleazar, who comes to the court of Adiabene for other reasons and only gives encouragement to a decision already underway (*Ant.* 20.38, 43–45). The rabbis (e.g., in the classic discussions of proselytes in *Num. Rab.* 8; Mek. R. Ish. Nezikin 18) know nothing of any Jewish mission to make proselytes; they assume (what seems to have been the case) that proselytes present themselves. Even in the famous story of Aquila the proselyte before Hadrian (Exod. Rab. 30:12), the only person who preaches the necessity of proselyte circumcision is Aquila himself.

Conclusion

To conclude: What evidence we have for Paul's proselyte-circumcision-preaching opponents suggests that they were themselves proselytes, "foreskins by nature" not "Jews by nature" (Paul's terms, Rom 2:27 and Gal 2:15, respectively). The participle περιτεμνόμενοι in Gal 6:13 is an important piece of evidence (thus rightly Munck), but it is just one of many: dogs, incisions, people whose god is the loins, who do not guard the law, who call themselves Jews, who transgress the commandment of eighth-day circumcision. In short: proselyte-circumcised gentiles. Meanwhile, in all of Paul's ranting about his certainly Jewish opponents, there is not the slightest hint that any of them preached proselyte circumcision. And if that were not enough, subsequent early Christian evidence (in Revelation, *Barnabas*, Ignatius, the *Didascalia*, and elsewhere) corroborates the hypothesis that it was gentile proselytes, not cradle Jews, among the Christ groups who were chiefly responsible for the vogue for proselyte circumcision therein. If the conclusion we have reached in this chapter seems counterintuitive, I suggest that is only because of certain unexamined, unfounded intuitions that we have absorbed from the standard handbooks and commentaries. We have been inured to thinking of Paul as "pro-gentile" and his opponents as "anti-gentile," or Paul as "gentile-inclusive" and his opponents as "gentile-exclusive." Of course, Paul is "pro-gentile" in the sense that he feels a loyalty to his gentile charges and wants (what he thinks is) best for them. But it does not follow that all gentiles-in-Christ will have found Paul's position obviously congenial and rallied to his side, nor – *a fortiori* – that Jews-in-Christ will have been predisposed to the opposite view. Surprisingly to us, perhaps, in the matter of the proselyte circumcision controversy, it was Paul versus the gentiles.

5 | *The Legalism of Paul*

And now, a thought experiment: Suppose that someone discovered, edited, translated, and published some previously unknown fragments, in Greek, from an anonymous ancient writer containing enough references to God, the messiah, the satan, Belial, Abraham, Isaac, Jacob, Moses, David, Elijah, Isaiah, Sinai, Jerusalem, Jews, gentiles, Pharisees, etc. that we could have a relatively high degree of confidence that this ancient writer was Jewish. (And let us stipulate, for the sake of this thought experiment, that we somehow know beyond a shadow of a doubt that these fragments are authentic, not a modern forgery. If only.)[1] And imagine that, alongside whatever else our anonymous author says about God, Abraham, the messiah, etc., he or she also includes frequent references to the νόμος, or law, or Torah, further confirming our suspicion that we have before us a Jewish text. Amongst these fragments, we make out the following logia:

> Do you not heed the law?
> As many as sinned in the law, through the law they shall be judged.
> The law is holy, and the commandment holy and right and good.
> We know that the law is pneumatic.
> Everyone who undergoes circumcision is obligated to do the whole law.
> It is not hearers of the law who are right with God, but doers of the law shall be proved right.
> God [acted] so that the upright deed of the law might be fulfilled among us.

---

[1] Cf. the tempest around the demonstrably forged *Gospel of Jesus Wife* fragment, documented by Ariel Sabar, *Veritas: A Harvard Professor, a Con Man, and the Gospel of Jesus's Wife* (New York: Doubleday, 2020); and the very different case of the *Secret Gospel of Mark* now reconstructed by Geoffrey S. Smith and Brent C. Landau, *The Secret Gospel of Mark: A Controversial Scholar, a Scandalous Gospel of Jesus, and the Fierce Debate over Its Authenticity* (New Haven: Yale University Press, 2023).

The one who loves another has fulfilled the law.
[My opponents] do not themselves guard the law.
We establish the law.
In respect of the law, I am a Pharisee; in respect of righteousness in the law, blameless.

Double Standards

If we read these lines in the fragments of our mysterious Hellenophone Jewish writer, what kind of impression would we form of him or her? How would we situate him or her on our mental map of ancient Jewish postures toward the Torah?[2] Faced with the evidence of those lines, we might well characterize our writer as some variety of halakhic rigorist, someone insistent on the exacting interpretation and observance of the commandments (as he or she understands them, of course). Certainly no seeker after smooth things, this writer: "They sought smooth things and preferred illusions, and they watched for breaks, and chose the fair neck" (CD 1:18–19, trans. Vermes).[3] Nor one of those extreme allegorists known to Philo: "There are some who, regarding laws in their literal sense in the light of symbols of matters belonging to the intellect, are overpunctilious about the latter, while treating the former with easy-going neglect" (*Migration* 89, trans. Colson and Whitaker in

---

[2] Like the catalogue of postures toward the Torah documented by John J. Collins, *The Invention of Judaism: Torah and Jewish Identity from Deuteronomy to Paul* (Berkeley: University of California Press, 2017). In addition to a great many early Jewish texts that do not know or do not care about the Torah of Moses (e.g., Third Isaiah, Qohelet, Esther, the documents from Elephantine), Collins catalogues texts that view the Torah as a narrative (e.g., Genesis Apocryphon, *Liber Antiquitatum Biblicarum*), texts that view the Torah as wisdom (e.g., Aramaic Levi, Ben Sira), texts that view the Torah as a system of philosophy (e.g., Philo's *Legum Allegoriae*), texts that take from the Torah just a few distinctive Jewish practices (e.g., Sibylline Oracles, Wisdom of Solomon), as well as some texts that view the Torah as a law proper (e.g., 1 Maccabees, Jubilees, 4QMMT). But this lattermost group is just one of a number of well-attested ancient Jewish ways of relating to the Torah.

[3] On whom, see James C. VanderKam, "Those Who Look for Smooth Things, Pharisees, and Oral Law," in *Emanuel: Studies in Hebrew Bible, Septuagint, and Dead Sea Scrolls in Honor of Emanuel Tov*, ed. Shalom M. Paul et al. (Leiden: Brill, 2003), 465–478.

Double Standards 113

LCL).⁴ Much less a fully assimilated diaspora Jew like Tiberius Julius Alexander, who, Josephus says, τοῖς γὰρ πατρίοις οὐκ ἐνέμεινεν οὗτος ἔθεσιν, "did not continue in his ancestral customs" (*Ant.* 20.100).⁵ No, our anonymous writer is unbending: The law is righteous. It is there to be fulfilled. God has shown us how to fulfil it. We (the author's group) do so; our opponents do not, to their shame. An old-fashioned term for this kind of perspective is, well, legalism.

Alas, these logia are too well known for most of us truly to be able to encounter them afresh in this way, so we must rely on our powers of imagination to run this hermeneutical experiment.⁶ Imagine that we encountered these logia not as familiar lines from the letters of Paul – who, we all learned from our mothers' knees, is the arch-anti-legalist⁷ – but as anonymous fragments of an ancient Jewish text. Had we done so, we could be forgiven for thinking that the writer of these lines was – analogously, perhaps, to Jubilees or 4QMMT, a halakhic rigorist, or, to use that old-fashioned term, a legalist.

Now, of course, in actual fact, we do not encounter these logia in the way I have suggested we imagine doing. We encounter them as sayings of the apostle Paul in their respective contexts in his several letters.

---

⁴ On whom see Harry Austryn Wolfson, *Philo: Foundations of Religious Philosophy in Judaism, Christianity, and Islam*, vol. 1 (Cambridge, MA: Harvard University Press, 1947), 66–71; Martin Goodman, *A History of Judaism* (London: Penguin, 2017), 170–181.
⁵ On whom see S. Etienne, "Réflexion sur l'apostasie de Tibérius Julius Alexander," *SPhA* 12 (2000): 122–142; John M. G. Barclay, "Deviance and Apostasy: Some Applications of Deviance Theory to First-Century Judaism and Christianity," in *Pauline Churches and Diaspora Jews* (Grand Rapids, MI: Eerdmans, 2016), 123–140.
⁶ See Graham Greene, *Monsignor Quixote* (New York: Simon & Schuster, 1982), 112: "A first reading is something special, like first love. I wish I could come on Saint Paul now by accident and read him for the first time."
⁷ E.g., C. H. Dodd, *The Meaning of Paul for Today* (New York: Doran, 1920), 122: "A legal religion lays all the emphasis on what a man does, or wills to do. The power of the will, the self-assertive element in us, is brought into the foreground. In direct contrast to this is the religion which says that not what we do, but what God does, is the root of the matter"; C. E. B. Cranfield, "St. Paul and the Law," *SJT* 17 (1964): 53: "The epistles reveal Paul's radical rejection of legalism... and of what is so inextricably bound up with legalism"; Richard N. Longenecker, *Paul, Apostle of Liberty* (Grand Rapids, MI: Eerdmans, 1964), 128: "At the heart of the Apostle's teaching is his conviction that the Law in its contractual aspect – and that means especially Jewish nomism – has come to its full completion and terminus in Christ." On anti-legalism as an animating force in much modern Pauline studies, see Thiessen, *Paul and the Gentile Problem*, 5.

Hence, to interpret these sayings plausibly (in a historical-critical sense, at least) is to make sense of them in these contexts, alongside other relevant sayings that make up the discourses of which they are all part.[8] "We establish the law" (Rom 3:31), but also, "a person is put right from trust, without works of the law" (Rom 3:28). And again, "In respect of the law, I am a Pharisee; in respect of righteousness in the law, blameless" (Phil 3:5–6), but also, "I suffer the loss of all things so that I may gain Christ and be found in him, not having my own righteousness from the law but that which is from Christ-faith" (Phil 3:8–9). And so on. But these latter logia of the apostle do not nullify the former ones, as he himself loudly insists on several occasions. "Do we, then, undo the law through trust? By no means!" (Rom 3:31) "Is the law, then, against the promises? By no means!" (Gal 3:21) The long history of interpretation, however, much of it overjoyed to discover an ostensibly Pauline warrant for casting off one contemporary burden or another (e.g., late medieval Catholic penance, the Elizabethan prayer book), has often missed this point.[9]

But it is not enough to explain away the legalism of Paul; we ought to be able to give an account of it. And let's be clear: When I speak of the legalism of Paul, I do not just mean the commonplace observation that he sometimes says positive things about the law.[10] That would be something less than legalism. I mean that Paul expresses ideas and attitudes that, when other people express them, those who use the term would call legalistic: for instance, a pettifogging obsessiveness with the

---

[8] As per the classic hermeneutical theory of James Barr, *The Semantics of Biblical Language* (Oxford: Oxford University Press, 1961).

[9] On the contexts and interests of these early modern interpreters of Paul and the law, see Michael Allen and Jonathan A. Linebaugh, eds., *Reformation Readings of Paul: Explorations in History and Exegesis* (Downers Grove, IL: InterVarsity, 2015); Stephen J. Chester, *Reading Paul with the Reformers: Reconciling Old and New Perspectives* (Grand Rapids, MI: Eerdmans, 2017). On their abiding relevance to the churches even now, see David E. Aune, ed., *Rereading Paul Together: Protestant and Catholic Perspectives on Justification* (Grand Rapids, MI: Baker, 2006). Consider, e.g., Longenecker, *Apostle of Liberty*, 265: "In his [Paul's] message there is a real corrective to constantly arising legalism. In a day when the 'Christian graces' are stressed without any thought of the centrality of Christ, and men seek divine favor through human effort." Yinger, "Quest for Jewish Legalism," 391 rightly diagnoses: "Much of the continued debate over legalism in first-century Judaism and in the NPP [New Perspective on Paul] amounts to a resurrection of Reformation debates over synergism."

[10] Thus, e.g., Femi Adeyemi, "Paul's 'Positive' Statements about the Mosaic Law," *Bibliotheca Sacra* 164 (2007): 49–58.

details of law observance, or a censorious attitude toward others' law observance or non-observance. There is a hermeneutical problem at work here. We tend unwittingly to follow something like Richard Nixon's rule for legality. "When the president does it, that means that it is not illegal." When the apostle Paul says it, that means that it is not legalistic – even though when someone else says the same thing it patently is.[11] There may be some theological logic according to which this works,[12] but not so for historical criticism. If the label is true of, say, Jubilees when it says x, then it should be true of Paul when he says x. The way forward is not to deny on *a priori* grounds that Paul could possibly express a legalistic view, but to explain how he can in fact express both view x (which, in another author, we would call legalistic) and also view y (which the interpretive tradition has valorized as anti-legalistic).[13]

Law-isms

Legalism, like pornography, is one of those things people claim to know when they see it but for which they struggle to supply a definition.[14] It is more *felt* than it is *thought*. The English word "legalism" and its cognates are first attested in the seventeenth-century theological writings of English nonconformist and Puritan thinkers (see OED, *ad loc.*). Thus, for instance, John Wheelwright: "He accuseth the

---

[11] This trend in New Testament scholarship is well documented by Yinger, "Quest for Jewish Legalism," 391: "Many attempts [in recent scholarship] founder on a deficient understanding of legalism. Too often, they identify some aspect of Jewish texts (e.g., casuistry, focus on doing) and inappropriately call it legalism. This is inappropriate because the very same aspect or emphasis in Pauline texts would not be called legalism."

[12] E.g., if the canon, or the *regula fidei*, or an early modern confession, or some other theological norm is allowed to constrain what meanings can and cannot be made of a Pauline or any other scriptural utterance. But that is a very different kind of language game (thus rightly Dale B. Martin, *Biblical Truths: The Meaning of Scripture in the Twenty-First Century* [New Haven: Yale University Press, 2017]).

[13] Of course, we might just as well opt to dispense with the term "legalism" altogether, as I generally do, following the lead of Rafael Neis, "The Seduction of Law: Rethinking Legal Studies in Jewish Studies," *JQR* 109 (2019): 119–138. But because the term remains so obstinately current in Pauline studies, I use it artificially in the present chapter as a means of forcing the question.

[14] As in US Supreme Court Justice Potter Stewart's famous obscenity ruling in 1964.

Magistrates and Ministers... [of a] manifest addiction of theirs to Legalisme, whil'st he declares them commonly intended by that expression, under a Covenant of works."[15] And Richard Baxter: "To make Salvation the end of Duty, is to be a Legalist."[16] For some 200 years, in fact, the word occurs almost exclusively in contexts of intra-Christian theological disputation, where it is a term of contempt for (what the respective writers judge to be) deficient forms of Christianity. Bernard Jackson has suggested that it did not occur to anyone to accuse *Jews* of legalism until as late as 1861, when the charge appears in Bishop Trench's *Commentary on the Epistles to the Seven Churches in Asia*.[17] I have been able to find a few earlier nineteenth-century instances. But Jackson's point stands: The "Jewish legalism" stereotype is not only (obviously) Christian, but very recent, too. Prior to the mid-nineteenth century, Christian writers traded in other anti-Jewish tropes, but not, for the most part, the familiar canard about legalism.[18]

No matter who the target, though – Roman Catholics, establishment Anglicans, Jews, or otherwise – the English word "legalism" has long been and still is used as a term of abuse, not of analysis. To invoke legalism is to pick a fight. To call someone a legalist is to insult her. Indeed, this is precisely why E. P. Sanders resorted to the word "nomism" in his bombshell book of 1977:[19] because, although in etymological terms "nomism" and "legalism" are effectively synonyms (from Greek νόμος and Latin *lex*, respectively, both meaning "law," thus: law-ism), "legalism" has nasty connotations, whereas "nomism" does not.[20] By using the latter term, then, Sanders was able to discuss

---

[15] John Wheelwright, *Mercurius Americanus* (1645) 19.
[16] Richard Baxter, *Saints Everlasting Rest* (1651) 1.1.6.8.
[17] Bernard S. Jackson, "Legalism," *JJS* 30 (1979): 6. See Richard Chenevix Trench, *Commentary on the Epistles to the Seven Churches in Asia* (London: Parker, Son, and Bourn, 1861), 77: "The first great battle which the Church had to fight was with Jewish legalism; this came to its head historically, and found its condemnation, in the Council of Jerusalem (Acts xv.1–31), dogmatically in St. Paul's Epistle to the Galatians, those who refused to accept the Church's decisions on the matter gradually forming themselves more and more into a schismatical heretical body."
[18] See further Neis, "Seduction of Law" on the modern genealogy of the association of law with Judaism.
[19] Sanders, *Paul and Palestinian Judaism*.
[20] Thus rightly Longenecker, *Apostle of Liberty*, 78n63: "The terms 'legalism' and 'nomism' are certainly synonymous in their primary and strict meanings.... Yet there is both a denotation and a connotation, an explication and a secondary meaning, to the terms." Longenecker himself sticks with this convention: "[I

serious theological and ethical issues pertaining to law without triggering a fight response in the lizard brains of his readers, as the word "legalism" would have done.[21] But the fact that "nomism" has no such connotations is a proof that "legalism" need not have developed them. The nasty connotations are a superfluous value judgment, not anything inherent in the idea of a "law-ism." In other words, it is only because particular groups of people (especially certain kinds of Protestant Christians) chose to heap scorn upon the word that the word strikes our ears in that way.[22]

By ceding "legalism" to its naysayers, Sanders missed the opportunity for a more radical criticism. As Philip Alexander has argued as far back as his 1986 review of Sanders's *Jesus and Judaism*, we ought to be asking ourselves: What's so bad about legalism?

> [Sanders's] answer to the charge of "legalism" seems, in effect, to be that Rabbinic Judaism, despite appearances, is really a religion of "grace." But does this not involve a tacit acceptance of a major element in his opponents' position – the assumption that "grace" is superior to "law"? The correct response to the charge must surely be: And what is wrong with "legalism," once we have got rid of abusive language about "hypocrisy" and "mere externalism"? It is neither religiously nor philosophically self-evident that a "legalistic" view of the world is inferior to one based on "grace." If we fail to

---

distinguish between] an 'acting legalism' and a 'reacting nomism'; i.e., between an ordering of one's life in external and formal arrangement according to the Law in order to gain righteousness and/or appear righteous, and the molding of one's life in all its varying relations according to the Law in response to the love and grace of God" (*Apostle of Liberty*, 78). Stephen Westerholm, *Perspectives Old and New on Paul: The "Lutheran" Paul and His Critics* (Grand Rapids, MI: Eerdmans, 2004), 332n109 reports that Sanders confirmed to him in conversation his view that the word "legalism" is irretrievably pejorative. Cf. Heikki Räisänen, "Legalism and Salvation by the Law," in *The Torah and Christ* (Helsinki: Finnish Exegetical Society, 1986), 25–54, who proposes a distinction between a benign "soft legalism" and a pernicious "hard legalism."

[21] Sanders, *Paul and Palestinian Judaism*, 75: "Briefly put, covenantal *nomism* is the view that one's place in God's plan is established on the basis of the covenant and that the covenant requires as the proper response of man his obedience to its commandments, while providing means of atonement for transgression" (emphasis added). Contrast ibid., 33–59 on "the persistence of the view of rabbinic religion as one of *legalistic* works-righteousness" (emphasis added). See further E. P. Sanders, "Covenantal Nomism Revisited," *JSQ* 16 (2009): 23–55.

[22] A point well made by Jackson, "Legalism," 1: "Legalism would not appear on the agenda of either the historian of Jewish thought or the jurist were it not for a challenge presented from the outside. That challenge is Christianity, especially in some of its Protestant manifestations."

take a firm stand on this point we run the risk of seriously misdescribing Pharisaic and Rabbinic Judaism, and of trying to make it over into a pale reflection of Protestant Christianity.[23]

Further to this final point about "a pale reflection of Protestant Christianity," Alexander argues in a 2001 essay that not only Sanders but his predecessors, too – Jewish as well as Christian scholars – were beholden to a Christianizing bias in this respect. Alexander writes:

These works [Moore, *Judaism*; Schechter, *Aspects of Rabbinic Theology*; Montefiore and Loewe, *Rabbinic Anthology*; Sanders, *Paul and Palestinian Judaism*], to a greater or lesser degree, have been influenced by liberal Protestantism. All seem tacitly to regard it as axiomatic that a religion of works-righteousness is inferior to a religion of grace. [Ferdinand] Weber had accused Judaism of legalistic works-righteousness. They [viz. Moore, Schechter, Montefiore, Sanders] set out to defend it against this charge, but nowhere does any of them radically question the premise that there is something wrong with a religion of works-righteousness.[24]

As is clear from these excerpts, Alexander disagrees with Sanders on the religious value judgment in question, but he gives Sanders the benefit of the doubt nonetheless. Jacob Neusner, writing around the same time, does not:

It is condescending because Sanders affirms that, if the Pharisees practiced "ritual," then they, and the Judaism that claims descent from them, would be subject to condemnation by Jesus and Paul.... It is clear Sanders is embarrassed by the particular rituals of Judaism. But I am not, and I do not thank him for apologizing for the rituals of my religion. As a believing Jew, I practice Judaism, and I do not require a gentile's defense of my religion that dismisses as unimportant or inauthentic what in my faith is very important indeed: the observance of rituals of various kinds. They are mine because they are the Torah's. I do not propose to apologize for them.... Nor do I value a defense of my religion that implicitly throughout and explicitly at many points accepts at face value what another religion values and rejects

---

[23] Philip S. Alexander, review of E. P. Sanders, *Jesus and Judaism*, in *JJS* 37 (1986): 105.

[24] Alexander, "Torah and Salvation in Tannaitic Literature," 272. On these figures in the history of research, see further Langton, *The Apostle Paul in the Jewish Imagination*.

what my religion deems authentic service to the living God.... With friends like Sanders, Judaism hardly needs any enemies.[25]

I think I understand Neusner's sentiment here, but it rather underplays just how many and how mortal Christian enemies of Judaism have been down the centuries.[26] In light of that history, one might be forgiven for thinking that friends, even erring ones, are preferable. As for Sanders's error, Neusner is right to say that Sanders *defends* ancient Jewish ritual, but wrong to say that Sanders *apologizes for* it (a subtle difference, but an important one). To be sure, Neusner, being Jewish, has a kind of knowledge of Judaism that Sanders, being a gentile Christian, simply cannot have. But neither Neusner nor Sanders is a first-century Pharisee or Qumran covenanter, so to that extent they are both – as are we all – foreigners to the strange old world of Roman Judea.[27] It may well be (and it probably is true) that Sanders reads too much liberal Protestantism into his ancient Jewish sources. But it may also be (and it probably is true) that Neusner, in his zeal to get the better of Sanders, swallows too uncritically the nineteenth-century (Weberian!) axiom that ancient Judaism was in fact a legalism.[28]

We should, however, take Neusner's and Alexander's point that legalism could, in principle, be a virtue rather than a vice.[29] If we strip the term "legalism" of all the layers of abuse and contempt that have attached to it over the centuries,[30] we might arrive at something like the way James Kugel describes the role of the Torah in historic Judaism under the rubric "a religion of laws."[31] Kugel writes:

---

[25] Jacob Neusner, "Mr. Sanders's Pharisees and Mine," *SJT* 44 (1991): 94–95.
[26] See Leon Poliakov's four-volume *History of Anti-Semitism* (Philadelphia: University of Pennsylvania Press, 2003).
[27] Here see Novenson, "Our Apostles, Ourselves."
[28] For evidence of the falsehood of this axiom, see especially Collins, *Invention of Judaism*.
[29] Cambell, *Deliverance of God*, 109 offers a very helpful four-quadrant schema of the valuations attached to "nomism" and "legalism" in recent scholarship: (1) attractive covenantal nomism (E. P. Sanders), (2) unattractive covenantal nomism (James Dunn), (3) attractive legalism (Philip Alexander), (4) unattractive legalism (the majority).
[30] Cf. Jackson, "Legalism," 17: "First, we must rid the charge [of legalism] of Protestant theological positions which are irrelevant to Judaism."
[31] Whether historic Judaism is in fact a religion of laws is, of course, debatable (see Neis, "Seduction of Law). But for those, like Kugel, who assume it is, this is an elegant summary of the idea.

This was the genius of a religion of laws. In all the little encounters of daily life... the Pentateuch set out the precise form of behavior that God had prescribed.... It seemed like there was no area of life about which the Torah did not have something to say – and that, for later Judaism, was the beauty of it. In doing each thing according to the way that God prescribed, a person could, as it were, turn life into a constant act of reaching out to God.[32]

One is tempted to say: If that kind of legalism is wrong, I don't want to be right.

As we have seen, however, people who use the word "legalism" at all usually use it in one or more pejorative senses. One helpful catalogue of these pejorative senses is provided by Simon Gathercole, who distinguishes five definitions of "legalism" as follows:[33]

1. Self-righteousness, puritanical self-satisfaction.
2. Concern for regulations, pettifogging obsession with correct definition of religious practice.
3. Association of Torah observance with the category of "getting in."
4. Merit theology (i.e., the idea that one earns credit with God for meritorious deeds done).
5. Belief in final vindication at the last judgment on the basis of works of the law.

---

[32] James Kugel, *How to Read the Bible: A Guide to Scripture, Then and Now* (New York: Free Press, 2007), 261.

[33] See Gathercole, *Where Is Boasting*, 30–33: "The first feature that can be isolated in a 'legalistic' religion is the 'self-righteousness' of its participants: a puritanical self-satisfaction... [But] I would argue that attitudes or psychological dispositions of the participants in the religion really lie outside the bounds of historical criticism of such texts... The second feature of legalism is more a description of the character of the religion than the inner disposition of its participants: that is, legalism as a characteristic of a religion at the center of which is a concern for regulations and a pettifogging obsession with correct definition of religious practice.... The third element, which has been associated with 'legalism' especially in terms of Sanders's opposition to it, is the association of Torah observance with the category of 'getting in'.... The fourth ingredient concerns merit, which combines both theology and the presumed religious attitude that must accompany it. Merit theology has received bad press because it is presumed that a petty-minded concern to accumulate merit, an insecurity about salvation, and a prideful desire to put God in one's debt must accompany it.... The fifth ingredient of legalism a distinction between salvation as *getting in* and *final* vindication at the last judgment." There are other rubrics of various types of legalism elsewhere in the secondary literature, but Gathercole's is as good and useful as any I have read.

Gathercole's sense 1, a psychological definition, is effectively inaccessible to the historian, as he rightly notes.[34] Sense 2, a practical definition, is important for our purposes, since, as we shall see, there are indeed points of religious practice which Paul regulates with (what could reasonably be called) a pettifogging obsession. Neither sense 3, the belief that one gets into covenant relationship with God by observing Torah, nor sense 4, the belief that one accumulates credit with God for meritorious deeds done, represents Paul's view. (Sense 4 may represent *Jesus's* view in the Synoptic Gospels, especially Matthew, but that is another matter.)[35] Sense 5, another theological definition, is also important for our purposes, since Paul does have something to say about the works (of the law or otherwise) that God takes into account at the last judgment.

Repaid According to Their Works

Apropos of Gathercole's legalism type 5 ("belief in final vindication at the last judgment on the basis of works of the law"), no little debate has swirled around Paul's own claim in Rom 2 that, on the day of judgment, "God will repay each person according to his works" (Rom 2:6).[36] This sounds, on the surface of it, conspicuously like legalism type 5, but if (*ex hypothesi*) Paul cannot be a legalist, then of course some other interpretation becomes necessary.[37] Douglas Campbell, to

---

[34] Likewise Longenecker, *Apostle of Liberty*, 79: "The first line of inquiry can lead nowhere, for, as I have noted above, our human powers of perception and analysis are at best inadequate in this area of motives and attitudes."

[35] See Nathan Eubank, *Wages of Cross-Bearing and Debt of Sin: The Economy of Heaven in Matthew's Gospel* (Berlin: De Gruyter, 2013).

[36] The whole relevant section is Rom 2:6–13: "*God will repay to each person according to his works* [Ps 61:13 OG = Prov 24:12 OG], to those who through endurance in good work seek glory and honor and incorruptibility he will repay life everlasting, but for those who are factious and disobey the truth but obey unrighteousness there will be wrath and anger. There will be tribulation and distress upon every human being who works evil, Jew first and also Greek, and glory and honor and peace for everyone who works the good, Jew first and also Greek. For there is no favoritism with God. As many as sinned lawlessly shall also perish lawlessly, and as many as sinned in the law shall be judged through the law. For it is not the case that hearers of the law are right with God, rather, doers of the law will be proved right."

[37] See, e.g., C. E. B. Cranfield, *The Epistle to the Romans*, ICC (London: T&T Clark, 2004 [1975]), 1:153: "It is absolutely vital to the true understanding of these verses to recognize that the statement of v. 6 is not made in a legalistic

cite one of the most interesting, takes the text to mean exactly what it says, but then concludes that Paul is quoting and deconstructing a thesis proposed by his opponent, not speaking for himself. Campbell's Paul quotes a legalist axiom, only in order to refute it.[38] This reading is bold and internally consistent, but unconvincing.[39] The more common, less interesting, and equally unconvincing maneuver is to let the words stand as Paul's, but then explain them away. For example, as something true in theory but not in reality: God would, in theory, judge everyone according to her works, but because God knows that that would end badly, he chooses to judge everyone according to *Christ's* works instead.[40] And other gymnastic interpretations beside.[41]

Recent research has seen one especially interesting effort to square this circle. Gabriele Boccaccini, widely renowned for his research on 1 Enoch, has stepped into one of the most well-worn debates in Pauline studies – does Paul have one path to salvation (for all people) or two (for Jews and gentiles, respectively)? – and cried: A plague on both your houses! Silly New Testament scholars, Paul has *three* paths to salvation: one for righteous Jews, a second for righteous gentiles, and a

---

sense – it is not an assertion of requital according to *deserts* – and that it is not implied in vv. 7 and 10 that the people referred to *earn* eternal life." I take Cranfield's point, but the protestations do begin to sound rather desperate.

[38] Campbell, *Deliverance of God*, 519–600.

[39] Thus rightly R. Barry Matlock, "Zeal for Paul but not according to Knowledge: Douglas Campbell's War on 'Justification Theory,'" *JSNT* 34 (2011): 115–149.

[40] E.g., F. F. Bruce, *The Epistle of Paul to the Romans: An Introduction and Commentary*, 2nd ed. (Grand Rapids, MI: Eerdmans, 1985), 85–86: "The course of his argument goes on to indicate that, while one who was a 'doer' of the law would be justified, yet, since no-one does it perfectly, there is no justification that way." Likewise the commentaries of Lietzmann, Wilckens, Knox, and Kuss, among others.

[41] Cranfield, *Romans*, 1:151 lists ten (!) possible interpretations of "repayment according to works" in Rom 2:6–11: (1) Paul is simply inconsistent; (2) Paul is only speaking hypothetically; (3) by "works" here Paul actually means faith; (4) by "works" here Paul actually means the byproduct of faith; (5) by "works" here Paul actually means the faith of ancient Israelites; (6) by "works" here Paul actually means the byproduct of the faith of ancient Israelites; (7) by "works" here Paul actually means the tacit faith of pagans; (8) by "works" here Paul actually means the byproduct of the tacit faith of pagans; (9) by "works" here Paul actually means the faith of ancient Israelites *and* pagans; (10) by "works" here Paul actually means the byproduct of the faith of ancient Israelites *and* pagans. The mind boggles.

third for sinners (whether Jew or gentile).[42] Boccaccini's thesis is deliberately provocative, and, in the end, not tenable. He is right, however, in many of his particular claims: Paul was and always remained a Jew. Paul agrees to a great extent with other Second Temple Jewish texts (including parts of 1 Enoch) and with other texts from the early Jesus movement; Paul's ideas are not *sui generis*. Paul's account of sin is irreducibly mythological, not simply moral-psychological. Paul does not class all human beings together as sinners in the same way. Justification (δικαίωσις) and salvation (σωτηρία) are quite distinct things in Paul's usage. When Paul says that God will repay everyone according to their works, he means exactly what he says. And much more.[43]

But Boccaccini is also wrong on some crucial points. Here is one: For Boccaccini, it is crucial that Paul – like Mark, Matthew, and Luke – takes Jesus to be "the Son of Man with authority on earth to forgive sins" (Mark 2:10; Matt 9:6; Luke 5:24; cf. John 5:27), a character Boccaccini traces to the eschatological drama of the Parables of Enoch (1 Enoch 50:1–5).[44] Conspicuously unlike the Synoptic Gospels, however, Paul *nowhere* refers to the Son of Man[45] and *almost nowhere* refers to forgiveness of sins.[46] Regarding the latter, the sole exception is Rom 4:6–8 quoting OG Ps 31:1–2, where Paul glosses the psalmist's ἄφεσις ἁμαρτιῶν ("forgiveness of sins") with λογίζεσθαι δικαιοσύνην ("to reckon righteousness"),[47] which admittedly does work well for

---

[42] Boccaccini, *Paul's Three Paths to Salvation*.

[43] For discussion of these and related points, see the reviews by Isaac Morales in *JTS* 73 (2022): 335–337; and Denys McDonald in *SR* 52 (2023): 290–292.

[44] 1 Enoch 50:1–5 is a crux for Boccaccini because it apparently envisions, at the final judgment, three groups of people: the righteous (who are blessed), the wicked (who are damned), and the others (who receive mercy from the Lord of Spirits). Contrary to Boccaccini's proposed parallel, however, this scene does not include the Son of Man character; rather, it is the Lord of Spirits himself who dispenses mercy.

[45] Which is puzzling, because Paul does allude to Daniel 7, the so-called Son of Man vision. On this puzzle, see J. Thomas Hewitt, *Messiah and Scripture: Paul's "In Christ" Idiom in Its Ancient Jewish Context*, WUNT 2/522 (Tübingen: Mohr Siebeck, 2020), 119–155.

[46] A point rightly emphasized by Stendahl, "Paul among Jews and Gentiles," 23–40 under the heading "justification rather than forgiveness."

[47] Rom 4:6–8: "David speaks a blessing upon the person to whom God reckons righteousness without works: *Blessed are they whose lawless acts are forgiven, whose sins are covered; blessed is the man to whom God does not reckon sin* [OG Ps 31:1–2]."

Boccaccini's reading, although it also works well for more traditional Protestant readings like that of Gathercole.[48] (There is also Col 1:14, "ransom, that is, the forgiveness of sins," which likewise works for Boccaccini's reading, but I regard this as deutero-Pauline.) My objection is: If the key that makes sense of Paul's whole speculative system is the Son of Man with authority on earth to forgive sins, then why does that character have to be read *between the lines* of Paul's letters, rather than appear explicitly as he does in the Synoptic Gospels? Surely that suggests that that character is not actually the key to Paul's system.

A second objection: For Boccaccini, it is crucial that Paul maps the *ethnic* categories Jew and gentile and the *moral* categories righteous and sinner onto a table of four quadrants: there are Jewish righteous, Jewish sinners, gentile righteous, and gentile sinners. This is a nice rubric, as tidy as it is humane, and it does fit some of our ancient sources,[49] but it does not fit Paul. As Boccaccini rightly notes, Paul says that all people are *under sin*, but only some people are *sinners*. But who are these some people? Contra Boccaccini's rubric, I think that Paul breezily, chauvinistically classes all Jews as ordinarily righteous, all gentiles as ordinarily sinners. "We Jews by nature, not gentile sinners" (Gal 2:15); "the passion of desire like the gentiles who do not know God" (1 Thess 4:5). In other words, Paul is both more optimistic about Jewish morality and more pessimistic about gentile morality than Boccaccini allows.[50]

Which has knock-on effects for how we understand the "paths to salvation" that are the burden of Boccaccini's argument. On his account, the top left quadrant (Jewish righteous) are saved by keeping the law of Moses, the top right (gentile righteous) by keeping the law of nature.[51] But the bottom left and bottom right quadrants (sinners, Jewish *and* gentile) are saved by the Christ gift. The top left and top

---

[48] See Simon Gathercole, "'Sins' in Paul," NTS 64 (2018): 143–161.
[49] See further Novenson, "Gentile Sinners" on the various ways ancient texts map ethnicity and morality.
[50] See further Chapter 6.
[51] In seeing an idea of natural law in Rom 2, Boccaccini is in good bibliographical company (e.g., Gregory E. Sterling, "A Law to Themselves: Limited Universalism in Philo and Paul," ZNW 107 [2016]: 30–47), but he is nevertheless mistaken. The only mention of φύσις in the passage speaks of "gentiles who *by nature* do not have the law" (Rom 2:14), as rightly argued by Simon Gathercole, "A Law unto Themselves: The Gentiles in Romans 2:14–15

right, for their part, have no need of the Christ gift. They would have reached the same beatific eschatological destination whether God had sent his son or not. And that, I am quite confident, cannot be Paul's view. (One could argue that it *is* Jesus's view in the Synoptics: "I came to call not the righteous but sinners" [Mark 2:17; Matt 9:13; Luke 5:32]. That is, there are righteous, and there are sinners, and Jesus only came for the latter.[52] But just here, Boccaccini reads a bit too much Jesus into his Paul.) Paul reasons, "I do not decline the gift of God. For if righteousness were through the law, then Christ died gratuitously" (Gal 2:21). But Christ cannot have died gratuitously, hence righteousness (in a maximal sense, at least) cannot be through the law. Q.E.D. It is a pristine piece of *ex post facto* logic, as Sanders rightly saw.[53]

For Boccaccini's Paul, however, righteousness *is* through the law. Hence Christ *did* die gratuitously, at least as regards all the righteous on the earth. Meanwhile, the *wicked* wicked (i.e., those who do not repent) will perish in any case.[54] What the messiah does, in Boccaccini's reading of Paul, is move a few more people over from the wicked column to the righteous column. That is a scenario attested in some ancient Jewish and Christian scenes of the last judgment, but it is not Paul's scenario. For Paul, the messiah confers eschatological righteousness upon *all* all, Jew and gentile, righteous and sinner.[55] It is the messiah's job to do so, because the law of Moses, as righteous as it is, is unable to transform mortal humans into immortal, superangelic beings, which is Paul's endgame. Only the messiah can do that, and the messiah does in fact do that. When these immortal, superangelic beings (Jew or gentile) are judged according to their works on

---

Revisited," *JSNT* 24 (2002): 27–49. There is no natural law doctrine in Rom 2, or indeed anywhere in Paul's letters.

[52] See E. P. Sanders, *Jesus and Judaism* (Philadelphia: Fortress, 1985), 174–211.
[53] Sanders, *Paul, the Law, and the Jewish People*, 27: "Put in propositional terms, they [Paul's premises] say this: God sent Christ; he did so in order to offer righteousness; this would have been pointless if righteousness were already available by the law ([Gal] 2:21); the law was not given to bring righteousness ([Gal] 3:21). That the positive statement about righteousness through Christ grounds the negative one about the law seems to me self-evident."
[54] Unlike in David Bentley Hart's strong universalist reading of Paul in his foreword to Boccaccini's book! And see further David Bentley Hart, *That All Shall Be Saved: Heaven, Hell, and Universal Salvation* (New Haven: Yale University Press, 2019).
[55] See Beverly Roberts Gaventa, "We, They, and All in Paul's Letter to the Romans," *Word & World* 39 (2019): 263–273.

the last day, they will receive glory and honour and peace, because that is what their works will merit.⁵⁶

The Three Deadly Sins

Although the idea of repayment according to works has caused the most hand-wringing among interpreters, there is another respect in which Paul is arguably even more legalistic. Recall Gathercole's sense 2: practical legalism, "a concern for regulations and a pettifogging obsession with correct definition of religious practice." This definition well fits a number of Pauline sayings such as: "Everyone who undergoes circumcision is obligated to do the whole law" (Gal 5:3), and "The naturally foreskinned person who fulfils the law shall judge you, who through the letter and circumcision are a transgressor of the law" (Rom 2:27). How are we to understand these occasional instances where Paul does not just say that the law in general is a good thing, but finely parses its commandments and insists on the exact performance thereof?

In a too-little-read section of his too-little-read book *The Mysticism of Paul the Apostle*,⁵⁷ Albert Schweitzer argues that there are, according to Paul, precisely three deadly sins (*Todsünden*), three things that, if a baptized person-in-Christ does them, will sever that person's union with Christ. These are: *porneia*, communion with demons, and proselyte circumcision. Schweitzer writes, "On the basis of his mysticism Paul this recognises three deadly sins – unchastity, accepting circumcision after baptism, and partaking in heathen sacrificial feasts. While all other sins are only prejudicial to the union with Christ these three destroy it at once. And since the obtaining of the resurrection state of existence at the Return of Jesus only takes place as a result of being-in-Christ, these sins cause death."⁵⁸ This theory of Schweitzer's has gone mostly ignored or dismissed in the secondary literature,⁵⁹ but it is basically right, and it goes a long way toward explaining the legalism of Paul that is our subject matter in this chapter.

---

⁵⁶ See further Nathan Eubank, "Configurations of Grace and Merit in Paul and His Interpreters," *IJST* 22 (2020): 7–17.
⁵⁷ On the composition and reception of this remarkable book, see James Carleton Paget, "Schweitzer and Paul," *JSNT* 33 (2011): 223–256.
⁵⁸ Schweitzer, *Mysticism*, 130.   ⁵⁹ Carleton Paget, "Schweitzer and Paul."

There are, of course, more than a few behaviors about which Paul voices disapproval, but only three that he says will, *ex opere operato*, destroy a Christ-believer. First, *porneia*:[60] "Don't you know that your bodies are members [i.e., body parts] of Christ? Shall I then take the members of Christ and make them members of a prostitute? No!.... Every other sin that a person does is outside the body, but the person who commits *porneia* sins into his own body" (1 Cor 6:15, 18). Which is why the man who has sex with his father's wife must be ritually destroyed in the assembly (1 Cor 5:4–5: παραδοῦναι τὸν τοιοῦτον τῷ σατανᾷ εἰς ὄλεθρον τῆς σαρκός).[61] Second, communion with demons: "What [gentiles] sacrifice, they sacrifice to demons and not to God. I do not want you to become partners with demons. You cannot drink the cup of the lord and the cup of demons; you cannot partake of the table of the lord and the table of demons" (1 Cor 10:20–21). Which is why Paul warns that one Christ-believer eating (innocuous) idol-food will actually destroy another Christ-believer if the latter person is thereby induced to commune with demons (1 Cor 8:10–12: ἀπόλλυται γὰρ ὁ ἀσθενῶν ἐν τῇ σῇ γνώσει).[62] Third and finally, proselyte circumcision: "If you undergo circumcision, Christ will profit you nothing... You are undone away from Christ, you who are getting rightwised by the law, you fall out from the gift" (Gal 5:2–4). Which is why Paul actually damns anyone who would teach a gentile-in-Christ to undergo proselyte circumcision (Gal 1:8–9: εἴ τις ὑμᾶς εὐαγγελίζεται παρ' ὃ παρελάβετε, ἀνάθεμα ἔστω).[63]

It is no coincidence that these are *the* three things about which Paul gives lengthy, detailed halakhah in his extant letters: *porneia* in 1 Corinthians 5–7, idol feasts in 1 Corinthians 8–10, and proselyte circumcision in Galatians 5–6.[64] What is more, all three of these are

---

[60] On the meaning of *porneia*, see David Wheeler-Reed, Jennifer W. Knust, and Dale B. Martin, "Can a Man Commit *Porneia* with His Wife?" *JBL* 137 (2018): 383–398.

[61] Dale B. Martin, *The Corinthian Body* (New Haven: Yale University Press, 1995), 168–174.

[62] Matthew T. Sharp, "Courting Daimons in Corinth: Daimonic Partnerships, Cosmic Hierarchies, and Divine Jealousy in 1 Corinthians 8–10," in *Demons in Early Judaism and Christianity*, ed. Hector M. Patmore and Josef Lössl, AJEC 113 (Leiden: Brill, 2022), 112–129.

[63] John G. Gager, *Curse Tablets and Binding Spells from the Ancient World* (Oxford: Oxford University Press, 1999), 183.

[64] Thus rightly Peter J. Tomson, *Paul and the Jewish Law: Halakha in the Letters of the Apostle to the Gentiles*, CRINT (Assen: Van Gorcum, 1990), 264: "His

likewise crux issues in the law of Moses: *porneia* in the seventh commandment of the Decalogue (οὐ μοιχεύσεις, "You shall not commit adultery"), idol feasts in the first and second commandments (οὐκ ἔσονταί σοι θεοὶ ἕτεροι πλὴν ἐμοῦ. οὐ ποιήσεις σεαυτῷ εἴδωλον, "There shall not be for you different gods, only me; you shall not make for yourself an idol"), and circumcision in the covenant with Abraham in Genesis 17 ("An uncircumcised male, the flesh of whose foreskin is not circumcised on the eighth day, that soul shall be destroyed from his people"). As Paula Fredriksen has pointed out, our traditional rubric of "Paul's law-free mission to gentiles" is a gross misnomer.[65] In point of fact, Paul strictly forbids gentiles-in-Christ from worshiping gentile gods and their images; he builds a wide, high fence around the commandment against adultery; and he gives a detailed (and controversial!) halakhah about post-eighth-day circumcisions. Whatever all this may be, the last thing it is *law-free*. Indeed, an interpreter not trained in Protestant theology might even call it legalistic.

Once we get past the initial *skandalon* of admitting that Paul does not nullify the law but in fact establishes it (Rom 3:31), we can perhaps see our way relatively easily to understanding the Pauline bans on *porneia* and communion with demons, which are, from the perspective of Paul and many of his Jewish contemporaries, both obvious and grave wrongs.[66] But what about circumcision? It does not fit that category (viz. obvious and grave wrongs), and yet Paul regards it, alongside *porneia* and demon-communion, as a union-with-Christ-destroying act. How can this be? Just here, that unfashionable term

letters contribute to our knowledge of an almost lost literary genre: grecized halakha. On the other hand this enhances his Pharisaic background, which... was not left behind after his 'conversion' on the Damascus road but accompanied him on his further travels, so much indeed that we actually find him formulating halakha for gentiles in Greek." Tomson thoroughly discusses Paul's halakhah on sex, food, and idols, but not circumcision, a lacuna now filled by Thiessen, *Paul and the Gentile Problem*; and Collman, *Apostle to the Foreskin*.

[65] Fredriksen, "Judaizing the Nations"; Paula Fredriksen, "Why Should a 'Law-Free' Mission Mean a 'Law-Free' Apostle?" *JBL* 134 (2015): 637–650.

[66] On *porneia*, see Hilary Lipka and Bruce Wells, eds., *Sexuality and Law in the Torah*, LHBOTS (London: T&T Clark, 2020); and Daniel Boyarin, *Carnal Israel: Reading Sex in Talmudic Culture* (Berkeley: University of California Press, 1993). On communion with demons, see Patmore and Lössl, eds., *Demons in Early Judaism and Christianity*; and Sara Ronis, *Demons in the Details: Demonic Discourse and Rabbinic Culture in Late Antique Babylonia* (Berkeley: University of California Press, 2022).

"legalism" can, ironically, be helpful. Interpreters of Paul are accustomed to saying that Paul *does not require* his gentiles to undergo circumcision, that they *need not* do so, that Paul makes circumcision (or the law *tout court*) adiaphora.[67] But as Beverly Gaventa memorably pointed out in a classic essay, that is the opposite of what Paul says in Galatians. He *requires* that gentiles-in-Christ *not* undergo circumcision. It is not that they *need not* do so; it is that they *must not* do so.[68] This is the furthest thing from an ethical adiaphoron, a matter of indifference. Here there is, from Paul's perspective, only one right course of action, and failure to take that course will mean destruction. As Schweitzer put it, "Paul's preaching of freedom from the Law is thus by no means conceived in a spirit of freethinking.... The champion of the freedom of Gentile Christianity is at the same time its tyrant."[69]

Gaventa explains this Pauline tyranny as a logical consequence of (what she calls) the singularity of Paul's gospel, its expulsive power to exclude all rival gospels, its refusal to make common cause with them.[70] And from one angle, this is true. But Paul's inflexible position

---

[67] For this claim, see literally almost any introduction to, commentary on, or theology of Paul. On the technical sense of adiaphora, see Brad Inwood, *Ethics and Human Action in Early Stoicism* (Oxford: Clarendon, 1985); James Jaquette, *Discerning What Counts: The Function of the Adiaphora Topos in Paul's Letters*, SBLDS 146 (Atlanta: Scholars Press, 1995); and Annalisa Phillips Wilson, *Paul and the Jewish Law: A Stoic Ethical Perspective on His Inconsistency*, APhR 8 (Leiden: Brill, 2022).

[68] Beverly Roberts Gaventa, "The Singularity of the Gospel," in *Our Mother Saint Paul* (Louisville, KY: Westminster John Knox, 2007), 101: "Paul's letter responds in the sharpest manner to those who find this 'other gospel' attractive, arguing that Gentile Christians *must not* take on the observance of the law" (emphasis original). Similarly Schweitzer, *Mysticism*, 193: "The simplest solution would have been if Paul had been able to declare [the law] an *adiaphoron*, a thing indifferent, neither harmful nor useful. In that case he would have been able to live at peace with the original Apostles and to look on the activities of Judaising emissaries with a gentle smile.... But the tragic thing was that he could not take up the ironic attitude towards this zealotry, but must needs treat it with all seriousness. For so was it required by the inexorable logic of the mystical doctrine of being-in-Christ."

[69] Schweitzer, *Mysticism*, 196.

[70] Gaventa, "Singularity of the Gospel," 103: "The governing theological antithesis in Galatians is between Christ or the new creation and the cosmos; the antithesis between Christ and the law and between the cross and circumcision are not the equivalent of this central premise but follow from it"; ibid., 110: "This new creation allows for no supplementation or augmentation by the law or any other power or loyalty."

on the proselyte circumcision controversy is, at the same time, a textbook example of legalism. Matthew Thiessen has provided a solution to this puzzle in his account of the contested halakhah around proselyte circumcision.[71] Thiessen shows that what we often think of as the official ancient Jewish view on conversion – that gentiles who wanted to could become Jews by taking on the whole law of Moses, up to and including male proselyte circumcision[72] – was in fact just one partisan view, and that a rival Jewish view said that gentile conversion was not just inadvisable but actually impossible.[73] The halakhic rationale for this view was that the covenant of circumcision in Genesis 17, according to the Greek text,[74] stipulates that circumcision be performed on the eighth day after birth *or not at all*, and in fact that *non*-eighth-day circumcisions are anathema.[75] If so, then proselyte circumcision is not just unnecessary but positively forbidden and even damnable. Jubilees certainly draws this conclusion,[76] and, Thiessen argues – persuasively, to my mind – Paul does, too.[77]

This account makes good sense of (what we might call) the conspicuous legalism of Galatians: "Everyone who undergoes circumcision is obligated to do the whole law" (Gal 5:3), that is, the whole law of circumcision, which proselyte circumcision – because it neglects the

---

[71] Thiessen, *Contesting Conversion*.
[72] For a classic discussion, see Cohen, *Beginnings of Jewishness*, ch. 5 "Crossing the Boundary and Becoming a Jew."
[73] An idea attested already in Ezra, as shown by Christine Hayes, *Gentile Impurities and Jewish Identities: Intermarriage and Conversion from the Bible to the Talmud* (Oxford: Oxford University Press, 2002).
[74] And the Samaritan Pentateuch, as well, but not the MT. See discussion in Thiessen, "The Text of Genesis 17:14."
[75] Gen 17:14 LXX: καὶ ἀπερίτμητος ἄρσην, ὃς οὐ περιτμηθήσεται τὴν σάρκα τῆς ἀκροβυστίας αὐτοῦ τῇ ἡμέρᾳ τῇ ὀγδόῃ, ἐξολεθρευθήσεται ἡ ψυχὴ ἐκείνη ἐκ τοῦ γένους αὐτῆς, ὅτι τὴν διαθήκην μου διεσκέδασεν, "An uncircumcised male, the flesh of whose foreskin is not circumcised *on the eight day*, that soul shall be destroyed from his people, for he has broken my covenant."
[76] See Jub. 15.25–27 (trans. mod. from Charles): "This law is for all the generations forever, and there is no circumcision of the days, and no omission of one day out of the eight days; for it is an eternal ordinance, ordained and written on the heavenly tablets. And everyone that is born, the flesh of whose foreskin is not circumcised on the eighth day, belongs not to the children of the covenant which the Lord made with Abraham, but to the children of destruction; nor is there, moreover, any sign on him that he is the Lord's, but (he is destined) to be destroyed and slain from the earth, and to be rooted out of the earth, for he has broken the covenant of the Lord our God."
[77] Thiessen, *Paul and the Gentile Problem*.

eighth-day clause – manifestly does not do. Hence a proselyte-circumcised gentile fails in his obligation to the law. "Those who are undergoing circumcision are not themselves guarding the law, but they want you to be circumcised so that they may boast in your flesh" (Gal 6:13), because to guard the law would be to obey the commandment as God gave it to Abraham; but proselyte circumcision actually *breaks* the commandment as God gave it to Abraham. The only thing it is good for, Paul says, is boasting in the sight of other human beings. All of this contributes to the rhetoric of Paul's argument against proselyte circumcision, but the actual reason for his absolute prohibition of the practice lies elsewhere, back in the strange but powerful logic of Schweitzer's three deadly sins.

Although on the face of it might seem a strange fit, for Paul, proselyte circumcision shares with *porneia* and demon-communion not only an effect (namely: destruction) but also an underlying cause for that effect. All and only these three acts constitute "body modifications" in the pneumatic body of Christ. As Ryan Collman explains, "These actions would theoretically create unions between Christ and something with which his body is completely incompatible. Since Paul cannot conceive of such things damaging the body of Christ, the one who participates in such acts is severed from the body like a gangrenous limb. They lose Christ's *pneuma* and are separated from his body and the benefits afforded to his members."[78] *Porneia* through sexual penetration, demon-communion through ingestion, proselyte circumcision through laceration: all three acts actually penetrate the body of Christ (at the site of one of its body parts or members: a particular Christ-believer), thereby threatening the pollution or loss of the *pneuma* of Christ.[79] This God cannot allow; hence the destruction

---

[78] Collman, *Apostle to the Foreskin*, 82. On the theory of pneuma's vulnerability to contamination, see further Giovanni B. Bazzana, *Having the Spirit of Christ: Spirit Possession and Exorcism in the Early Christ Groups* (New Haven: Yale University Press, 2020).

[79] With *porneia* in 1 Cor 5, the threat to the pneuma is evidently pollution; hence Paul's analogy to the activity of leaven in dough. With proselyte circumcision in Galatians, however, the threat to the pneuma is perhaps not pollution but loss. Thus plausibly Collman, *Apostle to the Foreskin*, 86: "In the case of circumcision, it is possible that the incision itself causes the *pneuma* to flow out of the individual in the same way that *pneuma* flows out of the wounds of an animal." Here Collman cites Galen, *On the Doctrines of Hippocrates and Plato* 7.3.30: "When the pneuma is let out through wounds, the animal immediately

(which is to say, amputation) of the offending member. "Shall we provoke the lord to jealousy? Are we stronger than he?" (1 Cor 10:22). As the incestuous man of 1 Cor 5 learned the hard way, the answer is no.

Conclusion

The foremost obstacle to achieving clarity on this issue clearly is a longstanding, discipline-wide habit of talking about legalism and antilegalism (or nomism and antinomianism) in broad, clumsy, binary terms, of imagining one great sliding scale from legalism on the one side to libertinism on the other.[80] And, relatedly, of classing all of Paul's sayings about the law as either positive or negative,[81] or perhaps, in moments of exceptional lucidity, as partly positive and partly negative. I hereby propose a moratorium on the commonplace observation that Paul has some positive statements about the law and other negative statements about it. That claim is arguably true if we content ourselves with extremely vague descriptions. But why should we settle for vagueness? We stand to make much more progress with these difficult questions if we insist on precision. Any solution to the hoary old problem of "Paul and the law" that is built on the positive-statements-versus-negative-statements rubric is insufficient, because sloppy. Solutions like: Paul's positive statements about the law pertain to its role as a mode of *revelation*, his negative statements to its role as an instrument of *salvation*.[82] Or: Paul's positive statements about the law imply "as it pertains to Jews," his negative statements about the law "as it pertains to gentiles."[83] And so on. There is a grain of truth in each of these, which is why they enjoy such popularity. But they buy

---

becomes like a corpse, but when it has been collected again the animal revives" (trans. De Lacy in CMG).

[80] As, e.g., in the title of John W. Drane, *Paul: Libertine or Legalist?* (London: SPCK, 1975), though Drane's actual analysis is more nuanced than his title might suggest.

[81] A move common among interpreters as different from one another as, e.g., Cranfield, "St Paul and the Law"; and Gager, *Reinventing Paul*.

[82] Thus, e.g., Otto Pfleiderer, *Paulinism: A Contribution to the History of Primitive Christian Theology*, trans. Edward Peters (London: Williams & Norgate, 1877), 82.

[83] Thus, e.g., Gager, *Reinventing Paul*, 58.

Conclusion

tidiness at the expense of precision, and hence, in the end, they prove unreliable guides.

If we are ever to understand the legalism of the apostle Paul, then we need to be attuned to his many subtle distinctions: between eighth-day circumcision and proselyte circumcision, between eating idol meat and communing with a demon, between prophylactic sex with one's spouse and sex in the passion of desire, between one commandment and another, between people who by nature have the law and those who do not, between doing the law and fulfilling it, between righteousness in the law and eschatological righteousness, and so on and on. Writing in a different context, I have put it in this way:

> We might be inclined to doubt that Paul could take *Jubilees*' side on the circumcision commandment because of our well worn image of the apostle as a libertine with respect to Torah. *But halakhic perspectives do not map onto a simple continuum from rigorist on one end to libertine on the other.* In 1 Maccabees, Mattathias and his sons aggressively enforce circumcision among the peoples under their jurisdiction (1 Macc 2:46), but they relax the Sabbath commandment to allow for warfare on the seventh day (1 Macc 2:29–41). Philo of Alexandria allegorizes commandments of Moses by the score, but he nevertheless insists on the proper, traditional observance of the Sabbath, feast days, and circumcision (*Migration* 89–93). By the same token, one can readily imagine Paul concluding that, in light of the present messianic ingathering of the gentiles, it is permissible – indeed, even necessary – for a Jew to violate [some Jews' definition of] kashrut in order to share in the one table of the lord (see Gal 2:11–21), and yet, at the same time, insisting that the eighth-day circumcision commandment is not to be violated, and in fact, for precisely the same eschatological reason: Jews enter the kingdom as Jews, gentiles as gentiles, but all share in the one messianic banquet.[84]

Depending on what, exactly, we mean by legalism, we can likely find evidence for it here and there in ancient Judaism, as we can in all human societies, religious or otherwise, in all times and places. Most ancient Jews were probably not legalists in any significant sense,[85] but

---

[84] Novenson, "The Self-Styled Jew of Romans 2 and the Actual Jews of Romans 9–11," 107 (emphasis added). On this theme, see further Fredriksen, "Judaizing the Nations." On the subtleties of Paul's halakhic reasoning, see Tomson, *Paul and the Jewish Law*, 55–96, 259–281.

[85] Which is not to say they did not *keep* Jewish law. As Yonatan Adler (*The Origins of Judaism: An Archaeological-Historical Reappraisal*, AYBRL [New Haven: Yale University Press, 2022]) has shown, at least from the Hasmonean period onward, many did.

some were, and the apostle Paul was one of them. (We can see this clearly if we practice the art of reading Paul's letters as if they were fragments of an anonymous ancient Jewish writer, as in the thought experiment in the introduction above.) My point in this chapter is not to suggest that Paul was more legalistic than his contemporaries, or that he was more legalistic than he was anything else, or otherwise to cast aspersions (or praise) on him. But it is the case that, measured by the rule people otherwise use when they speak of "legalism," Paul was a legalist. And to make this point is important because so many interpreters from the sixteenth century to the present have claimed that Paul's great, original contribution was precisely his anti-legalism. It was not. There were other Jewish thinkers, both before and after Paul, who were more anti-legalist than he, as well as others, both before and after, who were less so. Paul's big idea lay elsewhere.[86]

---

[86] Where exactly it lay is the subject of Chapters 8 and 9.

6 | *The Ethnic Chauvinism of Paul*

In an immortal stand-up comedy set that he performed in several variations in the early 1960s, Lenny Bruce said the following:

> Now I neologize Jewish and goyish. Dig: I'm Jewish. Count Basie's Jewish. Ray Charles is Jewish. Eddie Cantor's goyish. B'nai Brith is goyish; Hadassah, Jewish. Marine Corps – heavy goyim, dangerous. Kool-Aid is goyish. All Drake's cakes are goyish. Pumpernickel is Jewish, and, as you know, white bread is very goyish. Instant potatoes – goyish. Black cherry soda's very Jewish. Macaroons are very Jewish – very Jewish cake. Fruit salad is Jewish. Lime Jello is goyish. Lime soda is very goyish. Trailer parks are so goyish that Jews won't go near them. Jack Paar Show is very goyish. Underwear is definitely goyish. Balls are goyish. Titties are Jewish. Mouths are Jewish. All Italians are Jewish. Greeks are goyish – bad sauce. Eugene O'Neill – Jewish; Dylan Thomas – Jewish.[1]

The brilliance of this piece lies, in part, in the way it simultaneously reinforces (e.g., pumpernickel/white bread) and undermines (e.g., Ray Charles/Eddie Cantor) the familiar ethnic binary Jewish/goyish. It is a virtuoso improvisation on and deconstruction of ethnic stereotypes. The Jewish/goyish binary with which Bruce plays to great comic effect has a history stretching back at least to the Roman period, arguably earlier, although exactly how early is disputed. In any case, it is securely attested in the letters of Paul, who trades on it heavily, though without Bruce's sparkling wit. For Paul, some things are Jewish, others goyish (or rather, in Paul's Greek idiom: ἐθνικός, *ethnikos*, gentile). Paul is Jewish. The apostles are Jewish. The addressees of Paul's letters are goyish. Circumcision is Jewish. Having a foreskin is goyish. Idol temples are so goyish that Jews won't go near them. Lust is goyish. Men having sex with other men is definitely goyish. Torah study is

---

[1] Lenny Bruce, *The Essential Lenny Bruce*, comp. and ed. John Cohen (New York: Bell, 1970), 31.

Jewish. Diaspora Jews are Jewish. Judean Jews are very Jewish. Greeks are goyish – bad sauce.

As these examples illustrate, Paul's use of the Jew/gentile binary, unlike Bruce's, comes with heavy moral valuations attached. Nowadays we use the word "chauvinism" to mean any kind of bias in favor of one's in-group, especially in regard to gender.[2] But originally and most precisely, "chauvinism" (eponymous with Nicolas Chauvin, the legendary French soldier famous for his irrational patriotism)[3] signifies an intractable belief in the superiority of one's own *ethnos* or nation. That is the sense in which I use the term in this chapter, whose subject is Paul's own chauvinism. My usage of the term is admittedly old-fashioned, but it is more accurate than any of a number of closely related terms: racism, jingoism, nationalism, ethnocentrism, xenophobia, and other such.[4] The apostle has been much discussed, of course, in connection with *gendered* chauvinism on account of several notorious passages: "The head of every man is Christ, the head of woman is man, and the head of Christ is God" (1 Cor 11:3); "Let women be silent in the assemblies. For it is not permitted for them to speak, but they should be subordinate, just as the law says" (1 Cor 14:34); and so on. That fascinating discussion proceeds apace, but it is not my concern here.[5] For present purposes, I am interested, instead, in an underappreciated strand of ethnic chauvinism that runs through the authentic Pauline letters.

This strand lies hidden in plain sight, so to speak, across a number of passages in 1 Thessalonians, Galatians, 1 Corinthians, and Romans – familiar texts, all. Hidden, I think, because of a powerful interpretive tradition that associates the apostle so strongly with notions of trans-ethnic humanism and universalism that the idea of him harboring

---

[2] As in the phrase "male chauvinist pig," or Ariel Levy's more recent *Female Chauvinist Pigs* (New York: Free Press, 2005).

[3] See Gérard de Puymège, "Chauvin and Chauvinism: In Search of a Myth," *History and Memory* 6 (1994): 35–72.

[4] On the fine conceptual distinctions, see, e.g., Ronald R. Sundstrom and David Haekwon Kim, "Xenophobia and Racism," *Critical Philosophy of Race* 2 (2014): 20–45.

[5] See the excellent collection of essays in Amy-Jill Levine, ed., A *Feminist Companion to Paul: Authentic Pauline Writings* (London: T&T Clark, 2004); and the recent state-of-the-art essay by Kathy Ehrensperger, "Paul and Feminism," in *Oxford Handbook of Pauline Studies*, 622–636.

chauvinist attitudes becomes actually unthinkable.⁶ We may illustrate this interpretive tradition by citing several leading lights who, in other respects, represent quite different schools of thought. First, a more or less traditional Protestant exegete, N. T. Wright: "[Paul reasons] that, if there is one God – the foundation of all Jewish belief – there must be one people of God. Were there to be two or more 'peoples,' the whole theological scheme would lapse back into some sort of paganism, with each tribe or race possessing its own national deities."⁷ Second, a leading American Jewish interpreter of Paul, Daniel Boyarin: "Paul was motivated by a Hellenistic desire for the One, which among other things produced an ideal of a universal human essence, beyond difference and hierarchy."⁸ And third, the French Marxist philosopher Alain Badiou: "What Paul must be given exclusive credit for establishing is that the fidelity to such an event exists only through the termination of communitarian particularisms and the determination of a subject-of-truth who indistinguishes the One and the 'for all'.... Paul is a founder, in that he is one of the very first theoreticians of the universal."⁹ There is a lot that we could say about each of these three strong interpretations,¹⁰ but the salient point for now is that they all agree in ascribing to Paul the principled erasure of ethnic difference. To be sure, there is some evidence in Paul's letters that might admit of such an interpretation, and we will return to that. But the first and more important step is to consider the numerous texts in which – contrary to his reputation – Paul presupposes, reinscribes, and even valorises ethnic difference.

---

⁶ For a perceptive meta-criticism of this trend in interpretation, see Brigitte Kahl, "Galatians and the 'Orientalism' of Justification by Faith," in *The Colonized Apostle: Paul through Postcolonial Eyes*, ed. Christopher D. Stanley (Minneapolis: Fortress, 2011), 206–222.
⁷ N. T. Wright, *The Climax of the Covenant: Christ and the Law in Pauline Theology* (Minneapolis: Fortress, 1991), 170.
⁸ Boyarin, *Radical Jew*, 7.
⁹ Alain Badiou, *Saint Paul: The Foundation of Universalism*, trans. Ray Brassier (Stanford: Stanford University Press, 2003 [French original 1997]), 108.
¹⁰ For discussion see Ward Blanton, *A Materialism for the Masses: Saint Paul and the Philosophy of Undying Life* (New York: Columbia University Press, 2014); Benjamin H. Dunning, *Christ without Adam: Subjectivity and Sexual Difference in the Philosophers' Paul* (New York: Columbia University Press, 2014); Fatima Tofighi, *Paul's Letters and the Construction of the European Self* (London: T&T Clark, 2017).

Us and Them

Herodotus made the perceptive observation that barbarism is relative. Like most other Greek writers contemporary with and after him, Herodotus uses βάρβαρος, "barbarian," as a shorthand for any and all uncivilized peoples who do not speak Greek (e.g., Herodotus, *Hist.* 1.58; 2.57).[11] In his account of the career of King Necos II of Egypt, however, he notes that the Egyptians regard as barbarians all peoples who do not speak *their* indigenous language: "Necos stopped work [on the Red Sea canal], stayed by a prophetic utterance that he was toiling beforehand for the barbarian. The Egyptians call all people of other languages barbarians [βαρβάρους δὲ πάντας οἱ Αἰγύπτιοι καλέουσι τοὺς μὴ σφίσι ὁμογλώσσους]" (*Hist.* 2.158).[12] Most ancient writers were not so self-aware. Many operated with unreflective, folk-anthropological assumptions on which one might – though not all ancients did – wield a single taxon for all peoples outside one's own in-group: ἀλλόφυλοι, "people of another tribe" or "foreigners." This is the form of numerous well-known ancient ethnic binaries including Greeks vs. barbarians, Egyptians vs. barbarians, Jews vs. gentiles, and Christians vs. pagans.[13]

Which brings us to the case of Paul. Like many ancients (and many moderns, for that matter), Paul mostly perceives ethnic difference as binary, parochial, and asymmetrical. That is to say, by Paul's lights there are two kinds of people in the world: his own ethnic in-group (the Ἰουδαῖοι, "Jews") and everyone else (the ἔθνη, "nations" or "gentiles").[14] The people whom Paul calls gentiles generally would not

---

[11] See Edith Hall, *Inventing the Barbarian: Greek Self-Definition through Tragedy*, OCM (Oxford: Clarendon, 1991); Joseph E. Skinner, *The Invention of Greek Ethnography: From Homer to Herodotus* (Oxford: Oxford University Press, 2012).

[12] Translation modified from Godley in LCL.

[13] See Michael Avi-Yonah, *Hellenism and the East: Contacts and Interrelations from Alexander to the Roman Conquest* (Jerusalem: Hebrew University, 1978), 136: "The Egyptians, the Jews, and the Greeks are the only three nations of antiquity who, to our knowledge, drew a dividing line between themselves and all other people." But at least the Romans also did so, adopting the Greek custom and using *barbari* as a catch-all term for foreigners. Perhaps other ancient nations did not do so, or, I think more likely, we simply do not have enough of their literary remains to know.

[14] Glenn Snyder has recently argued that Paul regards himself as a Benjaminite (Rom 11:1; Phil 3:5) and therefore *not* as a Ἰουδαῖος, which Snyder translates

have called themselves gentiles (unless or until Paul taught them to do so) but rather Lycaonians, Asians, Thracians, Macedonians, Achaeans, or what have you.[15] As far as he is concerned, however, they are gentiles. In a few, rare cases Paul demonstrates some awareness of other ethnic self-designations – "Macedonians" in 2 Cor 9:2–4 and "Galatians" in Gal 3:1 – but his overwhelming pattern is to ignore all such distinctions and use "gentiles" throughout.[16] Precisely once, Paul parses the gentile side of the Jew/gentile binary more finely, when in Rom 1 he declares his apostolic obligation to all gentiles, Ἕλησίν τε καὶ βαρβάροις, "Greeks as well as barbarians" (Rom 1:14). Here, of course, Paul is using the conventional Hellenocentric ethnic binary noted above, but without the self-awareness of a Herodotus.[17]

In most instances and for most purposes, Paul sees the world as populated by a minority of Jews and an undifferentiated mass of gentiles (Rom 3:29; 9:24; 1 Cor 1:23; Gal 2:14, 15), or as he sometimes crassly puts it, circumcisions and foreskins (Rom 3:30; 4:9, 11, 12; Gal 2:7).[18] Like other Jewish writers of the early Roman period, he most

"Judahite" or "member of the tribe of Judah" ("Paul beyond the Jew/Gentile Dichotomy: A Perspective from Benjamin," *Expositions* 9 [2015]: 125–137). His argument is clever but, in my view, mistaken on the actual use of Ἰουδαῖος both in Paul and in other contemporary sources. See further my "*Ioudaios, Pharisee, Zealot.*"

[15] On this issue, see further Christopher D. Stanley, "Neither Jew nor Greek: Ethnic Conflict in Graeco-Roman Society," *JSNT* 64 (1996): 101–124; Christopher D. Stanley, "The Ethnic Context of Paul's Letters," in *Christian Origins and Hellenistic Judaism*, ed. Stanley E. Porter and Andrew W. Pitts (Leiden: Brill, 2012), 177–202; Terence L. Donaldson, *Gentile Christian Identity from Cornelius to Constantine: The Nations, the Parting of the Ways, and Roman Imperial Ideology* (Grand Rapids, MI: Eerdmans, 2020).

[16] For present purposes, I leave aside two further deutero-Pauline instances: Col 3:11: "Here there cannot be Greek and Jew, circumcision and foreskin, barbarian, Scythian, slave, free, but Christ is all, and in all"; and Titus 1:12–13: "One of themselves, a prophet of their own, said, 'Cretans are always liars, evil beasts, lazy gluttons.' This testimony is true."

[17] As George van Kooten has rightly noted, "There is no antithesis operative in antiquity between Jewish ethnocentrism versus Greek universalism; rather both sides are basically ethnocentric, focused on the continuation of their ancestral customs" ("Broadening the New Perspective on Paul: Paul and the Ethnographical Debate of His Time – The Criticism of Jewish and Pagan Ancestral Customs [1 Thess 2:13–16]," in *Abraham, the Nations, and the Hagarites*, ed. Martin Goodman et al. [Leiden: Brill, 2010], 319–344 at 321).

[18] Thus rightly Matlock, "Jews by Nature," 311: "When Paul touches explicitly on what we would regard as matters of 'ethnicity,' he does so in entirely conventional ways.... 'Ethnic identity' for Paul is a matter of genealogy,

often refers to himself and his co-ethnics with the prevailing ethnonym Ἰουδαῖος, "Judean" or "Jew,"[19] but also, depending on context, with heritage titles like Ἑβραῖος, "Hebrew" (2 Cor 11:22; Phil 3:5), and Ἰσραηλίτης, "Israelite" (2 Cor 11:22; Rom 9:4; 11:1).[20] Occasionally, in lieu of the binary "Jews and gentiles," Paul uses the binary "Jew and Greek" (Rom 1:16; 2:9, 10; 10:12; Gal 3:28), but there are straightforward linguistic reasons for this: Ἰουδαῖοι signifies the mass of all Jews and ἔθνη the mass of all gentiles, but whereas a singular Ἰουδαῖος is a Jewish *person*, a singular ἔθνος is a gentile *nation*, so the binary does not work in the grammatical singular. When, therefore, Paul wants to signify a singular gentile person, he uses Ἕλλην, "Hellene" or "Greek" (or alternatively ἀκροβυστία, "foreskin," as in Rom 2:26–27).[21] There are a few instances of the binary "Jews and Greeks," both plural (Rom 3:9; 1 Cor 1:22, 24; 10:32; 12:13), but this usage is explicable as an extension of the pattern established by grammatical necessity in the singular. Paul knows that, from a Greek perspective, not all gentiles are Greeks; many are barbarians (thus Rom 1:14). But from where he sits in the Hellenophone East, for all practical intents and purposes, any soul from among the gentiles can be called a Greek. All this, however, is not yet chauvinism, only ethnocentrism. Ethnocentrism grants particularity to one's own *ethnos* while classing all others together in an undifferentiated mass.[22] Chauvinism adds to this a layer of value judgment: Not only are all others alike; they are alike inferior to us.

---

language, and culture. And the boundary between Israel and the nations is a function of 'the cultural stuff' of the Torah.... So Paul is a 'primordialist,' then – not in any theoretical sense, but in the unreflective or folk-anthropological sort of way that ethnic actors tend to be."

[19] I continue to think that "Jew" is a reasonable English gloss for Greek Ἰουδαῖος, that it carries most of the ethnic, political, and geographical valences that scholars who insist on the gloss "Judean" are aiming for. Thus I follow, e.g., Daniel R. Schwartz, "Judaean or Jew? How Should We Translate *Ioudaios* in Josephus?" in *Jewish Identity in the Greco-Roman World*, ed. Jörg Frey et al. (Leiden: Brill, 2007), 3–27; against, e.g., Mason, "Jews, Judaeans, Judaizing."

[20] As Jennifer Eyl has shown, when Paul uses these latter terms, there are usually clear rhetorical reasons for his doing so. See Eyl, "I Myself Am an Israelite"; and further Novenson, "*Ioudaios*, Pharisee, Zealot."

[21] That is to say, Paul does *not* actually anticipate the later rabbinic use of *goy* to signify a singular gentile person, contra Ishay Rosen-Zvi and Adi Ophir, "Paul and the Invention of the Gentiles," *JQR* 105 (2015): 1–41.

[22] See further Tet-Lim N. Yee, *Jews, Gentiles, and Ethnic Reconciliation: Paul's Jewish Identity and Ephesians*, SNTSMS 130 (Cambridge: Cambridge

Paul's attitude toward gentiles, I propose, is not only ethnocentric but also chauvinist – and this in a specifically moral sense. Gentiles are sinners, as he puts it in Gal 2:15. This passage is part of Paul's report of his own words to Cephas (i.e., Peter)[23] when the latter withdrew from common meals with the Christ-gentiles in Antioch. Urging Cephas to repent of this policy, Paul appeals to a theologoumenon on which he thinks the two of them agree: that a person is rightwised not from works of Torah but from Christ-faith.[24] Significantly, although it is rarely commented on, Paul attributes the knowledge – or, conversely, the ignorance – of this theologoumenon to ethnic difference: "We who are by nature Jews and not sinners from among the gentiles ['Ημεῖς φύσει Ἰουδαῖοι καὶ οὐκ ἐξ ἐθνῶν ἁμαρτωλοί], knowing that a person is not rightwised from works of Torah except through the trust of Jesus Christ, we indeed trusted in Christ Jesus." In other words, that righteousness comes from Christ-faith is a truth acknowledged, Paul thinks, by natural Jews but not by gentile sinners.[25] Without exception, Paul uses the word φύσις, "nature," to signal features of species that seem to him normal, obvious, taken for granted: men sexually penetrating women in Rom 1:26–27; men wearing their hair short in 1 Cor 11:14; the growth of uncultivated trees in Rom 11:21–24; the subordinate status of gentile deities in Gal 4:8.[26] The English gloss "nature" might tempt one to think of a universal system of order, but that would be an over-interpretation. As Stanley Stowers notes, "When ancients appealed to nature they often meant merely that something was appropriate or inappropriate, just as today we often use the term without

---

University Press, 2005), 140–187, who, however, attributes too much ethnocentrism to other ancient Jewish thinkers and too little to Paul.

[23] From antiquity down to the present, interpreters have occasionally suggested that the Cephas of Gal 2 was not the apostle Peter, but it is overwhelmingly likely that he was. See Dale C. Allison, "Peter and Cephas: One and the Same," *JBL* 111 (1992): 489–495.

[24] On which see Chapter 3.

[25] In an unpublished but occasionally cited paper ("Who Rebuked Cephas? A New Interpretation of Galatians 2:14–17," SBL Annual Meeting 2013), Jeremy Hultin has argued – ingeniously but not, to my mind, persuasively – that this sentence is ascribed not to Paul (first person singular εἶπον, "I said") but to the "people from James" (third person plural εἶπον, "they said"). The actual form εἶπον is of course ambiguous, but the passage makes clearer sense on the premise that these are Paul's words.

[26] On "nature" in Paul, see further Martin, "Heterosexism and the Interpretation of Romans 1:18–32."

implying a theory of natural law."[27] Thus for Paul as for most ancient Greek-speakers, φύσις simply refers to what is perceived as normal. He and Peter are Jews φύσει, "by nature." Although he never uses the exact parallel phrase φύσει ἔθνη, "gentiles by nature," elsewhere he does characterize a hypothetical gentile person as ἡ ἐκ φύσεως ἀκροβυστία, "the foreskin from nature," that is, "the naturally foreskinned person" (Rom 2:27). This is a striking phrase, since we moderns tend to think of all human males as naturally foreskinned, because we think of circumcision as a surgical intervention in nature. Paul, however, did not think this way. By his lights, gentiles are naturally foreskinned, Jews naturally circumcised;[28] gentiles are naturally sinners, Jews naturally decent.[29]

Those who have commented on this aspect of Gal 2 have often been at pains to distance the apostle from the sentiment here expressed. James Dunn, for instance, writes, "The language ('gentile sinners') is the language of Jews who regarded the law as definitive of righteousness, and who therefore took it for granted that Gentiles 'by nature' were outside the law, out-laws, and therefore 'sinners,' unacceptable to God by definition. As such it is hardly likely to have been Paul's own choice of language, given his own much more pro-Gentile stance. Almost certainly, therefore, he is echoing the language of more traditional Jews."[30] But this is a rather desperate argument, and in any case, it is quite unnecessary. The view that gentiles – unlike Jews – are naturally and characteristically bad is entirely consistent

---

[27] Stowers, *Rereading of Romans*, 111.

[28] In this connection, both rabbinic midrash and later Islamic hadith imagine that certain patriarchs and prophets – e.g., Adam, Seth, Noah, Jacob, Moses, David, and for the hadith also Jesus and Muhammad – were actually born circumcised (see Menahem J. Kister, "And He Was Born Circumcised: Some Notes on Circumcision in Hadith," *Oriens* 34 [1994]: 10–30). Evidence for this idea is much thinner on the ground in the Second Temple Period, but see *LAB* 9.13 on the infant Moses: *puer natus est in testamento Dei et in testamento carnis eius*, "That boy was born in the covenant of God and in the covenant of his flesh" (and again in *LAB* 9.15) – if this idea goes back to the *Urtext* of *LAB* (see discussion in Howard Jacobson, *A Commentary on Pseudo-Philo's Liber Antiquitatum Biblicarum*, 2 vols. [Leiden: Brill, 1996], 1:425–429). Already for Jubilees (15.27) it is an axiom that the highest ranks of angels are by nature circumcised.

[29] Decent, though not in possession of perfect eschatological righteousness until they receive the divine pneuma; see further Chapter 8.

[30] James D. G. Dunn, "Echoes of Intra-Jewish Polemic in Paul's Letter to the Galatians," in *New Perspective on Paul*, 226.

with Paul's way of speaking throughout his authentic letters (and is perpetuated in some of the disputed Pauline letters, too).[31] So consistent, in fact, that Paul himself is a parade example of the ostensibly "more traditional Jews" from whom Dunn wants to distance him. The conceptual problem here lies in Dunn's appeal to Paul's "pro-gentile stance," which is, I suppose, an accurate characterization but is also irremediably vague. Paul is of course "pro-gentile," say, in the sense that he devotes his life to teaching gentiles, or in the sense that he has affection for the gentiles in his Christ assemblies. But none of this entails any more thoroughgoing kind of humanism or universalism, nor does it preclude the possibility that Paul means what he says when he speaks of "gentile sinners."

Gentile Sinners

And mean it he does. Although he does not use the phrase itself (ἐξ ἐθνῶν ἁμαρτωλοί, "sinners from among the gentiles") elsewhere, Paul frequently reiterates the point – which for him has the status of an axiom – that gentiles are naturally and characteristically immoral, Jews not so. This stereotype figures prominently in Paul's reasoning in Rom 9–11, where he undertakes to explain to himself the strange spectacle of gentiles thronging to the Christ sect while Jews, by and large, ignore or reject it. Paul interprets this perplexing state of affairs as follows: "Gentiles – who do not pursue righteousness [ἔθνη τὰ μὴ διώκοντα δικαιοσύνην] – laid hold of righteousness, that is, the righteousness from trust, but Israel – who pursue a law of righteousness ['Ισραὴλ δὲ διώκων νόμον δικαιοσύνης] – did not arrive at the law" (Rom 9:30–31). This explanation is predicated upon Paul's assumptions about what Jews and gentiles, respectively, do: Jews pursue the righteous law; that is the kind of people they are. Gentiles do not bother with righteousness. Indeed, they positively chase after ἀδικία, "unrighteousness" (Rom 1:18, 29); that is the kind of people they are.[32]

What is more, in a number of passages, Paul specifies particular gentile behaviors that he thinks demonstrate their natural sinfulness.

---

[31] On the latter phenomenon, see the essays in Isaac W. Oliver and Gabriele Boccaccini, eds., *The Early Reception of Paul the Second Temple Jew: Text, Narrative, and Reception History* (London: T&T Clark, 2019).

[32] On this text, see further Novenson, "The Self-Styled Jew of Romans 2 and the Actual Jews of Romans 9–11."

Typically for ancient (and indeed modern) stereotypes of ethnic others, the bad behaviors that Paul has in mind are especially sexual ones.[33] In an example from his earliest extant letter, Paul writes to his Christ-gentiles in Thessaloniki instructing the men among them to possess their wives without passion: "This is the will of God: your consecration, that you abstain from *porneia*, that each of you know how to possess his own vessel in consecration and honour, not in the passion of desire like the gentiles who do not know God [ἐν πάθει ἐπιθυμίας καθάπερ καὶ τὰ ἔθνη τὰ μὴ εἰδότα τὸν θεόν]" (1 Thess 4:3–5). In Paul's linguistic context, the word *porneia* signifies just any kind of sex the user of the word considers illicit.[34] Here, interestingly, Paul warns against not, say, sex with prostitutes (cf. 1 Cor 6:12–20) but against harboring the passion of desire (πάθει ἐπιθυμίας) toward one's own wife (figured as a σκεῦος, "vessel").[35] The latter is what "gentiles who do not know God" do with their wives. That is the key point for our purposes: The kind of sex that Paul considers illicit he also considers typical of gentiles.

This is even clearer in the notorious case of the man having sex with his father's wife in 1 Cor 5. In that letter, Paul scolds his Christ-gentiles in Corinth for a number of moral lapses – lapses exacerbated, perhaps, by Paul's own message of pneumatic liberty – asserting his apostolic authority over them.[36] Early in the letter, he flags up one particular sex act for censure, writing: "It is actually reported [that there is] *porneia* among you, and *porneia* of a kind that is not even [found] among the

---

[33] On this commonplace, see Jennifer Wright Knust, *Abandoned to Lust: Sexual Slander and Ancient Christianity* (New York: Columbia University Press, 2006), 15–50.

[34] See Wheeler-Reed, Knust, and Martin, "Can a Man Commit *Porneia* with His Wife?"; and more expansively David Wheeler-Reed, *Regulating Sex in the Roman Empire: Ideology, the Bible, and the Early Christians* (New Haven: Yale University Press, 2017); *pace* Kyle Harper's narrower account of ancient *porneia* in Kyle Harper, *From Shame to Sin: The Christian Transformation of Sexual Morality in Late Antiquity* (Cambridge, MA: Harvard University Press, 2013).

[35] Alternatively, it is possible that σκεῦος is a figure of speech for the male sexual organ, but in this context it more plausibly signifies the wife, especially in light of the following verse: "not transgressing and *not defrauding one's brother in this matter*, for the lord is an avenger in all these things" (1 Thess 4:7). See further Fatum, "Brotherhood in Christ."

[36] One principal reason for the Corinthian correspondence was a series of understandings, misunderstandings, and corrections between Paul and his audience in Corinth, as is powerfully demonstrated by Mitchell, *Paul, the Corinthians, and the Birth of Christian Hermeneutics*.

gentiles [τοιαύτη πορνεία ἥτις οὐδὲ ἐν τοῖς ἔθνεσιν]: someone has his father's wife" (1 Cor 5:1). Paul prescribes a ritual destruction of the man in the Christ-assembly, lest that man's *porneia* infect the entire group – a curious idea to modern sensibilities, perhaps, but one quite at home in Paul's conception of social ethics.[37] For our present purposes, again, the crucial thing is the way Paul expresses the extreme heinousness of this kind of *porneia* (τοιαύτη πορνεία): It is so bad that not even the gentiles do it. The unstated premise, of course, is that the gentiles are characteristically unscrupulous. Something that is taboo even among them must be horrible, indeed.

The stereotype of gentiles as sinners is by no means universal in ancient Jewish sources, but it is a recognizable trope.[38] There are hints of it in a few older biblical texts, for instance, Psalm 9:18: "The wicked [*resha'im*] shall depart to Sheol, all the nations [*goyim*] who forget God," or in the very similar Old Greek, "The sinners [ἁμαρτωλοί] shall depart to Hades, all the gentiles [ἔθνη] who forget God." Here ἁμαρτωλοί, "sinners," are coordinated with the undifferentiated ἔθνη, "nations" or "gentiles," but this is exceptional.[39] In Hellenistic-period Jewish texts, the coordination of gentiles with sinners becomes more common. We find it in the *Letter of Aristeas* (probably second-century BCE Alexandrian), which has Eleazar the priest explain the cloven-hoof criterion for kosher animals (Lev 11; Deut 14) as follows:

The symbolism conveyed by these things [viz. the cloven hoof in kashrut] compels us to make a distinction in the performance of all our acts, with righteousness as our aim. This moreover explains why we are distinct from all other men. The majority of other men defile themselves in their relationships, thereby committing a serious offense, and lands and whole cities take pride in it: they not only procure the males; they also defile mothers and

---

[37] See Martin, *Corinthian Body*, 163–197.
[38] See the fuller discussion in Novenson, "Gentile Sinners."
[39] And even this verse can be read to suggest that there are other gentiles who do *not* forget God, as, for instance, in t. Sanh. 13:2: "R. Eliezer says: None of the gentiles has a portion in the age to come, as it says: *The wicked shall depart to Sheol, all the gentiles who forget God* [Ps 9:18]. *The wicked shall depart to Sheol* are the wicked Israelites. R. Joshua said to him: If it had been written: *The wicked shall depart to Sheol, all the gentiles*, and then said nothing further, I should have maintained as you do. But in fact it is written: *all the gentiles who forget God*, thus indicating that there are also righteous people among the nations of the world, who do have a portion in the world to come."

daughters. We are quite separated from these practices. (Let. Aris. 151–152; trans. Shutt in *OTP*)

"The majority of other men [i.e., gentiles] defile themselves in their relationships," but "we [Jews] are quite separated from these practices." This is the gentile sinners stereotype in a nutshell.[40] Likewise 1 Maccabees (ca. turn of the first century BCE), praising Mattathias and his allies for their successes against the Seleucids, writes, "They rescued the law out of the hand of gentiles and kings [τῶν ἐθνῶν καὶ τῶν βασιλέων], and they did not give the horn [of victory] to the sinner [τῷ ἁμαρτωλῷ]" (1 Macc 2:48). Our author calls his enemies not – as he might have done – Seleucids, or Greeks, or Syrians, but gentiles, and in the second line he glosses "gentile" with "sinner." The Book of Jubilees (second century BCE), too, uses the stereotyped phrase "the sinners, the gentiles" in several scenes of military violence. "[The Lord] will rouse up against them [viz. a wicked generation in Israel] the sinners of the gentiles who have no mercy or grace for them and who have no regard for any persons old or young or anyone.... In those days, they will call out and cry and pray to be saved from the hands of the sinners, the gentiles, but there will be none who will be saved" (Jub. 23.23–24; trans. Wintermute, mod.). And again, "Isaac cursed the Philistines on that day, and he said, 'Cursed be the Philistines, for the day of wrath and anger from among all the nations. May the Lord make them as a scorn and a curse and (the object of) wrath and anger at the hands of the sinners, the gentiles, and in the hands of the Kittim'" (Jub. 24.28–29; trans. Wintermute, mod.). The Philistines themselves are gentiles, of course, but even so, Isaac calls down upon them the wrath of "the sinners, the gentiles," who in these passages are not so much sexually immoral as bloodthirsty. And we might multiply examples further, but this is enough to make the point.[41]

---

[40] See further Benjamin G. Wright III, *The Letter of Aristeas*, CEJL (Berlin: De Gruyter, 2015), 271–292.

[41] See the apt summary of E. P. Sanders, *Judaism: Practice and Belief, 63 BCE–66 CE* (London: SCM, 1992), 269: "It seems that Jews in general regarded the characteristic Gentile sins as being idolatry and sexual immorality, especially homosexual relations. How they reached those conclusions we cannot be sure. Both the appeal to nature and to 'Noachian' commandments were probably secondary rationalizations. They 'knew' that idolatry and homosexual practices were wrong.... I think that the practices that end up on various lists of things that make Gentiles *guilty* in God's eyes – rather than just *not Jewish* – were largely instinctive. Jews found some things repugnant. Idolatry is obvious. Sex

In light of this evidence, I cannot agree with the recent, ingenious argument of Adi Ophir and Ishay Rosen-Zvi that Paul himself actually invents the concept of the gentile.[42] Ophir and Rosen-Zvi argue that in Jewish sources prior to Paul, *goyim* or ἔθνη always has its etymological sense of "nations," that is, all nations, including Israel, each with its respective identity. On their account, it is Paul who first uses ἔθνη to mean all nations (except Israel) without distinction. They write, "The binary division of Jews and gentiles, in which the latter denotes all non-Jews in a generic manner, which does not apply only to groups but rather to each individual member of that group, appears for the first time in a systematic and explicit manner in Paul's own epistles."[43] I think this gives the apostle rather too much credit.[44] To be sure, some other Jewish writers – notably both Philo and Josephus – are better informed and subtler in their demography of non-Jewish nations. They know Idumeans, Pereans, Syrians, Phoenicians, Arabians, Egyptians, Cyrenians, and so on, whereas Paul knows only gentiles. And Ophir and Rosen-Zvi are quite right to criticize New Testament scholars for

and food come next, for the normal cultural reasons." On this issue in the Mishnah and Talmud (especially tractate Avodah Zarah), see now Mira Beth Wasserman, *Jews, Gentiles, and Other Animals: The Talmud after the Humanities* (Philadelphia: University of Pennsylvania Press, 2017), 75–78.

[42] Rosen-Zvi and Ophir, "Paul and the Invention of the Gentiles"; Ophir and Rosen-Zvi, *Goy*, especially 140–178.

[43] Ophir and Rosen-Zvi, *Goy*, 149. See further Ophir and Rosen-Zvi, "Paul and the Invention of the Gentiles," 15: "[Paul] took a marginal use [of the word *ethne*], radicalized it, and made it into a core of his thought. He was, in other words, the first author we know of to systematically capitalize on the possibilities that the shift in the meaning of *ethne* opens. It is this specific move that is not to be found in Qumran, in the books of Maccabees or, to the best of our knowledge, in any other pre-Pauline composition." And ibid., 18: "We cannot exclude the possibility that Paul actually invented the new *concept* of the gentile and made it into a constitutive element of a new discursive formation. But this does not mean that we have to go back to a conception of the history of 'great men' and ingenious authors and inventors. Our claim is that Paul's letters are the textual site for the first known appearance of a new discursive formation in which a generalized-individualized category of gentile – still pronounced in the plural, *ethne* – served as a key element for a whole conceptual constellation."

[44] As does Elad Lapidot, "Du, der mit Buchstaben und Beschneidung ein Gesetzübertreter bist: Paulus und die Grundlegung des Judentums," in *Täter und Opfer*, ed. Claudia Simone Dorchain and Tommaso Speccher (Würzburg: Königshausen & Neumann, 2014), 17–38, who credits Paul with inventing the category of the Jew. To be sure, Paul is an important ancient thinker, and he does important intellectual work with the notions of Jew and gentile, but he is not the inventor of either of them.

claiming that Paul comes along and demolishes an old, traditional Jew/gentile binary.[45] That binary is not ubiquitous in the sources, and Paul does not demolish it. But, *pace* Ophir and Rosen-Zvi, it is attested in Jewish sources both before and after Paul.[46] He is not alone in his ethnocentric and chauvinist taxonomy of humankind. It is only the prominence of this taxonomy in his rhetoric that perhaps gives this impression.

Just So Stories

Paul also – again like some of his co-ethnics – offers a diagnosis for the moral degeneracy of gentiles. Their immorality is not accidental or inexplicable. It is, as Paul sees it, causally related to their liturgical practice, the fact that gentiles venerate εἴδωλα, "idols," or better, "cult images" (see LSJ, *ad loc.*). Paul takes for granted that all gentiles venerate cult images. And in fact most did, although Greeks and Romans, not to mention others, also had their own very ancient traditions of aniconism, about which Paul either does not know or does not care.[47] He writes, for instance, to the Christ-gentiles in Corinth: "You know that, when you were gentiles, you were led away to mute idols [ὅτε ἔθνη ἦτε πρὸς τὰ εἴδωλα τὰ ἄφωνα ἀπαγόμενοι],

---

[45] See Ophir and Rosen-Zvi, *Goy*, 147–148: "Scholars unanimously ascribe the 'solution' to Paul, while the 'problem' and the categorization that undergirds it are treated as 'traditional'... This conception has ancient roots. The deutero-Pauline, second-century letter to the Ephesians presents Paul in a similar way.... But things are different for Paul. If there is any consistent effort in his letters, it is to *erect* 'the dividing wall' and not just to 'break [it] down,' as per Ephesians. Before the two can become one in Jesus (2:15), they must first appear as two; they must be radically and systematically differentiated."

[46] For the evidence, see Novenson, "Gentile Sinners"; and more generally on Ophir and Rosen-Zvi's hypothesis, Christine Hayes, "The Complicated Goy in Classical Rabbinic Sources," in *Perceiving the Other in Ancient Judaism and Early Christianity*, ed. Michal Bar-Asher Siegal et al., WUNT 394 (Tübingen: Mohr Siebeck, 2017), 147–168.

[47] See George H. van Kooten, "Pagan and Jewish Monotheism according to Varro, Plutarch, and St Paul," in *Flores Florentino: Dead Sea Scrolls and Other Early Jewish Studies in Honor of Florentino Garcia Martinez*, ed. A. Hilhorst et al. (Leiden: Brill, 2007), 633–651; Nathaniel B. Levtow, *Images of Others: Iconic Politics in Ancient Israel* (Winona Lake, IN: Eisenbrauns, 2008); Milette Gaifman, *Aniconism in Greek Antiquity* (Oxford: Oxford University Press, 2012); Chantziantoniou, "Paul and the Politics of Idolatry."

however you were led" (1 Cor 12:2).⁴⁸ And although these cult images are themselves powerless (ἄφωνα, "mute"), behind, below, and around them lurk a rogues' gallery of lower deities: στοιχεῖα, δαιμόνια, and so on.⁴⁹ As Paul writes to the Christ assemblies in Asia Minor: "At that time, when you did not know God, you were slaves to things that by nature are not gods [τοῖς φύσει μὴ οὖσιν θεοῖς]... the weak and poor elements [τὰ ἀσθενῆ καὶ πτωχὰ στοιχεῖα]" (Gal 4:8–9). And in a letter to Corinth: "What am I saying? That a cult image is something [ὅτι εἴδωλόν τί ἐστιν]? No, rather, that what [gentiles] sacrifice, they sacrifice to *daemons* and not to God [θύουσιν δαιμονίοις καὶ οὐ θεῷ]" (1 Cor 10:19–20). *Daemons* are not idols, but *daemons* loiter around idols, which is why Paul can say both that an idol is not a living thing (1 Cor 8:4–6) and that gentiles celebrate cultic meals with *daemons* (1 Cor 10:20–21).⁵⁰

So then, Paul looks out upon the Mediterranean cities in which he works and observes (what seem to him) two unassailable social facts: first, that gentiles venerate cult images and, second, that gentiles are wantonly immoral. He then infers a causal link between the two: It is not just that gentiles happen to do both, but that iconolatry actually leads to vice (and perhaps, conversely, aniconism to virtue, although Paul does not press the latter point). This causal link is implied in Paul's formulaic vice lists, which always include, alongside numerous stock evils deeds, the cultic use of images. Thus Gal 5:19–21: "The works of the flesh are plain: sexual immorality, impurity, sensuality, *worship of images* [εἰδωλολατρία], sorcery, hatred, strife, jealousy, anger, selfishness, dissension, partisanship, envy, drunkenness, debauchery, and the like. I warn you, as I warned you before, that those who do such things shall not inherit the kingdom of God." And similarly 1 Cor 6:9–10: "Do you not know that the unrighteous will not inherit the kingdom of God? Do not be deceived; neither the sexually immoral, *nor people who worship images* [εἰδωλολάτραι],

---

⁴⁸ That Paul speaks here of his auditors' gentile-ness in the past tense – "when you were gentiles" – is a puzzle, but see Concannon, *When You Were Gentiles*; and differently Joshua Garroway, *Paul's Gentile-Jews: Neither Jew nor Gentile but Both* (New York: Palgrave Macmillan, 2012).
⁴⁹ See further Sonja Anderson, "Idol Talk: The Discourse of False Worship in the Early Christian World" (PhD diss., Yale University, 2016).
⁵⁰ See further Sharp, "Courting Daimons in Corinth"; Martin Sanfridson, "Paul and Sacrifice in Corinth: Rethinking Paul's Views on Gentile Cults in 1 Corinthians 8 and 10" (PhD diss., McMaster University, 2022).

nor adulterers, nor soft men, nor sodomites, nor thieves, nor the greedy, nor drunkards, nor abusers, nor robbers will inherit the kingdom of God." All of these terms come from the lexicon of the moralists,[51] with the sole exception of εἰδωλολατρία, "worship of images," which refers not to *mores* but to cult. For most ancient people, offering cult to the gods at their established altars was just customary piety. It would not have occurred to them to single out for attention the presence of cult images, which were ubiquitous, much less to associate this religious commonplace with moral deviance.[52]

Paul, however, does make this inference. He comes from an aniconic tradition of Jewish piety, and what is more, he knows and republishes one particular etiological myth about how, long ago, the gentiles first began to worship images and to engage in debauchery, in turn. He relates this etiology in Romans 1:

The wrath of God is revealed from heaven upon all impiety and unrighteousness of people who suppress the truth in unrighteousness. For what can be known about God is plain to them, because God made it plain to them. Since the creation of the world, his invisible features – his eternal power and divinity – have been clearly perceived in the things that have been made, so that they are without excuse. For although they knew God they did not glorify him as God or give thanks, but they became futile in their thoughts, and their senseless heart was darkened. Claiming to be wise, they were made foolish, and exchanged the glory of the incorruptible God for the likeness of an image of humans or birds or animals or reptiles. Therefore God handed them over in the desires of their hearts to impurity, for the dishonoring of their bodies among them, who exchanged the truth of God for a falsehood and worshiped and offered cult to created things rather than the creator, who is blessed for ever, amen. For this reason God handed then over to passions of dishonor. Their females exchanged the natural use for that beyond nature, and the males likewise gave up the natural use of a female and were inflamed with their appetite for one another, males committing shamelessness with males and receiving in themselves the necessary recompense for their error. And just as they did not see fit to acknowledge God, God handed them over to an unfit mind, to do improper things. They were filled with all unrighteousness, wickedness, covetousness, and evil. (Rom 1:18–29)

[51] On the strong strand of moral philosophy in Paul, see Dingeldein, "Gaining Virtue, Gaining Christ."
[52] Indeed, the term εἰδωλολατρία is simply not current outside of Jewish and Christian Greek usage (see LSJ, *ad loc.*). See further Matthew V. Novenson, "On Christ and Idols, in Dialogue with Natalie Carnes" (forthcoming).

Although many interpreters have come to this passage looking for an account of the fall of humanity, Paul does not offer one.[53] Neither here nor anywhere else does Paul speak of a "fall." Here there is no mention of Adam (cf. 1 Cor 15:20–50; Rom 5:12–21), nor of Eve and the serpent (cf. 2 Cor 11:3). Here there is no "he," only "they." And *they* are people who "suppress the truth of God," "offer cult to created things," and "are inflamed with passions of dishonor" – in other words, gentiles.[54] Romans 1:18–32 is a chauvinist tale of the origins of gentile idolatry and immorality. Dale Martin accurately paraphrases as follows: "Once upon a time, even after the sin of Adam, all humanity was safely and securely monotheistic. At some point in ancient history most of humanity rebelled against God... As punishment for their invention of idolatry and polytheism, God 'handed them over' to depravity."[55]

Paul's version of this just-so story is the best known, but it is not the only nor even the first one. As interpreters have long noted, the first-century BCE Jewish author of Wisdom of Solomon explains the same phenomenon in almost exactly the same way: Gentiles long ago failed to acknowledge God for who he is, then mistook celestial bodies for gods, and finally manufactured ersatz gods from metal and stone:

All men who were ignorant of God were foolish by nature; and they were unable from the good things that are seen to know him who exists, nor did they recognize the craftsman while paying heed to his works; but they supposed that either fire or wind or swift air, or the circle of the stars, or turbulent water, or the luminaries of heaven were the gods that rule the

---

[53] Thus rightly Stowers, *Rereading of Romans*; and Martin, "Heterosexism and the Interpretation of Romans 1:18–32"; contra Morna D. Hooker, "Adam in Romans 1," *NTS* 6 (1960): 297–306; James D. G. Dunn, "Adam and Christ," in *Reading Paul's Letter to the Romans*, ed. Jerry L. Sumney (Atlanta: SBL Press, 2012), 125–138; and many others.

[54] It is often suggested that Rom 1:18–32 means to indict all humanity because of ἀνθρώπων in v. 18. But here the word is modified and thus restricted: ἀνθρώπων τῶν τὴν ἀλήθειαν ἐν ἀδικίᾳ κατεχόντων, "people *who suppress the truth in unrighteousness*," i.e., not all people without exception, but people who do such-and-such. By Paul's lights, all people are "under sin" (Rom 3:9), but not all people suppress the truth of God by worshiping idols.

[55] Martin, "Heterosexism and the Interpretation of Romans 1:18–32," 52–53. And see further Diana Swancutt, "The Disease of Effemination: The Charge of Effeminacy and the Verdict of God (Romans 1:18–2:16)," in *New Testament Masculinities*, ed. Stephen D. Moore and Janice Capel Anderson, SBLSS (Leiden: Brill, 2004), 193–234.

world... Miserable, with their hopes set on dead things, are the men who give the name "gods" to the works of men's hands, gold and silver fashioned with skill, and likenesses of animals, or a useless stone, the work of an ancient hand. (Wis 13:1–2, 10)

And, in Wisdom's telling as in Paul's, upon the gentiles' fateful decision to worship images, they fell prey to every kind of evil:

It was not enough for them to err about the knowledge of God, but they live in great strife due to ignorance, and they call such great evils peace. For whether they kill children in their initiations, or celebrate secret mysteries, or hold frenzied revels with strange customs, they no longer keep either their lives or their marriages pure, but they either treacherously kill one another, or grieve one another by adultery, and all is a raging riot of blood and murder, theft and deceit, corruption, faithlessness, tumult, perjury, confusion over what is good, forgetfulness of favors, pollution of souls, sex perversion, disorder in marriage, adultery, and debauchery. For the worship of idols not to be named is the beginning and cause and end of every evil. (Wis 14:22–27)

"The worship of idols is the beginning and cause and end of every evil"; that is the etiological myth in a nutshell. So close, in fact, is Wisdom's account to Paul's that there is now a firm majority opinion that the latter used the former as a source.

Consensus breaks down, however, on the question what Paul means by telling this tale: why he chooses to tell it, how it functions in his argument in Rom 1–3. The wrench in the works is the section immediately following the etiology, beginning at Rom 2:1: "You therefore are without excuse, O everyone who judges, for in the matter in which you judge the other person you condemn yourself, because you who judge do the same things." Because Rom 2:1–6 indicts the person who passes judgment on another, and because Rom 1:18–32 passes judgment on innumerable others (namely, gentile sinners), many interpreters take Paul to be qualifying, walking back, or even renouncing all that he had said in Rom 1:18–32. Some recent critics have even suggested that in Rom 1:18–32 Paul is actually parroting the view of his opponents, so that the passage represents not Paul's own view but its polar opposite.[56] More subtly, others have argued that Paul cites Wisdom's anti-idolatry polemic in order to implicate Jews and gentile god-fearers in it,

---

[56] See Campbell, *Deliverance of God*, 542–547.

as well, thereby gathering up all humanity in one great indictment.⁵⁷ This latter argument is more defensible, but even it tries too hard to avoid the implication that Paul means what Rom 1:18–32 says: that gentiles, being idolaters, are wicked in a way and to a degree that Jews are not. These modern interpreters want to be able to conclude that Wisdom of Solomon is chauvinist, but Paul is not. That conclusion, however, cannot be squared with the numerous other passages cited above. To be sure, Paul makes some subtle rhetorical moves in Rom 1–3, but the view of gentiles expressed in Rom 1:18–32 is Paul's own view.⁵⁸

Consequences

The account I have offered here both helps explain, and is further corroborated by, a notorious problem text in Rom 2, namely, the curious case of the virtuous pagan. The relevant part of the passage reads as follows: "Whenever gentiles – who by nature do not have the law [ἔθνη τὰ μὴ νόμον ἔχοντα φύσει] – do the things of the law, they who do not have the law are a law for themselves, who show the work of the law written on their hearts [τὸ ἔργον τοῦ νόμου γραπτὸν ἐν ταῖς καρδίαις αὐτῶν]" (Rom 2:14–15). My translation here presupposes one crucial decision: that the dative φύσει ("by nature") modifies not τὰ τοῦ νόμου ποιῶσιν ("they do the things of the law") but μὴ νόμον ἔχοντα ("they do not have the law"). That is, what Paul says is "natural" in this passage is not that gentiles sometimes obey the law but rather that gentiles lack the law. Admittedly, the syntax admits of either interpretation, but in the context of my argument above, the latter is by far the more likely: the natural state of gentiles, as Paul sees it, is to be without the law and without righteousness.⁵⁹ When, therefore, gentile sinners actually do the righteous deeds prescribed by the law, it can only be – in the most literal sense – an eschatological miracle. The gentiles whom

---

⁵⁷ See Linebaugh, "Announcing the Human"; Linebaugh, *God, Grace, and Righteousness*.
⁵⁸ As is the same portrait in the (post-Pauline, in my view) Eph 4:17–24, here v. 17: μηκέτι ὑμᾶς περιπατεῖν, καθὼς καὶ τὰ ἔθνη περιπατεῖ ἐν ματαιότητι τοῦ νοὸς αὐτῶν, "that you no longer walk as the gentiles walk in the futility of their mind." See the discussion by Matthew Thiessen, "The Construction of Gentiles in the Letter to the Ephesians," in *Early Reception of Paul the Second Temple Jew*, 13–25.
⁵⁹ *Pace*, among others, Sterling, "A Law to Themselves."

Paul describes here are not natural gentiles but pneumatic gentiles, gentiles filled with divine pneuma and thus endowed with moral superpower,[60] as Paul says about them in Rom 8: "God sent his son... so that the righteous precept of the law might be fulfilled in us [ἵνα τὸ δικαίωμα τοῦ νόμου πληρωθῇ ἐν ἡμῖν] who walk not according to the flesh but according to the pneuma" (Rom 8:3–4).

As this reading of Rom 2 illustrates, my hypothesis about Paul's ethnic chauvinism is not just a historical-psychological trifle; it impinges on other, more systemic and even theological aspects of the apostle's thought. One example is Paul's peculiar habit of speaking of the death and resurrection of Jesus as a χάρις, "gift" or "grace." John Barclay makes a related point in his recent, major study of grace in Paul, although he does not take the point as far as I am proposing. Barclay's point in this connection is that Paul especially emphasizes the *incongruousness* of the Christ-gift – the fact that God gives it without regard to the worthiness (or not) of the recipients. And Barclay further argues that Paul comes to this view in the context of and in defense of his gentile mission. Barclay writes, "The Christ-event *as gift* is thus the foundation of Paul's Gentile mission, in which Paul resists attempts to reinstitute preconstituted hierarchies of ethnic or social worth."[61] This is well said, but I would put a still finer point on it: That the sending of God's son is an incongruous gift is evident to Paul from the empirical fact that unscrupulous gentiles are the recipients of it. Were they not, Paul might not have interpreted it as a χάρις (as the Gospel of Matthew, for instance, does not do!). This, it seems to me, is roughly Paul's argument in Rom 4: "For this reason it is from trust [ἐκ πίστεως], so that it might be as a gift [κατὰ χάριν], in order that the promise be confirmed to all the seed, not only to that which is from Torah but also to that which is from the trust of Abraham, who is father of us all" (Rom 4:16). Paul's doctrine of grace – to borrow a later, theologizing term – presupposes and is actually predicated on his ethnic chauvinism.

A similar logic is at work in Paul's remarkably durable belief in the dawning new creation and the imminent parousia of Jesus. We know that the non-occurrence of the day of the lord posed an epistemic problem for early Christians (e.g., 2 Pet 3:4: "Scoffers will come and say, 'Where is the promise of his coming? For ever since the fathers fell

---

[60] As persuasively shown by Barclay, *Paul and the Gift*, 464–469.
[61] Ibid., 350.

asleep, all things have continued as they were from the beginning of creation'") and that many compensated by recasting their eschatology in less falsifiable terms. Thus 2 Peter gives a figurative interpretation of the passage of time ("With the lord one day is like a thousand years" [2 Pet 3:8 citing Ps 90:4]), and Hegesippus suggests that the kingdom of Christ is invisible rather than visible ("It was not a temporal nor an earthly kingdom, but a heavenly and angelic one, which would appear at the end of the world" [Hegesippus apud Eusebius, *Hist. eccl.* 3.20.6]). Paul, however, offers no such explanation. He does not experience the delay of the eschaton as an epistemic problem.[62] In fact, he does not realize that the eschaton is delayed at all. He thinks that he is beholding it with his own eyes. He writes to his gentiles in Asia Minor: "Did you experience such great things in vain [τοσαῦτα ἐπάθετε εἰκῇ] – if indeed it was in vain? He, then, who supplies you with the pneuma and works miracles among you [ὁ οὖν ἐπιχορηγῶν ὑμῖν τὸ πνεῦμα καὶ ἐνεργῶν δυνάμεις ἐν ὑμῖν], does he do so from works of Torah or from the hearing of trust?" (Gal 3:4–5) And to Rome: "I will not presume to speak of anything except what Christ worked through me for the obedience of the gentiles [ὑπακοὴν ἐθνῶν], by speech and work, in the power of signs and omens [ἐν δυνάμει σημείων καὶ τεράτων], in the power of the pneuma [ἐν δυνάμει πνεύματος]" (Rom 15:18–19). Paul believes *on empirical grounds* that the pneumatic transformation of all things is happening.[63] The evidence for this is that he sees gentiles living morally excellent lives, which – and this is the crucial premise – he thinks is an impossible feat. Had Paul been more charitable in his estimation of gentile moral capacity, he might have had to give up his apocalyptic certainty, but he was not, so he did not.

---

[62] A point well made by Wright, "Dogma of Delay," who, however, also tries to evade the issue entirely by claiming that the first generations after Jesus did not actually expect the end of the world as they knew it. In fact, they did. The interesting question for our purposes is how they interpreted the evidence of their senses in relation to this expectation.

[63] We often imagine the earliest Christ followers maintaining their apocalyptic belief in the face of empirical evidence to the contrary, a dynamic well theorized by John G. Gager, *Kingdom and Community: The Social World of Early Christianity* (Englewood Cliffs, NJ: Prentice Hall, 1975). In this instance, however, Paul thinks that he has the empirical evidence on his side (thus rightly Fredriksen, *Pagans' Apostle*). On Paul's interpretation of omens, now see Matthew T. Sharp, *Divination and Philosophy in the Letters of Paul*, ESRA (Edinburgh: Edinburgh University Press, 2023).

Objections

In sum, Paul's characteristic manner of talking about gentiles is a textbook example of ethnic chauvinism. Humanity comprises two subsets: Paul's own *ethnos*, the Jews, and all other *ethne* en bloc, the gentiles. Jews are naturally and normally virtuous, "gentile sinners" naturally and normally vicious. Gentiles' moral standards are lower, their conduct consistently worse, and their worst acts unspeakably awful. Their immorality is a direct consequence of their iconolatry; it began long ago when their ancestors first rejected the one true God and carved idols for themselves. (Paul's chauvinism therefore is not racism *sensu stricto*, because the fault lies not in gentile *seed* but in gentile *cult*.)[64] This is the view that Paul expresses across his authentic letters. I suspect, although I have no way of knowing, that he held this view relatively consistently for all of his adult life.[65] There is certainly no warrant for saying – as some New Perspective proponents have done – that Paul used to harbor ethnic chauvinism but renounced it upon his revelation of the risen Jesus.[66] Our evidence for what Paul thought prior to his revelation is close to nil, and all the evidence of ethnic chauvinism adduced in this chapter pertains to Paul *after* his revelation, Paul the apostle.

But someone will say, "There is no distinction [οὐ γάρ ἐστιν διαστολή], for all sinned and lack the glory of God, and are rightwised gratuitously by his gift through the ransom that is in Christ Jesus"

---

[64] On the terminological issue, see Isaac, *Invention of Racism*, here 24: "The major difference between racism and ethnic and other group prejudices is that such prejudices do not deny the possibility of change at an individual or collective level in principle. In these other forms of prejudice, the presumed group characteristics are not by definition held to be stable, unalterable, or imposed from the outside through physical factors: biology, climate, or geography." See also the time-worn but still valuable comment of Pierre L. Van den Berghe, *Race and Racism: A Comparative Perspective* (New York: Wiley, 1967), 12:
"[Racism] unlike ethnocentrism is not a universal phenomenon. Members of all human societies have a fairly good opinion of themselves compared with members of other societies, but this good opinion is frequently based on claims to cultural superiority.... Only a few human groups have deemed themselves superior because of the content of their gonads."

[65] See Hengel, *Pre-Christian Paul*; and Donaldson, *Paul and the Gentiles* for learned speculation on the views possibly held by the early Paul. And cf. my own more minimalist account in Novenson, "*Ioudaios*, Pharisee, Zealot."

[66] E.g., Dunn, *New Perspective on Paul*.

(Rom 3:22–24). Or again, "There is no distinction between Jew and Greek [οὐ γάρ ἐστιν διαστολὴ Ἰουδαίου τε καὶ Ἕλληνος], for the same lord is over them all, who is rich toward all who call upon him" (Rom 10:12). Or again, "We have charged that all, both Jews and Greeks, are under sin [Ἰουδαίους τε καὶ Ἕλληνας πάντας ὑφ' ἁμαρτίαν εἶναι]" (Rom 3:9). Or again, "There is neither Jew nor Greek [οὐκ ἔνι Ἰουδαῖος οὐδὲ Ἕλλην], there is neither slave nor free, there no male and female; for you are all one in Christ Jesus" (Gal 3:28). All these things Paul himself says. The question is how we are to square them with his other, more chauvinistic sayings discussed above. Many interpreters, swept up by the apostle's soaring rhetoric, simply give these texts hermeneutical pride of place over the others, concluding that while, say, Wisdom of Solomon may see a distinction between Jews and gentiles, Paul, for his part, renounces all such distinctions. But that is a non sequitur. As Origen already saw, the crucial thing in each of these texts is to grasp the particular distinction that Paul is denying, the particular sense in which he is saying that Jews and gentiles are one.[67] Indeed, precisely this hermeneutical question arises in Rom 3, where Paul emphatically denies the implication that he sees *no distinction whatsoever* between Jews and gentiles: "What then is the advantage of the Jew? Or what is the benefit of circumcision? Much in every way! First, they were entrusted with the oracles of God," and so on (Rom 3:1–2).

Upon closer inspection, the distinction-denying, pan-humanist sayings of Paul are entirely commensurable with the account of the apostle's chauvinism that I have offered above. "All people are under sin" (Rom 3:9) in the sense that sin holds sway over all mortals in the present evil age, from the primeval human to the messiah (Gal 1:4; Rom 5:12–21). But whereas gentiles' subjection to sin is evident to the naked eye (Paul's naked eye, at least: Rom 1:18–32), Jews' subjection to sin is non obvious. Paul says that he knows it only via the apocalyptic testimony of the Torah: "Scripture shut up everything under sin" (Gal 3:22); and again, "Whatever the law says it speaks to those who are in the law, so that every mouth may be shut and the

---

[67] Origen, *Commentary on Romans* 8.3.2. In the modern discussion, this methodological point is well made by Jouette M. Bassler, *Divine Impartiality: Paul and a Theological Axiom*, SBLDS 59 (Chico, CA: Scholars Press, 1982).

whole cosmos be liable to God" (Rom 3:19).[68] As he puts it in Romans 9–11, "God shut up all people in disobedience so that he might have mercy on all" (Rom 11:32). Whereas the gentiles' disobedience comprises their entire histories up to now (Rom 11:30), the Jews' disobedience comprises their present resistance to the news of the messiah (Rom 10:16; 11:28, 31).[69] "There is neither Jew nor Greek" (Gal 3:28) – just as "there is neither slave nor free, no male and female" – in the sense that the Torah no longer exercises its custodial function over these mundane social relations (Gal 3:23–25). In the dawning new creation, there is no more slavery, no more marriage, and no more gentile impurity.[70] It is not that Paul was once a chauvinist but then, when he met the risen Christ, repented of that attitude and became a humanist. Paul remained a chauvinist.[71] But he thought that, when gentile sinners trust in Christ and receive the divine pneuma, they cease to be constitutionally wicked and become miraculously virtuous.[72] (In this sense, they no longer present as gentiles, which is why Paul can write, "when you were gentiles..." [1 Cor 12:2]).[73] Meanwhile, Jews, when they trust in Christ and receive the divine pneuma, cease to be normally virtuous and become perfectly, perpetually virtuous. In that sense, "there is neither Jew nor Greek, for you are all one in Christ Jesus." In short, even these most universalizing sayings, so far from erasing or transcending ethnic difference, actually presuppose and underline the ethnic chauvinism of the apostle.

---

[68] On this crucial but too little understood point, see Novenson, "The Self-Styled Jew of Romans 2 and the Actual Jews of Romans 9–11." As Sharp, *Divination and Philosophy*, aptly puts it, Paul knows gentile sin via *omen* and Jewish sin via *oracle*.

[69] Thus rightly, Young, "Eschatological Myth of Jewish Sin."

[70] This is the import of Gal 3:28, as is powerfully shown by Karin B. Neutel, *A Cosmopolitan Ideal: Paul's Declaration "Neither Jew Nor Greek, Neither Slave Nor Free, Nor Male and Female" in the Context of First-Century Thought*. LNTS 513 (London: T&T Clark, 2015).

[71] On this point, especially in regard to the male-female clause, see Dale B. Martin, "The Queer History of Galatians 3:28," in *Sex and the Single Savior*, 77–90.

[72] Thus rightly, Fredriksen, "Pagan Justification by Faith," 807–808, although she unnecessarily restricts Paul's idea of pneumatic righteousness to gentiles.

[73] See Concannon, *When You Were Gentiles*, xi: "The *ethne*, constructed in Paul's rhetoric as people characterized by idolatry, have become not-*ethne* by changing their cultic practice. Paul's reasoning assumes a connection between cultic practice and ethnic identity: to change one's cultic practices and allegiances is also a means of changing one's ethnicity, becoming no longer *ethne* but now something else."

Conclusion

As with legalism in the previous chapter, my point here is not to suggest that Paul was more chauvinist than his contemporaries, or that he was more chauvinist than he was anything else, or otherwise to cast aspersions (or praise) on him. But it is the case that, measured by the rule we would use in any other case, Paul was an ethnic chauvinist. And to make this point is important because so many interpreters, especially in the wake of the New Perspective, have claimed that Paul's great, original contribution was precisely his anti-chauvinism. It was not. There were other Jewish thinkers, both before and after Paul, who were more anti-chauvinist than he,[74] as well as others, both before and after, who were less so. Paul's big idea lay elsewhere.[75] That the letters of the apostle should give voice to such chauvinism – which modern Christians (and indeed, modern people in general) rightly find objectionable – does of course pose a challenge for Christian theology and ethics. But it is no different in kind from the challenge posed by Paul's gender hierarchicalism (1 Cor 11:3–15), or his tolerance for chattel slavery (Philemon; 1 Cor 7:21–23), or his defence of the divine right of governments (Rom 13:1–7). It feels different, however, because we are still accustomed to thinking of Paul as an ally in the project of theorizing a trans-ethnic humanism.[76] He is not. He may turn out to be a valuable resource for us toward that end, but not without considerable constructive work on our part.[77]

---

[74] On these, see further Terence L. Donaldson, *Judaism and the Gentiles: Jewish Patterns of Universalism (to 135 CE)* (Waco, TX: Baylor University Press, 2007), especially his chapter 12 "Ethical Monotheism."

[75] Where exactly it lay is the subject of Chapters 8 and 9.

[76] See again Wright, Boyarin, and Badiou, cited at the beginning of this chapter. This habit of thought goes straight back to our disciplinary forebear F. C. Baur, who deliberately and effectively mediated Enlightenment cosmopolitanism to New Testament studies. See the essays in Bauspiess et al., *Baur and the History of Early Christianity*, especially Christof Landmesser, "Ferdinand Christian Baur as Interpreter of Paul: History, the Absolute, and Freedom," 147–176.

[77] A point well made by Charles H. Cosgrove, "Did Paul Value Ethnicity?" *CBQ* 68 (2006): 268–290, who answers his eponymous question by saying: not in the same way that we moderns do. As Troels Engberg-Pedersen has commented in a different context, we cannot responsibly discuss whether Paul's (or any ancient's) view is "a real option for us" until we have really, thoroughly understood that view in all its historical peculiarity. See Troels Engberg-Pedersen, *Paul and the Stoics* (Edinburgh: T&T Clark, 2000), 1–31, esp. 16–22; and Bernard Williams, *Ethics and the Limits of Philosophy* (London: Fontana, 1985), from whom Engberg-Pedersen takes the notion of "real options for us."

7 | Carnal Israel

Within a relatively short span of time – a century or two after the death of Jesus – it became fashionable for some early gentile Christians to think of themselves as Jews, as "the true Israel" over against the actual, empirical Israelites who lived alongside them in most of the great cities of the Mediterranean world. From the perspective of the history of religions, this is an entirely contingent and, in fact, rather strange development: that a religious sect should appropriate the ethnicity of its founding hero as a self-identifier. Muslims do not ordinarily style themselves "the true Arabs,"[1] nor Buddhists as "the true Indians," but many Christians, from antiquity down to the present, have persisted in imagining themselves as Jews – not as empirical Israel, but as true Israel, *verus Israel*, Israel in the eyes of God.

The earliest sure instance of this rhetorical *tour de force* is in Justin Martyr's mid-second century *Dialogue with Trypho the Jew*.[2] In the *Dialogue*, Justin undertakes to explain how Christianity, despite its apparent novelty, is in fact the legitimate flowering of Jewish scripture. One of Justin's themes is the identity of the people Israel, which he raises early in the *Dialogue*: Ἰσραηλιτικὸν γὰρ τὸ ἀληθινὸν πνευματικὸν καὶ Ἰούδα γένος καὶ Ἰακὼβ καὶ Ἰσαὰκ καὶ Ἀβραάμ... ἡμεῖς ἐσμεν, οἱ διὰ τούτου τοῦ σταυρωθέντος Χριστοῦ τῷ θεῷ προσαχθέντες, "For the true,

---

[1] On how the Christian and Muslim traditions, respectively, have navigated their relations to the ethnicity of the founding figure, see the perceptive discussion in Shabbir Akhtar, *The New Testament in Muslim Eyes: Paul's Letter to the Galatians* (London: Routledge, 2018).

[2] On this aspect of the *Dialogue*, see in particular Ben Zion Bokser, "Justin Martyr and the Jews," *JQR* 64 (1973): 97–122; David Rokeah, *Justin Martyr and the Jews,* JCP (Leiden: Brill, 2001). Matthijs den Dulk, *Between Jews and Heretics: Refiguring Justin Martyr's Dialogue with Trypho* (London: Routledge, 2018) has recently shown how much of Justin's polemic, ostensibly aimed at Jews, actually has Christian heretics in its sights. But the "true, spiritual Israel" motif, at least, seems to me to mean more or less exactly what it says.

Carnal Israel   161

spiritual Israelite race of Judah and Jacob and Isaac and Abraham...
are we who have been led to God through this crucified Christ" (Justin,
Dial. 11).³ Other ecclesiastical writers, taking a page from Justin's
book, perpetuated and elaborated upon the notion of a true or spiritual
Israel, namely Christians, in contrast to a carnal Israel comprising the
Jews.⁴ One key development, which is the focus of this chapter, is the
attribution of this idea by early Christian writers to the apostle Paul.
This attribution is well represented by Origen in his early third-century
work *De principiis*:⁵

The apostle, elevating our power of discernment, says somewhere, *Behold Israel according to the flesh* [1 Cor 10:18], as if there is an Israel according to the spirit [ὡς ὄντος τινὸς Ἰσραὴλ κατὰ πνεῦμα]. And in another place he says, *For it is not the children of the flesh that are the children of God* [Rom 9:8], *for not all who are descended from Israel belong to Israel* [Rom 9:6]. And, *neither is he a Jew who is one in the open, nor is that circumcision which is in the open, in the flesh; but he is a Jew who is one in secret, and circumcision is of the heart, in spirit not in letter* [Rom 2:28–29]. For if the determination of being a Jew depends upon what is in secret, it must be understood that, just as there is a race of bodily Jews, so also there is a race of those who are Jews in secret [ὥσπερ Ἰουδαίων σωματικῶν ἐστι γένος, οὕτω τῶν ἐν κρυπτῷ Ἰουδαίων ἐστί τι ἔθνος]. (Origen, *Princ*. 4.3.6)⁶

---

³ Greek text ed. Miroslav Marcovich, *Iustini Martyris Dialogus cum Tryphone* (Berlin: De Gruyter, 2005); translation mine.
⁴ On this whole tradition, see A. Lukyn Williams, *Adversus Judaeos: A Bird's-Eye View of Christian Apologiae until the Renaissance* (Cambridge: Cambridge University Press, 1935); Marcel Simon, *Verus Israel: A Study of the Relations between Christians and Jews in the Roman Empire, AD 135–425* (Oxford: Oxford University Press, 1986 [French original 1964]); Ora Limor and Guy G. Stroumsa, eds., *Contra Iudaeos: Ancient and Medieval Polemics between Christians and Jews*, TSMEMJ 10 (Tübingen: Mohr Siebeck, 1996); Graham Harvey, *The True Israel: Uses of the Names Jew, Hebrew, and Israel in Ancient Jewish and Early Christian Literature*, AGJU 35 (Leiden: Brill, 1996); Andrew S. Jacobs, *Remains of the Jews: The Holy Land and Christian Empire in Late Antiquity* (Stanford: Stanford University Press, 2004); Andrew S. Jacobs, *Christ Circumcised: A Study in Early Christian History and Difference* (Philadelphia: University of Pennsylvania Press, 2012); Buell, *Why This New Race*; Fredriksen, *Augustine and the Jews*.
⁵ On which theme see further Nicholas De Lange, *Origen and the Jews: Studies in Jewish-Christian Relations in Third-Century Palestine* (Cambridge: Cambridge University Press, 1976).
⁶ Text and trans. John Behr, *Origen, On First Principles*, 2 vols., OECT (Oxford: Oxford University Press, 2017).

Origen here provides a kind of *florilegium* of Pauline texts in support of the claim that there is such an entity as "Israel according to the spirit" or "a race of Jews-in-secret." For Origen, it is none other than Paul who "elevates our power of discernment" to enable us to perceive this invisible race.

A majority of modern New Testament scholars, it would seem, agree with this idea. From the four Pauline texts in Origen's *florilegium* – and several other, related passages – modern critics have reasoned that Paul is the author of the *verus Israel* motif, and indeed that salvation, for Paul, includes or even comprises entry into this true, spiritual Israel. What is more, this majority view cuts right across the various regions and traditions in which the study of Paul flourishes. From Germany and liberal Lutheranism, for instance, Udo Schnelle: "[The phrase] Ἰσραὴλ τοῦ θεοῦ ['the Israel of God,' Gal 6:16] can only mean the Galatian church in the inclusive sense... not empirical Israel."[7] From Britain and conservative Anglicanism, N. T. Wright: "Paul really does envisage people of any and every background being regarded as 'circumcision' and as 'Jew.'"[8] And from the United States and post-modern Judaism, Daniel Boyarin:

> [In Rom 2] Paul introduces his major concern throughout his ministry: producing a new, single human essence, one of "true Jews" whose "circumcision" does not mark off their bodies as ethnically distinct from any other human bodies.... "True Jewishness" ends up having nothing to do with family connection... but paradoxically consists of participating in a universalism, an allegory that dissolves those essences and meanings entirely.[9]

And we could cite many lesser lights, as well. It is Paul, we are told, who invented and bequeathed to Justin, Origen, and their successors the idea of a true, spiritual Israel comprising all and only Christians.

My purpose in this chapter is to argue that this influential idea is wrong, that Paul has a much more unreflective, essentialist understanding of Jewishness,[10] and that the *verus Israel* motif is a product of later gentile Christian theologizing. Our main task is to re-examine the several classic texts in which Paul supposedly redefines "Israel,"

---

[7] Udo Schnelle, *Apostle Paul: His Life and Theology*, trans. M. Eugene Boring (Grand Rapids, MI: Baker Academic, 2005 [German original 2003]), 590.
[8] Wright, *Paul and the Faithfulness of God*, 2:836–837.
[9] Boyarin, *Radical Jew*, 94–95.   [10] As per my argument in Chapter 6.

"Jew," and "circumcision" and to show that he does not actually do so. I will also suggest how this revisionist account fits in the bigger picture of the apostle's vision of God, Christ, Jews, and gentiles. So to the primary texts. There are six of them: three in the Letter to the Romans, and one each in Galatians, 1 Corinthians, and Philippians. We will discuss them in turn, focusing on the key question how Paul actually uses the ethnonyms "Israel" and "Jew" and the related term "circumcision."

Consider Israel According to the Flesh (1 Cor 10:18)

It is striking that the passage perhaps most cited in support of a "spiritual Israel" motif in Paul is one in which Paul says the (supposed) opposite. Recall Origen's reasoning: "The apostle says somewhere, *Behold Israel according to the flesh*, as if there were an Israel according to the spirit" (*Princ.* 4.3.6).[11] Origen's "as if there were" is an acknowledgment of a point that should be the first premise of any discussion of this issue: Paul never actually speaks of a "true Israel" or "spiritual Israel." Never and nowhere. And in fact, only once does he speak of "Israel according to the flesh." That one mention comes in 1 Cor 10, in the midst of a discussion of the ethics of the consumption of meat sacrificed at gentile shrines. Paul's point in the immediate context is that eating in a ritual meal makes the person who eats, a fellow of or participant with the deities involved. Of the Christ assembly, he says that their thanksgiving meal is a participation with the body and blood of Christ (1 Cor 10:16). Of sacred meals in gentile temples, he says that those who eat and drink the sacrifices are participants with *daemons* (1 Cor 10:20–21).[12] And as with the temple of Demeter in Corinth, so too with the temple of God in Jerusalem: βλέπετε τὸν Ἰσραὴλ κατὰ σάρκα· οὐχ οἱ ἐσθίοντες τὰς θυσίας κοινωνοὶ τοῦ θυσιαστηρίου εἰσίν; "Consider Israel according to the flesh. Are not those who eat the sacrifices

---

[11] Cf. Augustine's comment on the same verse in his *Adv. Jud.* 7.9: "This we know to be the carnal Israel; but the Jews do not grasp this meaning and as a result they prove themselves indisputably carnal." On this theme in Augustine, see further Fredriksen, *Augustine and the Jews*; Ra'anan S. Boustan, "Augustine as Revolutionary? Reflections on Continuity and Rupture in Jewish-Christian Relations in Paula Fredriksen's *Augustine and the Jews*," *JQR* 99 (2009): 74–87.

[12] On the mechanics of such participation, see Martin, *Corinthian Body*, 163–197; Sharp, "Courting Daimons in Corinth."

participants with the altar?" (1 Cor 10:18) That is, celebrants in the Jerusalem temple, too, are participants with their deity; not with *daemons*, as in Corinth, but with the altar of the one God over all.[13] "Israel according to the flesh" here means just Israel, the people whose temple is in their metropolis Jerusalem (thus rightly RSV: "Consider the people Israel").[14]

If so, then Origen's inference from this verse – "as if there were also an Israel according to the spirit" – is simply a *non sequitur*. The one does not entail the other. If we wanted to test it as a possible inference, then the most relevant evidence would be other places where Paul singles out particular persons or peoples "according to the flesh," of which there are in fact several. Jesus the son of God "comes from the seed of David according to the flesh [γενομένου ἐκ σπέρματος Δαυὶδ κατὰ σάρκα]" (Rom 1:3).[15] Abraham the patriarch is "our forefather according to the flesh [Ἀβραὰμ τὸν προπάτορα ἡμῶν κατὰ σάρκα]" (Rom 4:1).[16] The Israelites, Paul says, are "my brothers, my kinfolk according to the flesh [τῶν ἀδελφῶν μου τῶν συγγενῶν μου κατὰ σάρκα]" (Rom 9:3). Christ himself "comes from [Israel] according to the flesh [ἐξ ὧν ὁ Χριστὸς τὸ κατὰ σάρκα]" (Rom 9:5).[17]

Unsurprisingly, there is interpretive dispute around some of these parallel texts, too, but in any case, none of them either states or entails a counterpart "according to the spirit": a spiritual seed of David, a spiritual forefather Abraham, a spiritual messiah, etc. Daniel Boyarin, echoing Origen, comments on our verse, "Paul here is alluding to his

---

[13] This text gives the lie to the common post-70 CE Christian idea that the death and resurrection of Jesus had rendered the Jerusalem temple obsolete. Not so for Paul. See Jonathan Klawans, *Purity, Sacrifice, and the Temple: Symbolism and Supersessionism in the Study of Ancient Judaism* (Oxford: Oxford University Press, 2006), 213–246; Matthew Thiessen and Paula Fredriksen, "Paul and Israel," in *Oxford Handbook of Pauline Studies*, 371–388.

[14] This text, among others, suggests to me that Paul normally conflates, rather than distinguishes between, "Israel" and "Jews," contra Staples, *Resurrection of Israel*.

[15] On the syntax of this verse, see Nathan C. Johnson, "Romans 1:3–4: Beyond Antithetical Parallelism," *JBL* 136 (2017): 467–490.

[16] This phrase is clear enough, but the syntax of the verbal clause is less so. See the discussion in Hays, "Have We Found Abraham?"

[17] The much-discussed 2 Cor 5:16 is a red herring in this discussion, since here it is not Christ who is "according to the flesh," but rather Paul's (and others') *way of knowing* Christ; thus rightly J. Louis Martyn, "Epistemology at the Turn of the Ages," in *Theological Issues in the Letters of Paul* (London: T&T Clark, 1997), 89–110.

platonizing doctrine that external realities – things in the flesh – all have spiritual signifieds."[18] But in fact, Paul has no platonizing doctrine. Origen perhaps does,[19] but not Paul. As Troels Engberg-Pedersen has argued, Paul's cosmology is more Stoic (that is, monist and materialist) than it is anything else.[20] To be sure, Paul does sometimes trade on a flesh-versus-spirit contrast, though not a Platonic-cosmological one. Paul's formulaic contrast appears in discussions of moral discipline, not ethnicity, and he uses it to modify verbs, not nouns: "Walk by the pneuma, and do not gratify the desires of the flesh" (Gal 5:16); and so on.[21] In short, there is nothing about 1 Cor 10:18 to suggest that by saying "Israel according to the flesh" Paul means to imply that there is some other, parallel entity, a supposed Israel according to the spirit.

The Israel of God (Gal 6:16)

Although Paul never speaks of "Israel according to the spirit," in Galatians he does speak of "the Israel of God," which many interpreters have taken to be another way of saying the same thing. The phrase appears only once, at the very end of the letter, in a benediction formula. Just before this benediction, Paul summarizes the central exhortation of this polemical letter as follows: "Those who undergo circumcision do not even keep the law themselves, but they want you to undergo circumcision so that they may boast in your flesh. As for me, may I never boast except in the cross of our lord Jesus Christ, through whom the cosmos has been crucified to me, and I to the cosmos. For neither circumcision nor foreskin is anything, but: new creation" (Gal 6:13–15). There is an important clue here as to the identity of Paul's rivals, the anonymous "people who are troubling you" (whom the older commentaries mistakenly call "the Judaizers").

---

[18] Boyarin, *Carnal Israel*, 1.
[19] On the debate how far Origen can be classified as a middle Platonist, see Mark Julian Edwards, *Origen against Plato* (London: Ashgate, 2002).
[20] Engberg-Pedersen, *Paul and the Stoics*; Engberg-Pedersen, *Cosmology and Self*. The basic point stands, I think, even if Paul is not quite as maximally Stoic as Engberg-Pedersen suggests. Here see Stowers, "The Dilemma of Paul's Physics."
[21] So perhaps a Platonic moral psychology, in some texts, at least. See Wasserman, *Death of the Soul*; Dingeldein, "Gaining Virtue, Gaining Christ." But for a powerful argument that Paul is consistently Stoic-like even in his moral psychology, see Wilson, *Paul and the Jewish Law*.

Here they are called the περιτεμνόμενοι, "those who undergo circumcision," which, as Johannes Munck and others have argued, would seem to indicate not natural-born, eighth-day-circumcised Jews, but proselyte-circumcised gentiles.[22] "They undergo circumcision, and they want you to undergo circumcision." That observation will be important again when we consider Phil 3 shortly.

Following his peroration – "Neither circumcision nor foreskin is anything, but: new creation" – Paul adds a benediction, which reads as follows: καὶ ὅσοι τῷ κανόνι τούτῳ στοιχήσουσιν εἰρήνη ἐπ' αὐτοὺς καὶ ἔλεος καὶ ἐπὶ τὸν Ἰσραὴλ τοῦ θεοῦ (Gal 6:16). All the lexical items here are quite straightforward, but there is an ambiguity in the syntax: whether Paul means to issue a twofold blessing on one group of people, or two discrete, parallel blessings.[23] Most standard translations opt for the former interpretation, as, for example, the RSV: "Peace and mercy be upon all who walk by this rule, upon the Israel of God" (Gal 6:15–16). On this reading, "the Israel of God" stands in apposition to and effectively renames "all who walk by this rule." That is to say, Paul grants the name "Israel of God" to any and all people who comply with his solution to the circumcision controversy in Galatia. This, although it lacks the qualifiers "true" or "spiritual," would effectively be *verus Israel* theology by another name: Israel *according to the flesh* may comprise the Jewish people, but the Israel *of God* comprises all and only... Paulinists, people who take the apostle's point of view.[24]

But the syntax of the benediction need not be read this way, and in fact, the alternative construal is the more likely. On this alternative construal, it is not that Paul wishes peace and mercy upon a single group of people, named twice. Rather, he wishes peace upon one group of people, and mercy on another. The benediction comprises two, parallel clauses, as follows:

καὶ ὅσοι τῷ κανόνι τούτῳ στοιχήσουσιν εἰρήνη ἐπ' αὐτοὺς
καὶ ἔλεος καὶ ἐπὶ τὸν Ἰσραὴλ τοῦ θεοῦ

---

[22] Munck, *Paul and the Salvation of Mankind*; Collman, *Apostle to the Foreskin*. And see my fuller argument in Chapter 4.

[23] On the exegetical possibilities, see Ole Jakob Filtvedt, "God's Israel in Galatians 6.16: An Overview and Assessment of the Key Arguments," *CBR* 15 (2016): 123–140.

[24] The majority who read it this way usually call such people "gentile Christians," but in the context here, it is technically those who walk according to the rule pronounced by Paul in Gal 6:15.

> As many as walk by this rule, peace be upon them,
> and mercy also upon the Israel of God.

This translation leaves open the question who "the Israel of God" are, but it does eliminate the possibility that it is simply a title of honor granted by Paul to all who follow his rule. The next step, then, would be to inquire what the syntagm "Israel of God" would otherwise most naturally signify, to which the most likely answer by far is: the *ethnos* of the Jews.[25] (But the most relevant evidence in the Pauline corpus are the other texts under consideration in this chapter, so we cannot yet appeal to them for corroboration without begging the question.) In this connection, Susan Eastman has shown – against the assumption that Paul's benediction terminology is just vaguely benign – that ἔλεος, "mercy," is his particular term for God's posture toward Israel in Rom 9–11.[26] Hence nothing would be more natural than for Paul to wish mercy, in particular, upon Israel in Gal 6:16.[27] Perhaps, then we should render Ἰσραὴλ τοῦ θεοῦ, as Caroline Johnson Hodge suggests,[28] not "the Israel of God" – which might seem to suggest some Israel hitherto unknown – but simply "God's people Israel" – which sounds in English like the more conventional name that it is. E. P. Sanders reckoned that Gal 6:16 is the only time Paul ever uses "Israel" to mean something other than just the Jewish people.[29] I am suggesting that this passage is not an exception, after all. Paul wishes peace upon his gentiles-in-Christ, and he wishes mercy upon God's people Israel.

---

[25] Staples, *Idea of Israel*, argues that the ethnonym "Israel" always means the biblical twelve tribes, whereas "Judea" always means the old southern kingdom, the two tribes of Judah and Benjamin. But my own view, following Eyl, "I Myself Am an Israelite," is that – for Paul, at least – the two terms are more coextensive than that. "Israel" is the more baroque heritage name, useful for displays of ethnic authenticity, "Judea" the more prosaic, workaday label. See further Novenson, "*Ioudaios*, Pharisee, Zealot."
[26] Rom 9:23: "To make known the riches of his glory upon vessels of mercy which he prepared beforehand for glory"; Rom 11:31: "They presently do not comply with the mercy shown you, so that they too may receive mercy."
[27] Eastman, "Israel and the Mercy of God."
[28] Johnson Hodge, *If Sons Then Heirs*, 206n11.
[29] Sanders, *Paul, the Law, and the Jewish People*, 171–179, here 176: "Although Paul thought of the members of the church as heirs of the promises to Israel, he did not (with one exception [Gal 6:16]) give them the name."

We Are the Circumcision (Phil 3:3)

Thus far we have been looking at references to "Israel" in the letters of Paul, but the related terms "Jew" and "circumcision" also figure in this discussion. Indeed, a *crux interpretum* for those who find in Paul's letters a redefinition of Israel is the metonymic use of "circumcision" in Phil 3, where the apostle writes, ἡμεῖς γάρ ἐσμεν ἡ περιτομή, "We are the circumcision" (Phil 3:3). (RSV: "We are the *true* circumcision," but – tellingly – the word "true" is smuggled in by the translator.) Having just commended his colleague Epaphroditus to his audience, Paul writes,

Τὸ λοιπόν, ἀδελφοί μου, χαίρετε ἐν κυρίῳ. τὰ αὐτὰ γράφειν ὑμῖν ἐμοὶ μὲν οὐκ ὀκνηρόν, ὑμῖν δὲ ἀσφαλές. Βλέπετε τοὺς κύνας, βλέπετε τοὺς κακοὺς ἐργάτας, βλέπετε τὴν κατατομήν. ἡμεῖς γάρ ἐσμεν ἡ περιτομή, οἱ πνεύματι θεοῦ λατρεύοντες καὶ καυχώμενοι ἐν Χριστῷ Ἰησοῦ καὶ οὐκ ἐν σαρκὶ πεποιθότες.

Finally, my brothers, rejoice in the lord. To write the same things to you is not troublesome for me, and it is safe for you. Look out for the dogs. Look out for the bad workers. Look out for the mutilation. For we are the circumcision, who worship by the pneuma of God and boast in Christ Jesus and do not put confidence in the flesh. (Phil 3:1–3)

The passage is a warning against the influence of certain persons, rival teachers, but unfortunately we get precious little information about their program.[30] Here Paul only characterizes them, using colorful invective, as "the dogs, the bad workers, the mutilation." The first two terms tell us almost nothing of substance, but the third, κατατομή, "mutilation" or "incision" – a clear wordplay on περιτομή, "circumcision," in the following verse – strongly suggests that their program has something to do with that ritual; and the simplest, best explanation is that they advocate proselyte circumcision for gentile Christ-followers, as in Galatians. There is some corroboration for this hypothesis just a bit further on in the letter, where Paul writes,

---

[30] Attempts at reconstruction, some more valiant than others, include Klijn, "Paul's Opponents in Philippians III"; Lüdemann, *Opposition to Paul in Jewish Christianity*; Sumney, *Servants of Satan*; Kenneth Grayston, "The Opponents in Philippians 3," *ExTim* 97 (1986): 170–172; Demetrius K. Williams, *Enemies of the Cross of Christ: The Terminology of the Cross and Conflict in Philippians*, JSNTSup 223 (Sheffield: Sheffield Academic, 2002); Nina Nikki, *Opponents and Identity in Philippians* (Leiden: Brill, 2019).

"For many, of whom I often told you and now am telling you with tears, walk as enemies of the cross of Christ, whose end is destruction, whose god is the *koilia*, and whose glory is in their shame [ὧν ὁ θεὸς ἡ κοιλία καὶ ἡ δόξα ἐν τῇ αἰσχύνῃ αὐτῶν], who think on earthly things" (Phil 3:18–19). It is not certain but likely that this passage means to describe the same *dramatis personae* named in Phil 3:2 ("dogs, bad workers, mutilation").[31] The noun κοιλία, *koilia* ("belly" in polite modern versions) broadly signifies the abdomen, the lower parts of the trunk of the body (thus LSJ), and depending on context it can mean the stomach, the bowels, or the reproductive apparatus (male or female).[32] Similarly, αἰσχύνη, literally "shame," is often a euphemism for genitals (like Latin *pudendum*, or the quaint English expression "to cover one's modesty").[33] If these rival teachers advocate proselyte circumcision, then it makes good sense that Paul could call them "the mutilation" and say that "their god is the loins, their glory is in their genitals." (Harsh, yes, but by no means unusual by the standards of ancient invective.)[34]

But Paul insists that he, and not these people, represents περιτομή, "circumcision." "For we are the circumcision [ἡμεῖς γάρ ἐσμεν ἡ περιτομή], who worship by the pneuma of God and boast in Christ Jesus and do not put confidence in the flesh" (Phil 3:3). Paul snatches the title "circumcision" away from these people, suggesting that what they advocate is not circumcision at all but mutilation. But who are these people? The vast majority of critics have answered that, because they advocate circumcision, they must be so-called Jewish Christians, perhaps associated with or even identical with "the men from James" and "the circumcision party" mentioned in Gal 2.[35] On this premise, Paul is taking the title of honor "circumcision" away

---

[31] Contra those interpreters who unnecessarily multiply opponents here, e.g., Robert Jewett, "Conflicting Movements in the Early Church as Reflected in Philippians," *NovT* 12 (1970): 362–390.

[32] For this lattermost use, see LXX Deut 7:13; 28:4, 11, 18, 53; 30:9; 2 Kgdms 7:12 = 1 Chron 17:11; 2 Kgdms 16:11; 2 Chron 32:31; Ps 131:11. On this likely sense here, see Watson, *Paul, Judaism, and the Gentiles* (2nd ed.), 143–146. Further on κοιλία in the letters of Paul, see Karl Olav Sandnes, *Belly and Body in the Pauline Epistles*, SNTSMS 120 (Cambridge: Cambridge University Press, 2002).

[33] Paul himself uses this idiom in 1 Cor 12:23: "Our shameful parts have greater modesty."

[34] See further Collman, "Beware the Dogs"; Collman, *Apostle to the Foreskin*.

[35] On this majority view and my full argument against it, see Chapter 4.

from the Jews, to whom it traditionally belonged, and claiming it for (Pauline) "Christians" by means of an audacious act of redefinition. "Circumcision" now means just "worshiping by the pneuma of God and boasting in Christ Jesus." Scholars who take this view have marveled at the implications: That Paul would say that circumcision according to the law of Moses is mutilation and phallus-worship might seem incredible, but that just shows how radical a transvaluation he thinks follows from the Christ event![36]

But this is all wrong. That Paul would say that circumcision according to the law of Moses is mutilation and phallus-worship is actually not credible. And in fact, Paul does not say that what he excoriates here is circumcision according to the law of Moses. That is a modern inference, premised on the lazy and false assumption that Jews are for circumcision, gentiles against it. But as noted above, there are very good reasons to think that the proselyte-circumcision advocates whom Paul opposes are not Jews but gentiles who have recently undergone proselyte circumcision themselves (cf. περιτεμνόμενοι in Gal 6:13). Philippians 3 adds further evidence in favor of this reconstruction. "Dogs" and "bad workers" make good sense as inter-ethnic terms of abuse, by which Paul (a Jew) slanders his (gentile) opponents. (Recall how Jesus calls the Syro-Phoenician woman a "dog" in Mark 7:27–28; Matt 15:26–27).[37] "Mutilation" here means not traditional Jewish circumcision – which Paul praises moments later in Phil 3:5, not to mention elsewhere – but proselyte circumcision, the circumcision of adult male gentiles.[38] Eighth-day Jewish circumcision such as Paul's own (Phil 3:5) confers benefit (Rom 2:25), but proselyte circumcision is mutilation. Modern readers tend to think of all circumcision as more or less alike, with proselyte circumcision being just a "better late than

---

[36] Thus, e.g., Wright, *What Saint Paul Really Said*, 95.

[37] On the dog epithet as ethnic slander, see Nanos, "Wagging an Exegetical Dog"; Matthew Thiessen, "Gentiles as Impure Animals in the Writings of Early Christ Followers," in *Perceiving the Other in Ancient Judaism and Early Christianity*, 19–32. Alternatively, "dogs" here could be, like κοιλία and αἰσχύνη in this passage, yet another reference to the penis, as is argued by Collman, "Beware the Dogs."

[38] Andrew Rillera ("Paul's Philonic Opponent") argues that Paul calls this proselyte circumcision mutilation because of the particular procedure hypothetically used: *milah* as opposed to *periah* (to use the rabbinic terms of art). Maybe, but Paul nowhere makes this medical distinction himself. And moreover, it seems clear to me, Paul opposes proselyte circumcision for gentiles-in-Christ no matter what particular procedure is used.

It Is Not the Jew on Display (Rom 2:28–29)

never" alternative to eighth-day circumcision. But Paul (like Ezra and Jubilees before him) does not see it this way. He thinks that gentiles are naturally foreskinned (Rom 2:27), Jews naturally circumcised (Gal 2:15).[39] When, therefore, gentiles fetishize adult circumcision, Paul thinks, *that* amounts to pagan phallus worship (Phil 3:19). They are the κατατομή, "mutilation." "We" – Paul himself and other right-thinking, eighth-day circumcised apostles[40] – represent the περιτομή, "circumcision." So far from taking the title "circumcision" away from Jews and awarding it to gentiles, in Phil 3 Paul actually does the opposite. He takes it back from proselyte-circumcised gentiles and restores it to Jewish apostles like himself.

It Is Not the Jew on Display (Rom 2:28–29)

We turn now to the Letter to the Romans, in which many interpreters have detected a programmatic redefinition of Israel. The first of the three relevant passages in Romans has arguably done more mischief than any of the other texts discussed in this chapter, all because of a widespread and persistent mistranslation. This mistranslation is a fixture in many standard modern versions, but I will illustrate by referring to the RSV, which renders Rom 2:28–29 as follows: "For he is not a real Jew who is one outwardly, nor is true circumcision something external and physical. He is a Jew who is one inwardly, and real circumcision is a matter of the heart, spiritual and not literal. His praise is not from men but from God." I have claimed above that Paul never speaks of a "true Israel" or "spiritual Israel." According to the RSV and other standard translations, however, here in Rom 2 he does speak of "the real Jew" and "the true circumcision," which, on the face of it, looks like a smoking gun. And in fact, the majority who find a *verus Israel* theology in Paul point to Rom 2:28–29 as the decisive

---

[39] See Hayes, *Gentile Impurities*; Thiessen, *Contesting Conversion*; Thiessen, *Paul and the Gentile Problem*.
[40] To my mind, this is the most natural referent for the first-person plural pronoun here. Alternatively, it could mean the authors of the letter: Paul and Timothy (Phil 1:1). If the latter, that would seem to suggest that Timothy is an eighth-day circumcised Jew, which would contradict Acts 16:1–3. But then, Acts could just be wrong about Timothy.

evidence in favor of their hypothesis, the "true Jew" to contrast with "Israel according to the flesh."[41]

But against this interpretation stand two powerful objections.[42] First and most damning, the adjectives "true" and "real" are not in the Greek text of Rom 2:28–29 – anywhere in the manuscript tradition – but, yet again (!), are supplied by modern translators. And modern translators supply them precisely because of their prior, inherited assumption that this passage underwrites a *verus Israel* theology (as they do with "[true] circumcision" in Phil 3:3). A more honest translation, without these loaded additions, would read something like: "For he is not a Jew who is one outwardly, nor is circumcision external and physical..." and so on.[43] Such a translation would do away with the specious true-Jew-versus-counterfeit-Jew distinction suggested by the RSV. But it would still suggest, wrongly, that Paul's point here is to raise and to answer the question: Who is a Jew?[44] (Answer, according to the RSV: Not the literally, physically circumcised person but the "Jew inwardly.")

And here lies the second objection, which has to do with the syntax of the sentence. The Greek reads: οὐ γὰρ ὁ ἐν τῷ φανερῷ Ἰουδαῖός ἐστιν οὐδὲ ἡ ἐν τῷ φανερῷ ἐν σαρκὶ περιτομή, ἀλλ' ὁ ἐν τῷ κρυπτῷ Ἰουδαῖος καὶ περιτομὴ καρδίας ἐν πνεύματι οὐ γράμματι, οὗ ὁ ἔπαινος οὐκ ἐξ ἀνθρώπων ἀλλ' ἐκ τοῦ θεοῦ. My claim is that the more intelligible reading of the Greek takes "Jew" not as the predicate but as the subject of the sentence. In other words, the passage asks not, *Who is a Jew?* but rather, *Who gets praise from God?* Here I am following an

---

[41] E.g., Boyarin, *Radical Jew*, 79: "[Here] the ethical dualisms of the Bible are mapped onto hermeneutical, anthropological, and ontological dualisms of Plato in a way that often seems almost seamless"; Wright, *What Saint Paul Really Said*, 138: "God has called into being a new community (2:25–29), in which circumcision and uncircumcision are alike irrelevant, and in which what matters is whether or not one is – a Jew!" Collins (*Invention of Judaism*, 186), interestingly, assumes this majority interpretation of Rom 2:28–29, but then notes that it jars with Paul's usual idiom: "In one passage (Rom 2:28–29) Paul seems to redefine what it means to be a *Ioudaios*, but most often he uses that term for those who live by the law of Moses." Indeed. Perhaps, then, the problem lies with the majority interpretation of Rom 2:28–29.

[42] Here I make the case briefly and summarily. I discuss it at greater length and in greater detail in Novenson, "The Self-Styled Jew of Romans 2 and the Actual Jews of Romans 9–11."

[43] The NASB and NIV are better than the RSV and NRSV in this respect.

[44] This question is admittedly an important one in some Roman-period Jewish texts (on which see Cohen, *Beginnings of Jewishness*, 11–106), just not this one.

unpublished proposal by Hans Arneson.⁴⁵ As Arneson notes, the lone verb in this sentence is ἐστιν ("he, she, or it is") in the first clause, but the interpreter must decide on which side of the verb to read "Jew" – as subject or as predicate. The RSV and most others unthinkingly read "Jew" after the verb, as the predicate: "*He is a [real] Jew* who does so-and-so." But we can just as well – or better, in fact – read it before the verb, as the subject: "It is the Jew in secret, not the Jew on display, *whose praise is from God.*"⁴⁶ This rendering is more economical, using no more verbs than the sense demands, and does not smuggle in the specious notion of "the true Jew." Understood in this much more plausible way, our passage reads as follows: "For it is not the Jew on display, nor the circumcision on display in the flesh, but the Jew in secret, and the circumcision of the heart in pneuma, not in letter, whose praise comes not from people but from God."

The passage, then, is not about who is a real Jew, but about who gets praise from God. The two kinds of people Paul imagines who might hope for praise from God are "the Jew on display" (whose circumcision is on display in the flesh) and "the Jew in secret" (whose heart is circumcised). (N.B. "On display" versus "in secret," not "outward" versus "inward," which is yet another mistranslation, this one premised upon modern theories of religion as inwardness.)⁴⁷ But who are these two types? Under the long shadow of Christendom, interpreters

---

⁴⁵ Another compelling appeal to Arneson's proposal is Thiessen, "Paul's Argument against Gentile Circumcision"; Thiessen, *Paul and the Gentile Problem*, 57–59.

⁴⁶ Staples, *Resurrection of Israel*, raises the formidable – though not, in my view, decisive – objection that "Jew" must be the predicate of the clause due to the placement of the enclitic ἐστιν after Ἰουδαῖός rather than after οὐ γάρ. I concede that the more natural way to write the sentence (as I understand it) would have been to start with οὐ γάρ ἐστιν. But I do not concede that the way Paul actually writes it entails Staples's interpretation ("The person on display is not a Jew"). Wackernagel's Law, to which Staples appeals, is a "law" only in the linguistic sense: an observed pattern, not an obligation upon writers (not to mention its extremely high level of generalization). Like all such laws, it runs into numerous exceptions, of which I think Rom 2:28–29 is one. On this issue, see the caveats in David Goldstein, *Classical Greek Syntax: Wackernagel's Law in Herodotus* (Leiden: Brill, 2016), 5: "Wackernagel's Law has no explanatory power... [It] is an epiphenomenon that results from the syntactic and prosodic organization of the clause.... [It] is not a 'law' in the sense of a prescriptive linguistic convention."

⁴⁷ An important point well made by Barclay, "Paul and Philo on Circumcision," 554–555.

have most often taken them to mean Jews and Christians, respectively. But of course, circumcision of the heart is a very old Jewish idea, well known from the Torah (Lev 26:41; Deut 10:16; 30:6), prophets (Jer 4:4; 9:25; Ezek 44:9), and Dead Sea Scrolls (1QS 5:26; 1QH^a 21:5), where it does not exclude or replace but rather supplements circumcision of the (Jewish) penis.[48] Likewise, the idea that God praises modest Jewishness rather than ostentatious Jewishness is an inner-Jewish axiom,[49] not any kind of transferal of the title "Jew" to some other group. A century later, the gentile Justin Martyr will argue that Christians receive heart-circumcision *in lieu of* Jewish penis-circumcision.[50] But that idea never occurs to Paul, for whom circumcision of the heart is an index of *Jewish* piety,[51] as it is in all the other Jewish sources in which it appears. (Indeed, this intra-Jewish frame of reference might help explain why Rom 2:29 is the only verse in Paul, and indeed anywhere in the New Testament, that makes any reference at all to circumcision of the heart!)[52]

---

[48] See Werner E. Lemke, "Circumcision of the Heart: The Journey of a Biblical Metaphor," in *A God So Near: Essays on Old Testament Theology in Honor of Patrick D. Miller*, ed. Brent A. Strawn and Nancy R. Bowen (Winona Lake, IN: Eisenbrauns, 2003), 299–319.

[49] There is a near-perfect parallel in Jesus's sermon on the mount in Matt 6:1–6, here v. 1: "Take care not to do your righteousness before people, to be seen by them, for in that case you do not have a reward from your father in heaven." Indeed, Matt 6:4, 6 uses the very phrase (ἐν τῷ κρυπτῷ) that Paul does in Rom 2:29, on which parallel see W. D. Davies and Dale C. Allison, *The Gospel according to Saint Matthew*, 3 vols., ICC (London: T&T Clark, 2004 [1988]), 1:575–577.

[50] Justin, *Dial.* 19: "*You* [Jews], who are circumcised according to the flesh, have need of *our* [Christian, heart] circumcision. But we, having the latter, do not require the former." And *Dial.* 92: "We [Christians], in the foreskin of our flesh, trust God through Christ and have the circumcision that benefits us who receive it, namely: [circumcision] of the heart." On circumcision in Justin, see further Andrew S. Jacobs, "Dialogical Differences: (De-)Judaizing Jesus' Circumcision," *JECS* 15 (2007): 291–335.

[51] As Collman, *Apostle to the Foreskin*, demonstrates, Paul's view is that all Christ-believers receive the pneuma of God in their hearts, but only Jewish Christ-believers get circumcised hearts.

[52] On the significance of this almost total silence, see Collman, *Apostle to the Foreskin*; contra many interpreters who see heart circumcision as central to Paul's program, e.g., Wright, *Paul and the Faithfulness of God*; Staples, *Resurrection of Israel*; Kyle B. Wells, *Grace and Agency in Paul and Second Temple Judaism: Interpreting the Transformation of the Heart*, NovTSup 157 (Leiden: Brill, 2015).

There is, moreover, one further layer to this passage. I think, and have argued at length elsewhere,[53] that the particular target of Paul's criticism of "circumcision on display" that "wins praise from people" is proselyte circumcision, not traditional eighth-day Jewish circumcision. Important here is the beginning of this section at Rom 2:17: "You, if you call yourself a Jew and rest in the law… You, then, who teach another, do you not teach yourself?" (Rom 2:17–21). Building on the work of Runar Thorsteinsson, David Frankfurter, and Matthew Thiessen,[54] I propose that the person who "calls himself a Jew" in Rom 2:17 is not a representative of the Jews but, as the phrase suggests, a self-styled Jew, that is to say, a judaizing gentile.[55] In Rom 2:28–29, Paul concludes that proselyte circumcision is, by definition, ostentatious.[56] It is in the flesh and for display; hence it can only win praise from people, never from God.[57] In the near context, Paul explains, "Circumcision does confer benefit if you practice the Torah" (Rom 2:25), but proselyte circumcision violates the Torah's eighth-day commandment (Gen 17:14 LXX), so it is not only ostentatious but positively transgressive.[58] In sum, then, Rom 2 is emphatically not about taking the title of honor "Jew" away from Jews and bestowing it on "Christians," but rather – exactly like

---

[53] Novenson, "The Self-Styled Jew of Romans 2 and the Actual Jews of Romans 9–11."
[54] Thorsteinsson, *Paul's Interlocutor in Romans 2*; Frankfurter, "Jews or Not?"; Thiessen, *Contesting Conversion*; Thiessen, *Paul and the Gentile Problem*.
[55] The strongest objection known to me is Windsor, "The Named Jew and the Name of God." Windsor argues that ἐπονομάζῃ can only be passive, never middle-reflexive, thus: "are called," not "call oneself." While he is right about the best-attested forms of the verb, in my view his argument tries too hard to preclude a usage that is well within the range of the morphologically possible. But in any case, the crucial point is not the voice of the verb but the lexeme itself: Paul only allows that this person *is called*, not that he *is*, a Jew. He has the name but not the thing, as Origen (*Comm. Rom.* 2.11) rightly understood. See also Sloan, "Paul's Jewish Addressee," who rightly separates the question of the ethnicity of the interlocutor from the question of a supposed "critique of Judaism" (though, in my view, Sloan nevertheless misidentifies the interlocutor).
[56] Complementing Shaye Cohen's point in his essay "How Do You Know a Jew in Antiquity When You See One?" in *Beginnings of Jewishness*, 25–68: you generally did *not* know a Jew when you saw one, in part because Jewish infant circumcision was not ostentatious.
[57] Cf. the absolutely identical judgment in Gal 1:10; 5:11; 6:12!
[58] As he expressly says in Rom 2:27: σὲ τὸν διὰ γράμματος καὶ περιτομῆς παραβάτην νόμου, "you who through the letter and circumcision are a transgressor of the law."

Galatians and Philippians – about urging gentiles to choose Christ-faith, not proselyte circumcision, as their means of access to the one God. Standard translations notwithstanding, then, Rom 2:28–29 contributes precisely nothing to a supposed Pauline *verus Israel* theology.

Not All Those from Israel Are Israel (Rom 9:6)

Those interpreters who have thought – contrary to my argument in this chapter – that Rom 2 *is* about redefining Jewishness and circumcision have often pointed, by way of corroboration, to the beginning of Rom 9, where Paul writes οὐ γὰρ πάντες οἱ ἐξ Ἰσραὴλ οὗτοι Ἰσραήλ, "Not all those from Israel are Israel" (Rom 9:6). Here – so their argument goes – Paul expressly distinguishes between two Israels, which (these interpreters infer) we may take to be fleshly and spiritual, outward and inward, counterfeit and true, respectively, completing a tidy parallel with the other passages discussed here.[59] In fact, none of this follows. Here, however, the problem is not the translation, which is basically uncontroversial, but the inferences that interpreters draw from this verse.

At this point in the letter, Paul is trying to explain – to his audience and to himself – why, if the Torah and the prophets testify to God's sending of the messiah Jesus (Rom 3:21), the custodians of the Torah and the prophets, the Jews (Rom 3:2), do not believe Paul's announcement, while a surprising number of unwashed gentiles apparently do believe it (Rom 9:30–31). Paul's explanation of this state of affairs takes up all of Rom 9–11 and involves a number of different arguments.[60] Our passage (Rom 9:6: "Not all those from Israel are Israel") comes at the beginning of this discourse, where the burden is to explain

---

[59] E.g., N. T. Wright, "Romans 9–11 and the New Perspective," in *Pauline Perspectives*, 404: "[Here in Rom 9:6] Paul uses the word 'Israel' itself, as he does in Galatians 6.16, in a paradoxical and polemical way, to refer sometimes to 'Israel according to the flesh' and sometimes to that larger company of believing Jews and believing gentiles."

[60] See my longer discussion in *Paul, Then and Now*, 91–117; J. Ross Wagner, *Heralds of the Good News: Isaiah and Paul "in Concert" in the Letter to the Romans*, NovTSup 101 (Leiden: Brill, 2002); and the essays in Florian Wilk and J. Ross Wagner, eds., *Between Gospel and Election: Explorations in the Interpretation of Romans 9–11*, WUNT 257 (Tübingen: Mohr Siebeck, 2010); and Todd D. Still, ed., *God and Israel: Providence and Purpose in Romans 9–11* (Waco, TX: Baylor University Press, 2017).

why not all Jews, only a few, are on board with the apostolic message. It is in this context that Paul writes: Οὐχ οἷον δὲ ὅτι ἐκπέπτωκεν ὁ λόγος τοῦ θεοῦ. οὐ γὰρ πάντες οἱ ἐξ Ἰσραὴλ οὗτοι Ἰσραήλ· οὐδ' ὅτι εἰσὶν σπέρμα Ἀβραάμ πάντες τέκνα, ἀλλ'· ἐν Ἰσαὰκ κληθήσεταί σοι σπέρμα, "It is not as if the word of God has fallen. For not all those from Israel are Israel. Nor is it the case that all the children are seed of Abraham, but rather: *In Isaac your seed shall be called* [Gen 21:12]" (Rom 9:6–7). Paul is citing the story of Abraham's two sons, Ishmael and Isaac, to establish the motif of divine election, the choice of a few out of many.[61] He then corroborates by invoking the next generation, Isaac's two sons: "Jacob I loved, Esau I hated" (Rom 9:10–13). These examples illustrate what Paul means by saying that "Not all those from Israel are Israel": God chooses a few from among the many as the bearers of the divine purpose.[62] Hence the absence of the many does not mean that God has failed (Rom 9:6); it is just that he is deliberately using only a few, for the time being.

For the time being, because Paul will go on to claim that the many will all come around in due course (on this, more below). But Rom 9:6 – "Not all those from Israel are Israel" – is his effort to explain the present state of affairs in which Paul and other like-minded Jews are, from Paul's perspective, on the side of the angels (Rom 11:1), while most of his co-ethnics are not. He argues, first, that this is only temporary and, second, that it has venerable precedent in the history of the ancestors. The key thing, for our purposes, is the direction of Paul's distinction between "those from Israel" and "Israel": He reasons to fewer, not more,[63] and certainly not other. What the *verus Israel* hypothesis needs is an "Israel" that is *other than* and *more inclusive than* the nation of Israel (i.e., an "Israel" comprising the Christian church), but in Rom 9:6 Paul supplies precisely the opposite of this. So far from redefining and expanding Israel, he winnows Israel

---

[61] On which see Joel S. Kaminsky, *Yet I Loved Jacob: Reclaiming the Biblical Concept of Election* (Nashville: Abingdon, 2007).
[62] See Wagner, *Heralds of the Good News*, 45–51; Barclay, *Paul and the Gift*, 528–532.
[63] To his credit, Gathercole, *Where Is Boasting*, 207 rightly sees this issue, even if (in my view) he is still too beholden to the mistaken assumption that Paul redefines Israel. Gathercole writes, "Paul is not merely redefining these terms so that they include (some) gentiles; he is also redefining them in such a way as to exclude many Jews." There is, in fact, no redefinition here, but there is a remnant argument, the postulation of a (temporary) Israel within Israel.

down. "Not all those from Israel are Israel." There is nothing at all here about others who used to be outside Israel somehow finding a way in. "It is not the children of the flesh who are children of God, rather: the children of the promise will be counted as seed" (Rom 9:8). Admittedly, in Gal 3–4 Paul uses similar terms (children of flesh, children of promise, counted as seed) with reference to gentiles-in-Christ, but the context in Rom 9 is very different. Here the distinction is between Jews-currently-in-Christ and the rest of Israel. Paul thinks this distinction, in good prophetic fashion, by channelling classical remnant theology (Rom 9:27–29),[64] but does nothing at all to redefine or reassign ethnicity.

All Israel Will Be Preserved (Rom 11:26)

Paul's long discourse on God, Israel, and the gentiles (Rom 9–11) begins with the passage just discussed (Rom 9:6) and ends with our next and final passage. If Rom 9 is Paul's diagnosis of the present situation, Rom 11 is his remarkably optimistic vision of a future resolution: although presently only an elect few Jews recognize the righteousness of God (Rom 10:3), in due course all Jews will. It is inconceivable to Paul that they would not do so.[65] This is how I understand the logic of the discourse up to the end of Rom 11, where Paul writes, "For a hardening in part has come to Israel, until the fullness of the gentiles come in, and in this way all Israel will be preserved [καὶ οὕτως πᾶς Ἰσραὴλ σωθήσεται], as it is written, *The deliverer will come from Zion, he will turn away impiety from Jacob, and this is my covenant with them, when I take away their sins* [Isa 59:20–21 OG]" (Rom 11:25–27).

On this passage, at least, my reading would find more than a little agreement from other critics. For many, verse 25, in which "Israel" is expressly contrasted with "the gentiles" – "A hardening in part has come to *Israel*, until the fullness of *the gentiles* come in" – makes it overwhelmingly likely that "Israel" in the following sentence – "All Israel will be saved" – must also mean the

---

[64] Wagner, *Heralds of the Good News*, 92–117.
[65] Thus rightly, Paula Fredriksen, *Sin: The Early History of an Idea* (Princeton: Princeton University Press, 2012), 49: "Paul thus envisages a divine comedy, a cosmic happy ending."

ethnos of the Jews.⁶⁶ Thoroughgoing proponents of the *verus Israel* hypothesis, however, do not concede even this. Boyarin, for instance, writes, "Because the signifier Israel is and remains central for Paul, it has been transformed in its signification into another meaning, an allegory for which the referent is the new community of the faithful Christians."⁶⁷ And Wright: "Instead of saying, 'Israel in verse 25 is ethnic, so it must be in verse 26 as well,' we ought to say, 'Israel in verse 25 consists of the whole people of God, within which many Jews are presently 'hardened,' but into which many gentiles are being incorporated, so 'all Israel' in verse 26 must reflect that double existence."⁶⁸ But this interpretation – although I suppose it has the virtue of consistency – effectively leaves Paul bereft of any words at all with which he might signify his own co-ethnics, should he ever want to (which he does, very often!). Contra Boyarin and Wright, "all Israel" in Rom 11:26 means not a redefined "Israel" comprising both Jews and gentiles, but rather the whole Jewish people as opposed to the meager part who are presently on board with Paul's message when he writes his letter to Rome.⁶⁹

This is further confirmed by the citation from Old Greek Isaiah which Paul attaches to his declaration: "In this way all Israel will be preserved, as it is written, *The deliverer will come from Zion, he will turn away impiety from Jacob, and this is my covenant with them, when I take away their sins* [Isa 59:20–21 OG]" (Rom 11:26–27). On the great and final day that Paul imagines, the deliverer (by which I think Paul means the messiah, though he could instead mean

---

⁶⁶ Jason Staples ("What Do the Gentiles Have to Do with 'All Israel'? A Fresh Look at Romans 11:25–27," *JBL* 130 [2011]: 371–390; Staples, *Resurrection of Israel*) agrees that the referent here is an *ethnos*, but disagrees about which *ethnos*, exactly. He argues that "all Israel" in Rom 11:26 means all twelve tribes of Israel listed in the Hexateuch, as opposed to just the two southern tribes that would eventually become Roman Judea. But where Staples distinguishes between *Judah (and Benjamin)* on the one hand and *the ten lost tribes* on the other, Paul distinguishes between *Israel* on the one hand and *the gentiles* on the other. The source of the error here, in my view, is Staples's construction of an artificial "Jewish restoration eschatology," which forces the many, diverse Jewish eschatologies in our sources onto a single Procrustean bed. On the enduring allure of the ten lost tribes myth in cultural history, see Zvi Ben-Dor Benite, *The Ten Lost Tribes: A World History* (Oxford: Oxford University Press, 2009).
⁶⁷ Boyarin, *Radical Jew*, 202.
⁶⁸ Wright, *Paul and the Faithfulness of God*, 2:1244.
⁶⁹ On this point, see further Young, "Eschatological Myth of Jewish Sin."

God)[70] will come from Zion and turn away impiety from Jacob. Paul's use (of Deutero-Isaiah's use) of the patriarchal name "Jacob" here seems to me decisive, even though we could have arrived at the same conclusion even without it. Paul does call his gentiles-in-Christ "seed of Abraham," but they are not Jacob. Jacob is the father of the twelve tribes, the *ethnos* of Israel. In short, the "all Israel [who] will be preserved" refers to the whole (as opposed to a part) of the Jewish people, not to some other, newly minted entity.[71]

A great deal of confusion here stems from the word "saved," the English gloss most often used for the future passive σωθήσεται in Rom 11:26. To modern ears, it cannot help but connote evangelical conversionist rhetoric (e.g., the street evangelist asking, "Are you saved?"), which is grossly misleading in the context of Paul's Letter to the Romans. But that is our fault, not the fault of the Greek word σῴζω, or even of the poor old English gloss "save." As Paul uses it, this term has quite particularly to do with surviving (or "being preserved through") the great and terrible day of the lord:[72] "We shall be preserved through him [Christ] from the wrath" (Rom 5:9); "A person shall be preserved, as if through fire" (1 Cor 3:15); "The pneuma shall be preserved on the day of the lord" (1 Cor 5:5); and so on. On that fast-approaching day, one either perishes ("is destroyed," passive of ἀπόλλυμι) or survives ("is preserved," passive of σῴζω), which is why Paul – like the prophets before him – can call the selfsame day both a day of wrath and a day of preservation (2 Cor 6:2; Rom 2:5).[73] The point of Rom 11:26, then, is that all Israel will indeed survive the final

---

[70] Probably Stowers, *Rereading of Romans*, 206 is right: "'The deliverer will come from Zion' means that Christ, at his coming from heaven, will play some kind of role in the holy city." Stendahl, *Paul among Jews and Gentiles*, 1–7 suggests that Christ is conspicuously absent from Rom 9–11, but that is not true (see Rom 9:1, 3, 5, 32–33; 10:4, 6–7, 9, 17; 11:26). Stendahl's bigger point, however, that the key issue in this section is *God's* unwavering commitment to Israel is quite right.

[71] Thus I agree with Staples ("What Do the Gentiles Have to Do") that "all Israel" here means whole as opposed to part. But I disagree with Staples's claim that the particular whole Paul means is the twelve tribes as opposed to just two, because I think Paul has already expressly explained his part/whole distinction back in Rom 9:6–13 (discussed just above).

[72] Mark Nanos's gloss "be kept safe" is, in this respect, better than the usual one (Mark D. Nanos, "All Israel Will Be Saved, or Kept Safe?" in *Israel and the Nations: Paul's Gospel in the Context of Jewish Expectation*, ed. Frantisek Abel [Minneapolis: Fortress, 2021], 243–270). But even better, in my view, is the gloss "be preserved" (through the day of wrath, that is).

[73] As demonstrated by Tooth, *Eschatologies of 1 and 2 Thessalonians*.

judgment. (Of course, Paul thinks that all the righteous-in-Christ, too, will survive the final judgment, but that is not the point of this verse.) It is a traditional affirmation in the vein of – indeed, almost identical to – the famous theologoumenon in m. Sanh. 10:1: "All Israel have a share in the age to come."[74] But in the context of Rom 9–11, it is an affirmation in the face of Paul's present, empirical reality that most of Israel disagree with his interpretation of the divine will ("they are enemies as regards the [Christ] announcement" [Rom 11:28]). From this, Paul worries, one might mistakenly infer that the word of God had failed (Rom 9:6), or that God had forsaken his people (Rom 11:1), or that the call of God had been revoked (Rom 11:29). But it is not so. All Israel will survive the final judgment and enter into the kingdom of God. Gentiles-in-Christ will do likewise, of course, but they are not Israel. Only a gentile like Justin would ever think they were.[75]

What Kind of Animal Is a Gentile-in-Christ?

If, as I have argued, Paul's gentiles do not become part of a supposed "true, spiritual Israel" – an entity never imagined by the apostle – then what do they become? E. P. Sanders influentially argued that Paul perceived, though only dimly, what some second- and third-century writers would come to call the "third race" (τρίτον γένος, *tertium genus*) of the Christians.[76] In defense of this proposal, Sanders points to one passage in the letters, at the end of the idol-food discourse in 1 Cor 10:

Εἴτε οὖν ἐσθίετε εἴτε πίνετε εἴτε τι ποιεῖτε, πάντα εἰς δόξαν θεοῦ ποιεῖτε. ἀπρόσκοποι καὶ Ἰουδαίοις γίνεσθε καὶ Ἕλλησιν καὶ τῇ ἐκκλησίᾳ τοῦ θεοῦ, καθὼς

---

[74] That the Mishnah also itemizes certain exceptions to this rule (Epicureans, people who deny the resurrection, etc.) does not attenuate the force of the rule itself (thus rightly Sacha Stern, *Jewish Identity in Early Rabbinic Writings*, AGJU 23[Leiden: Brill, 1994], 30–31).

[75] Cf. the related point made by Schweitzer, *Mysticism*, 334: "Paul did not Hellenize Christianity; but he prepared the way for its Hellenization." On the continuing scandal of Rom 11:26 in Christian interpretation, see Jeremy Cohen, "The Mystery of Israel's Salvation: Romans 11:25–26 in Patristic and Medieval Exegesis," HTR 98 (2005): 247–281.

[76] Sanders, *Paul, the Law, and the Jewish People*, 173: "I do not doubt that he [Paul] would have been horrified to read that, in claiming that both Jew and Greek had to have faith in Christ, he had made of the Christian movement a third race."

κἀγὼ πάντα πᾶσιν ἀρέσκω μὴ ζητῶν τὸ ἐμαυτοῦ σύμφορον ἀλλὰ τὸ τῶν πολλῶν, ἵνα σωθῶσιν.

So then, whether you eat or drink or whatever you do, do all things to the glory of God. Be inoffensive to Jews and to Greeks and to the assembly of God, just as I, too, please all people in all things, not seeking my own advantage but that of the many, that they may be preserved. (1 Cor 10:31–33)

Jews, Greeks, and the assembly of God. Not for nothing does Sanders see in this phrase the seed of the third race theology of the apologists. And yet, if we were not already familiar with that idea from Aristides, Clement, Tertullian,[77] and others, I suspect that it would not have occurred to us to find it here.[78] Paul uses neither the lexicon of race (γένος, etc.) nor – here or anywhere – the word "Christians." The ἐκκλησίαι ("assemblies," a civic, not an ethnic term)[79] are comprised of Jews and gentiles (1 Thess 2:14; Rom 16:4). But in Paul's idiom, they are just Jews-in-Christ and gentiles-in-Christ, not some new, other ethnic thing.[80] They are "we whom [God] called not only from among the Jews but also from among the gentiles [Οὓς καὶ ἐκάλεσεν ἡμᾶς οὐ μόνον ἐξ Ἰουδαίων ἀλλὰ καὶ ἐξ ἐθνῶν]" (Rom 9:23–24).

So if not "spiritual Israel" or "the third race," is there another, more suitable category on offer? Joshua Garroway has lately argued, borrowing from Homi K. Bhabha's theory of hybridity, that Paul's charges become what Garroway calls "Gentile-Jews" or "non-Jewish

---

[77] Aristides, *Apol.* 2.1: "There are three races [τρία γένη] of people in the world: those who worship what are called gods by you [pagans], Jews, and Christians"; *Kerygma Petri*, apud Clement, *Strom.* 6.41.6: "The old things belong to Greeks and Jews, but we Christians worship him in a new way, as a third race [τρίτῳ γένει]"; Tertullian, *Nat.* 1.8.1: "We are said to be the third race [*tertium genus*]"; and cf. Tertullian, *Scorp.* 10.10.

[78] Thus rightly Erich S. Gruen, "Christians as a Third Race: Is Ethnicity at Issue?" in *Christianity in the Second Century*, ed. James Carleton Paget and Judith Lieu (Cambridge: Cambridge University Press, 2017), 236: "Paul's Letter to the Galatians does not so much as hint at the notion."

[79] Thus rightly George H. van Kooten, "*Ekklesia tou theou*: The 'Church of God' and the Civic Assemblies (*ekklesiai*) of the Greek Cities in the Roman Empire," *NTS* 58 (2012): 522–548.

[80] Paul, no less than the Christian apologists, is thoroughly enmeshed in ethnic reasoning (thus rightly Buell, *Why This New Race*), but Paul's particular construction is different from theirs in at least the respect I am explicating here.

Jews."⁸¹ In agreement with my argument here, Garroway points out that Paul never speaks of a "spiritual Israel," but against my argument, he does think that Paul's gentiles become Israel, full stop, just not in the conventional proselyte way: "Not 'spiritual' descendants of Abraham or 'spiritual' Israel, a qualification that Paul never employs because, on his reckoning, they are the genuine article: the descendants of Abraham, the Israel."⁸² Importantly, Garroway argues that when Paul calls Christ a διάκονος περιτομῆς, "servant of circumcision," in Rom 15:8, he means an *agent* of circumcision, a circumciser, that is, a mohel. On Garroway's interpretation, Paul claims that Christ circumcises gentiles, invisibly but nevertheless really. I find this argument ingenious but not finally convincing. I think that διάκονος περιτομῆς in Rom 15:8 means "servant of the circumcision" in the sense of "servant of the people Israel."⁸³ And as argued above, I think that Paul does not actually call his gentiles "Jews," "Israel," or "circumcision."

My argument finds closer points of contact in some recent discussion of the ancient halakhah surrounding conversion. Christine Hayes has highlighted those Jewish texts that follow the view associated with the Book of Ezra that the ethnic difference between Jews and gentiles is unbridgeable.⁸⁴ On Paul, in particular, she writes, "Paul's position on Gentiles must be seen as a paradoxical mix of exclusivistic and inclusivistic ideologies. Gentiles are included in the kingdom of God that it at hand – an inclusivistic ideology. Yet the seed of Abraham (Gentiles) can no more become the seed of Isaac (Jews) through a ritual of conversion than the seed of Isaac (lay Israelites) can become the seed of Aaron (priests) through a ritual of conversion – an exclusivistic ideology."⁸⁵ For Hayes, Paul's opposition to proselyte circumcision for gentiles-in-Christ comes not from any dissatisfaction with the Torah as such (as in much Christian interpretation) but rather from a belief in a divinely ordained ethnic fixity. Thinking along similar lines, Matthew Thiessen argues,

---

[81] Garroway, *Paul's Gentile-Jews*, 8–9; building on Homi K. Bhabha, *The Location of Culture* (London: Routledge, 1994).
[82] Garroway, *Paul's Gentile-Jews*, 6.
[83] Following Wagner, "Christ, Servant of Jew and Gentile."
[84] See Hayes, *Gentile Impurities*.   [85] Hayes, *Divine Law*, 150.

"[For Paul,] since the genealogical gap between Jew and gentile was divinely created, the only solution to the gentile problem was for God to overcome this gap by rewriting gentile genealogy so that they could become Abrahamic seed."[86]

I differ with Hayes and with Thiessen on a number of particular judgments about particular texts, but I think that their core observation – that the Ezran distinction between Israel and the nations is relevant to the case of Paul – is very much to the point. It makes clear, elegant sense of the fact that, as I have argued, Paul does not call his gentiles-in-Christ "Jews," true, spiritual, secret, or otherwise. By his lights, their being saved does not consist in their becoming Jews.[87] They remain gentiles. (There is only one apparent exception to this – 1 Cor 12:2: "When you were gentiles" – and it is not a genuine exception.)[88] But they join God's people Israel in attaining eschatological righteousness. Hence Rom 15:10, where Paul quotes from the Greek version of the song of Moses in Deut 32:43 LXX: εὐφράνθητε, ἔθνη, μετὰ τοῦ λαοῦ αὐτοῦ, "Rejoice, O gentiles, *along with* his people." (The Hebrew reads, "Praise his people, O nations").[89] Elsewhere Paul can say that gentiles-in-Christ become people of God (Rom 9:25 quoting Hos 2:25: "I will call not-my-people my people"), but – emphatically – not in such a way that they displace God's people Israel (Rom 11:29: "The gifts and the call of God are irrevocable").[90] Gentiles-in-Christ are *annexed to* the people Israel but do not *become* the people Israel. This is true even of that most notorious Pauline claim, namely, that gentiles-in-Christ become seed (σπέρμα) and sons (υἱοί) of Abraham (Gal 3; Rom 4).[91] Paul is consistently precise – though his interpreters have not been –

---

[86] Thiessen, *Paul and the Gentile Problem*, 162.

[87] Indeed, as Thiessen (*Paul and the Gentile Problem*, 56) rightly points out, if gentiles' salvation consisted in their becoming Jews, then God would be the god of Jews only, a possibility that Paul raises only to deny (Rom 3:29).

[88] Thus rightly Fredriksen, *Pagans' Apostle*, 117, who styles Paul's gentiles-in-Christ "ex-pagan pagans." And see further Concannon, *When You Were Gentiles*.

[89] On the significance of this citation, see Patrick McMurray, *Sacrifice, Brotherhood, and the Body: Abraham and the Nations in Romans* (Minneapolis: Fortress, 2021).

[90] Wagner, *Heralds of the Good News*, 78–92.

[91] On which see Johnson Hodge, *If Sons Then Heirs*; and Thiessen, *Paul and the Gentile Problem*.

in saying that gentiles-in-Christ become seed and sons of Abraham, but not of Isaac or of Jacob. This makes all the difference. Abraham is the father of us all (Rom 4:16); Jacob (which is to say, Israel) is not.

Abraham is a wonderfully malleable ancestor in this respect. We recall, of course, that even the Spartans were children of Abraham, according to 1 Maccabees:[92]

> This is a copy of the letter which they sent to Onias: "Arius, king of the Spartans, to Onias the high priest, greeting. It has been found in writing concerning the Spartans and the Jews that they are brothers and are from the clan of Abraham [εὑρέθη ἐν γραφῇ περί τε τῶν Σπαρτιατῶν καὶ Ιουδαίων ὅτι εἰσὶν ἀδελφοὶ καὶ ὅτι εἰσὶν ἐκ γένους Αβρααμ]. And now that we have learned this, please write us concerning your welfare; we on our part write to you that your cattle and your property belong to us, and ours belong to you. We therefore command that our envoys report to you accordingly." (1 Macc 12:19–23)

In this bit of kinship diplomacy, the Jews and Spartans are called brothers (read: allies) because, according to something that someone found written somewhere (!), both come ἐκ γένους Αβρααμ, "from the clan of Abraham." But it does not follow that the Spartans *are* Jews (or vice versa), for Spartans are not descendants of Isaac and of Jacob/Israel. Now, of course, Paul constructs his artificial Abrahamic genealogy differently from how 1 Maccabees does. For Paul it is not just one *ethnos* but all the *ethne* who stand to enjoy this privilege. For Paul, moreover, the novel genealogy is not discovered in the archives but achieved by incorporation into the messiah (Gal 3:16, 29).[93] Paul especially capitalizes on the fact that Abraham, unlike Isaac and Jacob, is – or was over the course of his life – both gentile and Jew, both a foreskinned pagan from Ur and the archetypal circumcised Israelite (Rom 4:10–11).[94] Thus Paul's gentiles-in-Christ can become seed of Abraham and people of God without thereby becoming Israel.

---

[92] See Jan N. Bremmer, "Spartans and Jews: Abrahamic Cousins?" in *Abraham, the Nations, and the Hagarites*, 47–60; Erich S. Gruen, "The Purported Jewish-Spartan Affiliation," in *Constructs of Identity in Hellenistic Judaism: Essays on Early Jewish Literature and History* (Berlin: De Gruyter, 2016), 153–167.

[93] See Matthew V. Novenson, "The Messiah ben Ahraham in Galatians," in *Paul, Then and Now*, 118–125; J. Thomas Hewitt, "Pneuma, Genealogical Descent, and Things That Do Not Exist," *NTS* 68 (2022): 239–252.

[94] The best discussion of this passage known to me is Neutel, "Restoring Abraham's Foreskin."

Conclusion

To summarize: In Paul's way of thinking ethnicity, Jews are Jews, and gentiles gentiles.[95] "Israel according to the flesh" (1 Cor 10:18) is just Israel. By the same token, "the Israel of God" (Gal 6:16) is also just Israel, though with emphasis on their election. The "all Israel [who] will be preserved" (Rom 11:26), again, is just Israel. The claim that "not all those from Israel are Israel" (Rom 9:6), so far from expanding or transferring the referent of "Israel," leaves it in place but narrows it, in an *homage* to the remnant motif in the classical prophets. "The true Jew" and "the true circumcision," despite their prominence in translations of the Epistle to the Romans, are phrases never uttered by the apostle. When Paul says, "We are the circumcision" (Phil 3:3), he means himself and other right-thinking, eighth-day-circumcised apostles as opposed to the mutilators of gentile foreskins. As for people in Christ, he calls them "people in Christ," "holy ones," "those who trust," "seed of Abraham," "assembly of God," and more,[96] but *never* "true Israel," "spiritual Israel," or any variation on these terms. It remained for gentile Christian thinkers like Justin, Origen, and Augustine to read between the lines, to supply missing terms, to imagine a spiritual Israel opposite Paul's carnal Israel.[97] Gentile Christians down to the present have perpetuated this exercise. For Paul, however, carnal Israel was the only Israel there was.

---

[95] East is east, and west is west, as in Kipling's poem. But, of course, even Kipling goes on to say that the twain do finally meet in the eschaton, as does Paul. See further Matlock, "Jews by Nature."

[96] See Paul Trebilco, *Self-Designations and Group Identity in the New Testament* (Cambridge: Cambridge University Press, 2012).

[97] In doing so, they used an old philosophical trope that Benjamin Edsall has referred to (in correspondence with me, citing an unpublished paper by Jonathan Norton) as the ethnicization of the worshiper. An example is Plutarch, *Isis and Osiris* 3, where the person who studies the meaning of the cult mysteries is truly worthy to be called a votary of Isis.

8 Liberty and Justice for All

Being a Christian socialist and a Jeffersonian, Francis Bellamy had considered making the final line of his 1892 pledge of allegiance to the American flag an encomium on "liberty, equality, *and fraternity* for all." Bellamy suspected, however, that this language risked sounding both too French and too utopian, in particular, that it signaled more expansive rights for women and black citizens than his fellow state school superintendents would be willing to endorse.[1] (This was the heyday of Jim Crow legislation and still a generation before the Nineteenth Amendment to the Constitution would guarantee women's suffrage.) "One nation, indivisible, with *liberty and justice* for all" it was, then – which is itself a pretty utopian slogan – and this refrain became fixed in the memories of generations of American schoolchildren down to the present, just as Bellamy intended.

It is fixed in my memory, as I once was one of those schoolchildren. I cannot help but hear Bellamy's words, therefore, when I read the apostle Paul's words in Rom 6: "Having been *liberated* from sin, you are enslaved to *justice*... For when you were slaves of sin, you were 'at *liberty*' in regard to *justice*... But now, having been *liberated* from sin and enslaved to God, you have your fruit unto consecration, the end [of which] is life everlasting" (Rom 6:18, 20, 22). As it happens, this is the only passage in the New Testament where "liberty" (ἐλευθερία) and "justice" (δικαιοσύνη) occur together. It is conceivable that Bellamy was thinking of Rom 6 when he wrote the final phrase of his pledge.[2]

---

[1] Francis Bellamy, "The Story of the Pledge of Allegiance to the Flag," *University of Rochester Library Bulletin* 8 (1953): "Just here arose the temptation of that historic slogan of the French Revolution which meant so much to Jefferson and his friends, 'Liberty, equality, fraternity.' No; that would be too fanciful, too many thousands of years off in realization. But we as a nation do stand square on the doctrine of liberty and justice for all. That's all any one nation can handle."

[2] His pledge is, more or less, the version that has come down to us, adopted by the United States Congress in 1942. But Bellamy used as a *Grundschrift* at least

Having studied theology and taken Baptist ordination, he was almost certainly familiar with the Pauline text. But I can find no mention of it in Bellamy's account of the writing of his pledge of allegiance. Be that as it may, this closing phrase – liberty and justice for all – is a near-perfect summary of the strange state of affairs Paul attempts to describe in the second quarter of his Letter to the Romans (Rom 5–8):[3] the phenomenology of moral experience on the part of immortal human beings.

The Science of Baptism

By the end of Rom 5, Paul has painted himself into a rhetorical corner in just the way that the diatribe form is designed to do.[4] "Where sin increased," he explains, "the gift abounded still more" (Rom 5:20). But if more sin yields more of the divine gift, then, one might ask, "Should we carry on in sin, so that the gift might increase?" (Rom 6:1) No, that suggestion is nonsense, Paul says, and the reason that it is nonsense is... science![5] In Rom 6, Paul does not – for the most part – *instruct* his gentiles-in-Christ not to carry on in sin. (Only three of the twenty-three verses in the chapter contain a second-person imperative [6:11, 13, 19].)[6] Rather, he *explains* the physics by which their doing so is prevented. He writes:

ἢ ἀγνοεῖτε ὅτι, ὅσοι ἐβαπτίσθημεν εἰς Χριστὸν Ἰησοῦν, εἰς τὸν θάνατον αὐτοῦ ἐβαπτίσθημεν; συνετάφημεν οὖν αὐτῷ διὰ τοῦ βαπτίσματος εἰς τὸν θάνατον, ἵνα ὥσπερ ἠγέρθη Χριστὸς ἐκ νεκρῶν διὰ τῆς δόξης τοῦ πατρός, οὕτως καὶ ἡμεῖς ἐν

George Thatcher Balch's 1885 version and possibly also an 1890 version by 13-year-old Frank Bellamy (whose likeness in name is, apparently, a total coincidence). See further Sam Roberts, "We Know the Pledge. Its Author, Maybe Not," *New York Times* (2 April 2022).

[3] This section of the letter has proved more puzzling to interpreters than other parts. But see now Beverly Roberts Gaventa, ed., *Apocalyptic Paul: Cosmos and Anthropos in Romans 5–8* (Waco, TX: Baylor University Press, 2013) for some incisive readings of these chapters.

[4] On this aspect of the letter, Stowers, *Diatribe and Paul's Letter to the Romans* is still unsurpassed.

[5] I owe thanks to my very clever children for suggesting this apt way of putting the point.

[6] Elsewhere Paul does, of course, issue more than a few second-person imperatives. People-in-Christ still do have moral agency, and therefore require exhortation, just to the extent that they still have mortal bodies (see further below). Thanks to John Barclay for helpful discussion on this point.

καινότητι ζωῆς περιπατήσωμεν. εἰ γὰρ σύμφυτοι γεγόναμεν τῷ ὁμοιώματι τοῦ θανάτου αὐτοῦ, ἀλλὰ καὶ τῆς ἀναστάσεως ἐσόμεθα· τοῦτο γινώσκοντες ὅτι ὁ παλαιὸς ἡμῶν ἄνθρωπος συνεσταυρώθη, ἵνα καταργηθῇ τὸ σῶμα τῆς ἁμαρτίας, τοῦ μηκέτι δουλεύειν ἡμᾶς τῇ ἁμαρτίᾳ· ὁ γὰρ ἀποθανὼν δεδικαίωται ἀπὸ τῆς ἁμαρτίας. εἰ δὲ ἀπεθάνομεν σὺν Χριστῷ, πιστεύομεν ὅτι καὶ συζήσομεν αὐτῷ, εἰδότες ὅτι Χριστὸς ἐγερθεὶς ἐκ νεκρῶν οὐκέτι ἀποθνῄσκει, θάνατος αὐτοῦ οὐκέτι κυριεύει. ὃ γὰρ ἀπέθανεν, τῇ ἁμαρτίᾳ ἀπέθανεν ἐφάπαξ· ὃ δὲ ζῇ, ζῇ τῷ θεῷ. οὕτως καὶ ὑμεῖς λογίζεσθε ἑαυτοὺς [εἶναι] νεκροὺς μὲν τῇ ἁμαρτίᾳ ζῶντας δὲ τῷ θεῷ ἐν Χριστῷ Ἰησοῦ.

Do you not know that as many of you as were immersed into Christ Jesus were immersed into his death? We were entombed, therefore, with him through immersion into his death, so that just as Christ was raised from among the corpses through the glory of the father, so also we might walk in newness of life. For if we have become conjoined to the likeness of his death, we shall also be to [the likeness] of the resurrection. This we know: that our old person was crucified with [him] such that the body of sin was rendered null, so that we are no longer slaves to sin. For the person who has died has been rightwised away from sin. And if we died with Christ, we trust that we shall also live with him, knowing that Christ, having been raised from among the corpses, no longer dies, for death no longer has mastery over him. For what he died, he died to sin, once for all; but what he lives, he lives to God. So too you, reckon yourselves corpses to sin, but living beings to God in Christ Jesus. (Rom 6:3–11)

The Christ-believer's ritual immersion in water was, Paul explains, a death and entombment. It joined her to the event of Christ's death and therefore also to the outcome of that death, namely, resurrection to sinless immortality.[7] The resurrection part may not yet have obtained in her own experience, though it very soon will do, but – crucially – the sinless immortality part has obtained. To be sure, Paul does not say here, as the author of Ephesians does, that the Christ-believer has been raised and has ascended with Christ (Eph 2:5–6). Rather, the Paul of Romans says, "If we died with Christ, we *trust that we shall* also live with him" (Rom 6:8).[8] Even in Romans, however, the death and

---

[7] With Schweitzer, *Mysticism*, and contra Boccaccini, *Paul's Three Paths to Salvation*, for Paul – differently from John the Baptizer and Jesus – baptism has nothing to do with forgiveness of sins. It is, rather, a ritual of metamorphosis, on which see Morton Smith, "Pauline Worship as Seen by Pagans," *HTR* 73 (1980): 241–249; Eyl, *Signs, Wonders, and Gifts*, 129–142.

[8] See Nils A. Dahl, "Ephesians and Qumran," in *Studies in Ephesians*, WUNT 131 (Tübingen: Mohr Siebeck, 2000), 107–144 on the problem of present versus

internal reconstitution with pneuma has already happened for the person who has been immersed into Christ.⁹ ὁ γὰρ ἀποθανὼν δεδικαίωται ἀπὸ τῆς ἁμαρτίας, "The person who has died has been rightwised away from sin" (Rom 6:7). Here δικαίωσις, "rightwising" or "justification," is coordinated with death, but, strikingly, not the death of Christ (except by extension); rather, the person-in-Christ herself dies in ritual immersion and thus is rightwised away from sin. Elsewhere, Paul can coordinate δικαίωσις with Christ's resurrection – ὃς παρεδόθη διὰ τὰ παραπτώματα ἡμῶν καὶ ἠγέρθη διὰ τὴν δικαίωσιν ἡμῶν, "[Christ] was handed over for our trespasses and was raised for our rightwising" (Rom 4:25) – but a shared logic underlies both of these claims. The mortal human is liable to sin and decay, but when she dies (with Christ, in ritual immersion), she escapes sin and decay, is rightwised away from them; henceforth she is, and will be, what the risen Christ is: pneumatic, incorruptible, altogether righteous.

In the present, brief, unusual, unexpected moment, the person-in-Christ is an immortal pneumatic being, but one still possessed of a θνητὸν σῶμα, a mortal body. She is a ghost in a shell, as it were, a divine pneuma still, fleetingly, encased in flesh and blood. As Paul writes several paragraphs later, εἰ δὲ Χριστὸς ἐν ὑμῖν, τὸ μὲν σῶμα νεκρὸν διὰ ἁμαρτίαν τὸ δὲ πνεῦμα ζωὴ διὰ δικαιοσύνην, "If Christ is in you, the body is a corpse on account of sin, but the pneuma is life on account of righteousness" (Rom 8:10). But "ghost in a shell" is potentially misleading, since "ghost" might suggest something immaterial. Paul's pneuma, however, is material (in a Stoic-like sense).¹⁰ Both the inner

---

future eschatologies; and Thomas D. McGlothlin, *Resurrection as Salvation: Development and Conflict in Pre-Nicene Paulinism* (Cambridge: Cambridge University Press, 2018), 199–200 on Origen's knowing conflation of these two different ideas in Rom 6 and Eph 2.

⁹ Thus rightly, Engberg-Pedersen, *Cosmology and Self*, 72: "The initial reception of the pneuma in baptism was almost certainly understood by Paul as a directly physical event that quite concretely began a transformation of the bodies of believers that would be played out in their present lives and eventually completed at the resurrection. At the beginning, God's love was literally poured into their hearts through the pneuma."

¹⁰ See Martin, *Corinthian Body*; Engberg-Pedersen, *Cosmology and Self*; Stowers, "Dilemma of Paul's Physics." N.B. To say that the pneuma is material is not to deny that it is personal; those are separate questions (thanks to Jay Thomas Hewitt and Jamie Davies for clarifying this issue with me in conversation). For Paul, the holy pneuma is both material and personal, because it is the stuff of God.

and the outer are material, but the inner material is indestructible, while the outer material is biodegradable. So not exactly a ghost in a shell, more like: an angel in a corpse. εἰ καὶ ὁ ἔξω ἡμῶν ἄνθρωπος διαφθείρεται, ἀλλ' ὁ ἔσω ἡμῶν ἀνακαινοῦται ἡμέρᾳ καὶ ἡμέρᾳ, "Even if our outer person is undergoing decay, nevertheless our inner [person] is being renewed day by day" (2 Cor 4:16). What Paul here calls "the outer person," that is, the body made of flesh and blood, undergoes decay and hence is physically incapable of inheriting the kingdom of God (1 Cor 15:50). Divine pneuma, however, is incorruptible stuff, stuff fit for the kingdom of God, stuff that does not decay but is perpetually self-renewing. It is the kind of stuff that, if a person were made of it, she would live forever.[11]

Consider the case of such a person. How would she experience moral decision-making? What would it feel like for her to exercise practical reason? Put thusly, it sounds like a science-fiction thought experiment, but this is precisely the question Paul addresses in the second half of Rom 6,[12] where the Bellamy-esque language of "liberty and justice" (or, alternatively, "freedom and righteousness") come to the fore. Paul writes:

ἐλευθερωθέντες δὲ ἀπὸ τῆς ἁμαρτίας ἐδουλώθητε τῇ δικαιοσύνῃ. Ἀνθρώπινον λέγω διὰ τὴν ἀσθένειαν τῆς σαρκὸς ὑμῶν. ὥσπερ γὰρ παρεστήσατε τὰ μέλη ὑμῶν δοῦλα τῇ ἀκαθαρσίᾳ καὶ τῇ ἀνομίᾳ εἰς τὴν ἀνομίαν, οὕτως νῦν παραστήσατε τὰ μέλη ὑμῶν δοῦλα τῇ δικαιοσύνῃ εἰς ἁγιασμόν. ὅτε γὰρ δοῦλοι ἦτε τῆς ἁμαρτίας, ἐλεύθεροι ἦτε τῇ δικαιοσύνῃ. τίνα οὖν καρπὸν εἴχετε τότε; ἐφ' οἷς νῦν ἐπαισχύνεσθε, τὸ γὰρ τέλος ἐκείνων θάνατος. νυνὶ δὲ ἐλευθερωθέντες ἀπὸ τῆς ἁμαρτίας δουλωθέντες δὲ τῷ θεῷ ἔχετε τὸν καρπὸν ὑμῶν εἰς ἁγιασμόν, τὸ δὲ τέλος ζωὴν αἰώνιον.

Having been *set free* from sin, you were enslaved to *righteousness*. (I am speaking humanly on account of the weakness of your flesh.) For just as you presented your limbs as slaves to impurity and lawlessness, unto lawlessness, so now present your limbs as slaves to *righteousness*, unto consecration. For when you were slaves of sin, you were *free* in relation to *righteousness*. What fruit did you have then? The kind of which you are ashamed now, for the end of those things is death. But now, having been *set free* from sin and enslaved

---

[11] See further David E. Aune, "Anthropological Duality in the Eschatology of 2 Corinthians 4:16–5.10," in *Paul beyond the Judaism/Hellenism Divide*, 215–240.
[12] As it rightly recognized by Engberg-Pedersen, *Cosmology and Self*, especially 106–138.

to God, you have your fruit unto consecration, the end [of which] is life everlasting. (Rom 6:18–22)

Before God sent his son, during the time Paul calls "the present evil aeon" (Gal 1:4), mortal human beings were subject to slavery and injustice – gentiles ostentatiously so, Jews subtly so, but, as per the testimony of the law, "all were under sin" (Rom 3:9, 19).[13] But in contrast to the slavery and injustice of that aeon, the new creation (Gal 6:15; 2 Cor 5:17) is characterized by liberty and justice for all.

A Homologia Pisteos, or Pledge of Allegiance

"Liberty" or "freedom," ἐλευθερία, is the absence of domination by the arbitrary power of another.[14] In Rom 6, the dominating power from which people-in-Christ find themselves freed is ἁμαρτία, failure or sin,[15] and this fits a broadly consistent pattern in Paul's letters. People are enslaved to or freed from sin, along with its attendants corruption and death. There is, of course, a long tradition in Christian (especially Protestant) theology of speaking of freedom *from the law*, but that is not Paul's idiom.[16] If we set aside the many references in Paul to workaday slave-master relations between human beings,[17] and look only at his figurative talk of human slavery to (or manumission from) non-human beings or things, we find the following. "You are slaves either of sin, unto death, or of obedience, unto righteousness" (Rom 6:16). "Having been freed from sin, you are slaves to righteousness" (Rom 6:18) or "slaves to God" (Rom 6:22). In the Letter to the

---

[13] See the argument of Chapter 6.
[14] On liberty and domination, see Jeffrey Stout, "Liberty for All: Democracy in Practice and Principle," *Commonweal* (20 September 2010); David Decosimo, "An *Umma* of Accountability: Al-Ghazali against Domination," *Soundings* 98 (2015): 260–288.
[15] On the roots of this notion in the classical and Hellenistic periods, see J. M. Bremer, *Hamartia: Tragic Error in the Poetics of Aristotle and in Greek Tragedy* (Amsterdam: Hakkert, 1969).
[16] On this key point, though with a focus on Galatians rather than Romans, see Charles K. Cisco, "The Philosophy of Freedom and Slavery in Paul's Epistle to the Galatians" (PhD diss., University of Edinburgh, 2023). On the whole problem in Protestant theology, see Jonathan A. Linebaugh, ed., *God's Two Words: Law and Gospel in the Lutheran and Reformed Traditions* (Grand Rapids, MI: Eerdmans, 2018).
[17] On which see J. Albert Harrill, *Slaves in the New Testament: Literary, Social, and Moral Dimensions* (Minneapolis: Fortress, 2006).

Galatians, gentile deities are classed on the side of sin, corruption, and death. The Galatian gentiles-in-Christ were formerly "enslaved to things that by nature are not gods" (Gal 4:8). Before the end of the ages arrived, Paul says, "we were enslaved to the elements of the cosmos" (Gal 4:3). In the new creation, by contrast, there is now freedom from all such forces, not only for humans but for other creatures, too. "The creation will be freed from its slavery to corruption" (Rom 8:21).[18] Paul sometimes coordinates the law with some of these enslaving forces ("sin takes an opportunity *afforded by* the law," etc.), but he also insists that the law itself is not one of them. There is one instance where Paul speaks of being freed from the law, but in that instance the liberating force is also the law: "The law of the pneuma of life in Christ Jesus freed you from the law of sin and of death" (Rom 8:2). Here and elsewhere in Paul, the actual mechanism by which Christ frees people from sin and death is the divine pneuma. "Where the pneuma of the lord is, there is freedom" (2 Cor 3:17).

"Justice" or "righteousness," δικαιοσύνη, is a state of ethical excellence, where all things are as they ought to be.[19] There is a paradox, or at least an irony, at the heart of Paul's talk of freedom, namely that freedom from sin and death does not mean an end to all domination whatsoever. Rather, people freed from sin are immediately enslaved to another power, namely righteousness, or God himself (another way of saying the same thing). Freedom, in Paul's idiom, consists in being dominated by a benevolent force rather than a malevolent one.[20] And the omni-benevolent force to whom Paul wants to see all people

---

[18] More on this, the fate of non-human created things, below in our discussion of Rom 8.

[19] See Westerholm, *Perspectives Old and New*, 261–296; Rim, "Messiah and Righteousness."

[20] Ernst Käsemann (in his *New Testament Questions of Today*, trans. W. J. Montague [Philadelphia: Fortress, 1969] and *Commentary on Romans*, trans. Geoffrey W. Bromiley [Grand Rapids, MI: Eerdmans, 1980]) famously found this to be a profound and thrilling idea. Recently, Concannon, *Profaning Paul*, has criticized it sharply: If Paul's highest utopian ideal is a state of enslavement, just to one power rather than another, then that betrays a failure of moral imagination on Paul's part. Käsemann and Concannon agree that this is Paul's view; they disagree whether it is morally and theologically tolerable to us.
I actually wonder whether it is in fact Paul's highest utopian ideal, given what he says in Rom 6:19: "I am speaking humanly on account of the weakness of your flesh." This suggests, I suspect, that Paul may already anticipate a version of Concannon's moral objection.

enslaved is δικαιοσύνη. Now, there is a kind of everyday righteousness, "righteousness in the law," Paul calls it, in respect of which it is possible to be more or less blameless (Phil 3:6), and which is certainly a great deal better than wickedness. But in Rom 6, as in most places where he uses the term, Paul means righteousness in a stronger sense, a maximal sense, in fact.[21] Such righteousness is what the eschatological kingdom of God itself consists in; it is not food and drink, but righteousness, peace, joy in the holy pneuma (Rom 14:17). The law of Moses (which is the law of God) is righteous and legislates righteousness, but it cannot effect this maximal, eschatological righteousness. "If a law had been given that could make alive, then righteousness would indeed be from the law" (Gal 3:21), Paul says, but it was not, so it is not. The kind of righteousness that can actually make alive Paul calls "the righteousness of God,"[22] and it only comes in the form of, or is mediated by, God's son, the messiah Jesus. Christ, Paul can say, just *is* this eschatological righteousness: "He became wisdom for us from God, that is, righteousness, consecration, and ransom" (1 Cor 1:30).[23] The person-in-Christ, therefore, experiences freedom from domination by sin and, in its place, a natural, internal compulsion by righteousness. When she acts in the world, she finds herself just doing love, joy, peace, patience, kindness, goodness, faithfulness, gentleness, and self-control, which is to say: δικαιοσύνη.[24]

Third and finally, "for all." This language, admittedly, does not occur in Rom 6, but it does occur frequently in Romans, including

---

[21] Cf. Westerholm's helpful distinction (in *Perspectives Old and New*, 263–284) between ordinary and extraordinary righteousness.

[22] See Sam K. Williams, "The Righteousness of God in Romans," *JBL* 99 (1980): 241–290.

[23] On this text, see Rim, "Messiah and Righteousness."

[24] About this ninefold "fruit of the pneuma," Paul writes, κατὰ τῶν τοιούτων οὐκ ἔστιν νόμος (Gal 5:23). The standard English versions translate this "Against such there is no law" (RSV, e.g.), but that is wrong. It means, rather, "The law is not over such things." That is, the law of Moses, although it is itself righteous, cannot generate virtues in people; only the pneuma of God can do that. See further Matthew V. Novenson, "'The Law Is Not Over Such Things': An Exegetical Note on Galatians 5:23," *Presbyterion* 47 (2021): 112–116. Logan Williams ("Being(s) above the Law: Ontology, Legislation, and Paul's Quotation of Aristotle's Politics in Galatians" [forthcoming]) argues, relatedly, that this sentence means "The law is not over such *people*," that is, pneuma-endowed people, spotting here a citation from Aristotle, *Pol.* 3.8 1284a. Citation it may be, but it seems to me that, in Paul's syntax, the antecedent of τοιούτων must be virtues just listed.

an important instance immediately preceding our passage: "Just as through one trespass [it came] to condemnation *for all people* [εἰς πάντας ἀνθρώπους], likewise through one just act [it came] to right-wising of life *for all people* [εἰς πάντας ἀνθρώπους]" (Rom 5:18). Some recent theological interpreters, especially (though not only) representing the so-called apocalyptic school, have made a point of emphasizing this and other references to "all people" in the Letter to the Romans.[25] They have done so especially (though not only) by way of response to the so-called Paul within Judaism school, which has entertained the contrasting claim that, for Paul, the righteousness effected by Christ extends to gentiles but not to Jews, since the latter have no need of it, being already provided for by God's covenant with the patriarchs.[26] (Actually, nowadays there is a lively debate over this question *amongst* members of the Paul within Judaism school.) My own view, which depends in part on Rom 5–6, is as follows: There are theologically significant respects in which Paul reasons that Jews and gentiles are deeply, even naturally different. In respect of attaining eschatological righteousness and life, however, they are in the same boat. As debauched as Paul says gentiles normally are, and as decent as he says Jews normally are, they are all mortal. And mortality is to sin as fire is to smoke. Death comes for everyone. Or it did, until Christ bested death and rose to pneumatic immortality.[27] With that event, Paul reckons, the general resurrection of the dead is underway. It remains for Christ to crush death fully and finally,[28] the evidence of which will be the emergence of the righteous dead from their tombs. When they emerge, they will find themselves unencumbered by sin and corruption and effortlessly, maximally virtuous, even as pneumatically endowed people-in-Christ already are.

---

[25] E.g., Gaventa, "We, They, and All in Paul's Letter to the Romans."
[26] E.g., Richard B. Hays, "The Gospel Is the Power of God for Salvation to Gentiles Only? A Critique of Stanley Stowers's *Rereading of Romans*," *CRBR* 9 (1996): 27–44, although Hays here attributes to Stowers a view that Stowers does not actually articulate or, I think, hold.
[27] The significance of this is rightly noted by Joseph Longarino, *Pauline Theology and the Problem of Death*, WUNT 2/558 (Tübingen: Mohr Siebeck, 2021).
[28] 1 Cor 15:26: ἔσχατος ἐχθρὸς καταργεῖται ὁ θάνατος, "Death is undone as the last enemy."

Paul's Religion and Ours

"Liberty and justice for all" as I am using it here – a state of affairs where both Jews and gentiles, transformed into undying pneumatic beings, fulfil the moral will of God perfectly, effortlessly, and forever – is about as good a summary of Paul's religious project as one is likely to find. But – and here, I think, lies the problem with most contributions to the Paul-and-Judaism debates – that project corresponds neither to Judaism nor to Christianity as the everyday lived religions that we normally mean by those terms. (Hence when, for instance, John Barclay insists that Paul goes beyond what any mainstream ancient Jew would say about the law,[29] while Paula Fredriksen insists that Paul does not underwrite Christian theologies straightforwardly, if at all,[30] in a significant sense, both are right.) To be sure, many high-minded Jews and Christians (and others), from Maimonides to Abraham Joshua Heschel, from Thomas Aquinas to Francis Bellamy, have dreamed of and worked toward something like a world of liberty and justice for all.[31] But that is the point. Paul did not dream of and work toward such a world. He simply announced that that world was now here. (That is what εὐαγγέλιον means!)[32] The fact that, to most observers then and ever since, that utopian world was *not* in fact here is not a problem for Paul's own theology, but it is a problem for Christian theologies built on Paul's letters, which is to say, most Christian theologies to one degree or another. This problem is not insuperable, but it does require honest and serious reckoning with.[33]

---

[29] John M. G. Barclay, "Paul, Judaism, and the Jewish People," in *The Blackwell Companion to Paul*, ed. Stephen Westerholm (Oxford: Wiley-Blackwell, 2011), 188–201.

[30] Fredriksen, *Pagans' Apostle*.

[31] For discussion see, e.g., Marc Rosenstein, *Contested Utopia: Jewish Dreams and Israeli Realities* (Lincoln: University of Nebraska Press, 2021); Joanne Maguire Robinson, *Waiting in Christian Traditions: Balancing Ideology and Utopia* (Lanham, MD: Lexington, 2015).

[32] On the term itself, see Steve Mason, "Paul's Announcement (*to euangelion*): 'Good News' and Its Detractors in Earliest Christianity," in *Josephus, Judea, and Christian Origins* (Peabody, MA: Hendrickson, 2009), 283–302.

[33] The task of reckoning with it does not fall within the scope of this book, nor entirely within my own professional competency. Being a Christian myself, however – and a Protestant, at that – I do have skin in the game, though I also must lean on my theologian colleagues for help thinking these constructive questions.

To illustrate this difficult-but-not-insuperable problem, consider two snapshots from the history of Pauline research, one of them a hundred years past, the other one present. Snapshot no. 1: Albert Schweitzer, in his 1931 *Mysticism of Paul the Apostle*, explains how it is that God's raising Christ from the dead in Rom 8:11 (ὁ ἐγείρας Χριστὸν ἐκ νεκρῶν) can entail God's giving life to believers' bodies through the pneuma (ζῳοποιήσει καὶ τὰ θνητὰ σώματα ὑμῶν διὰ τοῦ ἐνοικοῦντος αὐτοῦ πνεύματος) as follows:

> It is the resurrection of Jesus which led Paul to the adoption of the view that believers possess in the Messianic Kingdom the resurrection mode of existence... Paul's conception is that believers in mysterious fashion share the dying and rising again with Christ, and in this way are swept away out of their ordinary mode of existence, and form a special category of humanity.[34]

> His [Paul's] conviction that with the resurrection of Jesus the supernatural world-period has begun... determines also his conception of the Spirit.... The Spirit is the form of manifestation of the powers of the resurrection.... As a consequence of being in the Spirit, believers are raised above all the limitations of being-in-the-flesh.[35]

Snapshot no. 2: Stanley Stowers, in a 2022 essay, poses this question: Are Paul's moral teachings designed for ordinary humans? His answer, drawn in large part from Rom 8: an emphatic no.

> Participating in the pneumatic existence given to Christ in the resurrection allows those who are in Christ to become sons of God, divine beings. At baptism, the transformation into a mind like Christ's begins, but a fully pneumatic existence comes only at the resurrection for the tiny number who have died or, for most, who will still be alive, it will happen at the return of Christ. God's own pneuma forms the medium and does the work.[36]

> Such people [i.e., people-in-Christ, who have the pneuma of God] are no longer in the flesh. Contrary to the dominant 20th century interpretations inspired by Martin Heidegger and Rudolf Bultmann, the change is not existential, an attitude of finitude, but is ontological. Indeed, quite the opposite of their [Bultmann's, et al.] claim that Paul's gospel was about

---

[34] Schweitzer, *Mysticism*, 95–96. [35] Schweitzer, *Mysticism*, 166–167.
[36] Stanley K. Stowers, "Are Paul's Moral Teachings Designed for Ordinary Humans?" in *The Social Worlds of Ancient Jews and Christians: Essays in Honor of L. Michael White*, ed. Jaimie Gunderson et al., NovTSup 189 (Leiden: Brill, 2023), 4.

accepting human frailty and limitation, the apostle holds out the goal of a divinized mind and body.[37]

Schweitzer and Stowers are separated by a century, an ocean, and a disciplinary chasm: Schweitzer (typically for an early twentieth-century European academic) writes as a theologian, Stowers (typically for an early twenty-first-century American academic – sort of) as a critical scholar of religion.[38] These differences notwithstanding, however, their respective readings of Paul seem to me to agree to a quite remarkable extent. Schweitzer reasons from Jewish eschatology, Stowers from Stoic physics and Platonic moral psychology, but both arrive at an account of Paul as an architect of transhumanism,[39] on a mission from God to chaperone mortal humans through their necessary transformation into immortal, eternal form.

As already noted, this account of Paul has met with a rather cool reception in the field. When one reads J. T. Carlyon reviewing Schweitzer's *Mysticism of Paul* in the *Journal of Religion* in 1932, one can almost hear Carlyon shaking his head wearily: "A quarter of a century of continuous study and criticism has further intrenched Dr. Schweitzer in the position that Paul as well as Jesus can be understood only on the assumption of a thoroughgoing eschatology."[40] My own predecessor (several generations back) in New Testament at the University of Edinburgh, H. A. A. Kennedy, was even more candid in his assessment of Schweitzer's Paul: "A quite arbitrary emphasis has

---

[37] Stowers, "Ordinary Humans," 9.

[38] On these institutional dynamics, see Stephen D. Moore and Yvonne Sherwood, *The Invention of the Biblical Scholar: A Critical Manifesto* (Minneapolis: Fortress, 2011).

[39] The term "transhumanism" is rightly regarded with suspicion by many, implicated as it is with a number of contemporary projects that are foolish, or morally reprehensible, or both. But even so, it remains an apt term for certain aspects of Paul's, and some other ancient thinkers', visions of the human future, as illustrated by M. David Litwa, *We Are Being Transformed: Deification in Paul's Soteriology* (Berlin: De Gruyter, 2012); M. David Litwa, *Posthuman Transformation in Ancient Mediterranean Thought: Becoming Angels and Demons* (Cambridge: Cambridge University Press, 2021); Steven John Kraftchick, "Bodies, Selves, and Human Identity: A Conversation between Transhumanism and the Apostle Paul," *Theology Today* 72 (2015): 47–69; and, with theological sensitivity, Philip G. Ziegler, "'Those He Also Glorified': Some Reformed Perspectives on Human Nature and Destiny," *SCE* 32 (2019): 165–176.

[40] *JR* 12 (1932): 377.

been laid by Schweitzer on the eschatological implicates of Paul's conception of union with Christ.... This grotesque misconception of Paul's religious standpoint is an arresting instance of the results of 'consistent eschatology.'"[41]

Upon considering this reception, though, I cannot help but think that the distaste for "thoroughgoing eschatology" readings of Paul is not so much exegetical as it is theological. There are, to be sure, some pertinent objections to Schweitzer and, differently, to Stowers from certain passages in the letters. But many of the objections raised actually have to do with what is tolerable, or intolerable, to the critic's own (almost always Christian) sensibilities. Kennedy, for example – who was a good, pious Scots Presbyterian – just cannot stomach the idea that Paul would have countenanced the holy spirit working *ex opere operato* through baptism.[42] Stowers's criticism of Bultmann, cited above, is a fair one, in my view. But Bultmann at least knew and acknowledged that he was de-mythologizing Paul's letters.[43] Many – perhaps most – Christian interpreters of Paul, by contrast, think they

---

[41] H. A. A. Kennedy, *St. Paul and the Mystery Religions* (London: Hodder & Stoughton, 1913), 294–295.

[42] On which idea see further Schweitzer, *Mysticism*, 295–296: "In reality the dying and rising again with Christ is not a metaphorical but a quasi-physical conception. It results from the eschatological view of redemption, when this is understood in the light of the fact of Jesus' death and resurrection. From this concept, in itself quasi-physical, ethics follow directly.... The ethics result from the unique character of the condition of the world here presupposed. Since with the dying and rising again of Christ the super-earthly world has already begun to be, the believers who through the being-in-Christ already belong to it, can already exercise the temper of mind appropriate to their liberation from the natural world." Although both Kennedy and Schweitzer were Protestant, the former's criticism of the latter on Pauline baptism is a classic instance of Protestant anxiety about sacramental "magic," as per Jonathan Z. Smith, *Drudgery Divine: On the Comparison of Early Christianities and the Religions of Late Antiquity* (London; SOAS, 1990). On this aspect of the reception of Schweitzer, see further Carleton Paget, "Schweitzer and Paul"; and Fatima Tofighi, "The Reception of Pauline Mysticism: An Ideological Critique," *NTS* 68 (2022): 363–374.

[43] On Bultmann's demythologizing project, see Rudolf Bultmann, "New Testament and Mythology," in *New Testament and Mythology, and Other Basic Writings*, ed. and trans. Schubert M. Ogden (Philadelphia: Fortress, 1984), 1–44. On his existential interpretation of flesh in Paul, see his *Theology of the New Testament*, 1:232–246. In praise of Bultmann's self-awareness as an interpreter, see David W. Congdon, *The Mission of Demythologizing: Rudolf Bultmann's Dialectical Theology* (Minneapolis: Fortress, 2015).

are simply explicating the letters when in fact they are propounding their own Christian theologies.[44]

Resurrection Now!

It turns out that most of the (admittedly tricky) exegetical puzzles in Rom 8 find their resolution in Paul's very vivid, very imminent understanding of the resurrection of the dead, which is, as Stowers rightly notes, a matter of ontology.[45] Οὐδὲν ἄρα νῦν κατάκριμα τοῖς ἐν Χριστῷ Ἰησοῦ, "So then, there is now no death sentence for those who are in Christ Jesus" (Rom 8:1). As Markus Öhler has shown,[46] κατάκριμα means not "condemnation," the verbal action of condemning (that would be τὸ κατακρινεῖν), but rather "sentence," that is, the penalty assessed, as per its frequent usage in the papyri and inscriptions. We know from Rom 5:12–21, the only other place Paul uses the word, that "the sentence" he means is death itself. His claim in Rom 8:1, then, is that people-in-Christ are no longer subject to the sentence of death. How so? ὁ γὰρ νόμος τοῦ πνεύματος τῆς ζωῆς ἐν Χριστῷ Ἰησοῦ ἠλευθέρωσέν σε ἀπὸ τοῦ νόμου τῆς ἁμαρτίας καὶ τοῦ θανάτου, "The law of the pneuma of life in Christ Jesus freed you from the law of sin and death" (Rom 8:2–3). As noted above, despite a mountain of Christian theological discourse about a supposedly Pauline "freedom from law," the only place Paul ever expressly speaks of "freedom from law" is here, where one is freed *from* the law *by* the law: "The law... freed you from the law." Ironic, don't you think?

If we want to understand this νόμος τῆς ἁμαρτίας καὶ τοῦ θανάτου, "law of sin and death" from which the person in Rom 8:2 is liberated, we cannot neglect one of the only other places where all three of these loaded terms occur together, 1 Cor 15:56, at the crescendo of Paul's discourse on the resurrection: τὸ δὲ κέντρον τοῦ θανάτου ἡ ἁμαρτία, ἡ δὲ δύναμις τῆς ἁμαρτίας ὁ νόμος, "The sting of death is sin, and the power of sin is the law." The reference to the law might seem

---

[44] I discuss this phenomenon at length in my *Paul, Then and Now*.
[45] Most critics will grant that, in 1 Cor 15, at least, Paul is talking about ontology, but they hedge on Rom 5–8, insisting that here his language is merely relational and existential (which is to say, unfalsifiable!). But it is precisely this premise that I am challenging, suggesting that, if he uses much the same language in both contexts, then we need to take the ontological implications seriously.
[46] Markus Öhler, "Romans 8 in Light of the Epigraphic Sources" (forthcoming).

out of place here;⁴⁷ Paul has not mentioned it anywhere in 1 Cor 15 up to this point, and the immediate context is about God's final triumph over death ("Where, O death, is your victory?" etc.). But viewed alongside Rom 8, this mention of the law makes a certain clear sense: By Paul's lights, the law of Moses acknowledges, legislates for, and everywhere assumes the vicissitudes of human error and mortality. But the Christ-gift, as Paul sees it, does not assume those vicissitudes; it actually translates people-in-Christ beyond human error and mortality by making them into immortal sons of God.⁴⁸ ὁ νόμος τοῦ πνεύματος τῆς ζωῆς, "the law of the pneuma of life," then, is the same law of the same God,⁴⁹ but in a form suited for these immortal sons of God, beings who neither sin nor die. (This idea is in fact amply attested in the Jewish mystical tradition, as detailed by Gershom Scholem.)⁵⁰

Paul's shorthand phrase for beings who *do* sin and die, the kind of creatures for whom the law of Moses legislates, is σάρξ, "flesh." Flesh is, *eo ipso*, mortal, corruptible, and subject to error (ἁμαρτία).⁵¹ This is the main point of Paul's discourse about the primeval human, Adam, in Rom 5: error and mortality, sin and death, go hand-in-hand. It is not just that people die because they sin; it is also that they sin because they die. The former, more famous claim is what Paul writes in Rom 5:12a: δι' ἑνὸς ἀνθρώπου ἡ ἁμαρτία εἰς τὸν κόσμον εἰσῆλθεν καὶ διὰ τῆς ἁμαρτίας ὁ

---

⁴⁷ So much so that F. W. Horn, "1 Korinther 15,56 – ein exegetischer Stachel," *ZNW* 82 (1991): 88–105 judges the whole verse to be a post-Pauline interpolation, as did Von Soden, Bousset, Moffatt, and others before him. But there is no warrant for such a judgment, either in the manuscript tradition or in Paul's actual discourse. H. W. Hollander and J. Holleman, "The Relationship of Death, Sin and Law in 1 Cor 15:56," *NovT* 35 (1993): 270–291 rightly argue for the authenticity of the verse, though they fail to see the sense in which Paul says the law is in fact relevant to the new creation, on which see Chapter 9.
⁴⁸ This is explicit in Rom 5:21: "The [Christ-]gift reigns through righteousness into life everlasting."
⁴⁹ See further Chapter 9.
⁵⁰ On the idea, see Gershom Scholem, *On the Kabbalah and Its Symbolism*, trans. Ralph Manheim (New York: Schocken, 1965); and on the best documented historical example, Scholem, *Sabbatai Sevi: The Mystical Messiah, 1626–1676*, trans. R. J. Zwi Werblowsky (Princeton: Princeton University Press, 1973).
⁵¹ Martin, *Corinthian Body*, 123–129, 168–174; Engberg-Pedersen, *Cosmology and Self*; Wasserman, *Death of the Soul*; Stowers, "Dilemma of Paul's Physics"; Dingeldein, "Gaining Virtue, Gaining Christ." This link between flesh and sin is the crucial premise of Rom 8:3: "God, having sent his own son in the likeness of the flesh of sin, and for sin, condemned sin in the flesh."

θάνατος, "Through one person, sin came into the cosmos, and through sin, death." In other words, death follows sin. But the latter, much lesser known claim is what he writes in the following clause, Rom 5:12b: εἰς πάντας ἀνθρώπους ὁ θάνατος διῆλθεν, ἐφ' ᾧ πάντες ἥμαρτον, "Death came through to all people, upon which [event] all sinned." Most interpreters render this lattermost clause "*because* all sinned," making Paul repeat himself, making him say a second time that death is a *consequence* of sin. But this majority gloss is (1) redundant,[52] (2) not what the Greek text says,[53] and (3) a conspicuous instance of theological confirmation bias. The most obvious antecedent of the relative pronoun in the phrase ἐφ' ᾧ is the immediately preceding clause ("Death came through to all people"), an event.[54] Thus ἐφ' ᾧ πάντες ἥμαρτον means "upon which [event] all sinned." In other words, sin follows mortality. It is not just that people die because they sin; it is also that they sin because they die.

If one wants, therefore – as Paul emphatically does – to become the kind of person who never sins, one must become the kind of person who never dies.[55] Rom 6 and Rom 8 are two panels in a diptych making just this point: Rom 6 in relation to Christ, Rom 8 in relation

---

[52] Which is, bizarrely, often cited as a reason in its favor. Thus, e.g., the otherwise excellent Leander E. Keck, *Romans* ANTC (Nashville: Abingdon, 2005), 148: "This translation [viz. '...upon which event all sinned'], exact as it may be, suggests that the ubiquity of death resulted in the universality of sin – the opposite of what Paul had just said: Death *follows* sin." But that is the point! Paul is not merely repeating himself. He is making two interrelated points in the two clauses of the verse: Death follows sin, and thereafter sin follows mortality.

[53] Of course, the prepositional phrase admits of several different possible readings, but "upon which" is by far the most natural, and "because" is marginally possible, at best (thus rightly Lyonnet, "Le sens de *eph ho* en Rom 5,12 et l'exégèse des Pères grecs," Bib 36 [1955]: 436–456). ἐπί plus the dative relative pronoun can indeed signify cause ("upon which cause," "for which reason") [BDF §235 (2)]), but the cause signified is the *antecedent* of the relative pronoun, not the clause that follows it. Interpreters who translate the end of Rom 5:12 "because all sinned" reverse this syntax, however, for no other reason than theological confirmation bias.

[54] Thus rightly, Theodor Zahn, *Der Brief des Paulus an die Römer* (Leipzig: Deichert, 1910), 263–267. Joseph A. Fitzmyer, *Romans: A New Translation with Introduction and Commentary*, AYB (New Haven: Yale University Press, 2008 [1993]), 415 concedes that this is the best account of the syntax, but then goes on to argue, unnecessarily, for what he calls a "consecutive meaning" (where ἐφ' ᾧ effectively means ὥστε).

[55] Longarino, *Problem of Death*, grasps this essential point better than most.

to the pneuma.⁵⁶ In Rom 6, Paul writes about Christ and about all the baptized: ὁ ἀποθανὼν δεδικαίωται ἀπὸ τῆς ἁμαρτίας, "The person who has died is rightwised away from sin" (Rom 6:7). Χριστὸς ἐγερθεὶς ἐκ νεκρῶν οὐκέτι ἀποθνῄσκει, "Christ, having been raised from the dead, no longer dies" (Rom 6:9). ὃ ἀπέθανεν, τῇ ἁμαρτίᾳ ἀπέθανεν ἐφάπαξ· ὃ δὲ ζῇ, ζῇ τῷ θεῷ, "What he died, he died to sin once for all; but what he lives, he lives to God" (Rom 6:10). The risen Christ, because he died, now lives beyond sin and death. And those who are baptized into him do likewise (Rom 6:3–4; this is what made H. A. A. Kennedy so squeamish). Thus far Rom 6.

In Rom 8, meanwhile, the medium of mortal, sinful existence Paul again calls σάρξ, "flesh," while the medium of the life beyond sin and death he calls pneuma. In the idiom of Rom 8, to attain that life beyond sin and death is actually to be "not in the flesh" (Rom 8:9). Just here we find another striking parallel between our passage, Rom 8, and the resurrection discourse of 1 Cor 15.⁵⁷ In Rom 8:8 Paul writes: οἱ δὲ ἐν σαρκὶ ὄντες θεῷ ἀρέσαι οὐ δύνανται, "*Those who are in the flesh are not able* to please God." The key thing here is Paul's understanding of what flesh is and is not capable of (δύναται). Here he highlights a specifically *moral* inability of flesh: the capacity to please God. In 1 Cor 15, on the other hand, Paul highlights a *physical* inability of flesh: σὰρξ καὶ αἷμα βασιλείαν θεοῦ κληρονομῆσαι οὐ δύναται, "*Flesh and blood are not able* to inherit the kingdom of God" (1 Cor 15:50). "Pleasing God" is the counterpart to sin, while "inheriting the kingdom of God" is the counterpart to death. Flesh can do neither, Paul says, but pneuma can do both. Pneuma makes one morally able to please God and fulfil

---

⁵⁶ The much-misunderstood Rom 7 is not meant – despite its vivid first-person monologue – to provide a thick description of anyone's actual experience (whether Adam's, Eve's, Israel's, Paul's, or whatever). It is meant, as Paul expressly says at the start of the monologue in Rom 7:7 (!), to make the point that *the law is not sin*. It makes that point by arguing that, whenever "the person who knows the law" (Rom 7:1) sins, it is not the fault of the law, but of her flesh. On flesh in Rom 7, see Wasserman, *Death of the Soul*; Dingeldein, "Gaining Virtue, Gaining Christ." On the crucial point that Rom 7 is about the law, not the self, see Paul W. Meyer, "The Worm at the Core of the Apple: Exegetical Reflections on Romans 7," in *The Word in This World: Essays in New Testament Exegesis and Theology*, ed. John T. Carroll (Louisville, KY: Westminster John Knox, 2004), 57–77.

⁵⁷ As was perceived in part by Martinus C. De Boer, *The Defeat of Death: Apocalyptic Eschatology in 1 Corinthians 15 and Romans 5* (Sheffield: JSOT Press, 1988).

the law, and physically able to slip the bonds of mortality and attain life everlasting.[58]

Like the risen, heavenly Christ, Paul's auditors at Rome are full of divine, life-making pneuma. Unlike the risen, heavenly Christ, however, Paul's auditors at Rome have not quite yet finished with their mortal bodies. For just a little while longer, until Christ appears, they still carry around death in their body parts. As Paul puts it in our passage, εἰ δὲ Χριστὸς ἐν ὑμῖν, τὸ μὲν σῶμα νεκρὸν διὰ ἁμαρτίαν τὸ δὲ πνεῦμα ζωὴ διὰ δικαιοσύνην, "If Christ is in you, the body is a corpse on account of sin, but the pneuma is life on account of righteousness" (Rom 8:10). These people-in-Christ have the pneuma, and they have bodies, but they do not yet have pneumatic bodies, as the risen Christ has.[59] They have flesh bodies, clay vessels (as Paul puts it elsewhere, 2 Cor 4:7) newly infused with divine, life-making pneuma. As Troels Engberg-Pedersen aptly comments, "Paul is telling them that if Christ('s pneuma) is in them, then their bodies are only a hollow shell – and in this sense actually dead – to be contrasted with the pneuma inside the shell, which stands for life."[60]

The trouble is that – because sin always accompanies mortality, as per Rom 5 – these temporary flesh bodies still act out. They have a mind of their own, so to speak (τὸ φρόνημα τῆς σαρκός, Rom 8:6),[61] and they do the kinds of indecent things doing which will actually prevent a person from inheriting the kingdom of God (Gal 5:21; 1 Cor 6:9–10). εἰ γὰρ κατὰ σάρκα ζῆτε, μέλλετε ἀποθνῄσκειν, "If you live according to the flesh, you are about to die" (Rom 8:13). The only viable course of action for Paul's Roman auditors, then, is actually to weaponize the divine pneuma within them to kill the deeds of their flesh bodies. εἰ δὲ πνεύματι τὰς πράξεις τοῦ σώματος θανατοῦτε, ζήσεσθε, "If by the pneuma you put to death the deeds of the body, you will live" (Rom 8:13). The pneuma can be weaponized in this way because it, too, has a mind of its own (τὸ δὲ φρόνημα τοῦ πνεύματος, Rom 8:6). In this respect, Volker Rabens is right to insist that Pauline ethics are only, always pneumatic, or spirit-empowered.[62]

---

[58] Thus rightly, Stowers, "Ordinary Humans."
[59] See further Martin, *Corinthian Body*, 123–129.
[60] Engberg-Pedersen, *Cosmology and Self*, 52.
[61] See Jason Valdez, "The Body and the Problem of Agency in Romans 8" (forthcoming).
[62] Volker Rabens, *The Holy Spirit and Ethics in Paul: Transformation and Empowering for Religious-Ethical Life*, WUNT 2/283 (Tübingen: Mohr Siebeck, 2010).

The goal in all of this is to join the risen Christ in finishing with one's mortal flesh body once and for all. This happens via metamorphosis at Christ's parousia, when flesh will give way entirely to pneuma, the corruptible to incorruptibility, the mortal to immortality. That is Paul's idiom in 1 Cor 15, but he refers to the same event in our passage, in Rom 8:11: εἰ δὲ τὸ πνεῦμα τοῦ ἐγείραντος τὸν Ἰησοῦν ἐκ νεκρῶν οἰκεῖ ἐν ὑμῖν, ὁ ἐγείρας Χριστὸν ἐκ νεκρῶν ζωοποιήσει καὶ τὰ θνητὰ σώματα ὑμῶν διὰ τοῦ ἐνοικοῦντος αὐτοῦ πνεύματος ἐν ὑμῖν, "If the pneuma of him who raised Jesus from the dead dwells in you, he who raised Christ from the dead will also make alive your mortal bodies through his pneuma that dwells in you." What happens at the parousia is not escape from embodiment altogether, but rather a metamorphosis of the body:[63] "He will make alive your mortal body," that is, transform it into an immortal body, a σῶμα πνευματικόν. The divine pneuma is, in both 1 Cor 15 and Rom 8, a πνεῦμα ζωοποιοῦν, "life-making pneuma." It is about physics – the physics of resurrection – no less than it is about ethics.

Masters of the Universe

What ties together the first, more "ethical" half of Rom 8 (vv. 1–17) with the second, more "cosmological" half (vv. 18–39) is – the reader will not be surprised to hear me say – resurrection. κτίσις, "creation," in Rom 8:18–39 refers to the whole nonhuman world, the fate of which is tied to the fate of humanity. According to the scenario Paul sketches, the world cannot undergo transformation until human beings do. ἡ ἀποκαραδοκία τῆς κτίσεως τὴν ἀποκάλυψιν τῶν υἱῶν τοῦ θεοῦ ἀπεκδέχεται, "The expectation of creation awaits the revelation of the sons of God" (Rom 8:19). And again, αὐτὴ ἡ κτίσις ἐλευθερωθήσεται ἀπὸ τῆς δουλείας τῆς φθορᾶς εἰς τὴν ἐλευθερίαν τῆς δόξης τῶν τέκνων τοῦ θεοῦ, "The creation itself shall be set free from slavery to corruption into the freedom of the glory of the children of God" (Rom 8:21). This "revelation of the sons of God" is nothing other than their attainment of immortal bodies, either (for those few dead-in-Christ) through resurrection or (for the majority still alive at the parousia of Jesus) through direct transformation. Becoming "sons of God" in this sense means precisely getting bodies fit for the kingdom of God: υἱοθεσίαν ἀπεκδεχόμενοι, τὴν ἀπολύτρωσιν τοῦ σώματος ἡμῶν, "We await our establishment as sons,

---

[63] Thus rightly, Litwa, *We Are Being Transformed.*

that is, the ransoming of our body" (Rom 8:23). People-in-Christ attain their immortal, incorruptible form, and then in turn the nonuhuman creation attains its immortal, incorruptible form.[64]

The terms are admittedly different (κτίσις and κόσμος, respectively), but this is the same event Paul means in Rom 4 when he speaks of ἡ ἐπαγγελία τῷ Ἀβραὰμ ἢ τῷ σπέρματι αὐτοῦ, τὸ κληρονόμον αὐτὸν εἶναι κόσμου, "the promise to Abraham, or to his seed, that he would be heir of the cosmos" (Rom 4:13).[65] The sons of God, who are the seed of Abraham, actually inherit the cosmos when they, and it, enter into incorruptible glory. Just as παράγει τὸ σχῆμα τοῦ κόσμου τούτου, "The form of this cosmos is passing away" (1 Cor 7:31) but gives way to a new, incorruptible form, so also κτίσις gives way to καινὴ κτίσις, creation to new creation (Gal 6:15; 2 Cor 5:17).[66] Just as "if a person is in Christ, the new creation has come" (2 Cor 5:17), so also if a person is in Christ, she is effectively living the beatific life of resurrected dead.

People who are very soon to inherit the entire cosmos must, naturally, be made of sturdy stuff, not the flimsy χοῦς, "dust" (1 Cor 15:47–49 citing Gen 2:7) or ὄστρακον, "clay" (2 Cor 4:7) that make up flesh and blood bodies (according to the anatomical theory that Paul gets from Genesis 2).[67] They require bodies suited for the formidable task, bodies like, well, the body of the heavenly human, the risen Jesus. They need, in other words, to be conformed to his image. Thus Paul reasons in Rom 8: οὓς προέγνω, καὶ προώρισεν συμμόρφους τῆς εἰκόνος τοῦ υἱοῦ αὐτοῦ, εἰς τὸ εἶναι αὐτὸν πρωτότοκον ἐν πολλοῖς ἀδελφοῖς, "Those whom God foreknew, he also predetermined to be

---

[64] Thus rightly, Engberg-Pedersen, *Cosmology and Self*, 38: "What he wanted to talk about was the generation of an altogether new pneumatic world of eternal life in which everything that was tied to the lower elements of the present world of corruption and death would be transformed into a wholly different kind of heavenly existence."

[65] Cf. also Gal 3:14: "That in Christ Jesus the blessing of Abraham might come to the gentiles, that we might receive *the promise of the pneuma* through trust." This red thread in Paul's argument is ingeniously demonstrated by Thiessen, *Paul and the Gentile Problem*, 129–160.

[66] Paul uses καινός, not νέος, but I do not see a strong contrast implied by that word choice. Καινός can sometimes have the sense of "renewed" as opposed to "altogether novel," but, be that as it may, Paul's new creation is manifestly more than just a reboot of the *status quo ante*.

[67] Thus rightly, Stowers, "Dilemma of Paul's Physics," 245: "Adam's problem was that he was created out of earth of flesh and animal soul that are prone to passion, and thus sin and decay, as almost every commentator up to Augustine emphasized."

conformed to the image of his son, in order that he [Christ] would be the firstborn among many brothers" (Rom 8:29). To become a son of God is to become a brother of the firstborn son of God, Jesus, by gaining a ransomed body of the same glorious, pneumatic kind as his resurrected body. It is to be like Christ, physically as well as morally.[68] This is why, at the end of our chapter, Paul makes the point that no other superhuman beings (ἄγγελοι, ἀρχαί, δυνάμεις, etc. – what Schweitzer called "the angel powers") can stand in the way of people-in-Christ: because they, people-in-Christ, are actually higher up the chain of glory than angels, archons, powers, etc.[69] The holy people sit in judgment over angels (1 Cor 6:3). They are exalted over all things except their brother Christ and God the father himself.

Let us return, then, to those snapshots from the history of research. Schweitzer's argument from the Jewish apocalypses and Stowers's from the popular philosophers, different as they may at first appear, are not rival accounts (à la "Judaism versus Hellenism") but rather complementary.[70] Jewish eschatology provides scenarios for envisioning the utopian kingdom of God (scenarios, plural, not just one; on this issue, Schweitzer overreached).[71] But Jewish eschatology does not prescribe any particular physics. Paul's particular physics – or, for that matter, Philo's, or 2 Baruch's, or 2 Enoch's, etc. – he will have gotten from his own philosophical environment, which includes biblical and Jewish sources but also a great deal else beside.[72] It is certainly possible, therefore, and in my view it is in fact the case, that Schweitzer is basically right about what he calls "the resurrection mode of existence" and Stowers basically right about the physics of this scenario. Paul paints a portrait of the moral life of people who have transcended the human condition for which the law of Moses legislates, who are, in

---

[68] Stowers, "Dilemma of Paul's Physics," 246: "God recreated Jesus Christ out of his own *pneuma* in the resurrection to be the archetype of a new species."
[69] On this chain of glory in Deuteronomy and in Paul, see David A. Burnett, "A Neglected Deuteronomic Scriptural Matrix for the Nature of the Resurrection Body in 1 Corinthians 15:39–42," in *Scripture, Texts, and Tracings in 1 Corinthians*, ed. Linda L. Belleville and B. J. Oropeza (Lanham, MD: Lexington/Fortress, 2019), 187–212.
[70] See Engberg-Pedersen, ed., *Paul beyond the Judaism/Hellenism Divide*.
[71] On this weak spot in Schweitzer's account, see Novenson, *Christ among the Messiahs*.
[72] See Annette Yoshiko Reed, "Was There Science in Ancient Judaism? Historical and Cross-Cultural Reflections on Religion and Science," *SR* 36 (2007): 461–495.

that sense, "not in the flesh." To be sure, at the moment that Paul writes to these gentiles-in-Christ at Rome, they are still carrying around mortal bodies (θνητὰ σώματα), but those will very soon become immortal, pneumatic bodies.[73] And anyway, because their insides are already full of that coming pneuma, they are already capable of the kind of moral life lived by the immortal sons of God: the heavenly ἅγιοι (not "saints" but angels)[74] and the heavenly person himself, Jesus, into whose divine image they are being metamorphosed.

Conclusion

In his Letter to the Romans, Paul strains to describe a state of affairs that we might call the moral life of the resurrected dead. This state of affairs will obtain perfectly and entirely in the very near future when all the righteous dead are raised (1 Thess 4:13–18; 1 Cor 15:12–58), but it already obtains in the special case of Christ, who has experienced what the rest of the dead still await, and in the case of people-in-Christ whose insides are full of Christ's pneuma, which is the stuff of resurrected, celestial bodies. This moral life of the resurrected dead Paul characterizes in terms of liberty and justice for all. "Liberty," that is, freedom from the otherwise ubiquitous menace of sin, the physical decay that (Paul thinks) attends sin, and the inevitable end of that decay, namely death. "Justice," or an equally good translation, "righteousness," a state of perfect moral excellence where the upright statutes of the law are performed effortlessly and ceaselessly through pneumatically endowed virtue. "For all" in the sense that Paul clarifies both at the beginning and at the end of Romans: "If God, who will rightwise the circumcision from trust, is one, [he will also rightwise] the foreskin through [that same] trust" (Rom 3:30), and "There is no distinction between Jew and Greek, for the same Lord is over all" (Rom 10:12). Jews, Paul thinks, always had the promise of this eschatological liberty and justice, while gentiles had not even that; but in God's mercy all now have access to the thing itself. They can live the pneumatic life of the resurrected dead even now, during the short interval until the final ransom of their entire bodies.

[73] Troels Engberg-Pedersen, "Complete and Incomplete Transformation in Paul: A Philosophical Reading of Paul on Body and Spirit," in *Metamorphoses: Resurrection, Body, and Transformative Practices in Early Christianity*, ed. Turid Karlsen Seim and Jorunn Økland (Berlin: De Gruyter, 2009), 123–146.
[74] John J. Collins, "The Angelic Life," in *Metamorphoses*, 291–310.

9 | *The End of the Law and the Last Man*

Rabbi Eliyahu Kohen Ittamari (died 1729) was a prominent preacher and rabbinic jurist in Ottoman Izmir at the turn of the eighteenth century. He was also a kabbalist,[1] and although probably not a Sabbatean (that is, a loyalist of the messiah Sabbatai Zvi, 1626–1676),[2] he developed his own ingenious account of a change in the Torah in the messianic age. In one remarkable passage, commenting on why it is that Torah scrolls for liturgical use must be written without vowels or accents, Eliyahu Kohen reasons as follows:

The state of the Torah as it existed in the sight of God, before it was transmitted to the lower spheres. For he had before him numerous letters that were not joined into words as is the case today, because the actual arrangement of the words would depend on the way in which this lower world conducted itself. Because of Adam's sin, God arranged the letters before him into the words describing death and other earthly things, such as levirate marriage. Without sin there would have been no death. The same letters would have been joined into words telling a different story. That is why the scroll of the Torah contains no vowels, no punctuation, and no accents, as an allusion to the Torah which originally formed a heap of unarranged letters. The divine purpose will be revealed in the Torah at the coming of the Messiah, who will engulf death forever, so that there will be no room in the Torah for anything related to death, uncleanness, and the like.

---

[1] Not an especially famous one, though he receives due attention in Scholem, *Kabbalah and Its Symbolism*; and Shaul Magid, *From Metaphysics to Midrash: Myth, History, and the Interpretation of Scripture in Lurianic Kabbala* (Bloomington: Indiana University Press, 2008).

[2] Scholem speculates that perhaps he was a Sabbatean, though only ever a moderate, and that he may have repented of his Sabbateanism in his later years ("R. Elijah Ha-cohen Ha-itamari and the Sabbathaism," in *Alexander Marx Jubilee Volume* [New York: Jewish Theological Seminary, 1950], 451–470 [Hebrew]). Perhaps. Simpler, however, is the hypothesis that he was kabbalist though not Sabbatean.

For then God will annul the present combination of letters that form the words of our present Torah and will compose the letters into other words, which will form new sentences speaking of other things. This is the meaning of the words of Isaiah: *A Torah will proceed from me* [Isa 51:4], which was already interpreted by the ancient rabbis to mean: *A new Torah will proceed from me* [Lev. Rab. 13:3]. Does this mean that the Torah is not eternally valid? No, it means that the scroll of the Torah will be as it is now, but that God will teach us to read it in accordance with another arrangement of the letters, and enlighten us as to the division and combination of the words.[3]

Eliyahu Kohen subscribes to the traditional rabbinic belief in the eternity of the Torah,[4] but he also takes the (likewise traditional) view that when the messiah comes and the righteous dead are raised, death will be no more.[5] But if both these things are true, then there is a logical problem: The Torah manifestly legislates for *mortals* – people who are born, grow, eat, drink, marry, bear children, generate ritual impurity, inherit property, conduct business, and eventually die.[6] Hence the stated example of levirate marriage, according to which a man whose brother dies is obligated to marry the dead brother's widow (Deut 25:5–10). But like Jesus in Mark 12:18–27,[7] Eliyahu Kohen reckons that, in the resurrection, the kind of situation for which the law of the *levir* provides simply will not obtain. When marriage and death are no more, in the nature of the case, there can be no levirate marriage.[8]

---

[3] Rabbi Eliyahu Kohen Ittamari of Smyrna, apud Hayim Joseph David Azulai, *Devash le-Fi* (Livorno, 1801), 50a. Translation in Gershom Scholem, "The Meaning of the Torah in Jewish Mysticism," in *Kabbalah and Its Symbolism*, 32–86.

[4] Well summarized by George Foot Moore, *Judaism in the First Centuries of the Christian Era*, 3 vols. (Cambridge, MA: Harvard University Press, 1927–1930), 1:263–280.

[5] Well summarized by Moore, *Judaism*, 2:379–395.

[6] This is arguably the point of m. Abot 3:19: "R. Eleazar Hisma said: [The rules about] bird-offerings and the onset of menstruation – these are the essentials of the *halakhot*." That is, commandments regarding ritual impurity are paramount precisely because they provide for the conditions of human mortality.

[7] And close parallel in Matt 22:23–33. The parallel in Luke 20:27–40 changes Mark's sense to suggest that those who *will one day* be worthy of resurrection are those who *already now* renounce marriage and sex, on which see further Turid Karlsen Seim, "Children of the Resurrection: Perspectives on Angelic Asceticism in Luke-Acts," in *Asceticism and the New Testament*, ed. Leif E. Vaage and Vincent L. Wimbush (London: Routledge, 1999), 115–125.

[8] See Caroline Vander Stichele, "Like Angels in Heaven: Corporeality, Resurrection, and Gender in Mark 12:18–27," in *Begin with the Body: Corporeality, Religion, and Gender*, ed. Jonneke Bekkenkamp and Maaike de

Unlike Jesus, however, Eliyahu Kohen presses the question how it is, then, that the Torah can abide forever if the people for whom it legislates will be different kinds of beings entirely.

The End of the Law

It is an excellent question, and Eliyahu Kohen's answer is as good as any I know. But his is not the first answer, not by a long shot. The struggle to understand the relation between divine law and human mortality goes back to antiquity.[9] And this realization can help us to resolve what is perhaps the most notorious problem in the study of the apostle Paul, namely: his supposedly tortured stance toward the law of Moses. The late, great Heikki Räisänen wrote about Paul and the Torah:

> We find Paul struggling with the problem that a *divine* institution has been *abolished* through what God has done in Christ. Most of Paul's troubles can be reduced to this simple formula.... The problem of an abolition of a divine institution is clearly reflected in Paul's inability to give a satisfactory answer to the question, "Why then did God give this weak and imperfect law in the first place?".... If something is truly divine, it is hardly capable of being abrogated![10]

Let us grant for the sake of argument that Räisänen's terms "abolish" and "abrogate" are fitting for what Paul says about the law. (In fact, they are not, but we will deal with that later.) Räisänen's claim has a certain intuitive force, but it is actually a *non sequitur*. Or, perhaps better, it is a theological axiom – a thing asserted, not argued for. Why, we might ask, should a divine institution *not* admit of abrogation? Only because of certain presuppositions about what is worthy of the divine. But we have good reasons for doubting whether Paul – not to mention numerous other ancient and medieval Jews and Christians! – would have granted Räisänen's presuppositions.

Haardt (Leuven: Peeters, 1998), 215–232; Taylor G. Petrey, "The Resurrection Body," in *The Oxford Handbook of New Testament, Gender, and Sexuality*, ed. Benjamin H. Dunning (Oxford: Oxford University Press, 2019), 661–674.

[9] See Hayes, *Divine Law*.
[10] Heikki Räisänen, *Paul and the Law*, WUNT 29 (Tübingen: Mohr Siebeck, 1983), 264–265; emphasis original.

Eva Mroczek and Rebecca Scharbach Wollenberg have recently explored how, contra Räisänen's axiom, a conspicuous feature of ancient Jewish views of the Torah was precisely its capacity to undergo change, and in particular, to accommodate the changing condition of Israel.[11] One key text adduced by both Mroczek and Wollenberg is t. Sanh. 4:7, on how the script and language of the Torah underwent a change upon the return of the exiles from Babylon:

> Ezra was worthy that the Torah should have been given at his hand, if it hadn't been that Moses preceded him... Indeed the writing and language [as we have it] was given at his [Ezra's] hand, as it is said, *The writing of the message was Aramaic script and its interpretation was Aramaic* [Ezra 4:7].... As it is written, *He shall write for himself this mishneh ha-Torah* [Deut 17:18]. [*Mishneh ha-Torah* here means] a Torah that is destined to change.... The Torah was [originally] given to Israel in Aramaic writing, but when they sinned its language changed for them. Then when they repented in the days of Ezra, it returned for them to Aramaic writing. (t. Sanh. 4:7; trans. Wollenberg)

The Tosefta interprets the novel Assyrian script and Aramaic translation adopted in the Persian period as fulfilling the commandment in Deut 17 that the king should make a *mishneh ha-Torah*, understood here not as a *copy of* the Torah but rather as a *change in* the Torah. On this ingenious interpretation, God and Moses built into the Torah itself a capacity to adapt to new circumstances.[12] In this particular instance, the Tosefta reasons, the Torah changed to accommodate Israel's change in moral status: sinful and repentant, in turn.

---

[11] Eva Mroczek, "The Embarrassing Bible," public lecture at the University of San Francisco (22 March 2017), www.youtube.com/watch?v=nb3yL0UjKnA; Eva Mroczek, "Without Torah and Scripture: Biblical Absence and the History of Revelation," *Hebrew Studies* 61 (2020): 97–122; Rebecca Scharbach Wollenberg, "The Book That Changed: Narratives of Ezran Authorship as Late Antique Biblical Criticism," *JBL* 138 (2019): 143–160; Rebecca Scharbach Wollenberg, *The Closed Book: How the Rabbis Taught the Jews (Not) to Read the Bible* (Princeton: Princeton University Press, 2023). I owe thanks, too, to Logan Williams for several instructive conversations on this issue.

[12] Another *locus classicus* for this idea is the story of Moses receiving the law in two successive versions: the original inscribed by the finger of God but destroyed by Moses at the golden calf episode (Exod 31–32) and the second copy inscribed thereafter (Exod 34). Perhaps, some premodern interpreters reasoned, that former, lost version of the Torah was the Torah in its pristine, protological and eschatological state (Zohar I:26b; II:117b; III:124b, 153a, 255a; elaborating on b. Shabb. 146a). See further Scholem, "Meaning of the Torah," 66–71.

Wollenberg aptly comments on this passage: "The changes that Ezra introduced in the biblical text were directed at returning Torah to its original form after a sinful period in the history of Israel had caused the language of the Torah to change."[13] Mroczek generalizes about what she calls the ancient "biblical theology" that underlies this story: "The idea that the text of the Bible underwent processes of historical change and that its transmission was not wholly perfect or unbroken is not a discovery of modern historical-critical scholarship, but part of what premodern writers already assumed about their texts."[14] Whereas Tosefta Sanhedrin imagines a *past* change in the Torah at the return from exile, other premodern writers imagine a *future* change in the Torah at the eschaton. Eliyahu Kohen (who was early modern, not premodern, but still) is a case in point: The Torah is the divine institution *par excellence*, and yet, in the age to come, it will have to be something other than what it is now, because Israel will be something other than what it is now. As Mroczek puts it, "It is not simply that the Jews know and follow the Torah; the Torah also knows and follows the Jews."[15] Numerous premodern thinkers reckoned with this theological puzzle, and Paul was one of them. That is the argument of this final chapter.

There are many texts from the letters of Paul that are relevant here, and we will touch on a number of them below, but there is one that makes an especially good point of reference, both because it bears directly on the question and because it has been a bone of contention among interpreters. I mean Rom 10:4: τέλος γὰρ νόμου Χριστὸς εἰς δικαιοσύνην παντὶ τῷ πιστεύοντι, "For Christ is the end of the law unto righteousness for everyone who trusts." The verse is part of a paragraph in which Paul diagnoses his co-ethnics with what he calls "zeal without recognition," thus:

Brothers, the goodwill of my heart and my petition to God for [Israel] is for deliverance. For I testify for them that they have zeal for God, but not with recognition. For not recognizing the righteousness of God and seeking to establish their own, they did not submit to the righteousness of God. For Christ is the end of the law unto righteousness for everyone who trusts. For Moses writes [about] the righteousness from the law that *The person who*

---

[13] Wollenberg, "The Book That Changed," 154.
[14] Mroczek, "Without Torah and Scripture," 100.
[15] Mroczek, "The Embarrassing Bible."

does these things shall live in them [Lev 18:5]. *But the righteousness from trust says... The word is near you, in your mouth and in your heart* [Deut 30:14], *that is, the word of trust that we proclaim.* (Rom 10:1–8)

Despite its notoriety, our verse is not especially complicated. There is a question which term is the subject and which the predicate, in the absence of the article to disambiguate. Although τέλος is written first, this is probably for emphasis, and χριστός is actually the subject, thus "Christ is the end of the law," not "The end of the law is Christ."[16] It is a verbless clause, so we must supply a form of εἶναι. Julian Hills has argued that it should be the imperfect rather than the present,[17] but this is not necessary, and in any case not too much hangs on it. Some modern commentators dispute whether νόμος here is the Torah of Moses or a norm or principle more generally,[18] but there are no good reasons for thinking it means the latter. Most of the debate about this verse is lexical and focuses on τέλος, which is remarkably well matched by the English word "end." The commentators struggle mightily over the question whether τέλος here means "cessation" (one sense of English "end")[19] or rather "goal" (another sense of English "end").[20] Some also add a third possible gloss, "fulfillment," but those who make this move usually import the idea from the sermon on the mount in Matt 5:17: "I came not to abolish but to fulfill [πληρῶσαι] the law and the prophets."[21]

Perhaps unsurprisingly for the field of Pauline studies, interpretations of our verse are numerous, pedantic, and theologically fraught.[22] In particular, the debate whether to take τέλος here as cessation or goal is entangled with centuries-old Protestant

---

[16] Thus rightly Fitzmyer, *Romans*, 584.
[17] Julian V. Hills, "Christ Was the Goal of the Law (Romans 10:4)," *JTS* 44 (1993): 585–592.
[18] E.g., William Sanday and Arthur C. Headlam, *The Epistle to the Romans*, 5th ed., ICC (Edinburgh: T&T Clark 1902), 284.
[19] Thus, e.g., Augustine amongst ancient commentators, Käsemann amongst modern.
[20] Thus, e.g., Chrysostom amongst ancient commentators, Barth amongst modern.
[21] Thus, e.g., Erasmus. "Fulfillment" is not a normal sense of τέλος. And, what is more, in Paul's usage, unlike Matthew's, it is not *Christ* but *Christ-believers* who fulfil the law (Gal 5:14; Rom 13:8–10; and cf. Jas 2:8).
[22] See Robert Badenas, *Christ the End of the Law: Romans 10:4 in Pauline Perspective*, JSNTSup 10 (Sheffield: JSOT Press, 1985) for fulsome discussion of all the many debates.

controversies over the possibility of a so-called *tertius usus legis*, "third use of the law."²³ Nor are the schools of thought reduceable to just two. In a very thorough *Forschungsbericht*, Thomas Schreiner identifies eight main lines of interpretation of our verse, each with its own subdivisions! Schreiner's eight options, with exemplary proponents he identifies for each, are:²⁴

1. The law is abolished (e.g., Heikki Räisänen).
2. The messianic age puts an end to the age of the law (e.g., W. D. Davies).
3. The law is ended *as a way of salvation* (e.g., Richard Longenecker).
4. Christ puts an end to the *ceremonial* law (e.g., Christoph Haufe).
5. The *exclusivity* of the law is set aside (e.g., James D. G. Dunn).
6. Christ is the goal of the law (e.g., Lloyd Gaston).
7. Christ is the end *and* goal of the law (e.g., Ulrich Wilckens).
8. Christ puts an end to using the law *to establish one's own righteousness* (e.g., Rudolf Bultmann).

It is not my intention here to explore each of these views, much less to adjudicate among them. I am confident, nay, certain that most of the points of dispute are much more normative-theological than they are exegetical, which is fine. For present purposes, however, I am only interested in making sense of the text in its historical context.²⁵

Apropos of my historical-contextual interest, there is one school of thought in Schreiner's list that calls for some reconsideration, namely, the hypothesis that "the messianic age puts an end to the age of the law." This is a very unfashionable view nowadays. Schreiner dispatches it with a couple of sentences: "The fatal defect in this theory is the weakness of the alleged Jewish evidence. Adequate proof is lacking in rabbinic literature that the law would in fact be abrogated during the Messianic age."²⁶ In support of this judgment, Schreiner cites an excellent 1974 article by Peter Schäfer as having laid to rest the

---

[23] John Calvin took "Christ the End of the Law" as the title for his preface to the 1550 Geneva Bible. On the *tertius usus legis* debate, see the essays in Linebaugh, ed., *God's Two Words*.

[24] Thomas R. Schreiner, "Paul's View of the Law in Romans 10:4–5," *WTJ* 55 (1993): 113–124.

[25] On this methodological distinction, see Novenson, "Our Apostles, Ourselves."

[26] Schreiner, "Paul's View of the Law," 115.

Torah-in-the-messianic-age hypothesis.[27] In terms of bibliographical history, this is true. Almost all the great proponents of the hypothesis – Abba Hillel Silver, Albert Schweitzer, Leo Baeck, W. D. Davies, Alejandro Diez Macho, Hans-Joachim Schoeps, and Joseph Fitzmyer, among others[28] – wrote before Schäfer. Writing shortly after Schäfer, E. P. Sanders also decisively rejected the hypothesis in his *Paul and Palestinian Judaism*.[29] I suspect that the weight of Sanders's influence – along with the fact that the next generation of New Testament scholars has tended not to read rabbinics as Davies, Fitzmyer, and Sanders did – effectively took this venerable old hypothesis off the table.

It is not my intention to put it back on the table. The Torah-in-the-messianic-age hypothesis that Schäfer laid to rest deserved its fate. It was based above all on a slapdash reading of one particular passage in Bavli Sanhedrin:[30] "The Tanna debe Eliyahu teaches: The world is to exist six thousand years: Two thousand years of desolation, two thousand years for the Torah, and two thousand years for the messianic era. But through our many iniquities all these years have been lost" (b. Sanh. 97a–b). *Eureka*, New Testament scholars thought! A neat distinction between the age of the law and the age of the

---

[27] Peter Schäfer, "Die Torah der messianischen Zeit," ZNW 65 (1974): 27–42. See also the earlier criticisms raised by Samuel Sandmel, *The Genius of Paul: A Study in History* (New York: Farrar, Straus & Cudahy, 1958); and Ernst Bammel, "Nomos Christou," in *Studia Evangelica III*, ed. F. L. Cross (Berlin: Akademie Verlag, 1964), 120–128; and the discussion of the whole debate in Andrew Chester, *Messiah and Exaltation: Jewish Messianic and Visionary Traditions and New Testament Christology*, WUNT 207 (Tübingen: Mohr Siebeck, 2007), 497–536.

[28] Schweitzer, *Mysticism*, 177–204, especially 189–193; Abba Hillel Silver, *A History of Messianic Speculation in Israel* (New York: Macmillan, 1927), 3–35; Leo Baeck, "The Faith of Paul," *JJS* 3 (1952): 93–110; W. D. Davies, *Torah in the Messianic Age and/or the Age to Come* (Philadelphia: SBL, 1952); W. D. Davies, *The Setting of the Sermon on the Mount* (Cambridge: Cambridge University Press, 1966); Alejandro Diez Macho, "Cesara la Tora en la Edad Mesianica?" *EstBib* 12 (1953): 115–158; and *EstBib* 13 (1954): 5–51; H. J. Schoeps, *Paul: The Theology of the Apostle in the Light of Jewish Religious History*, trans. Harold Knight (London: Lutterworth, 1961), 168–175; Joseph Fitzmyer, "Saint Paul and the Law," *The Jurist* 27 (1967): 18–36.

[29] Sanders, *Paul and Palestinian Judaism*, 476–481, here 479–480: "It seems certain in any case that Paul did not base his view on such reasoning. He never appeals to the fact that the Messiah has come as a reason for holding the law invalid. He has many opportunities to do so.... If such reasoning governed his view, he kept it completely to himself."

[30] And parallel at b. Avod. Zar. 9a; cf. also b. Rosh Hash. 31a.

messiah, a ready-made theologoumenon taken over by the apostle. "The messiah is the end of the law." Q.E.D. But of course, it is not as simple as that. Even this text does not say that the Torah *comes to an end* in the messianic age, and other rabbinic discussions presuppose or even insist that it endures.[31] In this text, too, the division of ages is ideal, not real; the final clause says that the messianic age should have come by now but has not, due to Israel's transgressions.[32] Even more problematic than the dilettantish exegesis, however, is the way many twentieth-century New Testament scholars conceived the relation between the Talmud and the New Testament: the supposition that later rabbinic texts can be called upon, when needed, to supply dogmas to vindicate New Testament writers for ideas that might otherwise seem outlandish.[33] Many younger New Testament scholars nowadays, duly chastened during graduate school about doing this kind of thing, simply opt not to do Jewish studies. You cannot lose if you do not try. But that is not the way forward.[34]

Eschatological Anthropology

I have no interest in reviving the old Torah-in-the-messianic-age hypothesis. But I do think there is a subtler, more productive comparison to be made here.[35] I propose that we can make compelling sense of Paul as reflecting on the age-old puzzle of the relation of divine law to human mortality. We will, however, have to give up the instant gratification of a supposed Jewish dogma about the end of the law in

---

[31] Thus rightly Schäfer, "Die Torah der messianischen Zeit."
[32] See further Michael E. Stone, "Apocalyptic Historiography," in *Ancient Judaism: New Visions and Views* (Grand Rapids, MI: Eerdmans, 2011), 59–89.
[33] A habit accurately diagnosed by Sandmel, "Parallelomania" and Sanders, *Paul and Palestinian Judaism*, in particular in the widespread use of the Strack Billerbeck *Kommentar*, which has now been translated into English by Jacob Cerone and Joseph Longarino (Bellingham, WA: Lexham, 2021).
[34] Thus rightly Geza Vermes, "Jewish Studies and New Testament Interpretation," *JJS* 31 (1980): 1–17; William Horbury, "Introduction to the First Edition," in *Messianism among Jews and Christians: Biblical and Historical Studies*, 2nd ed. (London: T&T Clark, 2016), 29–50; Markus Bockmuehl, *Seeing the Word: Refocusing New Testament Study* (Grand Rapids, MI: Baker, 2006).
[35] Cf. the apt judgment of Chester, *Messiah and Exaltation*, 498–499: "The results of their [Davies et al.] studies have been mostly meagre and unconvincing. But this is at least partly, I would want to argue, because their approach has been both too limited and also in many ways the wrong way round."

the messianic age. This subtler, more productive comparison has to do with what we might call *eschatological anthropology*, that is, how exactly one imagines the conditions of human life in the age to come.[36] There are in fact a great many ways that one might imagine those conditions, many of which are expressly entertained in our primary sources.[37]

One important example is a dispute recorded in Bavli Shabbat:

R. Simeon b. Eleazar said: Perform [charity] while you can find [a beneficiary], you have the opportunity, and it is still in your power. Solomon in his wisdom, too, said: *Remember also your creator in the days of your youth, before the evil days come* – this refers to the days of old age – *and the years draw nigh when you shall say: I have no pleasure in them* [Eccl 12:1] – this refers to the messianic age, when there is neither merit nor guilt. Now he disagrees with Samuel, who said: The only difference between this world and the messianic age is in respect of servitude to [foreign] powers, for it is said, *For the poor shall never cease out of the land* [Deut 15:11]. (b. Shab. 151b)

Here, R. Simeon b. Eleazar (a contemporary of R. Judah the Patriarch, turn of the third c. CE) is said to attest the view that in the messianic age people will fulfill the law entirely and effortlessly, so that there will be neither merit (for obeying the commandments when one might have done otherwise) nor guilt (for transgressing the commandments). This is his gloss on Eccl 12:1: "the years to come when you shall say: I have no pleasure in them" – no pleasure because no merit or guilt, just

---

[36] A point well made by Morton Smith in his review of Davies, *Torah in the Messianic Age*, in *JBL* 72 (1953): 193: "Any study of the future of the Law should be closely connected with an account of the general concepts of future bliss." Sarah Harding, *Paul's Eschatological Anthropology* (Minneapolis: Fortress, 2015) perceptively puts her finger on this issue, though in my view her generous concession to (what she calls) the overlap of the eons causes her to lose sight of Paul's imminent eschatology. The best account known to me of the complicated idea of eschatological anthropology is Benjamin H. Dunning, *Specters of Paul: Sexual Difference in Early Christian Thought* (Philadelphia: University of Pennsylvania Press, 2011).

[37] Although the philosophical treatise on resurrection is an ancient Christian, not Jewish, genre, it is overstatement to say (as does Alan J. Avery-Peck, "Resurrection of the Body in Early Rabbinic Judaism," *Deuterocanonical and Cognate Literature Yearbook* 2009 [2009]: 243–266) that the rabbis neglect to discuss the nature of the resurrection. Discuss it they certainly do, just in their own, different literary mode.

undifferentiated law-abiding.[38] By contrast, the view here attributed to Samuel (i.e., Samuel bar Abba of Nehardea, fl. early third c. CE) is more modest. In the messianic age, according to this view, there will still be merit and guilt, which is to say that people will *not* be perfectly, effortlessly, perpetually righteous. The difference between the present age and the messianic age is not anthropological but political: When the messiah comes, Israel will no longer be dominated by foreign powers.[39] People, however, will still be then more or less what they are now. For instance, poverty, and therefore also almsgiving, will perdure, Samuel reasons from Deut 15:11: "The poor shall never cease out of the land."

Within the limited scope of this debate in b. Shab. 151b, the view of R. Simeon b. Eleazar is more optimistic than that of Samuel. But there are other views more optimistic than either of them, as, for instance, in a passage in Ecclesiastes Rabbah (post-Bavli, perhaps eighth c. CE). The midrash reads:

Another interpretation of *I wound and I heal* [Deut 32:39]: R. Hanina said in the name of R. Simeon b. Lakish, R. Joshua of Siknin in the name of R. Yohanan, and R. Levi in the name of R. Yohanan: It is not written here *I smite* but *I wound* [מחצתי] – that is, the distinction [מחיצה] which I made between the celestial creatures and the terrestrial ones, namely, that the former endure while the latter die, holds good only in this world, but in the time to come there will be no death at all, as it is stated, *He will swallow up death forever* [Isa 25:8]. R. Abba said: That distinction, too, I [God] shall heal; *I made a distinction* [מחצתי], and the distinction which I made *I heal*. (Eccl. Rab. 1.4.3)

---

[38] A scenario aptly characterized by Christine Hayes, writing in a different context: "For both of these prophets [Jer 31:31–34; Ezek 36:24–25], it is not the law that will change in the messianic future. The same laws and rules will continue to function as residency requirements for those who would live in Yahweh's land. What will change is *human nature*. Israel will be hardwired to obey Yahweh's will without effort or struggle.... With perfect knowledge of Yahweh's teaching, obedience to the divine law is automatic, a state we may refer to as 'robo-righteousness'" (Hayes, *Divine Law*, 48).

[39] A very widely attested scenario in ancient sources; see discussion in John J. Collins, *The Scepter and the Star: Messianism in Light of the Dead Sea Scrolls*, 2nd ed. (Grand Rapids, MI: Eerdmans, 2010); Matthew V. Novenson, *Grammar of Messianism: An Ancient Jewish Political Idiom and Its Users* (Oxford: Oxford University Press, 2017).

On this view of the messianic age, it is not just gentile domination that shall pass away, nor even just sin – as remarkable as that would surely be – but death itself. Israel will be not only free, not only righteous, but actually immortal. The midrash takes מחצתי in Deut 32:39[40] to mean not "I wound" but "I distinguish," namely, between mortal, terrestrial beings on the one hand and immortal, celestial beings on the other. In the age to come, however, God "heals" the "wound" – that is, God erases the distinction – between the two, so that the mortal shall become immortal, the perishable imperishable, the earthly heavenly.[41]

Ecclesiastes Rabbah does not enquire further into the actual mechanics of an immortal age to come, but other sources do. Bavli Berakot attributes to Rav (an early third-century amora) this much more specific account of the conditions that will obtain: "A favourite saying of Rav was: The world to come is not like this world. In the world to come there is no eating or drinking, nor propagation, nor business, nor jealousy, nor hatred, nor competition, but the righteous sit with their crowns on their heads, feasting on the brightness of the Shekhinah, as it says, *And they beheld God, and ate and drank* [Exod 24:11]" (b. Ber. 17a). This concluding scripture citation comes from the episode of the mysterious meal that Moses, Aaron, and the elders have with God atop Mount Sinai; the Talmud here takes the lemma to mean that beholding the divine presence itself *was* their food and drink. Now, the absence of jealousy, hatred, and competition (the last three things in Rav's list) would be consistent with a scenario where eschatological humans are righteous but nevertheless mortal. But the absence of eating, drinking, and childbirth (the first three things in Rav's list) suggests a scenario where they are not only righteous but also immortal. Our text does not think to ask what will become of the 613

---

[40] A verse frequently invoked by the rabbis in regard to resurrection; see Yifat Monnickendam, "I Bring Death and Give Life, I Wound and Heal (Deut 32:39): Two Versions of the Polemic on the Resurrection of the Dead," *Henoch* 35 (2013): 90–118.

[41] Not to put too fine a point on it: This is almost exactly what Paul writes in 1 Cor 15:53–54, citing the very same verse from Isaiah: "For this perishable [body] must put on imperishability, and this mortal [body] put on immortality. And when this perishable [body] puts on imperishability, and this mortal [body] puts on immortality, then shall come to pass the saying which stands written: *Death is swallowed up in victory* [Isa 25:8]."

Eschatological Anthropology 221

commandments in such a scenario, but one might well ask that question, and elsewhere the rabbis do ask it.[42]

The rabbis take diverse views on eschatological anthropology, but they are more unanimous when it comes to angelology: "The Torah was not given to ministering angels" (b. Ber. 25b; b. Yoma 30a; b. Qid. 54a; b. Meʻil. 14b) because of the species that angels are.[43] One crystalline statement of this widely attested idea comes from Pesiqta Rabbati:

> According to R. Aha, the angels said to God: It would truly be to your praise if you extended your majesty only to the heavens above [cf. Ps 8:2] – that is, if you gave your Torah to us only. The Holy One, Blessed Be He, replied: My Torah cannot remain with you. It would not be appropriate for it to remain in a realm of creatures who have [eternal] life... Why? Because it states, *I am the Lord your God* [Exod 20:2]. Do you ever deny my kingship? Are you not with me, and do you not see the likeness of my image every day? The Torah speaks further of *When a man dies in a tent* [Num 19:14]. Do you die? Again the Torah states, *These you may eat* [Lev 11:9], and *These you shall not eat* [Lev 11:4]. Do you eat or drink? Why then should you wish that I give my Torah to you? (Pes. Rab. 25, trans. mod. from Braude)[44]

In this episode, the angels want the Torah for themselves, so they ask God to give it to them, but God explains that the Torah is designed for creatures who eat, drink, sin, and die (as is clear from the subject

---

[42] See Moore, *Judaism*, 1:272–273: "With the Law in the Age to Come [as opposed to the interim messianic age] the case was different. The scene of that age was indeed the earth, but a transformed and glorified earth, where all the conditions of existence were so unlike those of human experience as to be imaginable only by contrast.... The new age began, so the Pharisees taught and the mass of the people believed, with the resurrection of the dead, who entered thus on a new and different life... It is evident that in such a world the greater part of the laws in the Pentateuch would have no application or relation to anything actual."

[43] On this rabbinic maxim, and its complex relation to rabbinic ethical exhortation, see Christine Hayes, "'The Torah Was Not Given to Ministering Angels': Rabbinic Aspirationalism," in *Talmudic Transgressions: Engaging the Work of Daniel Boyarin*, ed. Charlotte Fonrobert et al., JSJSup 181 (Leiden: Brill, 2017), 123–160. On rabbinic angelology more generally, see Mika Ahuvia, *On My Right Michael, On My Left Gabriel: Angels in Ancient Jewish Culture* (Berkeley: University of California Press, 2021).

[44] William G. Braude, trans., *Pesikta Rabbati*, 2 vols., YJS 18 (New Haven: Yale University Press, 1968).

matter of the commandments).⁴⁵ Since the angels do none of these things,⁴⁶ the Torah is not for them.

Elsewhere, fascinatingly, this very thing is actually portrayed as a bodily disability on the part of the angels. A discussion in Song of Songs Rabbah reads:

[The angels said:] "It is your happiness that your Torah should be in the heavens." God, however, said to them [the angels]: "You have no concern with it." R. Judan said: It is as if a man had a son with stumped fingers and took him to an embroiderer to teach him the art. The latter looked at his fingers and said: 'The very essence of this art depends upon the fingers. How can this one possibly learn it?' Thus you have no concern with it. So when the Holy One, blessed be He, sought to give the Torah to Israel, the ministering angels tried to thrust Israel away, and they thrust themselves before the Holy One, blessed be He, and said: 'Sovereign of the Universe, it is your happiness, your majesty, your honor that your Torah should be in the heavens.' He replied to them: 'You have no concern with it. It is written therein, *If a woman has a discharge of blood for many days* [Lev 15:25]. Is there any woman among you? So you have no concern with it. Further it is written therein, *When a man dies in a tent* [Num 19:14]. Is there death among you? So you have no concern with it.' And so scripture praises him [Moses] with the words, *You have ascended on high, you have taken your captive* [Ps

---

⁴⁵ In an earlier, longer parallel in b. Shabb. 88b–89a, it is Moses, not God, who teaches the angels this lesson. When Moses ascends Mount Sinai into the divine presence to receive the Torah, the angels resent him for intruding on their heavenly bliss. They complain to God, but God invites Moses to put them in their place by explaining how the Torah is fit for mortals, not immortals. On this story, see further Joseph P. Schultz, "Angelic Opposition to the Ascension of Moses and the Revelation of the Law," *JQR* 61 (1971): 282–307; and on the motif of which this story is an instance, see Peter Schäfer, *Rivalität zwischen Engeln und Menschen: Untersuchungen zur rabbinischen Engelvorstellung* (Berlin: De Gruyter, 1975).

⁴⁶ What about sex? Do angels do that? Here is a more complicated question. In most of our texts, they *cannot*: their bodies are not suitably equipped. In some of our texts, they *ought not*, but do. Thus, famously, the Book of the Watchers, in which male angels rape human women (1 Enoch 6:1–7:6), and the Animal Apocalypse, in which the body parts pertinent to the deed are described (1 Enoch 86:1–6; 88:3; 90:21); see further Megan R. Remington and Julianna Kaye Smith, "The Phallus in Our Stars: Sexual Violence in the Animal Apocalypse," *JSP* 32 (2022): 57–74. But in T. Reu. 5:6, significantly, the watchers must first metamorphose into male human bodies in order to carry out their crime! Angels are usually gendered male, if they are gendered at all; see Jub. 15:27, where the angels of the presence have circumcised penises. But there are also ancient examples of angels gendered female, on which see Mika Ahuvia, "Gender and the Angels in Late Antique Judaism," *JSQ* 29 (2022): 1–21.

68:19], on which R. Aha said: This applies to the rules which apply to human beings, such as those relating to men and women with a discharge, impure women, and women in childbirth. So 'you have no concern with it.' (Song Rab. 8.11.2, trans. mod. from Simon)

Whereas one might think of immortal angels as *more* able than humans, Song Rabbah[47] regards them as *disabled* in regard to the capacity to keep the Torah: just as (the text assumes that) a person lacking fingers cannot do embroidery, so also the angels who lack sexed, mortal bodies cannot do the Torah. On this rabbinic logic, angelic bodies are actually disabled.[48]

But if, at the resurrection, human beings become like the immortal angels, what would be the implications for *their* capacity to do the Torah? Not all ancient Jewish and Christian texts imagine resurrection as angelification, but a great many do, and understandably so.[49] The Epistle of Enoch, for instance, encourages the righteous with the promise that they will become like the angels (or like the stars, which is the same thing):[50]

---

[47] And the parallel in Midr. Teh. 8.2.

[48] On ancient ideas of disability in relation to imagined bodily perfection, see Candida R. Moss, *Divine Bodies: Resurrecting Perfection in the New Testament and Early Christianity* (New Haven: Yale University Press, 2019).

[49] On resurrection and/as angelification, see Collins, "Angelic Life"; Petrey, "Resurrection Body"; Martha Himmelfarb, *Ascent to Heaven in Jewish and Christian Apocalypses* (Oxford: Oxford University Press, 1993), 47–71; David Flusser, "Resurrection and Angels in Rabbinic Judaism, Early Christianity, and Qumran," in *The Dead Sea Scrolls, Fifty Years after Their Discovery*, ed. Lawrence H. Schiffman et al. (Jerusalem: Israel Exploration Society, 2000), 568–572; Kevin Patrick Sullivan, *Wrestling with Angels: A Study of the Relationship between Angels and Humans in Ancient Jewish Literature and the New Testament*, AGJU 55 (Leiden: Brill, 2004), 85–141. The motif is sometimes, though not always, related to the notion that humans were originally created in the image of the angels, following one ancient interpretation of Gen 1:26 ("Elohim said, 'Let us make humankind in our image, after our likeness'"), on which see Gabriel Barzilai, "Incidental Biblical Exegesis in the Qumran Scrolls and Its Importance for the Study of the Second Temple Period," *DSD* 14 (2007): 1–24.

[50] The notion that the stars *are* angels or gods has proved controversial in some recent research – e.g., Cook, "Paul and the Heavenly Bodies" – but in at least some primary texts, including those cited here, it seems to me very securely attested. See further Alan Scott, *Origen and the Life of the Stars: A History of an Idea* (Oxford: Clarendon, 1991), 150–163.

The angels in heaven make mention of you for good before the glory of the Great One, and your names are written before the glory of the Great One. Take courage, then, for formerly you were worn out by evils and tribulations, but now you will shine like the luminaries of heaven.... Take courage and do not abandon your hope, for you will have great joy like the angels of heaven.... Stay far from all their [the sinners'] iniquities, for you will be companions of the host of heaven. (1 Enoch 104:1–6, trans. Nickelsburg)

Likewise, the Syriac Apocalypse of Baruch describes the glorification of the righteous as a "change of shape" from one kind of body to another, namely, to an angelic body fit for "the undying world":[51]

Both the shape of those who are found to be guilty as also the glory of those who have proved to be righteous will be changed... [As for the righteous,] their splendour will then be glorified by transformations, and the shape of their face will be changed into the light of their beauty so that they may acquire and receive the undying world which is promised to them.... They will be changed into the splendor of angels. (2 Bar 51:1–5, trans. Klijn)

Here in 2 Baruch, just as in the Epistle of Enoch above, to be like the angels is to be like the stars: "Time will no longer make them older. For they will live in the heights of that world and they will be like the angels and will be equal to the stars" (2 Bar 51:10, trans. Klijn).

As in Jewish texts from this period, so also in Christian ones: for many of them, the life of the resurrected righteous is, in a word, the life of the angels. Thus, for instance, the Shepherd of Hermas describes the happy fate of the apostles in this way: "They [the apostles and teachers of the word] always proceeded in righteousness and truth, just as they received the holy spirit. And so their path lies with the angels" (Herm. Sim. 9.25.2, trans. Ehrman in LCL). And the happy fate of the bishops similarly: "Those who engage in such works [viz. the faithful bishops] are glorious before God and already have their place with the angels, if they continue serving the Lord until the end" (Herm. Sim. 9.27.3, trans. Ehrman).[52] And while we are on the topic of bishops, the Martyrdom of Polycarp (bishop of Smyrna) portrays the fate of the

---

[51] In fact, 2 Baruch imagines several variations, at least, on eschatological anthropology. Elsewhere, e.g., the eschaton is a state of affairs in which women still give birth, as they do in this world, but without labor pains (2 Bar 73:7), on which see Emily Gathergood, "The Midwifery of God" (PhD diss., University of Nottingham, 2022).

[52] See further Angelo P. O'Hagan, *Material Re-creation in the Apostolic Fathers* (Berlin: Akademie Verlag, 1968).

blessed martyrs in similar but, if anything, even clearer terms: "With the eyes of their hearts they [the martyrs] looked above to the good things preserved for those who endure, which no ear has heard nor eye seen, which have never entered into the human heart, but which the Lord revealed to them, who were no longer humans but already angels" (Mart. Pol. 2.3, trans. Ehrman).[53]

No longer humans, already angels! But if "the Torah was not given to ministering angels," then what happens when humans become angels? Ironically, one might well reason (along the lines of Song Rabbah) that such glorified humans, so far from becoming able to keep the commandments perfectly, would actually become constitutionally *unable* to keep the commandments.[54] Not because they are morally weak (they are not), but because they have the wrong kind of bodies.[55] Their very glorification renders them disabled, so to speak, in relation to God's law. Unless, that is, God had built into the law a change to accommodate this change in the human constitution, as Tosefta Sanhedrin says God did for the generation of Ezra. Might the Torah undergo a change, not because of any supposed doctrine of the

---

[53] See further William Horbury, "The Cult of Christ and the Cult of the Saints," NTS 44 (1998): 444–469; Candida R. Moss, *The Other Christs: Imitating Jesus in Ancient Christian Theologies of Martyrdom* (Oxford: Oxford University Press, 2010).

[54] The early Chabad Rebbe Dov Ber Shneuri, writing around the turn of the nineteenth century, draws precisely this conclusion: "In the future, the commandments will be annulled, for the process of spiritually refining the world will be complete. Being that the spirit of impurity [Zech. 13:2] will have departed completely, the spiritual refinement of good from evil upon which the entire scheme of the commandments is based – to depart from evil and do good, to distinguish between the impure and the pure – will not be feasible. Therefore the commandments will be annulled, for the same reason that the Torah was not given to the angels, since they are not able to murder and steal, etc." (Dov Ber Shneuri, *Shaarei Teshuvah*, vol. 2, ch. 32; trans. in Chaim Miller, ed., *Rambam: The 13 Principles of Faith* [New York: Kol Menachem, 2007]).

[55] Taylor G. Petrey, *Resurrecting Parts: Early Christians on Desire, Reproduction, and Sexual Difference* (London: Routledge, 2016); and Petrey, "Resurrection Body" aptly focuses on the sexed body, but in the primary sources the capacity for digestion is equally central as the capacity for reproduction. See, e.g., Gen. Rab. 14:3, where digestion, reproduction, and death are the features common to animals and humans, but not angels: "He created there four creatures above and four below. Below: He eats and drinks as an animal, procreates and fights as an animal, leaves droppings as an animal, and dies as an animal. Above: He stands as the ministering angels, and speaks and understands and sees as the ministering angels."

abolition of the Torah in the messianic age, but rather because of a change in anthropology? If the Torah was given to flesh and blood, can it adapt when that flesh and blood becomes something else?

Origen the Paulinist

Origen of Alexandria, a Christian contemporary of the first generation of amoraim (mid third century CE), puzzled over precisely this question, and he found an answer in the letters of Paul.[56] Like the rabbis in the passages discussed above, but unlike most other interpreters of Paul, ancient or modern, Origen keeps *mortality* at the front of his mind when thinking about the law of Moses. Modern readers of Paul, I think it is fair to say, usually assume that whatever Paul says about faith versus law, etc., complicated though it may be, is essentially describing "the way we [Christians] live now," the Christian pattern of religion over against its counterparts.[57] But Origen, to his great credit, does not assume that. Explicating our key verse, Rom 10:4 – "Christ is the end of the law unto righteousness for everyone who trusts" – in his mid-third century *Commentary on Romans*, Origen argues that Paul's two different righteousnesses, "the righteousness from the law" and "the righteousness from trust" (Rom 10:5–6), correspond to two different modes of human existence: the mortal life of the present age and the immortal life of the new creation.[58] He writes:

Consider the different kinds of righteousness in a similar manner as the different kinds of lives. For notice how the righteousness of God, that is, Christ, *who became for us righteousness from God* [1 Cor 1:30], and peace, says, *And this is eternal life, that they may know you, the only true God, and Jesus Christ, whom you have sent* [John 17:3]. Therefore, this righteousness offers not merely life but eternal life. But he has not said that the man who

---

[56] See Francesca Cocchini, "Origen's Pauline Commentaries," in *The Oxford Handbook of Origen*, ed. Ronald E. Heine and Karen Jo Torjesen (Oxford: Oxford University Press, 2022), 229–243; J. José Alviar, "Origen's Theological Anthropology," in ibid., 373–392; and J. A. McGuckin, "Origen's Eschatology," in ibid., 410–428.

[57] To borrow a phrase from Sanders, *Paul and Palestinian Judaism*.

[58] Westerholm, *Perspectives Old and New* rightly perceives Paul's distinction between "ordinary" and "extraordinary" righteousness (Westerholm's terms), but not, as Origen does, the corresponding distinction between mortal life and everlasting life.

does that righteousness of the law will live eternally, but only that *He will live in it* [Lev 18:5]. (Origen, *Comm. Rom.* 8.2.2)

Note that Origen reaches sideways in his biblical canon to John 17:3 for αἰώνιος ζωή, "life everlasting," but he need not have done so; Paul himself uses that phrase several times in both Galatians and Romans:

> The person who sows to his own flesh, from the flesh he will reap corruption; but the person who sows to the pneuma, from the pneuma he will reap life everlasting [ζωὴν αἰώνιον]. (Gal 6:8)

> To those who, by endurance in good work, seek glory and honor and incorruptibility, [God] will give life everlasting [ζωὴν αἰώνιον]. (Rom 2:7)

> Just as sin reigned in death, so also the gift might reign through righteousness to life everlasting [ζωὴν αἰώνιον], through Jesus Christ our lord. (Rom 5:21)

> Now that you have been freed from sin and enslaved to God, you have your fruit unto consecration, the end of which is life everlasting [ζωὴν αἰώνιον]. For the wages of sin is death, and the gift of God is life everlasting [ζωὴ αἰώνιος], in Christ Jesus our lord. (Rom 6:22–23)

It is this kind of life that Paul coordinates with the end of the law in Rom 10:4. Origen's incisive observation is that when, in the immediate context, Paul cites Moses as saying about the commandments that ὁ ποιήσας αὐτὰ ἄνθρωπος ζήσεται ἐν αὐτοῖς, "the person who does these things shall *live* in them" (Lev 18:5 in Rom 10:5), neither Moses nor Paul means life everlasting, the life of the new creation.[59] Rather, both Moses and Paul mean quotidian life, the mortal life of the present evil age.[60] In that age, for that kind of life, the righteousness from the law is what is on offer, and is a far cry better than the alternative, namely: unrighteousness. But the righteousness from trust, by contrast, pertains to the life everlasting of the new creation, and it has only just become

---

[59] Because in Gal 3:21 Paul expressly says that it cannot mean that.

[60] Likewise when Paul quotes the same logion of Moses, contrasting it with a prophecy of Habakkuk, in Gal 3:11–12: "It is clear that by the law no one is rightwised with God, for *The person who is righteous from trust shall live* [Hab 2:4 OG]; but the law is not from trust, but rather *The person who does these things shall live in them* [Lev 18:5 LXX]." Two kinds of righteousness, two kinds of life. In this respect, then, Rom 10:5 and Gal 3:12 are much closer to each other than is suggested by Friedrich Avemarie, "Paul and the Claim of the Law according to Scripture: Leviticus 18:5 in Galatians 3:12 and Romans 10:5," in *The Beginnings of Christianity*, ed. Jack Pastor and Menachem Mor (Jerusalem: Yad Ben-Zvi, 2005), 125–148.

available at the resurrection of Jesus, which is to say, at the beginning of the general resurrection.[61] That righteousness, naturally, lies beyond the jurisdiction of the law, because Moses legislated for mortals (as per the rabbinic texts discussed above), whereas people-in-Christ are actually immortals. Christ is the end of the law, then, just to the extent that Christ is the end of human mortality.[62]

On this point, Origen gets Paul's argument right where most modern interpreters get it wrong. Friedrich Avemarie perceptively notes that Origen's reading stands apart from most modern ones,[63] but in the end Avemarie himself sides with his fellow moderns, which is a shame. That modern majority opinion[64] is that Paul here sets up a zero-sum competition between rival means of attaining life everlasting (rival "soteriologies," in the common Christian idiom of the secondary literature): works vs. faith, Moses vs. Christ, Judaism vs. Christianity. Avemarie and others point to certain ancient Jewish texts that take Lev 18:5 ("the person who does these things shall live in them") as referring to the life of the age to come, and they argue that these texts add up to an ancient Jewish "soteriology" in which final salvation is by law-keeping. They "know" that Paul does not teach that (Rom 2:6–13 notwithstanding); hence, they conclude, Paul's point must be to reject one soteriology in favor of another one. The fatal flaw in this majority view is a naïve (not to say bizarre) Christianizing reading of ancient Jewish texts that are not, for their part, about "soteriology" at all. In fact – irony of ironies – not a few of these Jewish texts are wrestling with the selfsame theological question about

---

[61] I take this claim to be consistent with the compelling account of *pistis* offered by Schliesser, "Christ-Faith as an Eschatological Event," though Schliesser does not draw the thoroughgoing-eschatological conclusion that I do here.

[62] Christ is, for Paul, quite literally *the last man*, ὁ ἔσχατος Ἀδάμ (1 Cor 15:45), the last of the race of mortals made from dust, and, after his resurrection, the first of the race of sons of God (πρωτότοκος, Rom 8:29).

[63] Avemarie, "Paul and the Claim of the Law," 130.

[64] Including, e.g., Otto Michel, *Paulus und seine Bibel* (Gütersloh: Bertelsmann, 1929), 142–144; Ulrich Luz, *Das Geschichtsverständnis des Paulus* (Munich: Kaiser, 1968), 94; Daniel R. Schwartz, *Leben durch Jesus versus Leben durch die Torah* (Münster: Institutum Judaicum Delitschianum, 1993); Preston M. Sprinkle, *Law and Life: The Interpretation of Leviticus 18:5 in Early Judaism and in Paul*, WUNT 2/241 (Tübingen: Mohr Siebeck, 2008); Avemarie, "Paul and the Claim of the Law"; Gathercole, "Torah, Life, and Salvation."

law and mortality with which (I am arguing in this chapter) Paul himself wrestles.[65]

A couple of examples, both texts much cited in this discussion: Sifra, the early halakhic midrash on Leviticus, when it reaches Lev 18:5, poses the (eminently sensible) question what God can mean by saying, "The person who does these things shall live in them" if, in empirical fact, all Israelites, like all human beings generally, die. God cannot be either lying or mistaken, so he must mean something else.[66] Thus Sifra reasons, "*And he shall live in them* [Lev 18:5]: in the world to come. For if you say, in this world, is it not a person's end to die? How, then, is *And he shall live in them* [Lev 18:5] to be understood? In the world to come" (Sifra Aharei Mot 9:10). Second example: The late midrash Deuteronomy Rabbah poses the same question about the death of Moses at the end of the Pentateuch. Moses complains to God, "You said to me, *That man shall do and he shall live by them* [Lev 18:5], and I did them, yet you told me, *Die upon the mountain* [Deut 32:50]." But God answers Moses, clarifying what he meant: "*That man shall do* – in this world – *and he shall live by them* – in the world to come" (Deut. Rab. [Liebermann ed.], 44). Here, too, the point of the text is not at all to propose a soteriology; nor is it to answer the question, "What must I do to obtain eternal life?" The point, rather, is to resolve a contradiction: God promises life, but in fact Moses died, as do we all. How can this be? Answer: By "live" here, God must mean the life of the world to come, for scripture cannot be broken.

These rabbinic midrashim on "life" in Lev 18:5 are an exact corollary to Paul's famous (or infamous) discourse about the curse of the law (κατάρα τοῦ νόμου) in Gal 3. The uttermost curse that the Torah itself stipulates for transgressors is death:[67]

---

[65] On this aspect of these Jewish texts, see Ayelet Hoffmann Libson, *Law and Self-Knowledge in the Talmud* (Cambridge: Cambridge University Press, 2018), 128–129. Most interpreters of Paul, meanwhile, miss this crucial issue, though Boakye, *Death and Life*, and Longarino, *Problem of Death* are two brilliant exceptions. Even they, however, do not grasp the nettle sufficiently tightly, in my view.

[66] See Kugel, *How to Read the Bible*, on this ancient hermeneutical principle.

[67] A crucial point well made by Esau McCaulley, *Sharing in the Son's Inheritance: Davidic Messianism and Paul's Worldwide Interpretation of the Abrahamic Land Promise in Galatians*, LNTS 608 (London: T&T Clark, 2019); and Boakye, *Death and Life*. A mountain of secondary literature notwithstanding, Paul never says that the law *itself is* a curse, only that the curse of the law – that is, the curse *stipulated by* the law, namely: death – has been undone.

See, I have set before you this day life and good, death and evil. If you obey the commandments of the LORD your God which I command you this day, by loving the LORD your God, by walking in his ways, and by keeping his commandments and his statutes and his ordinances, then you shall live and multiply, and the LORD your God will bless you in the land which you are entering to take possession of it. But if your heart turns away, and you will not hear, but are drawn away to worship other gods and serve them, I declare to you this day, that you shall perish. (Deut 30:15–18 RSV)

But then, in empirical fact, the end of *all* people is death. Until it isn't. Because, Paul claims, with the resurrection of Christ, people can now actually escape death.[68] "Christ redeemed us from the curse of the law," that is, from the inevitability of death, "by becoming a curse for us," that is, by undergoing death and coming out the other side immortal. Just like Sifra and Deuteronomy Rabbah, Paul tries to square God's promises in scripture with the sad fact of human mortality. Differently from Sifra and Deuteronomy Rabbah, Paul does so by taking "life" in Lev 18:5 to refer to the present age, "life" in Hab 2:4 to refer to the new creation. Two kinds of righteousness, two kinds of life. This may not make good fodder for Christian polemics about a supposed "Jewish soteriology," but it is what Paul says.

Origen's conception of resurrection existence is not identical with Paul's. Most importantly, Origen concedes that the present age did not come to a prompt end at the resurrection of Jesus and therefore defers the resurrection to a more distant future than the apostle ever did.[69] Origen is also more of a Platonist than Paul is, notably in the former's highly developed theory of souls,[70] although both Origen and Paul agree in imagining resurrected humans in astral form, or something very much like it, as opposed to reanimated flesh.[71] In *De principiis*,

---

[68] Thus rightly Longarino, *Problem of Death*. De Boer, *Defeat of Death* begins well by recognizing this key point in 1 Cor 15 and Rom 5, but then takes his eye off the ball with his discussion of forensic versus cosmological schemas, etc.
[69] McGuckin, "Origen's Eschatology."
[70] Benjamin P. Blosser, *Become Like the Angels: Origen's Doctrine of the Soul* (Washington, DC: CUA Press, 2012).
[71] See Origen, *Cels.* 5.10, on why Jews do not worship the sun, moon, and stars as the gentiles do: "Concerning them the prediction was given to Abraham by the voice of the Lord to him: *Look up to the heaven and number the stars, if you can count them. And he said to him: So shall your seed be* [Gen 15:5]. A nation which had the hope to become as the stars in heaven would not have worshiped them; for they were to become like them as a result of understanding and

Origen scolds people who think that resurrected bodies will be equipped for sex and digestion, reasoning that such a view is both hedonist and – crucially – anti-Pauline:

> Certain persons, then, rejecting the labour of thinking and following the superficial view of the letter of the law, or yielding, rather, in some way to their own desires and lusts, being disciples of the letter alone, reckon that the promises of the future are to be looked for in the pleasure and luxury of the body; and especially because of this they desire to have again, after the resurrection, flesh of such a kind that never lacks the ability to eat and drink and to do all things that pertain to flesh and blood, not following the teaching of the apostle Paul regarding the resurrection of a spiritual body [1 Cor 15:44]. And consequently they say that there will be contracts of marriages and procreation of children even after the resurrection, picturing for themselves the rebuilding of the earthly city of Jerusalem. (Origen, *Princ.* 2.11.2, trans. Behr)

Here and elsewhere, Origen makes much of Paul's insistence in 1 Cor 15 that there is indeed a resurrection of the body, but not of the flesh. "Flesh and blood cannot inherit the kingdom of God" (1 Cor 15:50), but pneuma can; hence what is raised is a σῶμα πνευματικόν, pneumatic body (1 Cor 15:44). Origen is more explicit than Paul is about the passing away of bodily functions: eating, drinking, marrying, begetting. But Paul does in fact reason along precisely the same lines: "The kingdom of God is not *eating and drinking*" (Rom 14:17).[72] "*Food for the belly and the belly for food*, but God will nullify both the one and the other" (1 Cor 6:13).[73] "In Christ there is no *male and female*" (Gal 3:28).[74] "Let those who *have wives* be as if not having them... for the

---

keeping the law of God." See further Scott, *Origen and the Life of the Stars*, 150–163.

[72] Gary Steven Shogren, "Is the Kingdom of God about Eating and Drinking or Isn't It? (Romans 14:17)," *NovT* 42 (2000): 238–256 rightly identifies the puzzle that, whereas Jesus says the kingdom of God *is* about eating and drinking (Mark 14:25; Matt 26:29; Luke 22:16), Paul says it is *not* (Rom 14:17). Shogren balks, however, at the possibility that Paul means what he says, as in fact he does.

[73] I take this entire sentence to represent Paul's own view, not a so-called Corinthian slogan. See the fine discussion of this verse in Jonathan Rivett Robinson, "The Argument against Attributing Slogans in 1 Corinthians 6:12–20," *JSPL* 8 (2018): 147–166.

[74] That is, no binary sexual difference (Gen 2), but a metamorphosis into the androgynous image of God (Gen 1:27). See Martin, "Queer History of Galatians 3:28"; Dunning, *Specters of Paul*; Neutel, *Cosmopolitan Ideal*.

form of this cosmos is passing away" (1 Cor 7:29–31).[75] In this new creation, the righteous do not eat, drink, marry, or give in marriage. They are like... well, like the angels in heaven.[76]

But if there is no longer sex or digestion, are there body parts appropriate to those functions? What, in other words, is the actual *anatomy* of a resurrected body? Taylor Petrey has explored this question quite fruitfully, writing about the early Christian evidence:

> Key questions for early Christians [included]: What exactly is the flesh? What kinds of bodily parts count as flesh and what do not? How is a resurrected person different from her mortal self? What is the same between a resurrected person and her mortal self? Nowhere is this problem more vexing than on the issue of sexual desires, body parts, and practices.... In the early Christian treatises explaining the nature of future resurrected bodies, reproduction does not occur, bodily fluids cease to flow, and bodies are not penetrated, nor do they penetrate. This curated body was presented as a solution to the mortal body's seeming incompatibility with the heavenly realm. The solution, however, created a new problem of its own. Without reproduction, sexual intercourse, and bodily fluids, how might male and female bodies be distinguished? Are these differences simply of shape (morphology) between beings that are otherwise the same?[77]

---

[75] Here, binary sexual difference ("having a wife") is part of the soon-to-disappear present form of the cosmos. Despite their temporary mortal, sexed bodies, however, people-in-Christ can live the life of new form of the cosmos by renouncing marriage, sex, and procreation. On this idea, see further Jacob Taubes, *The Political Theology of Paul*, trans. Dana Hollander (Stanford: Stanford University Press, 2004); Judith M. Gundry, "Affliction for Procreators in the Eschatological Crisis: Paul's Marital Counsel in 1 Corinthians 7:28 and Contraception in Greco-Roman Antiquity," *JSNT* 39 (2016): 141–168.

[76] Thus rightly Martha Himmelfarb, review of Daniel Boyarin, *A Radical Jew*, in *AJS Review* 21 (1996): 150: "In 1 Corinthians 15:44, Paul tells his followers that they will be provided with 'spiritual bodies' at the resurrection. Boyarin tries hard to claim this most unpromising category for Platonism.... But the Judaism of Greek-speaking Jews was far more diverse than Boyarin's emphasis on Platonism suggests. A Hellenistic Judaism that included 2 Enoch, an apocalypse probably written in Egypt in Greek in the first century, as well as related apocalypses, would have suggested a different and, I believe, more persuasive background for spiritual bodies, the transformation of the body of the hero as he stands before the divine throne."

[77] Petrey, *Resurrecting Parts*, 2, referring in particular to Pseudo-Justin, *On the Resurrection*; the Nag Hammadi *Treatise on the Resurrection*; Athenagoras, *On the Resurrection*; Irenaeus, *Against Heresies*; and Tertullian, *On the Resurrection of the Flesh*. On this theme, see also Moss, *Divine Bodies*.

Tertullian, for example, creates a logical problem for himself by insisting, first, that there is no sex or reproduction in the resurrection but also, second, that resurrection bodies are indeed fleshly. Thus he wonders, quite sensibly, "What purpose are the loins, conscious of semen, and the other genitals in both sexes, as well as the enclosures of conception and the fountains of the breast, when sexual intercourse, pregnancy, and the nurturing of infants shall cease? Ultimately, what will be the use of the entire body, when clearly the whole is free from use?" (Tertullian, *Res.* 60.3, trans. Petrey). Fleshly bodies that do not do fleshly things would seem to be something of a waste of flesh. Tertullian recognises this, but he would rather live with an absurdity than concede the possibility that resurrected bodies are made of something other than flesh.[78]

Paul, for his part, does not provide an anatomy of the resurrected body, other than to say that it is the same shape (μορφή, εἰκών) as the body of the glorified Christ (1 Cor 15:49; Rom 8:29; Phil 3:21).[79] Origen goes further than this, though exactly how much further is a matter of dispute. Origen was famously condemned by the emperor Justinian for saying, among other things, that "in the resurrection the bodies of people rise spherical [σφαιροειδής],"[80] a charge repeated in the anathemas of the Second Council of Constantinople in 553 CE. But Origen never actually makes that claim in any of his extant works, at least in the form in which they have come down to us. In his edition of *De principiis*,[81] Paul Koetschau assumes that Justinian's charge is accurate and reasons that Rufinus must have redacted this claim out of his text of Origen, which would explain why we do not find it there. Perhaps, though this is speculation.[82]

---

[78] Caroline Walker Bynum, *The Resurrection of the Body in Western Christianity, 200–1336* (New York: Columbia University Press, 1995), 34–43.

[79] But what exactly is the anatomy of *Christ's* glorified body? Paul does not elaborate, though other early Christian writers certainly do. See further Guy G. Stroumsa, "Form(s) of God: Some Notes on Metatron and Christ," *HTR* 76 (1983): 269–288; Moss, *Divine Bodies*.

[80] *Letter of Justinian to Menas* (Mansi IX 516 D).

[81] Paul Koetschau, ed., *Origenes Werke, Band 5: De Principiis* (Hinrichs: Leipzig, 1913).

[82] Rufinus says in his preface that he has made some emendations where he suspects that heretics have corrupted the text of Origen, but the only issue he names in this connection is the doctrine of the trinity.

There is, in fact, one place where Origen might be understood to say what Justinian says he said, namely a passage in *De oratione* commenting on Phil 2:10: "So that at the name of Jesus, every knee might bow, of heavenly beings and earthly beings and chthonic beings." Are we to understand from this that the heavenly bodies have knees? Origen reasons:

> It is not in the least necessary to suppose that the bodies of the heavenly beings are so shaped as to have physical knees, since those who have discussed them in a scholarly way have proved that their bodies are spherical. Anyone unwilling to accept this will have to accept the notion that each limb has its uses, since otherwise God would have created parts for them which have no function – unless he is prepared shamelessly to deny the canons of reason. In either case he will fall into difficulties, whether he says that God has provided them with useless bodily limbs which have no proper function, or if he affirms that even in the case of the heavenly beings the digestive organs and the large intestines perform their characteristic function. (*Or.* 31.3, trans. Chadwick)

Paul portrays the celestial bodies as having knees, but, Origen reasons, this is a figure of speech. "Those who have discussed them in a scholarly way have proved that their bodies are spherical [σφαιροειδής]." Why they are spherical, he does not say, but several interpreters have quite sensibly pointed to Plato, *Timaeus* 33, where the demiurge creates the world spherical because the sphere is the perfect shape.[83] In any case, Origen's discussion in *De oratione* is about the sun, moon, and stars, not the resurrected righteous. Thus Chadwick reasons that Justinian condemns Origen for a view that Origen does not actually hold.[84]

Elsewhere, however, Origen does suggest that the resurrected righteous will have bodies very much like the stars.[85] Rebutting Celsus's taunt that Christians believe in a kind of zombie resurrection – they will rise from the dead into the same flesh they occupied before – Origen argues that that is the view of the Stoics, not the Christians.

---

[83] "Wherefore he made the world in the form of a globe, round as from a lathe, having its extremes in every direction equidistant from the centre, the most perfect and the most like itself of all figures; for he considered that the like is infinitely fairer than the unlike" (Plato, *Timaeus* 33, trans. Jowett).

[84] Henry Chadwick, "Origen, Celsus, and the Resurrection of the Body," *HTR* 41 (1948): 83–102.

[85] See Scott, *Origen and the Life of the Stars*, 150–163.

The Christians, Origen says, believe they will rise from the dead into celestial bodies:

> It teaches that the tabernacle of the soul, as it is called in the Bible, possesses a seminal principle [*logos spermatos*]. And in this tabernacle those who are righteous groan, being weighed down, and desiring not to put it off but to be clothed on top of it.... When the soul, which in its own nature is incorporeal and invisible, is in any material place, it requires a body suited to the nature of that environment... [At the resurrection,] it puts a body on top of that which it possessed formerly, because it needs a better garment for the purer, ethereal, and heavenly regions. (*Cels.* 7.32, trans. Chadwick)

Origen does not say that the resurrected righteous *are* stars, but he does say that they have the kind of bodies that stars have.[86] Conceivably, then, Origen actually does believe, as Justinian accuses him of believing, that the saints will raise from the dead spherical. Indeed, Wilfred Knox congratulated Origen for holding such an enlightened view: "Against this [viz. Origen's alleged view] Justinian maintains that the resurrection body is *orthion*, which appears to mean that it is erect or upright, like the human body.... Justinian seems to have overlooked the fact that the erect position of man was no longer necessary when he had ceased to contemplate heaven from below and was already standing above the firmament."[87]

The Last Man

Let us return to Eliyahu Kohen's ingenious theory of a divine reshuffling of the letters of the Torah. "Because of Adam's sin," he writes, "God arranged the letters [of the Torah] before him into the words describing death and other earthly things, such as levirate marriage. Without sin there would have been no death. The same letters would have been joined into words telling a different story." Would have been, *and will in fact be.* This, I propose, is more or less Paul's view of things. There is a crucial sense in which, Paul insists, that the law does

---

[86] Which is true, *mutatis mutandis*, of Paul, as well. Hence when Cook ("Paul and the Heavenly Bodies") criticizes Engberg-Pedersen (*Cosmology and Self*) on this score, his criticism is not exactly to the point. On this issue, see further David A. Burnett, "'So Shall Your Seed Be': Paul's Use of Genesis 15:5 in Romans 4:18 in Light of Early Jewish Deification Traditions," *JSPL* 5 (2015): 211–236.

[87] Wilfred L. Knox, "Origen's Conception of the Resurrection Body," *JTS* 39 (1938): 247.

not have jurisdiction over the new creation.[88] "The law was our custodian unto the messiah, so that we might be rightwised from trust. Now that trust has come, we are no longer under a custodian" (Gal 3:24–25; and see Gal 5:18; Rom 6:14). And yet, like Eliyahu Kohen, Paul is emphatic that this does not mean the law is abolished. "Do we then nullify the law through trust? No! Rather, we establish the law" (Rom 3:31). (Räisänen wrongly assumed that Paul could not possibly mean this when he said it.) Whatever exactly the righteousness of the new creation is like, it must be *the kind of thing* that is limned by the law, hence Paul's phrase δικαίωμα τοῦ νόμου (Rom 2:26; 8:4). This stands to reason, since by Paul's lights the law is not just holy, righteous, and good (Rom 7:12) but also pneumatic (Rom 7:14), which is to say, fit for the kingdom of God, as flesh and blood are not (1 Cor 15:50).[89] And yet, inasmuch as the righteousness of the age to come is a righteousness performed by immortal, godlike creatures,[90] it cannot be exactly the same as the righteousness prescribed by Moses, simply because most of the commandments are not apt. Paul's point is *not* that what is now forbidden will then be permitted.[91] It is, rather, that the very conditions for forbidding or permitting will not obtain. One can neither commit adultery nor remain monogamous if there is no such thing as marriage. One can neither murder nor save life if there is no such thing as dying. One can neither defile nor purify a holy place if there is no such thing as impurity. And so on. This, again, is the genius

---

[88] This is the (important) grain of truth in the many ham-fisted criticisms of the Paul-within-Judaism hypothesis from Christian interpreters.
[89] An important point well made by Gregory Tatum, "A Participationist Eschatological Reading of Justification in Galatians, Philippians, and Romans," *RevBib* 125 (2018): 223–238.
[90] Thus rightly Litwa, *We Are Being Transformed*.
[91] As it is, e.g., in Lev. Rab. 13:3: "R. Judan b. R. Simeon said: Behemoth and Leviathan are to engage in a wild beast contest before the righteous in the time to come, and whoever has not been a spectator at the wild beast contests of the gentiles in this world will be accorded the privilege of seeing one in the world to come. How will they be slaughtered? ... [Not in a kosher manner, but] R. Abin b. Kahana said: The Holy One, blessed be He, said: *Torah shall go forth from me* [Isa 51:4], meaning that: An exceptional temporary ruling shall go forth from me. R. Berekiah said in the name of R. Isaac: In the time to come, the Holy One, blessed be He, will make a banquet for his righteous servants, and whoever has not eaten *nebelah* [i.e., carrion, Lev 7:24] in this world will have the privilege of enjoying it in the world to come." Here the reward for keeping the commandments in the present is the promise of being allowed to break them in the eschaton, which is far more antinomian than anything Paul ever says.

of Origen's observation: the two different righteousnesses correspond to two different kinds of life.

Paul does not have a doctrine of an eschatological reshuffling of the letters of the Torah, *a la* Eliyahu Kohen. (If Paul was accustomed to reading the Torah in Greek, with its alphabetic vowels, it might never have occurred to him to imagine such a doctrine.) But Paul does have his own distinctions that do the same kind of work for him that Eliyahu Kohen's does for him. Paul distinguishes between the law as mortals encounter it in γράμματα, scripts of human languages, and the law as it is in pneuma, which is to say, in the sight of God (2 Cor 3:6–7; Rom 2:27–29; 7:6). (N.B. This is emphatically *not* our colloquial distinction between "the letter of the law" and "the spirit of the law.")[92] Paul distinguishes between *being under* the law, which is impossible in the new creation (Rom 6:14–15; 1 Cor 9:20; Gal 3:23; 4:4–5, 21; 5:18), and *fulfilling* the law, which is *only* possible in the new creation (Rom 8:4; 13:8, 10; Gal 5:14).[93] He distinguishes between the law of Moses and the law of Christ (1 Cor 9:21; Gal 6:2), which are not two discrete laws but the one law of God for two successive conditions of humankind. As Paul himself puts it elsewhere: a "law of sin and death" for the age of sin and death, and a "law of the pneuma of life" for the age of pneumatic life (Rom 8:2). He distinguishes between the law of Moses as such, which has a telos, and the *dikaioma* of the law, which abides forever (Rom 2:26; 8:4).

What exactly is this *dikaioma* of the law? Paul never says.[94] It is striking, however, that the only commandment he specifically cites as abiding in the new creation is Lev 19:18: "You shall love your neighbour as yourself" (at Rom 13:9–10; Gal 5:14).[95] Prophecy, tongues, and knowledge all cease, but love never passes away (1 Cor 13:8).[96]

---

[92] *Pace* Boyarin, *Radical Jew*, 86–105. On the law in letters and in pneuma, respectively, now see Yael Fisch, *Written for Us: Paul's Interpretation of Scripture and the History of Midrash*, JSJSup 202 (Leiden: Brill, 2023), 131–160.
[93] A point well made by Barclay, *Paul and the Gift*, 430–432.
[94] On the significance of this, see Garroway, "Paul: Within Judaism, Without Law."
[95] Here see Kengo Akiyama, *The Love of Neighbour in Ancient Judaism: The Reception of Leviticus 19:18 in the Hebrew Bible, the Septuagint, the Book of Jubilees, the Dead Sea Scrolls, and the New Testament* (Leiden: Brill, 2018), especially 138–154.
[96] Tellingly, Abot de Rabbi Nathan agrees that the immortal angels fulfill the commandment of Lev 19:18: "A man must love his neighbor [Lev 19:18] and

There is a fascinating analogy in a passage from Leviticus Rabbah that speculates about which of the temple prayers and sacrifices will remain in the age to come:

> R. Phinehas and R. Levi and R. Yohanan said in the name of R. Menahem of Gallia: In the time to come all sacrifices will be annulled, but that of thanksgiving will not be annulled; and all prayers will be annulled, but thanksgiving will not be annulled. This is [indicated by] what is written: *The voice of joy and the voice of gladness, the voice of the groom and the voice of the bride, the voice of them that say: Give thanks to the Lord of hosts* [Jer 33:11] – This refers to the thanksgiving; *that bring offerings of thanksgiving into the house of the Lord* – this refers to the sacrifice of thanksgiving. (Lev. Rab. 9.7[trans. Israelstam, mod.])[97]

According to this tradition (here attributed to R. Menahem of Gallia), thanksgiving abides even after sin and death are no more; hence the thanksgiving offering will still be offered.[98] This is a cultic counterpart, as it were, to Paul's point about love in Lev 19:18: Even absent birth, death, marriage, eating, drinking, etc., the resurrected righteous can still love, and they can still give thanks.

This very practical interest in eschatological anthropology is the key to another rabbinic text sometimes cited in the "Torah in the messianic age" debate. Bavli Niddah records a discussion about whether a burial shroud may include *kil'ayim* (mixed threads), which is of course not permitted in the garments of *living* Israelites:

> Our Rabbis taught: A garment in which *kil'ayim* [mixed threads, Lev 19:19] was lost may not be sold to an idolater, nor may one make of it a packsaddle for an ass, but it may be made into a shroud for a corpse. R. Joseph observed: This implies that the commandments will be abolished in the time to come. Abaye (or, some say, R. Dimi) said to him: But did not R. Manni in the name of R. Jannai state, "This was learned only in regard to the period of mourning, but for burial it is forbidden"? The other replied: But was it not stated in connection with it, "R. Yohanan ruled: Even for burial [it is

honor him. Can this not be inferred? If the ministering angels, who do not have the evil impulse, honor each other, then is it not reasonable that human beings, who have the evil impulse, should all the more honor each other? Where does scripture say that the ministering angels honor each other? It says, *And one called to the other and said*... [Isa 6:3]" (Abot R. Nat., version B, §26, trans. Saldarini). Thanks to Logan Williams for discussing this text with me.

[97] J. Israelstam, *Midrash Rabbah*, vol. 4 (London: Soncino, 1939).
[98] See further Klawans, *Purity, Sacrifice, and the Temple*, 199–201.

The Last Man 239

permitted]"? Thereby R. Yohanan followed his previously expressed view, for R. Yohanan stated: "What is the significance of the scriptural text, *Free among the dead* [Ps 88:6]? As soon as a man dies, he is free from the commandments." (b. Nid. 61b [trans. mod. from Soncino])

R. Yohanan's view is that, because Torah was given to mortal Israelites, once a person dies, he or she enters a state beyond the jurisdiction of the Torah. "As soon as a man dies, he is free from the commandments," which here glosses a curious expression in the lament Psalm 88: "I am reckoned among those who go down to the Pit, I am a man who has no strength, like one *free among the dead*" (Ps 88:5–6 MT).[99] Paul, for his part, makes an identical point in Rom 7:1: "The law has jurisdiction over a person [only] *for such time as he is alive.*"[100] Differently from R. Yohanan, however, Paul reckons that the righteous *have in fact just died* (ritually, but nevertheless really, in baptism) and crossed over to that immortal state: "Having died, we are now unemployed from the law" (Rom 7:5), which is the corollary to Paul's point a few paragraphs earlier: "A person who dies has been rightwised away from sin" (Rom 6:7). The law provides for mortals who sin, but those who have died now live beyond death, beyond sin, and therefore beyond the law (cf. 1 Cor 15:56).

It is an oft-repeated refrain in the secondary literature that what distinguishes Paul from his Jewish contemporaries is his extreme anthropological pessimism.[101] No other ancient Jew, we are told –

---

[99] RSV glosses this phrase "like one *forsaken* among the dead," which is surely the original sense, but the Talmud exploits the fact that חפשי literally means "free." This same interpretation is attested elsewhere at y. Kil. 9 (32a); y. Ket. 12 (34d); b. Shab. 30a, 151b.

[100] See further Peter J. Tomson, "'Death, Where Is Thy Victory?' Paul's Theology in the Twinkling of an Eye," in *Resurrection in the New Testament: Festschrift J. Lambrecht*, ed. R. Bieringer et al. (Leuven: Peeters, 2002), 357–386.

[101] For this refrain, see, among many others, Laato, *Paul and Judaism*; Sprinkle, *Law and Life*; Sprinkle, *Paul and Judaism Revisited*; Mikael Winninge, *Sinners and the Righteous: A Comparative Study of the Psalms of Solomon and Paul's Letters* (Stockholm: Almqvist & Wiksell, 1995), 264, 306; Stephen Westerholm, "Paul's Anthropological 'Pessimism' in Its Jewish Context," in *Divine and Human Agency in Paul and His Jewish Environment*, ed. John M. G. Barclay and Simon Gathercole (London: T&T Clark, 2006), 71–98; Klaus Haacker, *The Theology of Paul's Letter to the Romans* (Cambridge: Cambridge University Press, 2003); Jason Maston, *Divine and Human Agency in Second Temple Judaism and Paul*, WUNT 2/297 (Tübingen: Mohr Siebeck, 2010); James W. Thompson, *Moral Formation according to Paul: The Context and Coherence of Pauline Ethics* (Grand Rapids, MI: Baker, 2011).

except perhaps for the author of 4 Ezra, who complains to God: "You did not take away from them their evil heart!" – took such a radically dark view of the human condition. Ben Sira, Philo, the tannaim, and others, we are told, were more sanguine. They reckoned that human beings are pretty okay and just need a bit of training under the law in order to live their best lives. (And with this claim about anthropological pessimism, *voila!* Paul is made to be the apostolic ally of an Augustine or a Calvin.) Although there is a speck of truth in this generalization, for the most part, it gets things exactly the wrong way around. It would be far more accurate to say that it is, rather, Paul's anthropological *optimism* that distinguishes him from many of his near-contemporaries (Jewish, Christian, and otherwise). Like many ancient Jews and Christians, Paul believed that human beings would become perfect and immortal in the age to come. Unlike most ancient Jews and Christians – and, indeed, most modern Jews and Christians! – Paul believed that that metamorphosis was underway and indeed nearly complete, that in the immediate future all the righteous dead would be raised and the righteous living transformed, and God be all in all.[102] This, and not a supposed proto-Calvinist anthropology, determines what he says about the Torah of Moses. Paul does not think that humans are worms who cannot muster the will to keep even the smallest commandment. He thinks that humans, once they have God's pneuma, are demigods who can fulfil the *dikaioma* of the law perfectly, effortlessly, and forever.

Paul's belief in the end of the law (Rom 10:4) is of a piece with his belief in the end of the age (1 Cor 10:11). For people who sinned and died, the law of Moses was as good a custodian as one could hope for. But people who neither sin nor die have no need of a custodian. In a sense, people who neither sin nor die are no longer *people* in many of the relevant senses with which we normally mean that word.[103] Paul genuinely reckoned, in a way that very few of his later Christian interpreters would do, with the prospect that he and his

---

[102] George H. van Kooten, *Cosmic Christology in Paul and the Pauline School*, WUNT 2/171 (Tübingen: Mohr Siebeck, 2003), 103–107.

[103] Indeed, Paul himself says as much in 1 Cor 3:3: "When there is jealousy and strife among you, are you not fleshly and *behaving like people* [κατὰ ἄνθρωπον περιπατεῖτε]?" and Rom 6:19: "*I am speaking like a person* [Ἀνθρώπινον λέγω] on account of the weakness of your flesh."

contemporaries-in-Christ would actually no longer sin or die.[104] To the extent that Paul's later interpreters acknowledged that the age of sin and death did *not* come to an immediate end, they had to make different meaning out of his words. They had to make "the messiah is the end of the law unto righteousness" mean that God has abrogated the Torah, or that God has abrogated its ceremonial commandments, or that the Torah is superseded as a way of salvation, or that people should cease all their moral striving, or what have you, none of which is what Paul himself meant by "the messiah is the end of the law unto righteousness."[105] Paul, for his part, meant something close to what Origen wrote in the third century, or Eliyahu Kohen in the eighteenth. The law is what it is in relation to the people for whom it legislates. When they become different kinds of creatures, then the law becomes a different kind of thing, while nevertheless remaining itself.[106] In Paul's own terms, Christ is the end of the law (Rom 10:4) precisely because he is the last man (1 Cor 15:45), the last human being made of dust. By virtue of his resurrection, however, Christ is also the first of the newborn sons of God (Rom 8:29), who practice a kind of righteousness that agrees with but also transcends the righteousness prescribed by Moses.

Conclusion

Here, finally, the argument of this book draws to a close (a τέλος, one might say). What do we know now that we did not know before? First, the classic problem of "Paul and Judaism" emerges not from the letters themselves but from a particular reading strategy – the overwhelmingly dominant reading strategy through the long history of interpretation, it so happens – which views the letters not as artefacts of Paul's own

---

[104] Schweitzer, *Mysticism*, 39: "[Paul] built his system upon a conviction which ruled only in the first generation. But what was it that disappeared out of the first Christian generation? What but the expectation of the immediate dawn of the messianic kingdom of Jesus?"

[105] Elsa Tamez, *The Amnesty of Grace: Justification by Faith from a Latin American Perspective*, trans. Sharon H. Ringe (Nashville: Abingdon, 1991) shows how all of these well-known versions of "justification by faith" are (and always were) so many contingent, local, contextual reinterpretations of Paul. On this hermeneutical dynamic more generally, see Novenson, "Our Apostles, Ourselves."

[106] See Mroczek, "The Embarrassing Bible."

vividly eschatological Judaism but as founding documents of the Christianity that came after him. Second, contrary to this long-dominant reading approach, Paul himself never parts ways with Judaism, nor does he even reify it as a thing on which he could render judgment. The rare Greek word Ἰουδαϊσμός, which Paul uses twice in Gal 1, is evidence for, not against, this unimpeachable claim. That word Ἰουδαϊσμός means not "Judaism" – the religion of Jewish people – but rather (something like) "judaization" – a particular political program of which Paul was an adherent before his revelation of Christ.

Third, the "justification from works of the law" against which Paul remonstrates is not any pre-existing form of religious life (Jewish or otherwise) but Paul's own value-laden term for a response to the Christ-announcement which demurs from his, Paul's, thoroughgoing-eschatological conclusions and opts instead for a more conventional regimen of Jewish piety. One form of this response was the proposal that gentile men baptised into the name of the Jewish messiah should, naturally, undergo proselyte circumcision. Fourth, our extant evidence suggests that the people who actually advocated for this course of action were themselves proselyte-circumcised gentiles, not cradle Jews like Paul and the other apostles. To be sure, Paul did sometimes clash with certain other Jewish apostles, but not over circumcision. Contrary to F. C. Baur's popular but false hypothesis, the circumcision controversy was a case not of Paul versus Peter, but of Paul versus the gentiles.

Fifth, as Paul's adamantine opinion on proselyte circumcision illustrates, the influential view that Paul's great, world-changing idea was anti-legalism is completely wrong. The term "legalism" is a conceptual mess (which is perhaps the very feature that has rendered it so useful to so many), but if we were to insist on using the term – which we need not and should not do – we would have to concede that Paul is equally or more legalistic than many of the other Jewish writers to whom he is often compared. His big idea lay elsewhere. Sixth, likewise completely wrong is the influential view that Paul's great, world-changing idea was anti-chauvinism or anti-ethnocentrism. In fact, Paul everywhere assumes a binary, asymmetrical, parochial folk anthropology according to which gentiles (because their prehistoric ancestors chose to worship idols) are foreskinned and basically wicked, while Jews (because God gave them the moral prophylactic of the Torah) are circumcised and basically well-behaved. To be sure, Paul also says that

Conclusion 243

gentiles as well as Jews can now become sons of God, but in the sense Paul means it even this claim is not anti-chauvinist. His big idea lay elsewhere.

Seventh, Paul's actual big idea – about God sending his son to end sin and death and to effect the resurrection and new creation – entails gentiles sharing in the happy fate of Israel, but not *becoming* Israel. Contrary to a popular Christian view attested as early as the second century, for Paul, there is no such thing as a (supposedly) "true, spiritual Israel" to contrast with the actual, empirical Israel of which Paul was a member by birth. For Paul, in other words, "carnal Israel" was the only Israel there was. Eighth, what both Israel and the gentiles do stand to gain from the sending of God's son is: metamorphosis – the changing of their sinful, mortal bodies into the likeness of Christ's glorious, immortal body, and an attendant state of perfect liberty and justice. Ninth and finally, all of this suggests a decisive solution to the hoary old problem of "Paul and the law." Like some late ancient and medieval rabbis and mystics, Paul explored the outermost limits of the Torah, enquiring how a divine word custom-built for mortals could perdure once humans became immortal, as God long ago promised they would. Paul's contribution to this whole debate is the idea that the messiah is the end of the law because he is the last Adam, the last mere mortal. All of this is clear enough. The difficulty, if there is one, lies not in anything Paul says but in the empirical fact that we are – or at least I am, at the time of writing – still dust, and to dust we shall return.

Bibliography

Abegg, Martin. "4QMMT C 27, 31 and 'Works Righteousness.'" *DSD* 6 (1999): 139–147.

Adeyemi, Femi. "Paul's 'Positive' Statements about the Mosaic Law." *Bibliotheca Sacra* 164 (2007): 49–58.

Adler, Yonatan. *The Origins of Judaism: An Archaeological-Historical Reappraisal*. AYBRL. New Haven: Yale University Press, 2022.

Ahuvia, Mika. "Gender and the Angels in Late Antique Judaism." *JSQ* 29 (2022): 1–21.

On My Right Michael, On My Left Gabriel: Angels in Ancient Jewish Culture. Berkeley: University of California Press, 2021.

Akhtar, Shabbir. *The New Testament in Muslim Eyes: Paul's Letter to the Galatians*. London: Routledge, 2018.

Akiyama, Kengo. *The Love of Neighbour in Ancient Judaism: The Reception of Leviticus 19:18 in the Hebrew Bible, the Septuagint, the Book of Jubilees, the Dead Sea Scrolls, and the New Testament*. AJEC 105. Leiden: Brill, 2018.

Alexander, Philip S. Review of *Jesus and Judaism*, by E. P. Sanders. *JJS* 37 (1986): 103–106.

"Torah and Salvation in Tannaitic Literature." Pp. 261–302 in *Justification and Variegated Nomism, Volume 1*. Edited by D. A. Carson, Peter T. O'Brien, and Mark A. Seifrid. Tübingen: Mohr Siebeck, 2001.

Allen, Michael, and Jonathan A. Linebaugh, eds. *Reformation Readings of Paul: Explorations in History and Exegesis*. Downers Grove, IL: InterVarsity, 2015.

Allison, Dale C. *Constructing Jesus: Memory, Imagination, and History*. Grand Rapids, MI: Baker, 2010.

"Peter and Cephas: One and the Same." *JBL* 111 (1992): 489–495.

Alviar, J. José. "Origen's Theological Anthropology." Pp. 373–392 in *The Oxford Handbook of Origen*. Edited by Ronald E. Heine and Karen Jo Torjesen. Oxford: Oxford University Press, 2022.

Amir, Yehoshua. "The Term *Ioudaismos*: A Study in Jewish-Hellenistic Self-Identification." *Immanuel* 14 (1982): 34–41 (in Hebrew).

Amis, Kingsley. *Rudyard Kipling and His World.* London: Thames & Hudson, 1975.
Anderson, Sonja. "Idol Talk: The Discourse of False Worship in the Early Christian World." PhD diss., Yale University, 2016.
Aune, David E. "Anthropological Duality in the Eschatology of 2 Corinthians 4:16–5:10." Pp. 215–240 in *Paul beyond the Judaism/Hellenism Divide.* Edited by Troels Engberg-Pedersen. Louisville, KY: Westminster John Knox, 2001.
  ed. *Rereading Paul Together: Protestant and Catholic Perspectives on Justification.* Grand Rapids, MI: Baker, 2006.
Avemarie, Friedrich. "Paul and the Claim of the Law according to Scripture: Leviticus 18:5 in Galatians 3:12 and Romans 10:5." Pp. 125–148 in *The Beginnings of Christianity.* Edited by Jack Pastor and Menachem Mor. Jerusalem: Yad Ben-Zvi, 2005.
Avery-Peck, Alan J. "Resurrection of the Body in Early Rabbinic Judaism." *Deuterocanonical and Cognate Literature Yearbook* (2009): 243–266.
Avi-Yonah, Michael. *Hellenism and the East: Contacts and Interrelations from Alexander to the Roman Conquest.* Jerusalem: Hebrew University, 1978.
Azulai, Hayim Joseph David. *Devash le-Fi.* Livorno, 1801.
Bachmann, Michael. *Anti-Judaism in Galatians? Exegetical Studies on a Polemical Letter and on Paul's Theology.* Translated by Robert L. Brawley. Grand Rapids, MI: Eerdmans, 2008. German original 1999.
  "Was für Praktiken? Zur jüngsten Diskussion um die ἔργα νόμου." *NTS* 55 (2009): 35–54.
Badenas, Robert. *Christ the End of the Law: Romans 10:4 in Pauline Perspective.* JSNTSup 10. Sheffield: JSOT Press, 1985.
Badiou, Alain. *Saint Paul: The Foundation of Universalism.* Translated by Ray Brassier. Stanford: Stanford University Press, 2003. French original 1997.
Baeck, Leo. "The Faith of Paul." *JJS* 3 (1952): 93–110.
Baker, Cynthia M. *Jew.* New Brunswick, NJ: Rutgers University Press, 2016.
Bammel, Ernst. "Nomos Christou." Pp. 120–128 in *Studia Evangelica III.* Edited by F. L. Cross. Berlin: Akademie Verlag, 1964.
Barclay, John M. G. "Deviance and Apostasy: Some Applications of Deviance Theory to First-Century Judaism and Christianity." Pp. 123–140 in *Pauline Churches and Diaspora Jews.* Grand Rapids, MI: Eerdmans, 2016.
  Jews in the Mediterranean Diaspora: From Alexander to Trajan (323 BCE–117 CE). Edinburgh: T&T Clark, 1996.
  "Mirror-Reading a Polemical Letter: Galatians as a Test Case." *JSNT* 10 (1987): 73–93.

"'O wad some Pow'r the giftie gie us, To see oursels as others see us!': Method and Purpose in Comparing the New Testament." Pp. 9–22 in *The New Testament in Comparison: Validity, Method, and Purpose in Comparing Traditions*. Edited by John M. G. Barclay and B. G. White. LNTS 600. London: T&T Clark, 2020.

Obeying the Truth: A Study of Paul's Ethics in Galatians. Edinburgh: T&T Clark, 1988.

"Paul among Diaspora Jews: Anomaly or Apostate?" *JSNT* 18 (1996): 89–119.

Paul and the Gift. Grand Rapids, MI: Eerdmans, 2015.

"Paul and Philo on Circumcision: Rom 2:25–9 in Social and Cultural Context." *NTS* 44 (1998): 536–556.

"Paul, Judaism, and the Jewish People." Pp. 188–201 in *The Blackwell Companion to Paul*. Edited by Stephen Westerholm. Oxford: Wiley-Blackwell, 2011.

Pauline Churches and Diaspora Jews. Grand Rapids, MI: Eerdmans, 2016.

"Tertullian, Paul, and the Nation of Israel: A Response to Geoffrey D. Dunn." Pp. 98–103 in *Tertullian and Paul*. Edited by Todd D. Still and David E. Wilhite. London: T&T Clark, 2013.

Barr, James. *The Semantics of Biblical Language*. Oxford: Oxford University Press, 1961.

Barrett, C. K. "Jews and Judaizers in the Epistles of Ignatius." Pp. 220–244 in *Jews, Greeks, and Christians: Religious Cultures in Late Antiquity*. Edited by Robert Hamerton-Kelly and Robin Scroggs. Leiden: Brill, 1976.

"Paul's Opponents in 2 Corinthians." Pp. 60–86 in *Essays on Paul*. London: SPCK, 1982.

Barth, Karl. *Church Dogmatics*. Edited and translated by G. W. Bromiley and T. F. Torrance. London: T&T Clark, 2004.

The Epistle to the Romans. Translated by Edwyn C. Hoskyns. Oxford: Oxford University Press, 1968.

Barth, Markus. "St. Paul – A Good Jew." *HBT* 1 (1979): 7–45.

"Was Paul an Anti-Semite?" *JES* 5 (1968): 78–104.

Barton, Carlin A., and Daniel Boyarin. *Imagine No Religion: How Modern Abstractions Hide Ancient Realities*. New York: Fordham University Press, 2016.

Bartoš, Hynek, and Colin Guthrie King, eds. *Heat, Pneuma, and Soul in Ancient Philosophy and Science*. Cambridge: Cambridge University Press, 2020.

Barzilai, Gabriel. "Incidental Biblical Exegesis in the Qumran Scrolls and Its Importance for the Study of the Second Temple Period." *DSD* 14 (2007): 1–24.

Bassler, Jouette M. *Divine Impartiality: Paul and a Theological Axiom.* SBLDS 59. Chico, CA: Scholars Press, 1982.

Baur, F. C. "Die Christuspartei in der korinthischen Gemeinde, der Gegensatz des paulinischen und petrinischen Christentums in der ältesten Kirche, der Apostel Petrus in Rom." *TZTh* 3.4 (1831): 61–206.

——— *Paul the Apostle of Jesus Christ.* Translated by Eduard Zeller. Revised by A. Menzies. 2 vols. London: Williams & Norgate, 1876. German original 1845.

Bauspiess, Martin, Christof Landmesser, and David Lincicum, eds. *Ferdinand Christian Baur and the History of Early Christianity.* Translated by Robert F. Brown and Peter C. Hodgson. Oxford: Oxford University Press, 2017.

Baxter, Richard. *Saints Everlasting Rest.* 1651.

Bazzana, Giovanni B. *Having the Spirit of Christ: Spirit Possession and Exorcism in the Early Christ Groups.* New Haven: Yale University Press, 2020.

——— *Kingdom of Bureaucracy: The Political Theology of Village Scribes in the Sayings Gospel Q.* BETL 274. Leuven: Peeters, 2015.

Bellamy, Francis. "The Story of the Pledge of Allegiance to the Flag." *University of Rochester Library Bulletin* 8 (1953).

Ben-Dor Benite, Zvi. *The Ten Lost Tribes: A World History.* Oxford: Oxford University Press, 2009.

Berger, Peter L. *The Heretical Imperative: Contemporary Possibilities of Religious Affirmation.* New York: Doubleday, 1979.

Berkowitz, Beth A. *Defining Jewish Difference: From Antiquity to the Present.* Cambridge: Cambridge University Press, 2012.

Betz, Hans Dieter. *Galatians: A Commentary on Paul's Letter to the Churches in Galatia.* Hermeneia. Philadelphia: Fortress, 1979.

Betz, Otto. "Rechtfertigung in Qumran." Pp. 39–58 in *Jesus, der Messias Israels: Aufsätze zur biblischen Theologie.* WUNT 42. Tübingen: Mohr Siebeck, 1987.

Beyer, H. W. "Der Brief an die Galater." In *Die kleineren Briefe des Apostels Paulus.* Das Neue Testament Deutsch vol. 8. Göttingen: Vandenhoeck & Ruprecht, 1933.

Bhabha, Homi K. *The Location of Culture.* London: Routledge, 1994.

Biblia Hebraica Stuttgartensia. 5th ed. Stuttgart: Deutsche Bibelgesellschaft, 1997.

Bickerman, Elias. *The God of the Maccabees: Studies on the Origin and Meaning of the Maccabean Revolt.* SJLA 32. Leiden: Brill, 1979.

——— *The Jews in the Greek Age.* Cambridge, MA: Harvard University Press, 1988.

Bieringer, Reimund, and Didier Pollefeyt, eds. *Paul and Judaism: Crosscurrents in Pauline Exegesis and the Study of Jewish-Christian Relations*. LNTS 463. London: T&T Clark, 2012.

Bird, Michael F. *An Anomalous Jew: Paul among Jews, Greeks, and Romans*. Grand Rapids, MI: Eerdmans, 2016.

Blanton, Thomas R. *Constructing a New Covenant: Discursive Strategies in the Damascus Document and Second Corinthians*. WUNT 2/233. Tübingen: Mohr Siebeck, 2007.

Blanton, Ward. *A Materialism for the Masses: Saint Paul and the Philosophy of Undying Life*. New York: Columbia University Press, 2014.

Blass, F., and A. Debrunner. *A Greek Grammar of the New Testament and Other Early Christian Literature*. Translated by Robert W. Funk. Chicago: University of Chicago Press, 1961.

Bleek, F. *Einleitung in das Neue Testament*. Edited by W. Mangold. 3rd ed. Berlin: Reimer, 1875.

Blosser, Benjamin P. *Become Like the Angels: Origen's Doctrine of the Soul*. Washington, DC: CUA Press, 2012.

Boakye, Andrew K. *Death and Life: Resurrection, Restoration, and Rectification in Paul's Letter to the Galatians*. Eugene, OR: Pickwick, 2017.

Boccaccini, Gabriele. *Paul's Three Paths to Salvation*. Grand Rapids, MI: Eerdmans, 2020.

"The Three Paths to Salvation of Paul the Jew." Pp. 1–29 in *Paul the Jew: Rereading the Apostle as a Figure of Second Temple Judaism*. Edited by Gabriele Boccaccini and Carlos A. Segovia. Minneapolis: Fortress, 2016.

Bockmuehl, Markus. "1 Thessalonians 2:14–16 and the Church in Jerusalem." *TynBul* 52 (2001): 1–31.

Seeing the Word: Refocusing New Testament Study. Grand Rapids, MI: Baker, 2006.

Bokser, Ben Zion. "Justin Martyr and the Jews." *JQR* 64 (1973): 97–122.

Borgen, Peder. "Observations on the Theme 'Paul and Philo': Paul's Preaching of Circumcision in Galatia (Gal 5:11) and Debates on Circumcision in Philo." Pp. 85–102 in *Die Paulinische Literatur und Theologie*. Edited by S. Pedersen. Aarhus: Aros, 1980.

"Paul Preaches Circumcision and Pleases Men." Pp. 37–46 in *Paul and Paulinism: Essays in Honour of C. K. Barrett*. Edited by M. D. Hooker and S. G. Wilson. London: SPCK, 1982.

Paul Preaches Circumcision and Pleases Men, and Other Essays on Christian Origins. Trondheim: Tapir, 1983.

Bos, Abraham P. *Aristotle on God's Life-Generating Power and on Pneuma as Its Vehicle*. Albany, NY: SUNY Press, 2018.

Boustan, Ra'anan S. "Augustine as Revolutionary? Reflections on Continuity and Rupture in Jewish-Christian Relations in Paula Fredriksen's *Augustine and the Jews*." *JQR* 99 (2009): 74–87.

Boyarin, Daniel. *Carnal Israel: Reading Sex in Talmudic Culture*. Berkeley: University of California Press, 1993.

———. *Judaism*. New Brunswick, NJ: Rutgers University Press, 2019.

———. *A Radical Jew: Paul and the Politics of Identity*. Berkeley: University of California Press, 1994.

———. "Rethinking Jewish Christianity: An Argument for Dismantling a Dubious Category." *JQR* 99 (2009): 7–36.

———. "Why Ignatius Invented Judaism." Pp. 309–324 in *The Ways That Often Parted: Essays in Honor of Joel Marcus*. Edited by Lori Baron, Jill Hicks-Keeton, and Matthew Thiessen. Atlanta: SBL Press, 2018.

Braude, William G., trans. *The Midrash on Psalms*. YJS 13. New Haven: Yale University Press, 1959.

———, trans. *Pesikta Rabbati*. 2 vols. YJS 18. New Haven: Yale University Press, 1968.

Bremer, J. M. *Hamartia: Tragic Error in the Poetics of Aristotle and in Greek Tragedy*. Amsterdam: Hakkert, 1969.

Bremmer, Jan N. "Spartans and Jews: Abrahamic Cousins?" Pp. 47–60 in *Abraham, the Nations, and the Hagarites: Jewish, Christian, and Islamic Perspectives on Kinship with Abraham*. Edited by Martin Goodman, George H. van Kooten, and Jacques T. A. G. M. van Ruiten. TBN 13. Leiden: Brill, 2010.

Brown, Raymond E. "Not Jewish Christianity and Gentile Christianity but Types of Jewish/Gentile Christianity." *CBQ* 45 (1983): 74–79.

Brubaker, Rogers. *Ethnicity without Groups*. Cambridge, MA: Harvard University Press, 2004.

———. *Grounds for Difference*. Cambridge, MA: Harvard University Press, 2015.

Bruce, F. F. *The Epistle of Paul to the Romans: An Introduction and Commentary*. 2nd ed. Grand Rapids, MI: Eerdmans, 1985.

Bruce, Lenny. *The Essential Lenny Bruce*. Compiled and edited by John Cohen. New York: Bell, 1970.

Buell, Denise Kimber. *Why This New Race: Ethnic Reasoning in Early Christianity*. New York: Columbia University Press, 2005.

Bühner, Ruben A. *Paulus im Kontext des Diasporajudentums: Judenchristliche Lebensweise nach den paulinischen Briefen und die Debatten um "Paul within Judaism."* WUNT 511. Tübingen: Mohr Siebeck, 2023.

Bultmann, Rudolf. *Exegetische Probleme des zweiten Korintherbriefes*. Darmstadt: Wissenschaftliche Buchgesellschaft, 1963.

"New Testament and Mythology." Pp. 1–44 in *New Testament and Mythology, and Other Basic Writings*. Edited by and translated by Schubert M. Ogden. Philadelphia: Fortress, 1984.

Der Stil der paulinischen Predigt und die kynisch-stoische Diatribe. Göttingen: Vandenhoeck & Ruprecht, 1910.

Theology of the New Testament. 2 vols. Translated by Kendrick Grobel. New York: Scribner's, 1951–1955.

Burnett, David A. "A Neglected Deuteronomic Scriptural Matrix for the Nature of the Resurrection Body in 1 Corinthians 15:39–42." Pp. 187–212 in *Scripture, Texts, and Tracings in 1 Corinthians*. Edited by Linda L. Belleville and B. J. Oropeza. Lanham, MD: Lexington/Fortress, 2019.

"'So Shall Your Seed Be': Paul's Use of Genesis 15:5 in Romans 4:18 in Light of Early Jewish Deification Traditions." *JSPL* 5 (2015): 211–236.

Burton, Ernest De Witt. *A Critical and Exegetical Commentary on the Epistle to the Galatians*. ICC. New York: Scribner's, 1920.

Bynum, Caroline Walker. *The Resurrection of the Body in Western Christianity, 200–1336*. New York: Columbia University Press, 1995.

Byrne, Brendan. *Romans*. SacPag. Collegeville, MN: Liturgical Press, 1996.

Calvin, John. *Commentary on the Epistles of Paul the Apostle to the Corinthians*. Grand Rapids, MI: Baker, 1981.

Camelot, P. T., ed. *Ignace d'Antioche. Polycarpe de Smyrne. Lettres. Martyre de Polycarpe*. 4th ed. Sources chrétiennes 10. Paris: Éditions du Cerf, 1969.

Campbell, Douglas A. *The Deliverance of God: An Apocalyptic Rereading of Justification in Paul*. Grand Rapids, MI: Eerdmans, 2009.

"Galatians 5:11: Evidence of an Early Law-observant Mission by Paul?" *NTS* 57 (2011): 325–247.

Campbell, William S. "Reading Paul in Relation to Judaism: Comparison or Contrast?" Pp. 120–150 in *Earliest Christianity within the Boundaries of Judaism: Essays in Honor of Bruce Chilton*. Edited by Alan J. Avery-Peck, Craig A. Evans, and Jacob Neusner. BRLJ 49. Leiden: Brill, 2016.

Carleton Paget, James. "Barnabas 9:4: A Peculiar Verse on Circumcision." *VC* 45 (1991): 242–254.

"Paul and the Epistle of Barnabas." *NovT* 38 (1996): 359–381.

"Schweitzer and Paul." *JSNT* 33 (2011): 223–256.

"Some Observations on the Problem of the Delay of the Parousia in the Historiography of Its Discussion." *EC* 9 (2018): 9–36.

Carlson, Stephen C. *The Text of Galatians and Its History*. WUNT 2/385. Tübingen: Mohr Siebeck, 2015.

Carlyon, J. T. Review of *The Mysticism of Paul the Apostle*, by Albert Schweitzer. *JR* 12 (1932): 377.

Carras, George P. *Two Diaspora Jews: Josephus and Paul A Historical, Social, and Theological Comparison of Hellenistic Jewry*. Leiden: Brill, forthcoming.
Casey, Thomas G., and Justin Taylor, eds. *Paul's Jewish Matrix*. Rome: Gregorian & Biblical Press, 2011.
Castelli, Elizabeth A. *Imitating Paul: A Discourse of Power*. Louisville, KY: Westminster John Knox, 1991.
Chadwick, Henry. "Origen, Celsus, and the Resurrection of the Body." *HTR* 41 (1948): 83–102.
Chantziantoniou, Alexi. "Paul and the Politics of Idolatry: Ancient Mediterranean Cult Images and Iconic Ritual in the Letters of Paul." PhD diss., University of Cambridge, 2023.
Charles, R. H., trans. *The Book of Jubilees*. London: SPCK, 1917.
Charles, Ronald. *Paul and the Politics of Diaspora*. Minneapolis: Fortress, 2014.
Charlesworth, James H., ed. *Old Testament Pseudepigrapha*. 2 vols. New York: Doubleday, 1985.
Chester, Andrew. *Messiah and Exaltation: Jewish Messianic and Visionary Traditions and New Testament Christology*. WUNT 207. Tübingen: Mohr Siebeck, 2007.
Chester, Stephen J. *Reading Paul with the Reformers: Reconciling Old and New Perspectives*. Grand Rapids, MI: Eerdmans, 2017.
Cirafesi, Wally V. *John within Judaism: Religion, Ethnicity, and the Shaping of Jesus-Oriented Jewishness in the Fourth Gospel*. AJEC 112. Leiden: Brill, 2022.
Cisco, Charles K. "The Philosophy of Freedom and Slavery in Paul's Epistle to the Galatians." PhD diss., University of Edinburgh, 2023.
Clark, Ernest P. "Enslaved under the Elements of the Cosmos." PhD diss., University of St Andrews, 2018.
Cocchini, Francesca. "Origen's Pauline Commentaries." Pp. 229–243 in *The Oxford Handbook of Origen*. Edited by Ronald E. Heine and Karen Jo Torjesen. Oxford: Oxford University Press, 2022.
Cohen, Jeremy. "The Mystery of Israel's Salvation: Romans 11:25–26 in Patristic and Medieval Exegesis." *HTR* 98 (2005): 247–281.
Cohen, Shaye J. D. *The Beginnings of Jewishness: Boundaries, Varieties, Uncertainties*. Berkeley: University of California Press, 2001.
"How Do You Know a Jew in Antiquity When You See One?" Pp. 25–68 in *The Beginnings of Jewishness: Boundaries, Varieties, Uncertainties*. Berkeley: University of California Press, 2001.
"Judaism without Circumcision and 'Judaism' without 'Circumcision' in Ignatius." *HTR* 95 (2002): 395–415.

Why Aren't Jewish Women Circumcised? Gender and Covenant in Judaism. Berkeley: University of California Press, 2005.

Collins, John J. "The Angelic Life." Pp. 291–310 in *Metamorphoses: Resurrection, Body, and Transformative Practices in Early Christianity*. Edited by Turid Karlsen Seim and Jorunn Økland. Berlin: De Gruyter, 2009.

——— *The Invention of Judaism: Torah and Jewish Identity from Deuteronomy to Paul*. Berkeley: University of California Press, 2017.

——— *The Scepter and the Star: Messianism in Light of the Dead Sea Scrolls*. 2nd ed. Grand Rapids, MI: Eerdmans, 2010.

Collman, Ryan D. *The Apostle to the Foreskin: Circumcision in the Letters of Paul*. BZNW 259. Berlin: De Gruyter, 2023.

——— "Beware the Dogs! The Phallic Epithet in Phil 3.2," *NTS* 67 (2021): 105–120.

Concannon, Cavan W. "Paul Is Dead. Long Live Paulinism! Imagining a Future for Pauline Studies." *AJR*. 1 November 2016.

——— *Profaning Paul*. Chicago: University of Chicago Press, 2021.

——— *When You Were Gentiles: Specters of Ethnicity in Roman Corinth and Paul's Corinthian Correspondence*. New Haven: Yale University Press, 2014.

Congdon, David W. *The Mission of Demythologizing: Rudolf Bultmann's Dialectical Theology*. Minneapolis: Fortress, 2015.

Cook, John Granger. "1 Cor 15:40–41: Paul and the Heavenly Bodies." *ZNW* 113 (2022): 159–179.

Cosgrove, Charles H. "Did Paul Value Ethnicity?" *CBQ* 68 (2006): 268–290.

Cranfield, C. E. B. *The Epistle to the Romans*. 2 vols. ICC. London: T&T Clark, 2004.

——— "St. Paul and the Law." *SJT* 17 (1964): 43–68.

Dahl, Nils A. "Ephesians and Qumran." Pp. 107–144 in *Studies in Ephesians*. WUNT 131. Tübingen: Mohr Siebeck, 2000.

——— "Der Name Israel." *Judaica* 6 (1950): 161–170.

——— "One God of Jews and Gentiles." Pp. 178–191 in *Studies in Paul: Theology for the Early Christian Mission*. Minneapolis: Augsburg, 1977.

——— "Paul and the Church at Corinth according to 1 Corinthians 1:10–4:21." Pp. 40–61 in *Studies in Paul: Theology for the Early Christian Mission*. Minneapolis: Augsburg, 1977.

——— Review of *Paul and Palestinian Judaism*, by E. P. Sanders. *RSR* 4 (1978): 153–160.

Danby, Herbert, trans. *The Mishnah*. Oxford: Oxford University Press, 1933.

Danker, Frederick W., Walter Bauer, William F. Arndt, and F. Wilbur Gingrich. *Greek-English Lexicon of the New Testament and Other Early Christian Literature*. 3rd ed. Chicago: University of Chicago Press, 2000.
Davies, Jamie. "Why Paul Doesn't Mention the Age to Come." *SJT* 74 (2021): 199–208.
Davies, W. D. *Paul and Rabbinic Judaism: Some Rabbinic Elements in Pauline Theology*. London: SPCK, 1948.
— *The Setting of the Sermon on the Mount*. Cambridge: Cambridge University Press, 1966.
— *Torah in the Messianic Age and/or the Age to Come*. Philadelphia: SBL, 1952.
Davies, W. D. and Dale C. Allison. *The Gospel according to Saint Matthew*. 3 vols. ICC. London: T&T Clark, 2004.
De Boer, Martinus C. *The Defeat of Death: Apocalyptic Eschatology in 1 Corinthians 15 and Romans 5*. Sheffield: JSOT Press, 1988.
De Lacy, P. H., trans. *Galen: On the Doctrines of Hippocrates and Plato*. 3 vols. CMG. Berlin: Akademie Verlag, 1978–1984.
De Lange, Nicholas. *Origen and the Jews: Studies in Jewish-Christian Relations in Third-Century Palestine*. Cambridge: Cambridge University Press, 1976.
De Roo, Jacqueline C. R. *Works of the Law at Qumran and in Paul*. Sheffield: Sheffield Phoenix, 2007.
Decosimo, David. "An *Umma* of Accountability: Al-Ghazali against Domination." *Soundings* 98 (2015): 260–288.
den Dulk, Matthijs. *Between Jews and Heretics: Refiguring Justin Martyr's Dialogue with Trypho*. London: Routledge, 2018.
Diez Macho, Alejandro. "Cesara la Tora en la Edad Mesianica?" *EstBib* 12 (1953): 115–158 and *EstBib* 13 (1954): 5–51.
Dingeldein, Laura. "Gaining Virtue, Gaining Christ: Moral Development in the Letters of Paul." PhD diss., Brown University, 2014.
Dodd, C. H. *The Meaning of Paul for Today*. New York: Doran, 1920.
Doering, Lutz. "4QMMT and the Letters of Paul." Pp. 69–88 in *The Dead Sea Scrolls and Pauline Literature*. Edited by Jean-Sebastien Rey. STDJ 102. Leiden: Brill, 2014.
Donahue, Paul J. "Jewish Christianity in the Letters of Ignatius of Antioch." *VC* 32 (1978): 81–93.
Donaldson, Terence L. *Gentile Christian Identity from Cornelius to Constantine: The Nations, the Parting of the Ways, and Roman Imperial Ideology*. Grand Rapids, MI: Eerdmans, 2020.
— *Judaism and the Gentiles: Jewish Patterns of Universalism (to 135 CE)*. Waco, TX: Baylor University Press, 2007.

Paul and the Gentiles: Remapping the Apostle's Convictional World. Minneapolis: Fortress, 1997.

Downing, F. Gerald. *Cynics, Paul, and the Pauline Churches.* London: Routledge, 1998.

Drane, John W. *Paul: Libertine or Legalist?* London: SPCK, 1975.

Dunn, James D. G. "4QMMT and Galatians." Pp. 339–346 in *The New Perspective on Paul.* Rev. ed. Grand Rapids, MI: Eerdmans, 2008.

"Adam and Christ." Pp. 125–138 in *Reading Paul's Letter to the Romans.* Edited by Jerry L. Sumney. Atlanta: SBL Press, 2012.

"Echoes of Intra-Jewish Polemic in Paul's Letter to the Galatians." Pp. 227–246 in *The New Perspective on Paul.* Rev. ed. Grand Rapids, MI: Eerdmans, 2008.

The New Perspective on Paul. Rev. ed. Grand Rapids, MI: Eerdmans, 2008.

Review of *Paul within Judaism*, edited by Mark D. Nanos and Magnus Zetterholm. *JTS* 66 (2015): 782–784.

Dunn, James D. G. and James H. Charlesworth. "Qumran's Some Works of Torah and Paul's Galatians." Pp. 187–201 in *The Bible and the Dead Sea Scrolls, Volume 3.* Waco, TX: Baylor University Press, 2006.

Dunning, Benjamin H. *Christ without Adam: Subjectivity and Sexual Difference in the Philosophers' Paul.* New York: Columbia University Press, 2014.

Specters of Paul: Sexual Difference in Early Christian Thought. Philadelphia: University of Pennsylvania Press, 2011.

East, Brad. "Enter Paul." *LARB* (23 June 2019).

Eastman, Susan Grove. "Israel and the Mercy of God: A Re-reading of Galatians 6:16 and Romans 9–11." *NTS* 56 (2010): 367–395.

Paul and the Person: Reframing Paul's Anthropology. Grand Rapids, MI: Eerdmans, 2017.

Edwards, Mark Julian. *Origen against Plato.* London: Ashgate, 2002.

Ehrensperger, Kathy. "Paul and Feminism." Pp. 622–636 in *The Oxford Handbook of Pauline Studies.* Edited by Matthew V. Novenson and R. Barry Matlock. Oxford: Oxford University Press, 2022.

Eisenbaum, Pamela. *Paul Was Not a Christian: The Original Message of a Misunderstood Apostle.* San Francisco: HarperCollins, 2009.

Engberg-Pedersen, Troels. "Complete and Incomplete Transformation in Paul: A Philosophical Reading of Paul on Body and Spirit." Pp. 123–146 in *Metamorphoses: Resurrection, Body, and Transformative Practices in Early Christianity.* Edited by Turid Karlsen Seim and Jorunn Økland. Berlin: De Gruyter, 2009.

Cosmology and Self in the Apostle Paul: The Material Spirit. Oxford: Oxford University Press, 2010.

"Introduction: Paul beyond the Judaism/Hellenism Divide." Pp. 1–16 in *Paul beyond the Judaism/Hellenism Divide*. Edited by Troels Engberg-Pedersen. Louisville, KY: Westminster John Knox, 2001.

Paul and the Stoics. Edinburgh: T&T Clark, 2000.

ed. *Paul beyond the Judaism/Hellenism Divide*. Louisville, KY: Westminster John Knox, 2001.

ed. *Paul in His Hellenistic Context*. Edinburgh: T&T Clark, 1994.

Eskola, Timo. *A Narrative Theology of the New Testament*. WUNT 350. Tübingen: Mohr Siebeck, 2015.

Enslin, M. S. *Christian Beginnings*. New York: Harper, 1938.

Epstein, Isidore, ed. *The Talmud*. 35 vols. London: Soncino, 1935–1952.

Erasmus. *Novum Instrumentum Omne*. Basel, 1516.

Etienne, S. "Réflexion sur l'apostasie de Tibérius Julius Alexander." *SPhA* 12 (2000): 122–142.

Eubank, Nathan. "Configurations of Grace and Merit in Paul and His Interpreters." *IJST* 22 (2020): 7–17.

Wages of Cross-Bearing and Debt of Sin: The Economy of Heaven in Matthew's Gospel. Berlin: De Gruyter, 2013.

Eyl, Jennifer. "'I Myself Am an Israelite': Paul, Authenticity, and Authority." *JSNT* 40 (2017): 148–168.

"Semantic Voids, New Testament Translation, and Anachronism: The Case of Paul's Use of *Ekklesia*." *MTSR* 26 (2014): 315–339.

Signs, Wonders, and Gifts: Divination in the Letters of Paul. New York: Oxford University Press, 2019.

Fatum, Lone. "Brotherhood in Christ: A Gender Hermeneutical Reading of 1 Thessalonians." Pp. 183–198 in *Constructing Early Christian Families*. Edited by Halvor Moxnes. London: Routledge, 1997.

Feldman, Louis H. *Jew and Gentile in the Ancient World: Attitudes and Interactions from Alexander to Justinian*. Princeton: Princeton University Press, 1993.

Fewster, Gregory. "Archiving Paul: Manuscripts, Religion, and the Editorial Shaping of Ancient Letter Collections." *Archivaria* 81 (2016): 101–128.

Filtvedt, Ole Jakob. "God's Israel in Galatians 6.16: An Overview and Assessment of the Key Arguments." *CBR* 15 (2016): 123–140.

Fisch, Yael. *Written for Us: Paul's Interpretation of Scripture and the History of Midrash*. JSJSup 202. Leiden: Brill, 2023.

Fitzmyer, Joseph A. *Romans: A New Translation with Introduction and Commentary*. AYB. New Haven: Yale University Press, 2008.

"Saint Paul and the Law." *The Jurist* 27 (1967): 18–36.

Flusser, David. "Die Christenheit nach dem Apostelkonzil." Pp. 60–81 in *Antijudaismus im Neuen Testament?* Edited by W. Eckert, N. P. Levinson, and M. Stohr. Munich: Kaiser, 1967.

"Gesetzeswerke in Qumran und bei Paulus." Pp. 395–403 in vol. 1 of *Geschichte—Tradition—Reflexion: Festschrift für Martin Hengel zum 70 Geburtstag*. Edited by Hubert Cancik, Hermann Lichtenberger, and Peter Schäfer. 3 vols. Tübingen: Mohr Siebeck, 1996.

"Paul's Jewish-Christian Opponents in the *Didache*." Pp. 195–211 in *The Didache in Modern Research*. Edited by Jonathan A. Draper. Leiden: Brill, 1996.

"Resurrection and Angels in Rabbinic Judaism, Early Christianity, and Qumran." Pp. 568–572 in *The Dead Sea Scrolls, Fifty Years after Their Discovery*. Edited by Lawrence H. Schiffman, Emanual Tov, and James C. VanderKam. Jerusalem: Israel Exploration Society, 2000.

Fonrobert, Charlotte Elisheva. "The *Didascalia Apostolorum*: A Mishnah for the Disciples of Jesus." *JECS* 9 (2001): 483–509.

Forbes, Christopher. "Comparison, Self-Praise, and Irony: Paul's Boasting and the Conventions of Hellenistic Rhetoric." *NTS* 32 (1986): 1–30.

Foster, Paul. *Colossians*. BNTC. London: T&T Clark, 2016.

"Who Wrote 2 Thessalonians? A Fresh Look at an Old Problem." *JSNT* 35 (2012): 150–175.

Fraade, Steven D. "To Whom It May Concern: 4QMMT and Its Addressees." *RevQ* 19 (2000): 507–526.

Frankfurter, David. "Jews or Not? Reconstructing the 'Other' in Rev 2:9 and 3:9." *HTR* 94 (2001): 403–425.

Review of *Before Religion*, by Brent Nongbri. *JECS* 23 (2015): 632–634.

Fredriksen, Paula. "*Al Tirah* ('Fear Not!'): Jewish Apocalyptic Eschatology, from Schweitzer to Allison, and After." Pp. 15–38 in *"To Recover What Has Been Lost": Essays on Eschatology, Intertextuality, and Reception History in Honor of Dale C. Allison Jr.* Edited by Tucker S. Ferda, Daniel Frayer-Griggs, and Nathan C. Johnson. NovTSup 183. Leiden: Brill, 2021.

Augustine and the Jews: A Christian Defense of Jews and Judaism. New Haven: Yale University Press, 2008.

"Historical Integrity, Interpretive Freedom: The Philosopher's Paul and the Problem of Anachronism." Pp. 61–73 in *St. Paul among the Philosophers*. Edited by John D. Caputo and Linda Martin Alcoff. Bloomington, IN: Indiana University Press, 2009.

"Judaizing the Nations: The Ritual Demands of Paul's Gospel." *NTS* 56 (2010): 232–252.

Paul: The Pagans' Apostle. New Haven: Yale University Press, 2017.

"Paul's Letter to the Romans, the Ten Commandments, and Pagan Justification by Faith." *JBL* 133 (2014): 801–808.

"Philo, Herod, Paul, and the Many Gods of Ancient Jewish 'Monotheism.'" *HTR* 115 (2022): 23–45.

Review of *The Beginning of the Gospel*, by Joshua D. Garroway. *RBL*. June 2020.

Sin: The Early History of an Idea. Princeton: Princeton University Press, 2012.

"What 'Parting of the Ways?' Jews, Gentiles, and the Ancient Mediterranean City." Pp. 35–64 in *The Ways That Never Parted: Jews and Christians in Late Antiquity and the Early Middle Ages*. Edited by Adam H. Becker and Anette Yoshiko Reed. TSAJ 95. Tübingen: Mohr Siebeck, 2003.

"Why Should a 'Law-Free' Mission Mean a 'Law-Free' Apostle?" *JBL* 134 (2015): 637–650.

ed. and trans. *Augustine on Romans*. Chico, CA: Scholars Press, 1982.

Freedman, H., and Maurice Simon, eds. *Midrash Rabbah*. 9 vols. London: Soncino, 1939–1951.

Freiberger, Oliver. *Considering Comparison: A Method for Religious Studies*. Oxford: Oxford University Press, 2019.

Frey, Jean-Baptiste, ed. *Corpus inscriptioum judaicarum*. 2 vols. Rome: Pontifical Institute of Christian Archaeology, 1936–1952.

Frey, Jörg. "Contextualizing Paul's Works of the Law: MMT in New Testament Scholarship." Pp. 743–762 in *Qumran, Early Judaism, and New Testament Interpretation: Kleine Schriften III*. Edited by Jacob N. Cerone. WUNT 424. Tübingen: Mohr Siebeck, 2019.

Gager, John G. *Curse Tablets and Binding Spells from the Ancient World*. Oxford: Oxford University Press, 1999.

Kingdom and Community: The Social World of Early Christianity. Englewood Cliffs, NJ: Prentice Hall, 1975.

Reinventing Paul. Oxford: Oxford University Press, 2000.

Review of *The Mythmaker: Paul and the Invention of Christianity*, by Hyam Maccoby. *JQR* 79 (1988): 248–250.

Gaifman, Milette. *Aniconism in Greek Antiquity*. Oxford: Oxford University Press, 2012.

Gamble, Harry Y. "The Formation of the Pauline Corpus." Pp. 338–354 in *The Oxford Handbook of Pauline Studies*. Edited by Matthew V. Novenson and R. Barry Matlock. Oxford: Oxford University Press, 2022.

The Textual History of the Letter to the Romans. SD 42. Grand Rapids, MI: Eerdmans, 1977.

Garroway, Joshua D. *The Beginning of the Gospel: Paul, Philippi, and the Origins of Christianity*. London: Palgrave Macmillan, 2018.

"The Circumcision of Christ: Romans 15:7–13." *JSNT* 34 (2012): 303–322.

"Paul: Within Judaism, Without Law." Pp. 49–66 in *Law and Lawlessness in Early Judaism and Early Christianity*. Edited by David

Lincicum, Ruth Sheridan, and Charles M. Stang. WUNT 420. Tübingen: Mohr Siebeck, 2019.

Paul's Gentile-Jews: Neither Jew nor Gentile but Both. New York: Palgrave Macmillan, 2012.

"The Pharisee Heresy: Circumcision for Gentiles in the Acts of the Apostles." *NTS* 60 (2014): 20–36.

Gaston, Lloyd. *Paul and the Torah*. Vancouver: University of British Columbia Press, 1987.

Gathercole, Simon. "Justified by Faith, Justified by His Blood: The Evidence of Rom 3:21–4:25." Pp. 147–184 in *Justification and Variegated Nomism, Volume 2*. Edited by D. A. Carson, Peter T. O'Brien, and Mark A. Seifrid. Tübingen: Mohr Siebeck, 2004.

"A Law unto Themselves: The Gentiles in Romans 2:14–15 Revisited." *JSNT* 24 (2002): 27–49.

"'Sins' in Paul." *NTS* 64 (2018): 143–161.

"Torah, Life, and Salvation: Leviticus 18:5 in Early Judaism and the New Testament." Pp. 131–150 in *From Prophecy to Testament: The Function of the Old Testament in the New*. Edited by Craig A. Evans. Peabody, MA: Hendrickson, 2004.

Where Is Boasting: Early Jewish Soteriology and Paul's Response in Romans 1–5. Grand Rapids, MI: Eerdmans, 2002.

Gathergood, Emily. "The Midwifery of God." PhD diss., University of Nottingham, 2022.

Gaventa, Beverly Roberts, ed. *Apocalyptic Paul: Cosmos and Anthropos in Romans 5–8*. Waco, TX: Baylor University Press, 2013.

"Comparing Paul and Judaism: Rethinking Our Methods." *BTB* 10 (1980): 37–44.

"The Singularity of the Gospel." Pp. 101–112 in *Our Mother Saint Paul*. Louisville, KY: Westminster John Knox, 2007.

"We, They, and All in Paul's Letter to the Romans." *Word & World* 39 (2019): 263–273.

Georgi, Dieter. *The Opponents of Paul in Second Corinthians*. Edinburgh: T&T Clark, 1987. German original 1964.

Goldstein, David. *Classical Greek Syntax: Wackernagel's Law in Herodotus*. Leiden: Brill, 2016.

Goodblatt, David. *Elements of Ancient Jewish Nationalism*. Cambridge: Cambridge University Press, 2006.

Goodman, Martin. "Galatians 6:12 on Circumcision and Persecution." Pp. 275–280 in *Strength to Strength: Essays in Honor of Shaye J. D. Cohen*. Edited by Michael L. Satlow. Providence, RI: Brown Judaic Studies, 2018.

A History of Judaism. London: Penguin, 2017.

Mission and Conversion: Proselytizing in the Religious History of the Roman Empire. Oxford: Clarendon, 1994.
Goulder, Michael. *St. Paul versus St. Peter: A Tale of Two Missions*. Louisville, KY: Westminster John Knox, 1994.
Grayston, Kenneth. "The Opponents in Philippians 3." *ExpTim* 97 (1986): 170–172.
Greene, Graham. *Monsignor Quixote*. New York: Simon & Schuster, 1982.
Gruen, Erich S. "Christians as a Third Race: Is Ethnicity at Issue?" in *Christianity in the Second Century*. Edited by James Carleton Paget and Judith Lieu. Cambridge: Cambridge University Press, 2017.
"The Purported Jewish-Spartan Affiliation." Pp. 153–167 in *Constructs of Identity in Hellenistic Judaism: Essays on Early Jewish Literature and History*. Berlin: De Gruyter, 2016.
Gundry, Judith M. "Affliction for Procreators in the Eschatological Crisis: Paul's Marital Counsel in 1 Corinthians 7:28 and Contraception in Greco-Roman Antiquity." *JSNT* 39 (2016): 141–168.
Gunther, John J. *St. Paul's Opponents and Their Background: A Study of Apocalyptic and Jewish Sectarian Teachings*. NovTSup 35. Leiden: Brill, 1973.
Haacker, Klaus. *The Theology of Paul's Letter to the Romans*. Cambridge: Cambridge University Press, 2003.
Hall, Edith. *Inventing the Barbarian: Greek Self-Definition through Tragedy*. OCM. Oxford: Clarendon, 1991.
Hardin, Justin K. "'If I Still Proclaim Circumcision' (Gal 5:11a): Paul, the Law, and Gentile Circumcision." *JSPL* 3 (2013): 145–164.
Harding, Sarah. *Paul's Eschatological Anthropology*. Minneapolis: Fortress, 2015.
Harker, Christina. *The Colonizers' Idols: Paul, Galatia, and Empire in New Testament Studies*. WUNT 2/460. Tübingen: Mohr Siebeck, 2018.
von Harnack, Adolf. *Marcion: The Gospel of the Alien God*. Translated by John E. Steely and Lyle D. Bierma. Durham, NC: Labyrinth, 1990.
Harper, Kyle. *From Shame to Sin: The Christian Transformation of Sexual Morality in Late Antiquity*. Cambridge, MA: Harvard University Press, 2013.
Harrill, J. Albert. *Slaves in the New Testament: Literary, Social, and Moral Dimensions*. Minneapolis: Fortress, 2006.
Hart, David Bentley. "Foreword." Pp. ix–xv in *Paul's Three Paths to Salvation*, by Gabriele Boccaccini. Grand Rapids, MI: Eerdmans, 2020.
That All Shall Be Saved: Heaven, Hell, and Universal Salvation. New Haven: Yale University Press, 2019.
Hart, Patrick. *A Prolegomenon to the Study of Paul*. MTSRSup 15. Leiden: Brill, 2020.

Harvey, A. E. "The Opposition to Paul." Pp. 319–332 in *Studia Evangelica*, vol. 4. Berlin: Akademie Verlag, 1968.

Harvey, Graham. *The True Israel: Uses of the Names Jew, Hebrew, and Israel in Ancient Jewish and Early Christian Literature.* AGJU 35. Leiden: Brill, 1996.

Hawkins, John Gale. "The Opponents of Paul in Galatia." PhD diss., Yale University, 1971.

Hayes, Christine. "The Complicated Goy in Classical Rabbinic Sources." Pp. 147–168 in *Perceiving the Other in Ancient Judaism and Early Christianity*. Edited by Michal Bar-Asher Siegal, Wolfgang Grünstäudl, and Matthew Thiessen. WUNT 394. Tübingen: Mohr Siebeck, 2017.

Gentile Impurities and Jewish Identities: Intermarriage and Conversion from the Bible to the Talmud. Oxford: Oxford University Press, 2002.

"'The Torah Was Not Given to Ministering Angels': Rabbinic Aspirationalism." Pp. 123–160 in *Talmudic Transgressions: Engaging the Work of Daniel Boyarin*. Edited by Charlotte Fonrobert, Ishay Rosen-Zvi, Aharon Shemesh, and Moulie Vidas. JSJSup 181. Leiden: Brill, 2017.

What's Divine about Divine Law? Princeton: Princeton University Press, 2015.

Hays, Richard B. "Galatians." Pp. 181–348 in vol. 11 of *The New Interpreter's Bible*. Nashville: Abingdon, 2000.

"The Gospel Is the Power of God for Salvation to Gentiles Only? A Critique of Stanley Stowers's *Rereading of Romans*." CRBR 9 (1996): 27–44.

"Have We Found Abraham to Be Our Forefather according to the Flesh? A Reconsideration of Rom 4:1." NovT 27 (1985): 76–98.

"Psalm 143 and the Logic of Romans 3." JBL 99 (1980): 107–115.

Hengel, Martin. *Judaism and Hellenism: Studies in Their Encounter in Palestine During the Early Hellenistic Period.* 2 vols. Translated by John Bowden. Philadelphia: Fortress, 1974.

The Pre-Christian Paul. Translated by John Bowden. London: SCM, 1991.

"Die Synagogeninschrift von Stobi." ZNW 57 (1966): 145–183.

Hengel, Martin. and Ulrich Heckel, eds. *Paulus und das antike Judentum.* WUNT 58. Tübingen: Mohr Siebeck, 1991.

Hewitt, J. Thomas. *Messiah and Scripture: Paul's "In Christ" Idiom in Its Ancient Jewish Context.* WUNT 2/522. Tübingen: Mohr Siebeck, 2020.

"Pneuma, Genealogical Descent, and Things That Do Not Exist according to Paul." NTS 68 (2022): 239–252.

Hills, Julian V. "Christ Was the Goal of the Law (Romans 10:4)." JTS 44 (1993): 585–592.

Himmelfarb, Martha. *Ascent to Heaven in Jewish and Christian Apocalypses*. Oxford: Oxford University Press, 1993.
"Judaism and Hellenism in 2 Maccabees." *Poetics Today* 19 (1998): 19–40.
"Judaism in Antiquity: Ethno-Religion or National Identity." *JQR* 99 (2009): 65–73.
Review of *A Radical Jew: Paul and the Politics of Identity*, by Daniel Boyarin. *AJS Review* 21 (1996): 148–151.
Hirsch, E. "Zwei Fragen zu Galater 6." *ZNW* 29 (1930): 192–197.
Hockey, Katherine M., and David G. Horrell, eds. *Ethnicity, Race, Religion: Identities and Ideologies in Early Jewish and Christian Texts and in Modern Biblical Interpretation*. London: T&T Clark, 2018.
Hodge, Caroline Johnson. *If Sons Then Heirs: A Study of Kinship and Ethnicity in the Letters of Paul*. Oxford: Oxford University Press, 2007.
Hoklotubbe, T. Christopher. *Civilized Piety: The Rhetoric of Pietas in the Pastoral Epistles and the Roman Empire*. Waco, TX: Baylor University Press, 2017.
Holladay, Carl R. "Paul and His Predecessors in the Diaspora: Some Reflections on Ethnic Identity in the Fragmentary Hellenistic Jewish Authors." Pp. 429–460 in *Early Christianity and Classical Culture: Comparative Studies in Honor of Abraham J. Malherbe*. Edited by John T. Fitzgerald, Thomas H. Olbricht, and L. Michael White. NovTSup 110. Leiden: Brill, 2003.
Hollander, H. W., and J. Holleman. "The Relationship of Death, Sin and Law in 1 Cor 15:56." *NovT* 35 (1993): 270–291.
Holleman, Joost. *Resurrection and Parousia: A Traditio-Historical Study of Paul's Eschatology in 1 Corinthians 15*. NovTSup 84. Leiden: Brill, 1996.
Hooker, Morna D. "Adam in Romans 1." *NTS* 6 (1960): 297–306.
"Were There False Teachers in Colossae?" Pp. 121–136 in *From Adam to Christ: Essays on Paul*. Cambridge: Cambridge University Press, 1990.
Horbury, William. "The Cult of Christ and the Cult of the Saints." *NTS* 44 (1998): 444–469.
"Introduction to the First Edition." Pp. 29–50 in *Messianism among Jews and Christians: Biblical and Historical Studies*. 2nd ed. London: T&T Clark, 2016.
"Jewish-Christian Relations in the Epistle of Barnabas and Justin Martyr." Pp. 127–161 in *Jews and Christians in Contact and Controversy*. Edinburgh: T&T Clark, 1998.
Horky, Phillip Sidney, ed. *Cosmos in the Ancient World*. Cambridge: Cambridge University Press, 2019.
Horn, F. W. "1 Korinther 15,56 — ein exegetischer Stachel." *ZNW* 82 (1991): 88–105.

Hübner, Hans. "Gal 3,10 und die Herkunft des Paulus." *KD* 19 (1973): 215–231.
Hultgren, Arland J. "On Translating and Interpreting Galatians 1:13." *Bible Translator* 26 (1975): 146–148.
———. "Paul's Pre-Christian Persecutions of the Church: Their Purpose, Locale, and Nature." *JBL* 95 (1976): 97–111.
Hultin, Jeremy F. "Who Rebuked Cephas? A New Interpretation of Galatians 2:14–17." Unpublished paper. SBL Annual Meeting 2013.
Huttunen, Niko. *Paul and Epictetus on Law: A Comparison*. LNTS 405. London: T&T Clark, 2009.
Inwood, Brad. *Ethics and Human Action in Early Stoicism*. Oxford: Clarendon, 1985.
Isaac, Benjamin. *The Invention of Racism in Classical Antiquity*. Princeton: Princeton University Press, 2004.
Jackson, Bernard S. "Legalism." *JJS* 30 (1979): 1–22.
Jackson-McCabe, Matt. *Jewish-Christianity and the History of Judaism*. AYBRL. New Haven: Yale University Press, 2020.
Jacobs, Andrew S. *Christ Circumcised: A Study in Early Christian History and Difference*. Philadelphia: University of Pennsylvania Press, 2012.
———. "Dialogical Differences: (De-)Judaizing Jesus' Circumcision." *JECS* 15 (2007): 291–335.
———. *Epiphanius of Cyprus: A Cultural Biography of Late Antiquity*. Berkeley: University of California Press, 2021.
———. *Remains of the Jews: The Holy Land and Christian Empire in Late Antiquity*. Stanford: Stanford University Press, 2004.
Jacobson, Howard. *A Commentary on Pseudo-Philo's Liber Antiquitatum Biblicarum*. 2 vols. AGJU 31. Leiden: Brill, 1996.
Jaquette, James. *Discerning What Counts: The Function of the Adiaphora Topos in Paul's Letters*. SBLDS 146. Atlanta: Scholars Press, 1995.
Jervis, L. Ann. *Paul and Time: Life in the Temporality of Christ*. Grand Rapids, MI: Baker, 2024.
Jewett, Robert. "The Agitators and the Galatian Congregation." *NTS* 17 (1971): 198–212.
———. "Conflicting Movements in the Early Church as Reflected in Philippians." *NovT* 12 (1970): 362–390.
———. *Romans*. Hermeneia. Minneapolis: Fortress, 2006.
Johnson, Luke Timothy. *Constructing Paul*. Grand Rapids, MI: Eerdmans, 2020.
Johnson, Nathan C. "Romans 1:3–4: Beyond Antithetical Parallelism." *JBL* 136 (2017): 467–490.
Johnson-DeBaufre, Melanie, and Laura S. Nasrallah. "Beyond the Heroic Paul: Toward a Feminist and Decolonizing Approach to the Letters of

Paul." Pp. 161–174 in *The Colonized Apostle: Paul through Postcolonial Eyes*. Edited by Christopher D. Stanley. Minneapolis: Fortress, 2011.

Jones, F. Stanley. *An Ancient Jewish Christian Source on the History of Christianity: Pseudo-Clementine Recognitions 1.27–71*. Atlanta: Scholars Press, 1995.

Jowett, Benjamin, trans. *The Dialogues of Plato*. 5 vols. New York: Macmillan, 1892.

Kabisch, Richard. *Die Eschatologie des Paulus*. Göttingen: Vandenhoeck & Ruprecht, 1893.

Kahl, Brigitte. "Galatians and the 'Orientalism' of Justification by Faith." Pp. 206–222 in *The Colonized Apostle: Paul through Postcolonial Eyes*. Edited by Christopher D. Stanley. Minneapolis: Fortress, 2011.

Kaminsky, Joel S. *Yet I Loved Jacob: Reclaiming the Biblical Concept of Election*. Nashville: Abingdon, 2007.

Kampen, John, and Moshe J. Bernstein, eds. *Reading 4QMMT: New Perspectives on Qumran Law and History*. Atlanta: Scholars Press, 1996.

Käsemann, Ernst. *Commentary on Romans*. Translated by Geoffrey W. Bromiley. Grand Rapids, MI: Eerdmans, 1980.

——— "Die Legitimität des Apostels: Eine Untersuchung zu II Korinther 10–13." ZNW 41 (1942): 33–71.

——— *New Testament Questions of Today*. Translated by W. J. Montague. Philadelphia: Fortress, 1969.

Keck, Leander E. *Romans*. ANTC. Nashville: Abingdon, 2005.

Kennedy, H. A. A. *St. Paul and the Mystery Religions*. London: Hodder & Stoughton, 1913.

Kipling, Rudyard. *Barrack-Room Ballads and Other Verses*. London: Methuen, 1892.

Kister, Menahem J. "And He Was Born Circumcised: Some Notes on Circumcision in Hadith." *Oriens* 34 (1994): 10–30.

Klawans, Jonathan. *Purity, Sacrifice, and the Temple: Symbolism and Supersessionism in the Study of Ancient Judaism*. Oxford: Oxford University Press, 2006.

Klijn, A. F. J. "Paul's Opponents in Philippians III." *NovT* 7 (1965): 278–284.

Knox, John. "Romans." In vol. 9 of *The Interpreter's Bible*. Nashville: Abingdon, 1954.

Knox, Wilfred L. "Origen's Conception of the Resurrection Body." *JTS* 39 (1938): 247–248.

Knust, Jennifer Wright. *Abandoned to Lust: Sexual Slander and Ancient Christianity*. New York: Columbia University Press, 2006.

Koester, Helmut. "Gnomai Diaphorai: The Origin and Nature of Diversification in the History of Early Christianity." Pp. 114–157 in

Trajectories through Early Christianity. Edited by James M. Robinson and Helmut Koester. Philadelphia: Fortress, 1971.

Koetschau, Paul, ed. *Origenes Werke, Band 5: De Principiis*. Hinrichs: Leipzig, 1913.

Kohler, Kaufmann. "Saul of Tarsus." Pp. 79–87 in vol. 11 of *The Jewish Encyclopedia*. New York: Funk & Wagnalls, 1906.

Kraft, Robert A. "The Epistle of Barnabas: Its Quotations and Their Sources." PhD diss., Harvard University, 1961.

Kraftchick, Steven John. "Bodies, Selves, and Human Identity: A Conversation between Transhumanism and the Apostle Paul." *Theology Today* 72 (2015): 47–69.

Kreitzer, L. Joseph. *Jesus and God in Paul's Eschatology*. JSNTSup 19. Sheffield: Sheffield Academic, 1987.

Krostenko, Brian A. *Cicero, Catullus, and the Language of Social Performance*. Chicago: University of Chicago Press, 2001.

Kugel, James. *How to Read the Bible: A Guide to Scripture, Then and Now*. New York: Free Press, 2007.

Kuss, Otto. *Der Römerbrief*. 3 vols. Regensburg: Pustet, 1957–1978.

Kwon, Yon-Gyong. *Eschatology in Galatians*. WUNT 2/183. Tübingen: Mohr Siebeck, 2004.

Laato, Timo. *Paul and Judaism: An Anthropological Approach*. Atlanta: Scholars Press, 1995. German original *Paulus und das Judentum: Anthropologische Erwagungen*. Åbo: Åbo Academy Press, 1991.

Lampe, G. W. H. *A Patristic Greek Lexicon*. Oxford: Clarendon, 1961.

Landmesser, Christof. "Ferdinand Christian Baur as Interpreter of Paul: History, the Absolute, and Freedom." Pp. 147–176 in *Ferdinand Christian Baur and the History of Early Christianity*. Edited by Martin Bauspiess, Christof Landmesser, and David Lincicum. Translated by Robert F. Brown and Peter C. Hodgson. Oxford: Oxford University Press, 2017.

Lang, T. J. "Cosmology and Eschatology." Pp. 507–524 in *The Oxford Handbook of Pauline Studies*. Edited by Matthew V. Novenson and R. Barry Matlock. Oxford: Oxford University Press, 2022.

Langford, Andrew M. "Diagnosing Deviance: Pathology and Polemic in the Pastoral Epistles." PhD diss., University of Chicago, 2018.

Langton, Daniel R. *The Apostle Paul in the Jewish Imagination: A Study in Modern Jewish-Christian Relations*. Cambridge: Cambridge University Press, 2010.

Lapidot, Elad. "Du, der mit Buchstaben und Beschneidung ein Gesetzübertreter bist: Paulus und die Grundlegung des Judentums." Pp. 17–38 in *Täter und Opfer: Verbrechen und Stigma im europäisch-jüdischen Kontext*. Edited by Claudia Simone Dorchain and Tommaso Speccher. Würzburg: Königshausen & Neumann, 2014.

Larsen, Matthew D. C. *Early Christians and Incarceration: A Cultural History*. Oxford: Oxford University Press, forthcoming.
Lee, Yongbom. "Getting in and Staying in: Another Look at 4QMMT and Galatians." *EvQ* 88 (2017): 126–142.
Lemke, Werner E. "Circumcision of the Heart: The Journey of a Biblical Metaphor." Pp. 299–319 in *A God So Near: Essays on Old Testament Theology in Honor of Patrick D. Miller*. Edited by Brent A. Strawn and Nancy R. Bowen. Winona Lake, IN: Eisenbrauns, 2003.
Levine, Amy-Jill, ed. *A Feminist Companion to Paul: Authentic Pauline Writings*. London: T&T Clark, 2004.
Levine, Lee I. *The Ancient Synagogue: The First Thousand Years*. New Haven: Yale University Press, 2005.
Levtow, Nathaniel B. *Images of Others: Iconic Politics in Ancient Israel*. Winona Lake, IN: Eisenbrauns, 2008.
Levy, Ariel. *Female Chauvinist Pigs*. New York: Free Press, 2005.
Libson, Ayelet Hoffmann. *Law and Self-Knowledge in the Talmud*. Cambridge: Cambridge University Press, 2018.
Liddell, Henry George, Robert Scott, and Henry Stuart Jones. *A Greek-English Lexicon*. 9th ed. Oxford: Clarendon, 1996.
Lietzmann, Hans. *An die Römer*. HNT 8. 3rd ed. Tübingen: Mohr Siebeck, 1928.
——— "Die Synagogeninschrift in Stobi/Ausgrabungen in Doura-Europos." *ZNW* 32 (1933): 93–95.
Lim, Timothy H. "Why did Paul cite Habakkuk 2:4b?" *ExpTim* 133 (2022): 225–232.
Limor, Ora, and Guy G. Stroumsa, eds. *Contra Iudaeos: Ancient and Medieval Polemics between Christians and Jews*. TSMEMJ 10. Tübingen: Mohr Siebeck, 1996.
Linebaugh, Jonathan A. "Announcing the Human: Rethinking the Relationship between Wisdom of Solomon 13–15 and Romans 1:18–2:11." *NTS* 37 (2011): 214–237.
——— *God, Grace, and Righteousness in Wisdom of Solomon and Paul's Letter to the Romans*. NovTSup 152. Leiden: Brill, 2013.
——— ed. *God's Two Words: Law and Gospel in the Lutheran and Reformed Traditions*. Grand Rapids, MI: Eerdmans, 2018.
Lipka, Hilary, and Bruce Wells, eds. *Sexuality and Law in the Torah*. LHBOTS. London: T&T Clark, 2020.
Litwa, M. David. *Posthuman Transformation in Ancient Mediterranean Thought: Becoming Angels and Demons*. Cambridge: Cambridge University Press, 2021.
——— *We Are Being Transformed: Deification in Paul's Soteriology*. BZNW 187. Berlin: De Gruyter, 2012.

Longarino, Joseph. *Pauline Theology and the Problem of Death*. WUNT 2/558. Tübingen: Mohr Siebeck, 2021.

Longenecker, Bruce W. *Eschatology and the Covenant: A Comparison of 4 Ezra and Romans 1–11*. JSNTSup 57. Sheffield: JSOT Press, 1991.

Longenecker, Richard N. *Paul, Apostle of Liberty*. Grand Rapids, MI: Eerdmans, 1964.

Luckensmeyer, David. *The Eschatology of First Thessalonians*. NTOA 71. Göttingen: Vandenhoeck & Ruprecht, 2009.

Lüdemann, Gerd. *Opposition to Paul in Jewish Christianity*. Translated by M. Eugene Boring. Minneapolis: Fortress, 1989. German original 1983. *Paulus und das Judentum*. Munich: Kaiser, 1983.

Lütgert, Wilhelm. *Freiheitspredigt und Schwarmgeister im Korinth*. Gütersloh: Bertelsmann, 1908.

Luther, Martin. *Commentary on St. Paul's Epistle to the Galatians*. Philadelphia: Smith, English & Co., 1860.

Luz, Ulrich. *Das Geschichtsverständnis des Paulus*. Munich: Kaiser, 1968.

Lyonnet, S. "Le sens de *eph ho* en Rom 5,12 et l'exégèse des Pères grecs." *Bib* 36 (1955): 436–456.

Maccoby, Hyam. *The Mythmaker: Paul and the Invention of Christianity*. New York: Barnes & Noble, 1986.

Magid, Shaul. *From Metaphysics to Midrash: Myth, History, and the Interpretation of Scripture in Lurianic Kabbala*. Bloomington, IN: Indiana University Press, 2008.

Marcovich, Miroslav, ed. *Iustini Martyris Dialogus cum Tryphone*. Berlin: De Gruyter, 2005.

Marmorstein, A. "The Synagogue of Claudius Tiberius Polycharmus at Stobi." *JQR* 27 (1937): 373–384.

Marshall, John W. *Parables of War: Reading John's Jewish Apocalypse*. ESCJ 10. Waterloo, ON: Wilfrid Laurier University Press, 2001.

Martin, Dale B. *Biblical Truths: The Meaning of Scripture in the Twenty-First Century*. New Haven: Yale University Press, 2017.

The Corinthian Body. New Haven: Yale University Press, 1995.

"Heterosexism and the Interpretation of Romans 1:18–32." Pp. 51–64 in *Sex and the Single Savior: Gender and Sexuality in Biblical Interpretation*. Louisville, KY: Westminster John Knox, 2006.

"Paul and the Judaism/Hellenism Dichotomy: Toward a Social History of the Question." Pp. 29–62 in *Paul beyond the Judaism/Hellenism Divide*. Edited by Troels Engberg-Pedersen. Louisville, KY: Westminster John Knox, 2001.

"Paul without Passion: On Paul's Rejection of Desire in Sex and Marriage." Pp. 65–76 in *Sex and the Single Savior: Gender and Sexuality in Biblical Interpretation*. Louisville, KY: Westminster John Knox, 2006.

"The Queer History of Galatians 3:28." Pp. 77–90 in *Sex and the Single Savior: Gender and Sexuality in Biblical Interpretation*. Louisville, KY: Westminster John Knox, 2006.

Martyn, J. Louis. "Epistemology at the Turn of the Ages." Pp. 89–110 in *Theological Issues in the Letters of Paul*. London: T&T Clark, 1997.

Galatians: A New Translation with Introduction and Commentary. AB 33A. New York: Doubleday, 1997.

Mason, Steve. "Jews, Judaeans, Judaizing, Judaism: Problems of Categorization in Ancient History." *JSJ* 38 (2007): 457–512.

"Paul without Judaism: Historical Method over Perspective." Pp. 9–40 in *Paul and Matthew among Jews and Gentiles: Essays in Honour of Terence L. Donaldson*. Edited by Ronald Charles. LNTS 628. London: T&T Clark, 2021.

"Paul's Announcement (*to euangelion*): 'Good News' and Its Detractors in Earliest Christianity." Pp. 283–302 in *Josephus, Judea, and Christian Origins*. Peabody, MA: Hendrickson, 2009.

Maston, Jason. *Divine and Human Agency in Second Temple Judaism and Paul*. WUNT 2/297. Tübingen: Mohr Siebeck, 2010.

Matlock, R. Barry. "Jews by Nature: Paul, Ethnicity, and Galatians." Pp. 304–315 in *Far From Minimal: Celebrating the Work and Influence of Philip R. Davies*. Edited by Duncan Burns and J. W. Rogerson. London: T&T Clark, 2012.

"Zeal for Paul but not according to Knowledge: Douglas Campbell's War on 'Justification Theory.'" *JSNT* 34 (2011): 115–149.

Matt, Daniel C., trans. *The Zohar: Pritzker Edition*. 12 vols. Stanford: Stanford University Press, 2018.

Mbiti, John S. *New Testament Eschatology in an African Background*. Oxford: Oxford University Press, 1971.

McCaulley, Esau. *Sharing in the Son's Inheritance: Davidic Messianism and Paul's Worldwide Interpretation of the Abrahamic Land Promise in Galatians*. LNTS 608. London: T&T Clark, 2019.

McDonald, Denys. Review of *Paul's Three Paths to Salvation*, by Gabriele Boccaccini. *SR* 52 (2023): 290–292.

McGlothlin, Thomas D. *Resurrection as Salvation: Development and Conflict in Pre-Nicene Paulinism*. Cambridge: Cambridge University Press, 2018.

McGrath, Alister E. *Iustitia Dei: A History of the Christian Doctrine of Justification*. 4th ed. Cambridge: Cambridge University Press, 2020.

McGuckin, J. A. "Origen's Eschatology." Pp. 410–428 in *The Oxford Handbook of Origen*. Edited by Ronald E. Heine and Karen Jo Torjesen. Oxford: Oxford University Press, 2022.

McMurray, Patrick. *Sacrifice, Brotherhood, and the Body: Abraham and the Nations in Romans*. Minneapolis: Fortress, 2021.

McNamara, Martin. "Some Targum Themes." Pp. 303–356 in *Justification and Variegated Nomism, Volume 1*. Edited by D. A. Carson, Peter T. O'Brien, and Mark A. Seifrid. Tübingen: Mohr Siebeck, 2001.

Metzger, Bruce M. *A Textual Commentary on the Greek New Testament*. London: United Bible Societies, 1971.

Meyer, Paul W. "The Worm at the Core of the Apple: Exegetical Reflections on Romans 7." Pp. 57–77 in *The Word in This World: Essays in New Testament Exegesis and Theology*. Edited by John T. Carroll. Louisville, KY: Westminster John Knox, 2004.

Michaelis, W. "Judaistische Heidenchristen," *ZNW* 30 (1931): 83–89.

Michel, Otto. *Paulus und seine Bibel*. Gütersloh: Bertelsmann, 1929.

Miller, Chaim, ed. *Rambam: The 13 Principles of Faith*. New York: Kol Menachem, 2007.

Miller, David M. "Ethnicity Comes of Age: An Overview of Twentieth-Century Terms for *Ioudaios*." *CBR* 10 (2012): 293–311.

——— "The Meaning of *Ioudaios* and Its Relationship to Other Group Labels in Ancient 'Judaism.'" *CBR* 9 (2010): 98–126.

Mitchell, Margaret M. *The Heavenly Trumpet: John Chrysostom and the Art of Pauline Interpretation*. Louisville, KY: Westminster John Knox, 2002.

——— "Paul and Judaism now, Quo vadimus?" *JJMJS* 5 (2018): 55–78.

——— *Paul and the Emergence of Christian Textuality: Early Christian Literary Culture in Context*. WUNT 393. Tübingen: Mohr Siebeck, 2017.

——— *Paul, the Corinthians, and the Birth of Christian Hermeneutics*. Cambridge: Cambridge University Press, 2010.

Moll, Sebastian. *The Arch-heretic Marcion*. WUNT 250. Tübingen: Mohr Siebeck, 2010.

Monnickendam, Yifat. "I Bring Death and Give Life, I Wound and Heal (Deut 32:39): Two Versions of the Polemic on the Resurrection of the Dead." *Henoch* 35 (2013): 90–118.

Moore, George Foot. *Judaism in the First Centuries of the Christian Era*. 3 vols. Cambridge, MA: Harvard University Press, 1927–1930.

Moore, Stephen D., and Yvonne Sherwood. *The Invention of the Biblical Scholar: A Critical Manifesto*. Minneapolis: Fortress, 2011.

Moore-Gilbert, Bart. "Kipling and Postcolonial Literature." Pp. 155–168 in *The Cambridge Companion to Rudyard Kipling*. Edited by Howard J. Booth. Cambridge: Cambridge University Press, 2011.

Morales, Isaac. Review of *Paul's Three Paths to Salvation*, by Gabriele Boccaccini. *JTS* 73 (2022): 335–337.

Moss, Candida R. *Divine Bodies: Resurrecting Perfection in the New Testament and Early Christianity*. New Haven: Yale University Press, 2019.

The Other Christs: Imitating Jesus in Ancient Christian Theologies of Martyrdom. Oxford: Oxford University Press, 2010.

"The Secretary: Enslaved Workers, Stenography, and the Production of Early Christian Literature." *JTS* 74 (2023): 20–56.

Mroczek, Eva. "The Embarrassing Bible." Public lecture at the University of San Francisco (22 March 2017). www.youtube.com/watch?v=nb3yL0UjKnA

"Without Torah and Scripture: Biblical Absence and the History of Revelation." *Hebrew Studies* 61 (2020): 97–122.

Muir, Alexander W. "Paul and Seneca on Consolation." PhD diss., University of Edinburgh, 2022.

Munck, Johannes. *Paul and the Salvation of Mankind.* Translated by Frank Clarke. Richmond, VA: John Knox, 1959. German original 1954.

Murray, Michele. *Playing a Jewish Game: Gentile Christian Judaizing in the First and Second Centuries CE.* ESCJ 13. Waterloo, ON: Wilfrid Laurier University Press, 2004.

Nanos, Mark D. "All Israel Will Be Saved, or Kept Safe?" Pp. 243–270 in *Israel and the Nations: Paul's Gospel in the Context of Jewish Expectation.* Edited by Frantisek Abel. Minneapolis: Fortress, 2021.

The Irony of Galatians: Paul's Letter in First-Century Context. Minneapolis: Fortress, 2002.

"Paul's Reversal of Jews Calling Gentiles 'Dogs' (Philippians 3.2): 1600 Years of an Ideological Tale Wagging an Exegetical Dog." *BibInt* 17 (2009): 448–482.

Reading Paul within Judaism. Eugene, OR: Cascade, 2017.

Nanos, Mark D. and Magnus Zetterholm, eds. *Paul within Judaism: Restoring the First-Century Context to the Apostle.* Minneapolis: Fortress, 2015.

Nasrallah, Laura Salah. *Archaeology and the Letters of Paul.* Oxford: Oxford University Press, 2019.

Neander, A. *Geschichte der Pflanzung und Leitung der christlichen Kirche durch die Apostel,* vol. 1. 4th rev. ed. Hamburg: Friedrich Perthes, 1847.

Neis, Rafael. "The Seduction of Law: Rethinking Legal Studies in Jewish Studies." *JQR* 109 (2019): 119–138.

Neusner, Jacob. "Comparing Judaisms." *HR* 18 (1978): 117–191.

"Mr. Sanders's Pharisees and Mine: A Response to E. P. Sanders, *Jewish Law from Jesus to the Mishnah.*" *SJT* 44 (1991): 73–96.

Neutel, Karin B. "Circumcision Gone Wrong: Paul's Message as a Case of Ritual Disruption." *Neot* 50 (2016): 373–396.

A Cosmopolitan Ideal: Paul's Declaration "Neither Jew Nor Greek, Neither Slave Nor Free, Nor Male and Female" in the Context of First-Century Thought. LNTS 513. London: T&T Clark, 2015.

"Restoring Abraham's Foreskin: The Significance of *akrobustia* for Paul's Argument about Circumcision in Romans 4:9–12." *JJMJS* 8 (2021): 53–74.

Niese, Benedict, ed. *Flavii Iosephi opera*. 4 vols. Berlin: Weidmann, 1887–1890.

Nikki, Nina. *Opponents and Identity in Philippians*. NovTSup 173. Leiden: Brill, 2019.

Noam, Vered. *4QMMT*. OCDSS. Oxford: Oxford University Press, forthcoming.

"The Gentileness of Gentiles: Two Approaches to the Impurity of Non-Jews." Pp. 27–41 in *Halakhah in Light of Epigraphy*. Edited by Albert I. Baumgarten, Hanan Eshel, Ranon Katzoff, and Shani Tzoref. JAJSup 3. Göttingen: Vandenhoeck & Ruprecht, 2011.

Nock, Arthur Darby. *Conversion: The Old and the New in Religion from Alexander the Great to Augustine of Hippo*. Oxford: Oxford University Press, 1933.

Nongbri, Brent. *Before Religion: A History of a Modern Concept*. New Haven: Yale University Press, 2013.

"The Concept of Religion and the Study of the Apostle Paul." *JJMJS* 2 (2015): 1–26.

"To See Paul as Paul Saw Himself." *Syndicate*. 2 June 2020.

Novenson, Matthew V. *Christ among the Messiahs: Christ Language in Paul and Messiah Language in Ancient Judaism*. Oxford: Oxford University Press, 2012.

"Did Paul Abandon Either Judaism or Monotheism?" Pp. 46–66 in *Paul, Then and Now*. Grand Rapids, MI: Eerdmans, 2022.

"Gentile Sinners: A Brief History of an Ancient Stereotype." Pp. 159–179 in *Negotiating Identities: Conflict, Conversion, and Consolidation in Early Judaism and Christianity (200 BCE–600 CE)*. Edited by Karin Hedner Zetterholm, Anders Runesson, Cecilia Wassen, and Magnus Zetterholm. Minneapolis: Fortress, 2022.

The Grammar of Messianism: An Ancient Jewish Political Idiom and Its Users. Oxford: Oxford University Press, 2017.

"*Ioudaios*, Pharisee, Zealot." Pp. 24–45 in *Paul, Then and Now*. Grand Rapids, MI: Eerdmans, 2022.

"'The Law Is Not Over Such Things': An Exegetical Note on Galatians 5:23." *Presbyterion* 47 (2021): 112–116.

"The Messiah ben Abraham in Galatians." Pp. 118–125 in *Paul, Then and Now*. Grand Rapids, MI: Eerdmans, 2022.

ed. *Monotheism and Christology in Greco-Roman Antiquity*. NovTSup 180. Leiden: Brill, 2020.

"On Christ and Idols, in Dialogue with Natalie Carnes" (forthcoming).

"Our Apostles, Ourselves." Pp. 1–12 in *Paul, Then and Now*. Grand Rapids, MI: Eerdmans, 2022.

Paul, Then and Now. Grand Rapids, MI: Eerdmans, 2022.

Review of *Paul, A New Covenant Jew*, by Brant Pitre, Michael P. Barber, and John A. Kincaid. *SJT* 74 (2021): 93–94.

"Romans and Galatians." Pp. 67–90 in *Paul, Then and Now*. Grand Rapids, MI: Eerdmans, 2022.

"The Self-Styled Jew of Romans 2 and the Actual Jews of Romans 9–11." Pp. 91–117 in *Paul, Then and Now*. Grand Rapids, MI: Eerdmans, 2022.

"Whither the Paul within Judaism *Schule*?" *JJMJS* 5 (2018): 79–88.

Novum Testamentum Graece. Stuttgart: Deutsche Bibelgesellschaft, 2012.

O'Hagan, Angelo P. *Material Re-creation in the Apostolic Fathers*. Berlin: Akademie Verlag, 1968.

Öhler, Markus. "Romans 8 in Light of the Epigraphic Sources" (forthcoming).

Oliver, Isaac W., and Gabriele Boccaccini, eds. *The Early Reception of Paul the Second Temple Jew: Text, Narrative, and Reception History*. LSTS 92. London: T&T Clark, 2019.

Ophir, Adi, and Ishay Rosen-Zvi. *Goy: Israel's Multiple Others and the Birth of the Gentile*. Oxford: Oxford University Press, 2018.

Origen. *Commentary on the Epistle to the Romans*. Translated by Thomas P. Scheck. 2 vols. Washington, DC: CUA Press, 2012.

On First Principles. Edited and translated by John Behr. 2 vols. OECT. Oxford: Oxford University Press, 2017.

Oudshoorn, Daniel. *Pauline Eschatology: The Apocalyptic Rupture of Eternal Imperialism*. Eugene, OR: Cascade, 2020.

Parks, Sara. *Gender in the Rhetoric of Jesus: Women in Q*. Minneapolis: Fortress, 2019.

Pearson, Birger A. *The Pneumatikos-Psychikos Terminology in 1 Corinthians*. SBLDS 12. Missoula, MT: SBL, 1973.

"1 Thessalonians 2:13–16: A Deutero-Pauline Interpolation." *HTR* 64 (1971): 79–94.

Petrey, Taylor G. *Resurrecting Parts: Early Christians on Desire, Reproduction, and Sexual Difference*. London: Routledge, 2016.

"The Resurrection Body." Pp. 661–674 in *The Oxford Handbook of New Testament, Gender, and Sexuality*. Edited by Benjamin H. Dunning. Oxford: Oxford University Press, 2019.

Petroelje, Benjamin. *The Pauline Book and the Dilemma of Ephesians*. LNTS 665. London: T&T Clark, 2022.

Pfleiderer, Otto. *Paulinism: A Contribution to the History of Primitive Christian Theology*. Translated by Edward Peters. London: Williams & Norgate, 1877.

Pietersma, Albert, and Benjamin G. Wright, eds. *A New English Translation of the Septuagint*. Oxford: Oxford University Press, 2007.

Pitre, Brant, Michael P. Barber, and John Kincaid. *Paul, a New Covenant Jew: Rethinking Pauline Theology*. Grand Rapids, MI: Eerdmans, 2019.

Plevnik, Joseph. "Paul's Eschatology." *TJT* 6 (1990): 86–99.

Plumer, Eric, trans. *Augustine's Commentary on Galatians*. OECS. Oxford: Oxford University Press, 2003.

Poliakov, Leon. *History of Anti-Semitism*. 4 vols. Philadelphia: University of Pennsylvania Press, 2003.

Porter, Stanley E., ed. *Paul and His Opponents*. Leiden: Brill, 2005.

de Puymège, Gérard. "Chauvin and Chauvinism: In Search of a Myth." *History and Memory* 6 (1994): 35–72.

Qimron, Elisha, and John Strugnell, eds. *Qumran Cave 4 V: Miqsat Ma'aseh ha-Torah*. DJD 10. Oxford: Clarendon, 1994.

Rabens, Volker. *The Holy Spirit and Ethics in Paul: Transformation and Empowering for Religious-Ethical Life*. WUNT 2/283. Tübingen: Mohr Siebeck, 2010.

Rahlfs, A., ed. *Septuaginta*. 9th ed. Stuttgart: Württemberg Bible Society, 1935.

Räisänen, Heikki. "Legalism and Salvation by the Law." Pp. 25–54 in *The Torah and Christ*. Helsinki: Finnish Exegetical Society, 1986.

———. *Paul and the Law*. WUNT 29. Tübingen: Mohr Siebeck, 1983.

Reed, Annette Yoshiko. *Jewish-Christianity and the History of Judaism*. TSAJ 171. Tübingen: Mohr Siebeck, 2018.

———. "Was There Science in Ancient Judaism? Historical and Cross-Cultural Reflections on Religion and Science." *SR* 36 (2007): 461–495.

Reinhartz, Adele. *Cast out of the Covenant: Jews and Anti-Judaism in the Gospel of John*. Minneapolis: Fortress, 2018.

Reinhartz, Adele, Steve Mason, Daniel Schwartz, Annette Yoshiko Reed, Joan Taylor, Malcolm Lowe, Jonathan Klawans, Ruth Sheridan, and James Crossley. "Jew and Judean." *Marginalia*. August 2014.

Remington, Megan R., and Julianna Kaye Smith. "The Phallus in Our Stars: Sexual Violence in the Animal Apocalypse." *JSP* 32 (2022): 57–74.

Rey, Jean-Sebastien, ed. *The Dead Sea Scrolls and Pauline Literature*. STDJ 102. Leiden: Brill, 2014.

Richardson, Peter. *Israel in the Apostolic Church*. SNTSMS 10. Cambridge: Cambridge University Press, 1969.

Riches, John. *Galatians through the Centuries*. Oxford: Wiley-Blackwell, 2008.

Rillera, Andrew R. "Paul's Philonic Opponent: Unveiling the One Who Calls Himself a Jew in Romans 2:17." PhD diss., Duke University, 2021.

Rim, Manse. "Messiah and Righteousness in Paul and His Context." PhD diss., University of Edinburgh, 2023.

Roberts, Alexander, and James Donaldson, eds. *Ante-Nicene Fathers*. 10 vols. Grand Rapids, MI: Eerdmans, 1986.
Roberts, Sam. "We Know the Pledge. Its Author, Maybe Not." *New York Times*. 2 April 2022.
Robinson, James M., ed. *The Nag Hammadi Library in English*. San Francisco: HarperCollins, 1990.
Robinson, Joanne Maguire. *Waiting in Christian Traditions: Balancing Ideology and Utopia*. Lanham, MD: Lexington, 2015.
Robinson, Jonathan Rivett. "The Argument against Attributing Slogans in 1 Corinthians 6:12–20." *JSPL* 8 (2018): 147–166.
Rodriguez, Rafael. *If You Call Yourself a Jew: Reappraising Paul's Letter to the Romans*. Eugene, OR: Cascade, 2014.
Rodriguez, Rafael, and Matthew Thiessen, eds. *The So-Called Jew in Paul's Letter to the Romans*. Minneapolis: Fortress, 2016.
Roetzel, Calvin J. *Paul, a Jew on the Margins*. Louisville, KY: Westminster John Knox, 2003.
Rokeah, David. *Justin Martyr and the Jews*. JCP 5. Leiden: Brill, 2001.
Rollens, Sarah E. *Framing Social Criticism in the Jesus Movement: The Ideological Project in the Sayings Gospel Q*. WUNT 2/374. Tübingen: Mohr Siebeck, 2014.
Ronis, Sara. *Demons in the Details: Demonic Discourse and Rabbinic Culture in Late Antique Babylonia*. Berkeley: University of California Press, 2022.
Ropes, J. H. *The Singular Problem of the Epistle to the Galatians*. HTS 14. Cambridge, MA: Harvard University Press, 1929.
Rosen-Zvi, Ishay, and Adi Ophir. "Paul and the Invention of the Gentiles." *JQR* 105 (2015): 1–41.
Rosenstein, Marc. *Contested Utopia: Jewish Dreams and Israeli Realities*. Lincoln, NE: University of Nebraska Press, 2021.
Rothschild, Clare K. "Soteriology and the Allegorical Construction of Opponents in the Epistle of Barnabas." Pp. 561–576 in *Soteria: Salvation in Early Christianity and Antiquity*. Edited by David S. du Toit, Christine Gerber, and Christiane Zimmerman. NovTSup 175. Leiden: Brill, 2019.
Runesson, Anders. "The Question of Terminology: The Architecture of Contemporary Discussion on Paul." Pp. 53–78 in *Paul within Judaism: Restoring the First-Century Context to the Apostle*. Edited by Mark D. Nanos and Magnus Zetterholm. Minneapolis: Fortress, 2015.
Sabar, Ariel. *Veritas: A Harvard Professor, a Con Man, and the Gospel of Jesus's Wife*. New York: Doubleday, 2020.
Said, Edward W. "Introduction." Pp. 7–46 in *Kim*. By Rudyard Kipling. London: Penguin, 1987.

Saldarini, Anthony J., trans. *The Fathers according to Rabbi Nathan*. Leiden: Brill, 1975.
Sanday, William, and Arthur C. Headlam. *The Epistle to the Romans*. 5th ed. ICC. Edinburgh: T&T Clark, 1902.
Sanders, E. P. "Covenantal Nomism Revisited." *JSQ* 16 (2009): 23–55.
Jesus and Judaism. Philadelphia: Fortress, 1985.
Judaism: Practice and Belief, 63 BCE–66 CE. London: SCM, 1992.
Paul and Palestinian Judaism: A Comparison of Patterns of Religion. Philadelphia: Fortress, 1977.
Paul, the Law, and the Jewish People. Philadelphia: Fortress, 1983.
Sandmel, Samuel. *The Genius of Paul: A Study in History*. New York: Farrar, Straus & Cudahy, 1958.
"Parallelomania." *JBL* 81 (1962): 1–13.
Sandnes, Karl Olav. *Belly and Body in the Pauline Epistles*. SNTSMS 120. Cambridge: Cambridge University Press, 2002.
Sanfridson, Martin. "Paul and Sacrifice in Corinth: Rethinking Paul's Views on Gentile Cults in 1 Corinthians 8 and 10." PhD diss., McMaster University, 2022.
Satlow, Michael L. *How the Bible Became Holy*. New Haven: Yale University Press, 2014.
"Paul, a Jew from Jerusalem." *Bible and Interpretation*. September 2014.
"Paul's Scriptures." Pp. 257–274 in *Strength to Strength: Essays in Honor of Shaye J. D. Cohen*. Edited by Michael L. Satlow. Providence, RI: Brown University Press, 2018.
Schäfer, Peter. *Rivalität zwischen Engeln und Menschen: Untersuchungen zur rabbinischen Engelvorstellung*. Berlin: De Gruyter, 1975.
"Die Torah der messianischen Zeit." *ZNW* 65 (1974): 27–42.
Schliesser, Benjamin. "Christ-Faith as an Eschatological Event (Galatians 3.23–26): A Third View on *Pistis Christou*." *JSNT* 38 (2016): 277–300.
Schmithals, Walter. "The False Teachers of Romans 16:17–20." Pp. 219–238 in *Paul and the Gnostics*. Nashville: Abingdon, 1972.
Schnelle, Udo. *Apostle Paul: His Life and Theology*. Translated by M. Eugene Boring. Grand Rapids, MI: Baker Academic, 2005. German original 2003.
Schoeps, H. J. *Paul: The Theology of the Apostle in the Light of Jewish Religious History*. Translated by Harold Knight. London: Lutterworth, 1961.
Scholem, Gershom. "The Meaning of the Torah in Jewish Mysticism." Pp. 32–86 in *On the Kabbalah and Its Symbolism*. Translated by Ralph Manheim. New York: Schocken, 1965.
On the Kabbalah and Its Symbolism. Translated by Ralph Manheim. New York: Schocken, 1965.

"R. Elijah Ha-cohen Ha-itamari and the Sabbathaism." Pp. 451–470 in *Alexander Marx Jubilee Volume*. New York: Jewish Theological Seminary, 1950 (in Hebrew).

Sabbatai Sevi: The Mystical Messiah, 1626–1676. Translated by R. J. Zwi Werblowsky. Princeton: Princeton University Press, 1973.

Schott, H. A. *Epistolae Pauli ad Thessalonicenses et Galatas*. Leipzig: Barth, 1834.

Schreiner, Thomas R. "Paul's View of the Law in Romans 10:4–5." *WTJ* 55 (1993): 113–124.

Schremer, Adiel. "Thinking about Belonging in Early Rabbinic Literature: Proselytes, Apostates, and 'Children of Israel.'" *JSJ* 43 (2012): 249–275.

Schrenk, Gottlob. "Was bedeutet 'Israel Gottes'?" *Judaica* 5 (1949): 81–94.

Schultz, Joseph P. "Angelic Opposition to the Ascension of Moses and the Revelation of the Law." *JQR* 61 (1971): 282–307.

Schüssler Fiorenza, Elisabeth. "Rhetorical Situation and Rhetorical Reconstruction in 1 Corinthians." *NTS* 33 (1987): 386–403.

Schwartz, Daniel R. "Judaean or Jew? How Should We Translate *Ioudaios* in Josephus?" Pp. 3–27 in *Jewish Identity in the Greco-Roman World*. Edited by Jörg Frey, Daniel R. Schwartz, and Stephanie Gripentrog. AJEC 71. Leiden: Brill, 2007.

Leben durch Jesus versus Leben durch die Torah. Münster: Institutum Judaicum Delitschianum, 1993.

Schwartz, Seth. "How Many Judaisms Were There?" *JAJ* 2 (2011): 208–238.

Schweitzer, Albert. *The Mysticism of Paul the Apostle*. Translated by William Montgomery. New York: Seabury, 1968.

Scott, Alan. *Origen and the Life of the Stars: A History of an Idea*. Oxford: Clarendon, 1991.

Sechrest, Love L. *A Former Jew: Paul and the Dialectics of Race*. LNTS 410. London: T&T Clark, 2009.

Segal, Alan F. *Paul the Convert: The Apostolate and Apostasy of Paul the Pharisee*. New Haven: Yale University Press, 1990.

Seim, Turid Karlsen. "Children of the Resurrection: Perspectives on Angelic Asceticism in Luke-Acts." Pp. 115–125 in *Asceticism and the New Testament*. Edited by Leif E. Vaage and Vincent L. Wimbush. London: Routledge, 1999.

Sharp, Matthew T. "Courting Daimons in Corinth: Daimonic Partnerships, Cosmic Hierarchies, and Divine Jealousy in 1 Corinthians 8–10." Pp. 112–129 in *Demons in Early Judaism and Christianity*. Edited by Hector M. Patmore and Josef Lössl. AJEC 113. Leiden: Brill, 2022.

Divination and Philosophy in the Letters of Paul. ESRA. Edinburgh: Edinburgh University Press, 2023.

Shogren, Gary Steven. "Is the Kingdom of God about Eating and Drinking or Isn't It? (Romans 14:17)." *NovT* 42 (2000): 238–256.
Silver, Abba Hillel. *A History of Messianic Speculation in Israel*. New York: Macmillan, 1927.
Simon, Marcel. *Verus Israel: A Study of the Relations between Christians and Jews in the Roman Empire, AD 135–425*. Oxford: Oxford University Press, 1986. French original 1964.
Skinner, Joseph E. *The Invention of Greek Ethnography: From Homer to Herodotus*. Oxford: Oxford University Press, 2012.
Sloan, Paul T. "Paul's Jewish Addressee in Romans 2–4: Revisiting Recent Conversations." *JTS* (2023).
Smit, Peter-Ben. "In Search of Real Circumcision: Ritual Failure and Circumcision in Paul." *JSNT* 40 (2017): 73–100.
Smith, Geoffrey S., and Brent C. Landau. *The Secret Gospel of Mark: A Controversial Scholar, a Scandalous Gospel of Jesus, and the Fierce Debate over Its Authenticity*. New Haven: Yale University Press, 2023.
Smith, Jonathan Z. *Drudgery Divine: On the Comparison of Early Christianities and the Religions of Late Antiquity*. London: SOAS, 1990.
—— "In Comparison a Magic Dwells." Pp. 19–35 in *Imagining Religion: From Babylon to Jonestown*. Chicago: University of Chicago Press, 1982.
Smith, Morton. "Pauline Worship as Seen by Pagans." *HTR* 73 (1980): 241–249.
—— Review of *Torah in the Messianic Age*, by W. D. Davies. *JBL* 72 (1953): 192–194.
Smith, Wilfred Cantwell. *The Meaning and End of Religion*. Minneapolis: Fortress, 1991.
Snyder, Glenn. "Paul beyond the Jew/Gentile Dichotomy: A Perspective from Benjamin." *Expositions* 9 (2015): 125–137.
Soon, Isaac T. *A Disabled Apostle: Impairment and Disability in the Letters of Paul*. Oxford: Oxford University Press, 2023.
—— "'In Strength' Not 'By Force': Rereading the Circumcision of the Uncircumcised ἐν ἰσχύι in 1 Macc 2:46." *JSP* 29 (2020): 149–167.
—— "Satan and Circumcision: The Devil as the *angelos poneros* in Barnabas 9:4." *VC* 76 (2021): 60–72.
Soulen, R. Kendall. *The God of Israel and Christian Theology*. Minneapolis: Fortress, 1996.
Sprinkle, Preston M. *Law and Life: The Interpretation of Leviticus 18:5 in Early Judaism and in Paul*. WUNT 2/241. Tübingen: Mohr Siebeck, 2008.
—— *Paul and Judaism Revisited: A Study of Divine and Human Agency in Salvation*. Downers Grove, IL: InterVarsity, 2013.

Stanley, Christopher D. "The Ethnic Context of Paul's Letters." Pp. 177–201 in *Christian Origins and Hellenistic Judaism*. Edited by Stanley E. Porter and Andrew W. Pitts. Leiden: Brill, 2012.

"Neither Jew nor Greek: Ethnic Conflict in Graeco-Roman Society." *JSNT* 64 (1996): 101–124.

Paul and the Language of Scripture: Citation Technique in the Pauline Epistles and Contemporary Literature. SNTSMS 74. Cambridge: Cambridge University Press, 1992.

Staples, Jason A. *The Idea of Israel in Second Temple Judaism.* Cambridge: Cambridge University Press, 2021.

Paul and the Resurrection of Israel. Cambridge: Cambridge University Press, 2023.

"What Do the Gentiles Have to Do with 'All Israel'? A Fresh Look at Romans 11:25–27." *JBL* 130 (2011): 371–390.

Stendahl, Krister. *Final Account: Paul's Letter to the Romans.* Minneapolis: Fortress, 1995.

Paul among Jews and Gentiles. Philadelphia: Fortress, 1976.

"Paul among Jews and Gentiles." Pp. 7–23 in *Paul among Jews and Gentiles*. Philadelphia: Fortress, 1976.

Sterling, Gregory E. "A Law to Themselves: Limited Universalism in Philo and Paul." *ZNW* 107 (2016): 30–47.

Stern, Sacha. *Jewish Identity in Early Rabbinic Writings.* AGJU 23. Leiden: Brill, 1994.

Still, Todd D., ed. *God and Israel: Providence and Purpose in Romans 9–11.* Waco, TX: Baylor University Press, 2017.

Stone, Michael E. "Apocalyptic Historiography." Pp. 59–89 in *Ancient Judaism: New Visions and Views*. Grand Rapids, MI: Eerdmans, 2011.

Stout, Jeffrey. "Liberty for All: Democracy in Practice and Principle." *Commonweal.* 20 September 2010.

"What Is the Meaning of a Text?" *New Literary History* 14 (1982): 1–12.

Stowers, Stanley. "Are Paul's Moral Teachings Designed for Ordinary Humans?" Pp. 3–18 in *The Social Worlds of Ancient Jews and Christians: Essays in Honor of L. Michael White*. Edited by Jaimie Gunderson, Tony Keddie, and Douglas Boin. NovTSup 189. Leiden: Brill, 2023.

The Diatribe and Paul's Letter to the Romans. SBLDS 57. Missoula, MT: Scholars Press, 1981.

"The Dilemma of Paul's Physics: Features Stoic-Platonist or Platonist-Stoic?" Pp. 231–253 in *From Stoicism to Platonism: The Development of Philosophy, 100 BCE–100 CE*. Edited by Troels Engberg-Pedersen. Cambridge: Cambridge University Press, 2017.

"Kinds of Myth, Meals, and Power: Paul and the Corinthians." Pp. 105–150 in *Redescribing Paul and the Corinthians*. Edited by Ron Cameron and Merrill P. Miller. Atlanta: SBL Press, 2011.

A Rereading of Romans: Justice, Jews, and Gentiles. New Haven: Yale University Press, 1994.

Strack, Hermann L., and Paul Billerbeck. *Kommentar zum Neuen Testament aus Talmud und Midrasch*. 4 vols. Munich: Beck, 1922–1928. ET *Commentary on the New Testament from the Talmud and Midrash*. Translated by Jacob Cerone and Joseph Longarino. Bellingham, WA: Lexham, 2021.

Strecker, Georg. *Das Judenchristentum in den Pseudoklementinen*. Berlin: Akademie Verlag, 1958.

"On the Problem of Jewish Christianity." Pp. 241–285 in Walter Bauer, *Orthodoxy and Heresy in Early Christianity*. Translated by Robert A. Kraft and Gerhard Kroedel. Philadelphia: Fortress, 1971.

Stroumsa, Guy G. "Form(s) of God: Some Notes on Metatron and Christ." *HTR* 76 (1983): 269–288.

Sullivan, Kevin Patrick. *Wrestling with Angels: A Study of the Relationship between Angels and Humans in Ancient Jewish Literature and the New Testament*. AGJU 55. Leiden: Brill, 2004.

Sumney, Jerry L. *Identifying Paul's Opponents: The Question of Method in 2 Corinthians*. JSNTSup 40. Sheffield: Sheffield Academic, 1990.

Servants of Satan, False Brothers, and Other Opponents of Paul. JSNTSup 188. Sheffield: Sheffield Academic, 1999.

Sundstrom, Ronald R., and David Haekwon Kim. "Xenophobia and Racism." *Critical Philosophy of Race* 2 (2014): 20–45.

Sussman, Robert Wald. *The Myth of Race: The Troubling Persistence of an Unscientific Idea*. Cambridge, MA: Harvard University Press, 2014.

Swancutt, Diana. "The Disease of Effemination: The Charge of Effeminacy and the Verdict of God (Romans 1:18–2:16)." Pp. 193–234 in *New Testament Masculinities*. Edited by Stephen D. Moore and Janice Capel Anderson. SBLSS 45. Leiden: Brill, 2004.

Tamez, Elsa. *The Amnesty of Grace: Justification by Faith from a Latin American Perspective*. Translated by Sharon H. Ringe. Nashville: Abingdon, 1991.

Tatum, Gregory. "A Participationist Eschatological Reading of Justification in Galatians, Philippians, and Romans." *RevBib* 125 (2018): 223–238.

Taubes, Jacob. *The Political Theology of Paul*. Translated by Dana Hollander. Stanford: Stanford University Press, 2004.

Taylor, Joan E. "The Phenomenon of Early Jewish-Christianity: Reality or Scholarly Invention?" *VC* 44 (1990): 313–334.

Thackeray, Henry St. John. *The Relation of St. Paul to Contemporary Jewish Thought*. New York: Macmillan, 1900.

Thiessen, Matthew. "Conjuring Paul and Judaism Forty Years after *Paul and Palestinian Judaism*." *JJMJS* 5 (2018): 7–20.

Contesting Conversion: Genealogy, Circumcision, and Identity in Ancient Judaism and Christianity. Oxford: Oxford University Press, 2011.

"The Construction of Gentiles in the Letter to the Ephesians." Pp. 13–25 in *The Early Reception of Paul the Second Temple Jew: Text, Narrative, and Reception History*. Edited by Isaac W. Oliver and Gabriele Boccaccini. LSTS 92. London: T&T Clark, 2019.

"Gentiles as Impure Animals in the Writings of Early Christ Followers." Pp. 19–32 in *Perceiving the Other in Ancient Judaism and Early Christianity*. Edited by Michal Bar-Asher Siegal, Wolfgang Grünstäudl, and Matthew Thiessen. WUNT 394. Tübingen: Mohr Siebeck, 2017.

A Jewish Paul: The Messiah's Herald to the Gentiles. Grand Rapids, MI: Baker, 2023.

Paul and the Gentile Problem. Oxford: Oxford University Press, 2016.

"Paul's Argument against Gentile Circumcision in Romans 2:17–29." *NovT* 56 (2014): 373–391.

"The Text of Genesis 17:14." *JBL* 128 (2009): 625–642.

Thiessen, Matthew, and Paula Fredriksen. "Paul and Israel." Pp. 371–388 in *The Oxford Handbook of Pauline Studies*. Edited by Matthew V. Novenson and R. Barry Matlock. Oxford: Oxford University Press, 2022.

Thompson, James W. *Moral Formation according to Paul: The Context and Coherence of Pauline Ethics*. Grand Rapids, MI: Baker, 2011.

Thorsteinsson, Runar M. *Commentary on Romans* (forthcoming).

"Not Everyone Will Be Justified Before Him by Works of the Law: A Fresh Reading of Romans 3:20" (forthcoming).

Paul's Interlocutor in Romans 2: Function and Identity in the Context of Ancient Epistolography. ConBibNT 40. Stockholm: Almqvist & Wiksell, 2003.

Thrall, Margaret. *2 Corinthians 8–13*. ICC. London: T&T Clark, 2004.

Tofighi, Fatima. *Paul's Letters and the Construction of the European Self*. London: T&T Clark, 2017.

"The Reception of Pauline Mysticism: An Ideological Critique." *NTS* 68 (2022): 363–374.

Tomson, Peter J. "'Death, Where Is Thy Victory?' Paul's Theology in the Twinkling of an Eye." Pp. 357–386 in *Resurrection in the New Testament: Festschrift J. Lambrecht*. Edited by R. Bieringer, V. Koperski, and B. Lataire. BETL 165. Leuven: Peeters, 2002.

Paul and the Jewish Law: Halakha in the Letters of the Apostle to the Gentiles. CRINT. Assen: Van Gorcum, 1990.

Tooth, Sydney. *The Eschatologies of 1 and 2 Thessalonians*. WUNT. Tübingen: Mohr Siebeck, forthcoming.

Trebilco, Paul. *Self-Designations and Group Identity in the New Testament*. Cambridge: Cambridge University Press, 2012.

Trench, Richard Chenevix. *Commentary on the Epistles to the Seven Churches in Asia*. London: Parker, Son, and Bourn, 1861.

Trivedi, Harish. "Reading Kipling in India." Pp. 187–199 in *The Cambridge Companion to Rudyard Kipling*. Edited by Howard J. Booth. Cambridge: Cambridge University Press, 2011.

Ullucci, Daniel C. *The Christian Rejection of Animal Sacrifice*. Oxford: Oxford University Press, 2012.

Valdez, Jason. "The Body and the Problem of Agency in Romans 8" (forthcoming).

Van den Berghe, Pierre L. *Race and Racism: A Comparative Perspective*. New York: Wiley, 1967.

Vander Stichele, Caroline. "Like Angels in Heaven: Corporeality, Resurrection, and Gender in Mark 12:18–27." Pp. 215–232 in *Begin with the Body: Corporeality, Religion, and Gender*. Edited by Jonneke Bekkenkamp and Maaike de Haardt. Leuven: Peeters, 1998.

VanderKam, James C. "Those Who Look for Smooth Things, Pharisees, and Oral Law." Pp. 465–478 in *Emanuel: Studies in Hebrew Bible, Septuagint, and Dead Sea Scrolls in Honor of Emanuel Tov*. Edited by Shalom M. Paul, Robert A. Kraft, Lawrence H. Schiffman, and Weston W. Fields. Leiden: Brill, 2003.

van Henten, Jan Willem. *The Maccabean Martyrs as Saviours of the Jewish People: A Study of 2 and 4 Maccabees*. JSJSup 57. Leiden: Brill, 1997.

van Kooten, George H. "Broadening the New Perspective on Paul: Paul and the Ethnographical Debate of His Time—The Criticism of Jewish and Pagan Ancestral Customs (1 Thess 2:13–16)." Pp. 319–344 in *Abraham, the Nations, and the Hagarites: Jewish, Christian, and Islamic Perspectives on Kinship with Abraham*. Edited by Martin Goodman, George H. van Kooten, and Jacques T. A. G. M. van Ruiten. TBN 13. Leiden: Brill, 2010.

Cosmic Christology in Paul and the Pauline School. WUNT 2/171. Tübingen: Mohr Siebeck, 2003.

"*Ekklesia tou theou*: The 'Church of God' and the Civic Assemblies (*ekklesiai*) of the Greek Cities in the Roman Empire." NTS 58 (2012): 522–548.

"Pagan and Jewish Monotheism according to Varro, Plutarch, and St Paul." Pp. 633–651 in *Flores Florentino: Dead Sea Scrolls and*

Other Early Jewish Studies in Honor of Florentino Garcia Martinez, ed. A. Hilhorst, Emile Puech, and Eibert Tigchelaar. JSJSup 122. Leiden: Brill, 2007.

Vermes, Geza, trans. *The Complete Dead Sea Scrolls in English*. 7th ed. London: Penguin, 2012.

"Jewish Studies and New Testament Interpretation." *JJS* 31 (1980): 1–17.

Voltaire. "Idol, Idolator, Idolatry." *Encyclopedia of Diderot & d'Alembert Collaborative Translation Project*. Translated by Erik Liddell. Ann Arbor: University of Michigan Library, 2006. French original *Encyclopédie ou Dictionnaire raisonné des sciences, des arts et des métiers*. Paris, 1765.

von Weissenberg, Hanne. *4QMMT: Reevaluating the Text, the Function, and the Meaning of the Epilogue*. STDJ 82. Leiden: Brill, 2008.

Vos, Geerhardus. *The Pauline Eschatology*. Grand Rapids, MI: Baker, 1930.

Wagner, J. Ross. "The Christ, Servant of Jew and Gentile: A Fresh Approach to Romans 15:8–9." *JBL* 116 (1997): 473–485.

Heralds of the Good News: Isaiah and Paul "in Concert" in the Letter to the Romans. NovTSup 101. Leiden: Brill, 2002.

Walker, William O. *Interpolations in the Pauline Letters*. JSNTSup 213. Sheffield: Sheffield Academic, 2001.

Wasserman, Emma. *Apocalypse as Holy War: Divine Politics and Polemics in the Letters of Paul*. AYBRL. New Haven: Yale University Press, 2018.

The Death of the Soul in Romans 7: Sin, Death, and the Law in Light of Hellenistic Moral Psychology. WUNT 2/256. Tübingen: Mohr Siebeck, 2008.

Wasserman, Mira Beth. *Jews, Gentiles, and Other Animals: The Talmud after the Humanities*. Philadelphia: University of Pennsylvania Press, 2017.

Watson, Francis. *Paul and the Hermeneutics of Faith*. London: T&T Clark, 2004.

Paul, Judaism, and the Gentiles. SNTSMS 56. Cambridge: Cambridge University Press, 1986.

Paul, Judaism, and the Gentiles. 2nd rev. ed. Grand Rapids, MI: Eerdmans, 2007.

Weizsäcker, K. H. "Paulus und die Gemeinde in Korinth." *JDT* 21 (1876): 603–653.

Welborn, Larry L. *An End to Enmity: Paul and the "Wrongdoer" of Second Corinthians*. BZNW 185. Berlin: De Gruyter, 2011.

Wells, Kyle B. *Grace and Agency in Paul and Second Temple Judaism: Interpreting the Transformation of the Heart*. NovTSup 157. Leiden: Brill, 2015.

Wendt, Heidi. *At the Temple Gates: The Religion of Freelance Experts in the Roman Empire*. Oxford: Oxford University Press, 2016.

Westerholm, Stephen. "Paul's Anthropological 'Pessimism' in Its Jewish Context." Pp. 71–98 in *Divine and Human Agency in Paul and His Jewish Environment*. Edited by John M. G. Barclay and Simon Gathercole. London: T&T Clark, 2006.

Perspectives Old and New on Paul: The "Lutheran" Paul and His Critics. Grand Rapids, MI: Eerdmans, 2004.

Wheeler-Reed, David. *Regulating Sex in the Roman Empire: Ideology, the Bible, and the Early Christians*. New Haven: Yale University Press, 2017.

Wheeler-Reed, David, Jennifer W. Knust, and Dale B. Martin. "Can a Man Commit *Porneia* with His Wife?" *JBL* 137 (2018): 383–398.

Wheelwright, John. *Mercurius Americanus*. 1645.

White, Benjamin L. *Remembering Paul: Ancient and Modern Contests over the Image of the Apostle*. Oxford: Oxford University Press, 2014.

Wilckens, Ulrich. *Der Brief an die Römer*. 3 vols. EKK. Neukirchen-Vluyn: Neukirchener Verlag, 1978.

Wilk, Florian, and J. Ross Wagner, eds. *Between Gospel and Election: Explorations in the Interpretation of Romans 9–11*. WUNT 257. Tübingen: Mohr Siebeck, 2010.

Wilken, Robert L. *John Chrysostom and the Jews: Rhetoric and Reality in the Late 4th Century*. Berkeley: University of California Press, 1983.

Williams, A. Lukyn. *Adversus Judaeos: A Bird's-Eye View of Christian Apologiae until the Renaissance*. Cambridge: Cambridge University Press, 1935.

Williams, Bernard. *Ethics and the Limits of Philosophy*. London: Fontana, 1985.

Williams, Demetrius K. *Enemies of the Cross of Christ: The Terminology of the Cross and Conflict in Philippians*. JSNTSup 223. Sheffield: Sheffield Academic, 2002.

Williams, Logan. "Being(s) above the Law: Ontology, Legislation, and Paul's Quotation of Aristotle's *Politics* in Galatians" (forthcoming).

Williams, Margaret H. "The Meaning and Function of *Ioudaios* in Graeco-Roman Inscriptions." *ZPE* 116 (1997): 249–262.

Williams, Sam K. "The Righteousness of God in Romans." *JBL* 99 (1980): 241–290.

Wilson, Annalisa Phillips. *Paul and the Jewish Law: A Stoic Ethical Perspective on His Inconsistency*. APhR 8. Leiden: Brill, 2022.

Wilson, Stephen G. *Related Strangers: Jews and Christians, 70–170 CE*. Minneapolis: Fortress, 1995.

Windischmann, F. *Erklärung des Briefes an die Galater*. Mainz: Schott & Thielmann, 1843.

Windsor, Lionel J. "The Named Jew and the Name of God: The Argument of Romans 2:17–29 in Light of Roman Attitudes to Jewish Teachers." *NovT* 63 (2021): 229–248.
Winninge, Mikael. *Sinners and the Righteous: A Comparative Study of the Psalms of Solomon and Paul's Letters.* ConBibNT 26. Stockholm: Almqvist & Wiksell, 1995.
Winter, Sean F. "Paul's Attitudes to the Gentiles." Pp. 138–153 in *Attitudes to Gentiles in Ancient Judaism and Early Christianity.* Edited by David C. Sim and James S. McLaren. London: T&T Clark, 2013.
Wire, Antoinette Clark. *The Corinthian Women Prophets: A Reconstruction through Paul's Rhetoric.* Minneapolis: Fortress, 1995.
Wolfson, Harry Austryn. *Philo: Foundations of Religious Philosophy in Judaism, Christianity, and Islam*, vol. 1. Cambridge, MA: Harvard University Press, 1947.
Wollenberg, Rebecca Scharbach. "The Book That Changed: Narratives of Ezran Authorship as Late Antique Biblical Criticism." *JBL* 138 (2019): 143–160.
The Closed Book: How the Rabbis Taught the Jews (Not) to Read the Bible. Princeton: Princeton University Press, 2023.
Wright, Benjamin G. *The Letter of Aristeas.* CEJL. Berlin: De Gruyter, 2015.
Wright, N. T. "4QMMT and Paul: Justification, 'Works' and Eschatology." Pp. 332–355 in *Pauline Perspectives: Essays on Paul, 1978–2013.* Minneapolis: Fortress, 2013.
The Climax of the Covenant: Christ and the Law in Pauline Theology. Minneapolis: Fortress, 1991.
Galatians. Grand Rapids, MI: Eerdmans, 2021.
"Hope Deferred? Against the Dogma of Delay." *EC* 9 (2018): 37–82.
Paul and the Faithfulness of God. 2 vols. London: SPCK, 2013.
"Romans 9–11 and the New Perspective." Pp. 392–406 in *Pauline Perspectives: Essays on Paul, 1978–2013.* Minneapolis: Fortress, 2013.
What Saint Paul Really Said: Was Paul of Tarsus the Real Founder of Christianity? Grand Rapids, MI: Eerdmans, 1997.
Wyschogrod, Michael. *Abraham's Promise: Judaism and Jewish-Christian Relations.* Grand Rapids, MI: Eerdmans, 2004.
Yee, Tet-Lim N. *Jews, Gentiles, and Ethnic Reconciliation: Paul's Jewish Identity and Ephesians.* SNTSMS 130. Cambridge: Cambridge University Press, 2005.
Yinger, Kent L. "The Continuing Quest for Jewish Legalism." *BBR* 19 (2009): 375–391.
Young, James O., and Conrad G. Brunk, eds. *The Ethics of Cultural Appropriation.* Oxford: Wiley-Blackwell, 2012.

Young, Stephen L. "Paul's Eschatological Myth of Jewish Sin." *NTS* (forthcoming).

Zahn, Theodor. *Der Brief des Paulus an die Römer*. Leipzig: Deichert, 1910.

Zellentin, Holger M. *Law beyond Israel: From the Bible to the Quran*. Oxford: Oxford University Press, 2022.

Zetterholm, Karin Hedner. "Jewish Teachings for Gentiles in the Pseudo-Clementine Homilies." *JJMJS* 6 (2019): 68–87.

Zetterholm, Magnus. *Approaches to Paul: A Student's Guide to Recent Scholarship*. Minneapolis: Fortress, 2009.

Ziegler, Philip G. "'Those He Also Glorified': Some Reformed Perspectives on Human Nature and Destiny." *SCE* 32 (2019): 165–176.

Zuntz, Günther. *The Text of the Epistles: A Disquisition upon the Corpus Paulinum*. Oxford: British Academy, 1953.

Index of Subjects

Abraham, 2, 27, 46, 58, 70, 73–74, 83, 92, 97, 111, 128, 131, 154, 161, 164, 177, 180, 183–186, 196, 206, 230
Adam, 137, 142, 151, 201, 203, 206, 209, 235, 243
age to come, 74, 145, 181, 213, 218, 220, 228, 236, 238, 240
age, messianic, 209, 215, 217–218, 220–221, 226, 238
age, present, 1–2, 71, 219, 226, 230
Alexandria, 20, 61, 63, 76, 86, 133, 226
anatomy, 206, 232–233
ancestors, 43, 68, 156, 177, 242
ancestry, 5, 43
angels, 28, 80, 142, 177, 207–208, 221–225, 232, 237
aniconism, 148–150
anomalous, 14, 18–19
anomaly, 14, 18, 40
anthropology, 218, 221, 224, 226, 238, 240, 242
Antioch, 31, 36, 58, 65, 70, 82, 106, 141
apocalyptic, 18, 20, 33, 70, 155, 157, 195
Apollos, 24, 47, 80–81, 85–87
apostasy, 30, 113

baptism, 75, 103, 126, 188–189, 197, 199, 239
barbarian, 37, 138–139
Barnabas, 70, 80, 82, 106–107, 110
Belial, 57, 111
benediction, 48, 165–166

Cephas, 24, 65, 67, 70, 80–83, 85, 141
chauvinism, 27, 136, 140, 154, 156–157, 159, 242
Christianismos, 105–106

circumcision, 6, 14, 37, 43–45, 47, 60–61, 63, 70–71, 76–77, 80–82, 84, 86–89, 91–92, 94–101, 104–111, 126–131, 133, 139, 142, 157, 161–163, 165–166, 168–176, 183, 186, 208, 242
commandments, 17, 60, 89–90, 103, 107, 112, 117, 126, 128, 133, 146, 210, 218, 220, 222, 225, 227, 230, 236, 238–239, 241
comparison, 13–16, 48, 73, 92, 217
conversion, 32, 128, 130, 183
corpus Paulinum, 22
cosmos, 2, 62, 64, 129, 158, 165, 193, 202, 206, 232
covenant, new, 12, 17, 20
creation, new, 1, 28, 48, 129, 154, 158, 165–166, 192–193, 201, 206, 226–227, 230, 232, 236–237, 243
cult, 5, 91, 148–151, 156, 186
curse, 146, 229

day of the lord, 2, 79, 154, 180
death, 54, 68, 165, 195, 201–203, 220, 229, 239
Decalogue, 72, 128
demons, 126–128
deutero-Pauline, 124, 139, 148
diaspora, 15, 18, 20, 43, 63, 76, 82, 113
diatribe, 62, 96–97, 188
disability, 222–223
dogs, 91–93, 95–96, 110, 168, 170
domination, 192–193, 219
dust, 206, 228, 241, 243

Ebionites, 102
Egyptians, 108, 138, 147
elements, 10, 14, 18, 61, 149, 193, 206
eschatology, 2, 6–7, 12, 16, 20, 25, 28, 155, 179, 198–199, 207, 218

285

ethnicity, 2, 4, 6, 8, 20, 25, 27–28, 37, 51, 67, 79, 81, 94, 102–103, 124, 139, 158, 160, 165, 175, 178, 186
ethnocentrism, 136, 139–140, 156, 242
ethnos, 3–4, 35, 48–49, 136, 140, 156, 167, 179–180, 185
etymology, 36–38, 40
ex opere operato, 127, 199

flesh, 23, 53, 61, 68, 73, 87, 91–93, 99, 107, 128, 130–131, 142, 149, 154, 161, 163–166, 168–169, 172–176, 178, 186, 190–191, 193, 197, 199, 201, 203–206, 208, 226–227, 230–234, 236, 240
foreskin, 31, 48, 60, 70, 87, 97–98, 105, 128, 130, 135, 139–140, 142, 165, 174, 208
forgiveness, 73, 75, 123, 189
future, 2, 7, 25, 28, 91, 107, 178, 180, 190, 198, 208, 213, 218–219, 225, 230–232, 240

gender, 41, 136, 159, 222
gentileness, 2, 4–5, 79
glory, 95–96, 121, 125, 150, 156, 167, 169, 182, 189, 205–207, 223, 227
grace, 15, 70, 99, 117–118, 146, 154

halakhah, 60, 75, 82, 127–128, 130, 183
Hasmoneans, 45, 133
heart, 13, 55, 69, 99, 107, 113, 150, 161, 171, 173–174, 213, 225, 230, 240
Hellenism, 10–11, 30, 41, 138, 191, 207
heresy, 80, 88, 102–103
hermeneutics, 24–25, 113–115, 157, 172, 229, 241
history, 2, 4, 8–9, 26, 28, 50–51, 58, 69–70, 89, 95, 114, 118–119, 135, 147, 151, 160, 177, 179, 197, 207, 213, 216, 241
homeland, 5, 82
humanism, 136, 143, 159
hybridity, 182

idolatry, 50, 60, 76, 146, 151–152, 158
ignorance, 67, 70, 141, 152

immortality, 27, 74, 189, 195, 205, 220
inscriptions, 39, 43, 200
interlocutor, 62, 64, 68, 175
intermarriage, 57, 59
interpolation, 79, 100, 201
Ioudaismos, 5, 12, 26, 29, 31, 39–40, 105
Ishmael, 109, 177
Israel, 4, 8, 10, 27, 30, 32–33, 43, 45, 48–49, 57, 60, 69–70, 89, 91–93, 99, 128, 140, 143, 146–148, 160–168, 171–174, 176, 178–182, 184–186, 203, 212–213, 216–217, 219–220, 222–223, 243

Jerusalem, 2, 19, 41, 79, 81–83, 90, 105, 111, 116, 138, 163, 223, 227, 231
Jewish Christianity, 27, 33, 38, 77–78, 101–104, 106, 168
Jewishness, 2, 4–5, 13, 27, 34, 37–38, 40, 46, 79, 86–87, 92, 102, 108, 130, 162, 172, 174–176
judaize, 30–31, 34–36, 38, 48, 65, 67, 89, 104
Judean, 33–34, 44, 92, 136, 140
justice, 72, 187, 191–192, 196, 208, 243
justification, 26, 47, 50–53, 55–56, 59, 61–62, 64–65, 67, 70–71, 73, 75–76, 122–123, 190, 241–242

kabbalah, 201, 209–210
kingdom, 7, 27, 71, 108, 133, 149, 155, 167, 181, 183, 191, 194, 203–205, 207, 231, 236, 241
koilia, 95, 99, 169

legalism, 27, 113–117, 119–121, 126, 129–130, 132–133, 159, 242
letters, 2, 4–5, 7–8, 10, 21–24, 26–27, 64–65, 67, 69, 72, 75, 78–80, 87, 90, 94, 96, 101, 109, 113, 124–125, 127–128, 134–137, 143, 147–148, 156, 159, 168–169, 181, 192, 196, 199, 209, 213, 226, 235, 237, 241
libertine, 95, 132–133
liberty, 144, 187, 191–192, 196, 208, 243

Index of Subjects

life everlasting, 2, 121, 187, 192, 201, 204, 227–228
love, 60, 113, 117, 190, 194, 237–238
Lutheran, 32, 70, 117, 192

manuscript, 58, 79, 100, 172, 201
Marcion, 31
marriage, levirate, 209–210, 235
martyrs, 41, 225
mercy, 48, 53, 73, 123, 146, 158, 166–167, 208
merit, 61, 120, 126, 218
messiah, 1–2, 9, 48, 55, 66, 68, 70–71, 75–76, 111, 125, 157, 164, 176, 179, 185, 194, 209–210, 217, 219, 236, 241–243
midrash, 142, 219–220, 229
milah, 170
mohel, 183
Moses, 2, 42–43, 55–56, 61, 63, 69, 76, 81, 84, 90, 99, 103–104, 106, 111–112, 124–125, 128, 130, 133, 142, 170, 172, 184, 194, 201, 207, 211–214, 220, 222, 226–229, 236–237, 240

nationalism, 136
Nazarenes, 102
neologism, 41, 105
New Perspective, 8–9, 12, 51–52, 70, 114, 156, 159
nomism, 16, 113, 116, 119, 132

opponents, 27, 35–36, 48, 58, 77, 79–80, 83, 87, 90–93, 95–96, 99–100, 103, 109–110, 112–113, 117, 152, 169–170

pagans, 38, 72, 122, 137–138, 153, 171, 182, 184–185
parousia, 7–8, 154, 205
patriarchs, 2, 28, 142, 195
Paul within Judaism, 8, 10–12, 17, 29, 81, 195
Paulinism, 25, 28, 61, 108, 132, 190
penis, 94–95, 170, 174, 222
periah, 170
persecution, 41, 46
Pharisee, 17, 19, 30, 34, 82, 91–92, 104, 107, 112, 114, 119, 139–140, 156, 167

Philistines, 146
philosophy, 80, 84, 112, 150
physics, 1, 27, 74, 188, 198, 205, 207
piety, 56, 64, 72, 76, 150, 174, 242
pneumatic, 28, 60, 74, 84, 111, 131, 144, 154–155, 158, 190, 195–197, 204, 206–208, 231, 236–237
porneia, 60, 126–128, 131, 144
proselyte, 18–19, 40, 45, 60, 63, 76–77, 80–82, 87–88, 90–92, 94–96, 98–99, 101, 104–105, 107–110, 126–127, 130–131, 133, 166, 168, 170, 175, 183, 242
Protestant, 17, 26, 114, 117–119, 124, 128, 137, 192, 196, 199, 214
pseudonymous, 14, 22, 80
purity, 43, 57, 108

Qumran, 9, 20, 56–59, 63, 119, 147, 189, 223

rabbis, 62–63, 109, 210, 218, 220–221, 226, 243
racism, 3, 136, 156
racist, 3
Reformed, 70, 192, 198
religion, 4, 6, 11, 13, 15–16, 26, 28, 30–31, 33–37, 39, 41–43, 47, 49–51, 71, 73–74, 113, 117–119, 173, 198, 226, 242
remnant, 177–178, 186
resurrection, 1, 74, 114, 126, 154, 164, 181, 189–190, 195, 197, 199–200, 203, 205, 207, 210, 218, 220–221, 223, 228, 230–235, 241, 243
revolt, Maccabean, 40
righteousness, 12, 27–28, 32, 48, 51, 54–57, 59–60, 65–66, 69–70, 72–76, 91, 97, 112, 114, 117–118, 120, 123, 125, 133, 141–143, 145, 153, 158, 174, 178, 184, 190–195, 201, 204, 208, 213, 215, 219, 224, 226–227, 230, 236, 241
ritual failure, 94

Sabbateans, 209
salvation, 33, 59, 64, 120, 122, 124, 132, 162, 184, 215, 228, 241
Satan, 78–80, 86, 107, 168
sectarian, 36, 42, 49, 57, 59

seed, 46, 73–74, 83, 92, 154, 156, 164, 177–178, 180, 182–186, 206, 230
sexual, 131, 144, 146, 149, 231–233
shame, 1, 67–68, 82, 95–96, 113, 169, 228
Sinai, 111, 220, 222
sinners, 47, 65–66, 69, 71, 90, 123–124, 141–143, 145–146, 152–153, 156, 158, 224
skandalon, 2, 69–70, 128
slavery, 158–159, 192, 205
Son of Man, 123
Sonderweg, 10
soteriology, 15, 73, 228–230
Spartans, 185
stars, 74, 151, 223–224, 230, 234–235
Stoic, 68, 74, 129, 165, 190, 198
super-apostles, 83–84, 86, 92–93
synagogue, 33, 39

temple, 2, 43, 68, 163, 238
theology, 1, 8, 11, 18, 26, 68–69, 120, 128, 159, 166, 171–172, 176, 178, 182, 188, 192, 196, 213

Thessaloniki, 67, 144
Torah, 2, 10, 17, 30, 36, 55–60, 70–71, 73, 75–76, 90, 102–103, 111–112, 117–121, 128, 133, 135, 140–141, 154–155, 157, 174–176, 183, 209–214, 216–218, 221–223, 225, 228–229, 235–242
transhumanism, 198
translation, 34, 37, 59, 65, 153, 161, 167, 172, 176, 202, 208, 212

uniqueness, 4, 14, 19
universalism, 136, 139, 143, 162

women, 24, 97, 136, 141, 187, 222–224
works of the law, 12, 27, 32, 47, 50–56, 58–67, 69–71, 73, 75–76, 114, 120–121, 242

zeal, 43–44, 69, 91, 119, 213

Index of Ancient Sources

1QH^a 21:5, 174

1QS 5:26, 174

4Q394, 56

4Q395, 56

4Q396, 56

4Q397, 56

4Q398, 56

4Q398 14–17 ii, 57

4Q399, 56

4QMMT, 56, 58–60, 75, 108, 113

Abot R. Nat., version B, §26, 238

Acts
  6:14, 42
  15:1–31, 116
  15:5, 82, 104, 107
  16:1–3, 81, 171
  16:3, 46
  18:24, 86
  19:1, 86
  23:6, 104
  26:5, 104
  28:17, 42

Aramaic Levi, 112

Aristides, *Apol.* 2.1, 178

Aristotle, *Pol.* 3.8 1284a, 194

Augustine, *Adv. Jud.* 7.9, 163

Augustine, *Exp. Gal.* 7.2, 32

b. Avod. Zar. 9a, 216

b. Ber.
  17a, 220
  25b, 221

b. Meʻil. 14b, 221

b. Nid. 61b, 239

b. Qidd. 54a, 221

b. Rosh Hash. 31a, 216

b. Sanh. 97a–b, 216

b. Shabb.
  30a, 239
  88b–89a, 222
  146a, 212
  151b, 218, 239

b. Yoma 30a, 221

2 Baruch, 207
  51:1–5, 224
  51:10, 224
  73:7, 224

Ben Sira, 15, 112, 240

Cassius Dio, *Roman History*
  37.17.1, 92

CD 1:18–19, 112

1 Chronicles
  17:11 OG, 96, 169

2 Chronicles
  32:31 OG, 169

CIJ 537, 39

CIJ 694, 39

Clement, *Strom.* 6.41.6,
  182

Colossians
  1:14, 124
  2:8, 80
  2:16, 80
  2:18, 80
  3:11, 139

1 Corinthians
  1:1, 21
  1:11, 97
  1:12, 81, 85
  1:22, 140
  1:23, 69, 100, 139
  1:24, 140
  1:30, 194, 226
  2:2, 69
  3:3, 240
  3:4, 47, 85
  3:5, 85
  3:6, 85
  3:10, 85
  3:15, 180
  3:22, 85
  4:6, 85
  5, 131–132
  5:1, 145
  5:4–5, 127
  5:5, 180
  5–7, 127
  6:3, 207
  6:9–10, 149, 204
  6:12–20, 144
  6:13, 231
  6:15, 127
  6:18, 127
  7, 97
  7:19, 82

7:21–23, 159
7:29–31, 232
7:31, 2, 206
8:4–6, 149
8:10–12, 127
8–10, 127
9:19–23, 46
9:20, 237
9:21, 237
10, 69
10:6, 69
10:11, 2, 240
10:16, 100, 163
10:18, 48, 161, 164–165,
  186
10:19–20, 149
10:20–21, 127, 149, 163
10:22, 132
10:31–33, 182
10:32, 140
11, 97
11:3, 136
11:3–15, 159
11:14, 138
12:2, 67, 149, 158, 184
12:13, 140
12:23, 94, 169
13:8, 237
14:34, 136
15, 200, 205, 230
15:12–58, 208
15:20–50, 151
15:26, 195
15:34, 68
15:44, 231–232
15:45, 2, 228, 241
15:47–49, 206
15:49, 233
15:50, 191, 203, 231, 236
15:53–54, 220
15:56, 200, 239
16:12, 85

2 Corinthians
  1:1, 20–21
  3:6, 12, 18
  3:6–7, 237
  3:7, 48
  3:14, 67
  3:14–15, 69

Index of Ancient Sources 291

3:17, 193
4:7, 204, 206
4:16, 191
5:10, 28
5:16, 164
5:17, 192, 206
6:2, 180
9:2-4, 139
9:5, 100
9:6, 100
10:14-15, 84
10-13, 83-84, 86
11, 92-93
11:2, 84
11:3, 151
11:4, 84-85
11:5, 83
11:5-6, 84
11:13, 83
11:21-22, 83
11:22, 92, 140
12:11, 83
12:12, 83

3 Corinthians, 22

Daniel
7, 123

Deuteronomy
7:13 LXX, 96, 169
10:16, 99, 174
14, 145
15:11, 219
17, 212
17:18, 212
25:5-10, 210
28:4 LXX, 96, 169
28:11 LXX, 96, 169
28:18 LXX, 96, 169
28:53 LXX, 96, 169
30:6, 174
30:9 LXX, 96, 169
30:14, 55
30:15-18, 230
32:39, 219-220
32:43 LXX, 184
32:50, 229

Deut. Rab. 44, 229

Didache 6:2, 108

Didascalia Apostolorum 9, 102, 104
23-26, 104
25, 104
26, 103-104

Ecclesiastes, 112
12:1, 218

Eccl. Rab. 1.4.3, 219

1 Enoch, 15
6:1-7:6, 222
50:1-5, 123
86:1-6, 222
88:3, 222
90:21, 222
104:1-6, 224

2 Enoch, 207, 232

Ephesians
2:5-6, 189
2:15, 148
4:17-24, 80, 153

Epiphanius, *Panarion*
29.7.1, 102
29-30, 102

Epistle of Barnabas
3:6, 106
9, 103
9:4, 107

Epistula Apostolorum, 7

Esther, 112
8:17 OG, 37

Eusebius, *Hist. eccl.* 3.20.6, 155

Eusebius, *Praep. ev.* 9.22.5, 37

Exodus
4:24-26 LXX, 81
20:2, 221
20:26 LXX, 96

Exodus (cont.)
 24:11, 220
 31–32, 212
 32, 34, 69, 212

Exod. Rab. 30:12, 109

Ezekiel
 36:24–25, 219
 44:9, 174

4 Ezra, 1, 14–15, 240
 7:28–32, 1

Ezra, 171, 183–184
 4:7, 212

Galatians
 1, 31, 242
 1:1–2, 21
 1:4, 151, 192
 1:8–9, 127
 1:13, 12, 32, 45–47
 1:13–14, 12, 26, 30, 32, 38, 43, 49
 1:16, 30
 1:18, 81
 1:23, 46
 1–2, 81
 2, 141–142, 169
 2:1, 81
 2:1–10, 81
 2:2, 81
 2:4, 81
 2:6, 81
 2:7, 5, 82, 139
 2:7–8, 48
 2:8, 47, 82
 2:9, 81–83
 2:11–21, 133
 2:12, 82
 2:14, 30, 36, 38, 49, 65, 139
 2:14–17, 141
 2:15, 90, 110, 124, 139, 141, 171
 2:15–16, 47, 65, 67, 69
 2:16, 12, 51
 2:19, 12
 2:21, 51, 125
 3, 184, 229
 3:1, 68, 139
 3:3, 61, 68
 3:4–5, 155
 3:6, 58
 3:11, 51, 53
 3:11–12, 227
 3:12, 55, 227
 3:14, 74, 100, 206
 3:16, 185
 3:21, 51, 75, 114, 125, 194, 227
 3:22, 157
 3:23, 237
 3:23–25, 158
 3:24, 51
 3:24–25, 236
 3:28, 140, 157–158, 231
 3:29, 185
 3–4, 178
 4:3, 192
 4:4–5, 237
 4:8, 141
 4:8–9, 149, 193
 4:21, 55, 237
 5:2–12, 49
 5:2–4, 127
 5:3, 89, 126, 130
 5:4, 51
 5:7, 47
 5:7–12, 47
 5:10, 47–48
 5:11, 44, 46, 96, 100
 5:12, 47
 5:14, 214, 237
 5:16, 165
 5:18, 236–237
 5:19–21, 149
 5:21, 204
 5:23, 194
 5–6, 98, 127
 6:2, 237
 6:8, 227
 6:12, 96
 6:12–13, 47
 6:13, 87, 89–90, 110, 131, 170
 6:13–15, 165
 6:15, 48, 192, 206
 6:15–16, 166
 6:16, 48, 162, 166–167, 176, 186

Galen, *On the Doctrines of Hippocrates and Plato* 7.3.30, 131

Index of Ancient Sources

Genesis
  1:26, 223
  1:27, 231
  2, 231
  2:7, 206
  15:5, 74, 230
  15:6, 58
  17, 128, 130
  17:14, 90, 130, 175
  21:12, 177

Gen. Rab. 14:3, 225

Genesis Apocryphon, 112

Gospel of Jesus's Wife, 111

Habakkuk
  2:4, 53–54, 227, 230

Hebrews, 22

Herm. Sim.
  9.25.2, 224
  9.27.3, 224

Herodotus, *Hist.*
  1.58, 138
  2.57, 138
  2.158, 138
  4.144, 38

Hos 2:25, 184

Ignatius, *Magn.* 10.3, 31, 37

Ignatius, *Phld.* 6.1, 31, 105

IJO 1 Mac. 1, 39

Isaiah
  6:3, 238
  25:8, 219
  51:4, 210, 236
  59:20–21 OG, 179

James
  2:8, 214

Jeremiah
  4:4, 99, 174
  9:25, 174
  31:31–34, 219
  33:11, 238

JIWE 2.584, 39

John
  5:27, 123
  7:22–23, 108
  17:3, 226

Josephus, *Ant.*
  1.21, 64
  3.101, 72
  4.139, 42
  18.117, 72
  20.34–48, 109
  20.38, 109
  20.43–45, 109
  20.100, 113

Josephus, *War*
  2.454, 463, 37

Jubilees, 112–113, 130, 133, 171
  15.25–27, 130
  15.27, 142, 222
  23.23–24, 146
  24.28–29, 146

Julian, *Ep.* 84, 38

Justin, *Dial.*
  11, 161
  19, 174
  47.4, 104
  92, 174

Kerygma Petri, 182

2 Kingdoms
  7:12, 96, 169
  16:11, 169

1 Kings
  19, 69

LAB, 112
  9.13, 142
  9.15, 142

Let. Aris. 151–152, 146

Leviticus
 7:24, 236
 11, 145
 11:4, 221
 11:9, 221
 15:25, 222
 18:5, 55, 214, 227–230
 18:5 LXX, 227
 19:18, 237–238
 19:19, 238
 26:41, 174

Lev. Rab.
 9:7, 238
 13:3, 210, 236

Libanius, Or. 11.103, 37

Luke
 5:24, 123
 5:32, 125
 20:27–40, 210
 22:16, 231

m. Abot 3:19, 210

m. Sanh. 10:1, 181

1 Maccabees, 46, 112
 2:29–41, 133
 2:46, 46, 133
 2:48, 146
 12:19–23, 185

2 Maccabees
 2:21, 39, 41
 4:13, 38, 40
 8:1, 39, 41
 14:38, 39, 41

4 Maccabees
 4:26, 39

Mark
 2:10, 123
 2:17, 125
 7:27, 93
 7:27–28, 170

 12:18–27, 210
 13:32, 7
 14:25, 231

Mart. Pol. 2.3, 225

Matthew, 154
 5:17, 214
 6:1–6, 174
 8:11, 27
 9:6, 123
 9:13, 125
 15:26, 93
 15:26–27, 170
 22:23–33, 210
 23:15, 109
 26:29, 231
 28:19–20, 107

Mek. R. Ish. Nezikin 18, 109

Midr. Teh. 8.2, 223

Numbers
 19:14, 221–222
 31:23, 5

Num. Rab. 8, 109

Origen, Cels.
 5.10, 230
 7.32, 235

Origen, Comm. Rom.
 2.11, 175
 8.2.2, 227
 8.3.2, 157

Origen, Or.
 31.3, 234

Origen, Princ.
 2.11.2, 231
 4.3.6, 161, 163

Pesiq. Rab. 25, 221

2 Peter, 7
 3:4, 8, 154
 3:8, 155

Index of Ancient Sources

Philippians
  1:1, 21, 171
  2:10, 234
  3, 92, 98, 100
  3:1–3, 168
  3:2, 93, 96
  3:2–7, 91, 93, 95
  3:3, 82, 91, 94, 168–169, 172, 186
  3:4–6, 76
  3:5, 48, 94, 138, 140, 170
  3:5–6, 43, 114
  3:6, 46, 194
  3:8–9, 114
  3:9, 51
  3:17–18, 96
  3:18–19, 95, 169
  3:19, 171
  3:21, 233
  4:2, 97

Philo, *Creation* 3, 62

Philo, *Legum Allegoriae*, 112

Philo, *Migration*
  89, 112
  89–93, 133
  92, 61

Philemon, 80, 159
  1, 21

Plato, *Timaeus* 33, 234

Plutarch, *Cicero* 7.6, 37

Plutarch, *Isis and Osiris* 3, 186

Porphyry, *Against the Christians*, 7

Proverbs
  24:12 OG, 121

Psalms
  8:2, 221
  9:18, 145
  13:3 OG, 100
  31:1–2 OG, 123
  61:13 OG, 121
  68:19, 223
  88:5–6 MT, 239
  88:6, 239
  90:4, 155
  131:11 OG, 96, 169
  142 OG, 53
  142:2 OG, 53

Ps.-Clem. Rec.
  1.33, 108
  5.34, 109

Psalms of Solomon, 15

Ptolemy, *Tetrabiblos* 2.2.9, 27

Q, 107

Revelation
  2:9, 108
  3:9, 108
  6:15, 96

Romans
  1:3, 164
  1:14, 139–140
  1:16, 140
  1:17, 54
  1:18, 143
  1:18–29, 150
  1:18–32, 151–152, 157
  1:26–27, 141
  1:28, 68
  1:29, 143
  1–2, 62
  1–3, 62, 152–153
  2, 71, 92, 97, 125, 154, 162
  2:1, 152
  2:1–6, 152
  2:4, 68
  2:5, 180
  2:6, 121
  2:6–11, 122
  2:6–13, 121, 228
  2:7, 227
  2:9, 140
  2:10, 140
  2:14, 99, 124
  2:14–15, 153
  2:17, 62, 98

Romans (cont.)
  2:17–21, 175
  2:25, 94, 98, 170, 175
  2:25–27, 98
  2:26, 236–237
  2:26–27, 140
  2:27, 110, 126, 142, 171, 175
  2:27–29, 237
  2:28–29, 161, 171, 173, 175
  2:28–3:1, 99
  2:29, 174
  2–4, 97, 99
  3, 53, 157
  3:1, 82
  3:1–2, 157
  3:2, 68, 176
  3:7, 47
  3:9, 140, 151, 157, 192
  3:12, 100
  3:19, 158, 192
  3:20, 51, 53, 73
  3:21, 176
  3:22–24, 157
  3:28, 51, 114
  3:29, 139, 184
  3:30, 70, 97, 139, 208
  3:31, 114, 128, 236
  4, 97, 184
  4:1, 164
  4:3, 58
  4:6–8, 123
  4:9, 82, 139
  4:10–11, 185
  4:11, 139
  4:11–12, 97
  4:12, 139
  4:13, 206
  4:16, 154, 185
  4:18, 74
  4:25, 190
  5, 230
  5:9, 180
  5:12, 201
  5:12–21, 151, 157, 200
  5:18, 195
  5:20, 188
  5:21, 201, 227
  5–6, 195
  5–8, 200
  6:1, 188
  6:3–11, 189
  6:3–4, 203
  6:7, 190, 203, 239
  6:8, 189
  6:9, 203
  6:10, 203
  6:11, 188
  6:13, 188
  6:14, 236
  6:14–15, 237
  6:16, 192
  6:18, 192
  6:18–22, 187, 192
  6:19, 188, 193, 240
  6:22, 192
  6:22–23, 227
  7, 203
  7:1, 239
  7:5, 239
  7:6, 237
  7:12, 72, 236
  7:14, 236
  8:1, 200
  8:1–17, 205
  8:2, 193, 200, 237
  8:2–3, 200
  8:3, 201
  8:3–4, 154
  8:4, 236–237
  8:6, 204
  8:8, 203
  8:9, 203
  8:10, 190, 204
  8:11, 197, 205
  8:13, 204
  8:18–39, 205
  8:19, 205
  8:21, 193, 205
  8:23, 206
  8:29, 207, 228, 233, 241
  9:1, 180
  9:3, 164, 180
  9:4, 140
  9:4–5, 68
  9:4–5, 43
  9:5, 164, 180
  9:6, 48, 161, 177, 181, 186
  9:6–13, 180
  9:6–7, 177
  9:8, 161, 178

Index of Ancient Sources 297

9:10–13, 177
9:14–29, 48
9:23, 167
9:23–24, 182
9:24, 139
9:25, 184
9:27, 48
9:27–29, 178
9:30–10:4, 76
9:30–31, 143, 176
9:31, 48, 71–72
9:31–32, 49
9:32–33, 180
9:33, 100
9–11, 48, 143, 158, 167, 176
10:1–8, 214
10:2–3, 69
10:3, 49, 69, 178
10:4, 12, 180, 213, 226–227, 240–241
10:5, 55, 227
10:5–6, 226
10:5–8, 55
10:6–7, 180
10:9, 180
10:12, 140, 157, 208
10:16, 158
10:17, 180
10:19, 48
10:21, 48
11, 69
11:1, 138, 140, 177, 181
11:2, 48
11:5, 69
11:7, 48
11:9, 100
11:19, 47
11:21–24, 141
11:25, 48
11:25–27, 178
11:25–32, 48
11:26, 48, 179–180, 186
11:26–27, 179
11:28, 158, 181
11:29, 181, 184
11:30, 158
11:31, 158, 167
11:32, 158
12:2, 68
13:1–7, 159
13:8, 237
13:8–10, 214
13:9–10, 237
13:10, 237
14:10, 28
14:13, 100
14:17, 194, 231
15, 100
15:8, 97, 183
15:10, 184
15:18–19, 155
15:29, 100
16, 97, 100
16:4, 182
16:7, 80
16:11, 80
16:17, 100
16:17–20, 99–100
16:21, 80
16:22, 21
16:25–27, 22

Secret Gospel of Mark, 111

Sextus Empiricus, *Math.* 1.246, 38

Sibylline Oracles, 112

Sifra, Acharei Mot 9:10, 229

Sifre Numbers 158, 5

Song Rab. 8.11.2, 223

T. Reu. 5:6, 222

t. Sanh
  4:7, 212
  13:2, 145

Tertullian, *Marc.* 5.2, 32

Tertullian, *Nat.* 1.8.1, 182

Tertullian, *Res.* 60.3, 233

Tertullian, *Scorp.* 10.10, 182

Theodotus, *On the Jews*, 37

1 Thessalonians
  1:1, 21
  1:9, 48
  2:14, 182
  2:14–16, 79
  4:3–5, 144
  4:4, 67
  4:5, 124
  4:7, 144
  4:13–18, 208

2 Thessalonians
  2:2, 79

Third Isaiah, 112

Thucydides 3.62, 38

1 Timothy 80

2 Timothy 80

Titus, 80
  1:12–13, 139

Wisdom of Solomon, 15, 112
  2:12, 52
  13:1–2, 152
  13:10, 152
  14:22–27, 152

y. Ketub. 12 (34d), 239

y. Kil. 9 (32a), 239

Zechariah
  13:2, 225

Index of Modern Authors

Abegg, Martin, 58–59
Abel, Frantisek, 180
Adeyemi, Femi, 114
Adler, Yonatan, 133
Ahuvia, Mika, 221–222
Akhtar, Shabbir, 160
Akiyama, Kengo, 237
Alcoff, Linda Martin, 26
Alexander, Philip S., 56, 117–119
Allen, Michael, 114
Allison, Dale C., 7–8, 141, 174
Alviar, J. José, 226
Amir, Yehoshua, 39–40
Amis, Kingsley, 3
Anderson, Janice Capel, 151
Anderson, Sonja, 149
Arneson, Hans, 173
Aune, David E., 114, 191
Avemarie, Friedrich, 227–228
Avery-Peck, Alan J., 13, 218
Avi-Yonah, Michael, 138

Bachmann, Michael, 30, 58
Badenas, Robert, 214
Badiou, Alain, 137, 159
Baeck, Leo, 216
Baker, Cynthia M., 34
Bammel, Ernst, 216
Barber, Michael P., 17, 20
Barclay, John M. G., 14–15, 18–19, 32, 36, 60, 63–64, 73–74, 89, 99, 113, 154, 173, 177, 188, 196, 237, 239
Baron, Lori, 31
Barr, James, 114
Barrett, C. K., 61, 83, 106
Barth, Karl, 32, 51, 214
Barth, Markus, 17, 89
Barton, Carlin A., 36
Bartoš, Hynek, 74
Barzilai, Gabriel, 223

Bassler, Jouette M., 157
Bauer, Bruno, 21
Baumgarten, Albert I., 5
Baur, F. C., 21, 78, 81, 83, 90, 101, 105, 159, 242
Bauspiess, Martin, 78, 159
Baxter, Richard, 116
Bazzana, Giovanni B., 107, 131
Becker, Adam H., 28
Behr, John, 161, 231
Bekkenkamp, Jonneke, 210
Bellamy, Francis, 187, 196
Belleville, Linda L., 207
Benite, Zvi Ben-Dor, 179
Berger, Peter, 42
Berkowitz, Beth A., 33
Bernstein, Moshe J., 57
Betz, Hans Dieter, 32–33
Betz, Otto, 59
Beyer, H. W., 89
Bhabha, Homi K., 182
Bickerman, Elias J., 41, 64
Bieringer, Reimund, 29, 239
Bierma, Lyle D., 31
Billerbeck, Paul, 64, 217
Bird, Michael F., 18
Blanton, Thomas R., 83–84
Blanton, Ward, 137
Bleek, F., 89
Blosser, Benjamin P., 230
Boakye, Andrew K., 54, 229
Boccaccini, Gabriele, 17, 71, 123–125, 189
Bockmuehl, Markus, 79, 217
Bokser, Ben Zion, 160
Borgen, Peder, 61
Boring, M. Eugene, 77, 162
Bos, Abraham P., 74
Bousset, Wilhelm, 201
Boustan, Ra'anan S., 163

Bowen, Nancy R., 174
Boyarin, Daniel, 17, 31, 33, 36, 38, 77, 105, 128, 137, 159, 162, 164, 172, 179, 221, 232, 237
Brawley, Robert L., 30
Bremer, J. M., 192
Bremmer, Jan N., 185
Bromiley, Geoffrey W., 32, 193
Brown, Raymond E., 101
Brown, Robert F., 78
Brubaker, Rogers, 4
Bruce, F. F., 122
Brunk, Conrad G., 34
Buell, Denise Kimber, 3–4, 161, 182
Bühner, Ruben A., 82
Bultmann, Rudolf, 32–33, 51, 83, 96, 197, 199, 215
Burnett, David A., 207, 235
Burns, Duncan, 67
Burton, Ernest De Witt, 66
Bynum, Caroline Walker, 231
Byrne, Brendan, 100

Calvin, John, 85, 215, 240
Cameron, Ron, 7
Campbell, Douglas A., 45–46, 91, 99, 119, 121–122, 152
Campbell, William S., 13
Cancik, Hubert, 59
Caputo, John D., 26
Carleton Paget, James, 8, 106, 126, 182, 199
Carlson, Stephen C., 66
Carlyon, J. T., 198
Carnes, Natalie, 150
Carras, George P., 15
Carroll, John T., 203
Carson, D. A., 52, 56
Casey, Thomas G., 29
Castelli, Elizabeth A., 84
Cerone, Jacob N., 58, 217
Chadwick, Henry, 234–235
Chantziantoniou, Alexi, 50, 148
Charles, R. H., 130
Charles, Ronald, 9, 18
Charlesworth, James H., 1, 59
Chester, Andrew, 216–217
Chester, Stephen J., 114
Cirafesi, Wally V., 108
Cisco, Charles K., 192

Clark, Ernest P., 61–62
Cocchini, Francesca, 226
Cohen, Jeremy, 181
Cohen, Shaye J. D., 4–5, 13, 19, 31, 34, 37–38, 89, 92, 97, 105, 130, 172, 175
Collins, John J., 112, 119, 172, 208, 219, 223
Collman, Ryan D., 46, 87, 94, 99, 128, 131, 166, 169–170, 174
Concannon, Cavan W., 4, 23, 25–26, 67, 149, 158, 184, 193
Congdon, David W., 199
Cook, John Granger, 74, 223, 235
Cosgrove, Charles H., 159
Cranfield, C. E. B., 113, 121–122, 132
Cross, F. L., 216
Crossley, James, 34
Cullmann, Oscar, 8

Dahl, Nils A., 15, 48, 81, 97, 189
Davies, Jamie, 2, 190
Davies, W. D., 5, 10, 18, 29, 174, 215–217
De Boer, Martinus C., 203, 230
de Haardt, Maaike, 211
De Lange, Nicholas, 161
de Puymège, Gérard, 136
De Roo, Jacqueline C. R., 59
Decosimo, David, 192
den Dulk, Matthijs, 160
Diez Macho, Alejandro, 216
Dingeldein, Laura, 68, 150, 165, 201, 203
Dodd, C. H., 113
Doering, Lutz, 60
Donahue, Paul J., 106
Donaldson, James, 32
Donaldson, Terence L., 5, 9, 35, 45, 67, 139, 156, 159
Dorchain, Claudia Simone, 147
Downing, F. Gerald, 18
Drane, John W., 132
Draper, Jonathan A., 108
du Toit, David S., 107
Dunn, Geoffrey D., 32
Dunn, James D. G., 9, 12–13, 51–52, 58, 64, 119, 142–143, 151, 156, 215
Dunning, Benjamin H., 137, 211, 218, 231

Index of Modern Authors

East, Brad, 7
Eastman, Susan Grove, 6, 48, 167
Edsall, Benjamin, 186
Edwards, Mark Julian, 165
Ehrensperger, Kathy, 136
Ehrman, Bart D., 224–225
Eisenbaum, Pamela, 9, 11, 36, 51, 68, 70–71
Elliott, Neil, 15
Engberg-Pedersen, Troels, 10, 20, 68, 74, 85, 159, 164, 190–191, 201, 204, 206, 235
Enslin, M. S., 89
Eskola, Timo, 65
Etienne, Stephane, 113
Eubank, Nathan, 121, 126
Eyl, Jennifer, 30, 85, 92, 140, 189

Fatum, Lone, 67, 144
Feldman, Louis H., 28, 37, 74
Ferda, Tucker S., 8
Fewster, Gregory, 23
Filtvedt, Ole Jakob, 166
Fisch, Yael, 237
Fitzgerald, John T., 18
Fitzmyer, Joseph A., 202, 216
Flusser, David, 59, 89, 108, 223
Fonrobert, Charlotte, 102–103, 221
Forbes, Christopher, 84
Foster, Paul, 79–80
Fraade, Steven D., 59
Frankfurter, David, 36, 108, 175
Fredriksen, Paula, 5–9, 11, 26, 28, 32, 45, 48, 60, 71–72, 85, 100, 128, 133, 155, 158, 161, 163–164, 178, 184, 196
Freiberger, Oliver, 13
Frey, Jean-Baptiste, 39
Frey, Jörg, 58, 60, 140

Gabriele Boccaccini, 17, 71, 122, 143
Gager, John G., 5, 10, 19, 36, 71, 127, 132, 155
Gaifman, Milette, 148
Gamble, Harry, 22, 100
Garcia Martinez, Florentino, 148
Garroway, Joshua D., 12, 45, 82, 97, 104, 107, 149, 182–183, 237
Gaston, Lloyd, 2, 36, 53, 75, 215

Gathercole, Simon, 52, 55, 59, 64, 120–121, 124, 126, 177, 228, 239
Gathergood, Emily, 224
Gaventa, Beverly Roberts, 13, 125, 129, 188, 195
Georgi, Dieter, 83–85
Goldstein, David, 173
Goodblatt, David, 13
Goodman, Martin, 74, 89, 109, 113, 139
Goulder, Michael, 77
Grayston, Kenneth, 168
Greene, Graham, 113
Grobel, Kendrick, 32
Gruen, Erich S., 182, 185
Gunderson, Jaimie, 197
Gundry, Judith M., 232
Gunther, John J., 78

Haacker, Klaus, 239
Hall, Edith, 138
Hamerton-Kelly, Robert, 106
Hardin, Justin K., 45
Harding, Sarah, 218
Harker, Christina, 60
Harnack, Adolf, 31
Harper, Kyle, 144
Harrill, J. Albert, 192
Hart, David Bentley, 125
Hart, Patrick, 21, 23
Harvey, A. E., 88–89
Harvey, Graham, 161
Haufe, Christoph, 215
Hawkins, John Gale, 88–89
Hayes, Christine, 72, 130, 148, 171, 183–184, 211, 219, 221
Hays, Richard B., 53, 69, 97, 164, 195
Headlam, Arthur C., 214
Heckel, Ulrich, 29
Heidegger, Martin, 197
Heine, Ronald E., 226
Hengel, Martin, 10, 29, 35, 39, 156
Heschel, Abraham Joshua, 196
Hewitt, J. Thomas, 123, 185, 190
Hilhorst, A., 148
Hills, Julian V., 214
Himmelfarb, Martha, 13, 41, 223, 232
Hirsch, E., 89
Hockey, Katherine M., 4
Hodge, Caroline Johnson, 4, 167, 184

Hodgson, Peter C., 78
Hoklotubbe, T. Christopher, 72
Holladay, Carl R., 18
Hollander, Dana, 232
Hollander, H. W., 201
Holleman, Joost, 6, 201
Holmes, Peter, 32
Holob, Kelly, 81
Hooker, Morna D., 61, 80, 151
Horbury, William, 106, 217, 225
Horky, Phillip Sidney, 74
Horn, F. W., 201
Horrell, David G., 4
Hoskyns, Edwyn C., 51
Hübner, Hans, 35
Hultgren, Arland J., 43
Hultin, Jeremy, 141
Huttunen, Niko, 15

Inwood, Brad, 129
Isaac, Benjamin, 3, 156
Israelstam, J., 238

Jackson, Bernard, 116–117, 119
Jackson-McCabe, Matt, 101
Jacobs, Andrew S., 102, 161, 174
Jacobson, Howard, 142
Jaquette, James, 129
Jervis, L. Ann, 2
Jewett, Robert, 44, 100, 169
Johnson, Luke Timothy, 22
Johnson, Nathan C., 164
Johnson-DeBaufre, Melanie, 15, 24–25, 81
Jones, F. Stanley, 109

Kabisch, Richard, 6
Kahl, Brigitte, 137
Kaminsky, Joel S., 177
Kampen, John, 57
Käsemann, Ernst, 83, 193, 214
Keck, Leander E., 202
Kennedy, H. A. A., 198–199, 203
Kim, David Haekwon, 136
Kincaid, John, 18
King, Colin Guthrie, 74
Kipling, Rudyard, 2–3, 27
Kister, Menahem J., 142
Klawans, Jonathan, 34, 164, 238
Klijn, A. F. J., 95, 168, 224

Knight, Harold, 216
Knox, John, 100, 122
Knox, Wilfred, 235
Knust, Jennifer W., 127, 144
Koester, Helmut, 101
Koetschau, Paul, 233
Kohen, Eliyahu, 209–211, 213, 235, 237, 241
Kohler, Kaufmann, 16
Kraft, Robert A., 103, 106
Kraftchick, Steven John, 198
Kreitzer, L. Joseph, 6
Krostenko, Brian A., 37
Kugel, James L., 119, 229
Kuss, Otto, 122
Kwon, Yon-Gyong, 6

Laato, Timo, 5, 29, 239
Ladd, G. E., 8
Lambrecht, Jan, 239
Landau, Brent C., 111
Landmesser, Christof, 78, 159
Lang, T. J., 7
Langford, Andrew M., 80
Langton, Daniel R., 17, 118
Lapidot, Elad, 147
Larsen, Matthew D. C., 92
Lee, Yongbom, 59
Lemke, Werner E., 174
Levine, Amy-Jill, 136
Levine, Lee I., 39
Levtow, Nathaniel B., 148
Levy, Ariel, 136
Libson, Ayelet Hoffmann, 229
Liddell, Erik, 50
Lietzmann, Hans, 40, 88, 122
Lieu, Judith, 182
Lim, Timothy H., 53
Limor, Ora, 161
Lincicum, David, 12, 78
Linebaugh, Jonathan A., 6, 14–15, 67, 69, 114, 153, 192, 215
Lipka, Hilary, 128
Litwa, David, 86, 198, 205, 236
Loewe, H. M. J., 118
Longarino, Joseph, 195, 202, 217, 229
Longenecker, Bruce W., 14–15
Longenecker, Richard N., 113–114, 116, 121, 215
Lössl, Josef, 127–128

Index of Modern Authors

Lowe, Malcolm, 34
Luckensmeyer, David, 7
Lüdemann, Gerd, 5, 29, 77, 91, 168
Lütgert, Wilhelm, 84
Luther, Martin, 30, 32, 51–52
Luz, Ulrich, 228
Lyonnet, S. J., 202

Maccoby, Hyam, 19
Magid, Shaul, 209
Manheim, Ralph, 201
Marcovich, Miroslav, 161
Marmorstein, A., 39
Marshall, John W., 108
Martin, Dale B., 10, 67, 115, 127, 141, 145, 151, 158, 163, 190, 201, 204, 231
Martyn, J. Louis, 33, 44, 46, 77, 164
Mason, Steve, 9, 12, 26, 31, 33–34, 38, 40, 42–43, 140, 196
Maston, Jason, 239
Matlock, R. Barry, 7, 67, 122, 139, 186
Mbiti, John S., 6
McCaulley, Esau, 229
McDonald, Denys, 123
McGlothlin, Thomas D., 190
McGrath, Alister E., 51
McGuckin, J. A., 226, 230
McLaren, James S., 67
McMurray, Patrick, 184
McNamara, Martin, 56
Metzger, Bruce M., 1, 66
Meyer, Paul W., 203
Michaelis, W., 89, 101
Michel, Otto, 228
Miller, Chaim, 225
Miller, David M., 33
Miller, Merrill P., 7
Mitchell, Margaret M., 23–24, 144
Moffatt, James, 201
Moll, Sebastian, 31
Monnickendam, Yifat, 220
Montague, W. J., 193
Montefiore, C. G., 118
Montgomery, William, 10, 12
Moore, George Foot, 118, 210, 221
Moore, Stephen D., 151, 198
Moore-Gilbert, Bart, 3
Mor, Menachem, 227
Morales, Isaac, 123

Moss, Candida R., 21, 223, 225, 232–233
Moxnes, Halvor, 67
Mroczek, Eva, 212–213, 241
Muir, Alexander, 15
Munck, Johannes, 88–91, 110, 166
Murray, Michele, 104–105

Nanos, Mark D., 9, 12, 17, 29, 77, 93, 170, 180
Nasrallah, Laura S., 15, 21, 24–25, 81
Neander, A., 89
Neis, Rafael, 115–116, 119
Neusner, Jacob, 15, 118
Neutel, Karin, 94, 97, 158, 185, 231
Nickelsburg, George W. E., 224
Niese, Benedikt, 42
Nikki, Nina, 168
Noam, Vered, 5, 57
Nock, Arthur Darby, 73
Nongbri, Brent, 14, 21, 36
Norton, Jonathan, 186
Novenson, Matthew V., 7, 9, 11–12, 29, 49, 67, 69, 82, 87, 92, 107, 119, 124, 133, 140, 143, 145, 148, 150, 156, 158, 167, 172, 185, 194, 207, 215, 219, 241

O'Hagan, Angelo P., 224
Ogden, Schubert M., 199
Öhler, Markus, 200
Økland, Jorunn, 208
Oliver, Isaac W., 143
Ophir, Adi, 4, 140, 147
Oropeza, B. J., 207
Oudshoorn, Daniel, 7

Parks, Sara, 107
Pastor, Jack, 227
Patmore, Hector M., 127–128
Paul, Shalom M., 112
Pearson, Birger A., 79, 84–85
Pedersen, S., 61
Petrey, Taylor G., 211, 223, 225, 232–233
Petroelje, Benjamin, 21, 80
Pfleiderer, Otto, 132
Pitre, Brant, 17–18
Pitts, Andrew W., 139
Plevnik, Joseph, 6
Plumer, Eric, 32

Poliakov, Leon, 119
Pollefeyt, Didier, 29
Porter, Stanley E., 78, 139

Qimron, Elisha, 57

Rabens, Volker, 204
Rahlfs, Alfred, 37–38
Räisänen, Heikki, 117, 211, 215, 236
Reed, Annette Yoshiko, 28, 34, 101–102, 109, 207
Reinhartz, Adele, 15, 34, 108
Remington, Megan R., 222
Rey, Jean-Sebastien, 20
Richardson, Peter, 89
Riches, John, 30
Rillera, Andrew R., 62, 170
Rim, Manse, 70, 193–194
Roberts, Alexander, 32
Roberts, Sam, 188
Robinson, James M., 101
Robinson, Joanne Maguire, 196
Robinson, Jonathan Rivett, 231
Rodriguez, Rafael, 98
Roetzel, Calvin, 17
Rogerson, J. W., 67
Rokeah, David, 160
Rollens, Sarah E., 107
Ronis, Sara, 128
Ropes, J. H., 89
Rorty, Richard, 77
Rosenstein, Marc, 196
Rosen-Zvi, Ishay, 4, 140, 147
Rothschild, Clare, 107
Runesson, Anders, 11, 15

Sabar, Ariel, 111
Said, Edward W., 3
Saldarini, Anthony J., 238
Sanday, William, 214
Sanders, E. P., 5, 8, 15, 18, 29, 48–49, 54, 64, 73, 116, 118–119, 125, 146, 167, 181, 216–217, 226
Sandmel, Samuel, 62–63, 216–217
Sandnes, Karl Olav, 169
Sanfridson, Martin, 149
Satlow, Michael L., 19, 89
Schäfer, Peter, 215–217, 222
Schechter, Solomon, 118
Schiffman, Lawrence H., 223

Schliesser, Benjamin, 54, 228
Schmithals, Walter, 100
Schnelle, Udo, 162
Schoeps, Hans-Joachim, 216
Scholem, Gershom, 201, 209–210, 212
Schott, H. A., 89
Schreiner, Thomas R., 215
Schremer, Adiel, 33
Schrenk, Gottlob, 48
Schultz, Joseph P., 222
Schüssler Fiorenza, Elisabeth, 84
Schwartz, Daniel R., 34, 140, 228
Schwartz, Seth, 33
Schweitzer, Albert, 7, 10, 12, 25, 74, 126, 129, 131, 181, 189, 197–199, 207, 216, 241
Scott, Alan, 223, 231
Scroggs, Robin, 106
Sechrest, Love, 17
Segal, Alan, 18, 30
Segovia, Carlos A., 17
Seim, Turid Karlsen, 208, 210
Shanks, Hershel, 57
Sharp, Matthew T., 127, 149, 155, 158, 163
Sheridan, Ruth, 34
Sherwood, Yvonne, 198
Shneuri, Dov Ber, 225
Shogren, Gary Steven, 231
Siegal, Michal Bar-Asher, 93, 148
Silver, Abba Hillel, 216
Sim, David C., 67
Simon, Marcel, 161
Skinner, Joseph E., 138
Sloan, Paul T., 98, 175
Smit, Peter-Ben, 94
Smith, Geoffrey S., 111
Smith, Jonathan Z., 13, 16, 19, 199
Smith, Julianna Kaye, 222
Smith, Morton, 189, 218
Smith, Wilfred Cantwell, 50
Snyder, Glenn, 138
Soon, Isaac, 46, 94, 107
Soulen, R. Kendall, 49
Speccher, Tommaso, 147
Spinoza, Baruch, 25
Sprinkle, Preston M., 5, 59, 228, 239
Stanley, Christopher D., 15, 53, 137, 139
Staples, Jason A., 69, 93, 164, 167, 174, 179–180

Steely, John E., 31
Stendahl, Krister, 7, 43, 49, 123, 180
Sterling, Gregory E., 124, 153
Stern, Sacha, 181
Still, Todd D., 32, 176
Stone, Michael E., 217
Stout, Jeffrey, 13, 192
Stowers, Stanley K., 7, 26, 36, 47, 67–68, 73–74, 96–97, 141, 153, 165, 180, 188, 190, 195, 197–201, 204, 206–207
Strack, Hermann L., 64, 217
Strawn, Brent A., 174
Strecker, Georg, 103, 109
Stroumsa, Guy G., 161, 233
Strugnell, John, 57
Sullivan, Kevin Patrick, 223
Sumney, Jerry L., 78, 80, 83, 151, 171
Sundstrom, Ronald R., 136
Sussman, Robert Wald, 3
Swancutt, Diana, 151

Tamez, Elsa, 241
Tatum, Gregory, 15, 236
Taubes, Jacob, 232
Taylor, Joan, 34, 101, 104
Taylor, Justin, 29
Thackeray, Henry St. John, 5
Thiessen, Matthew, 4–5, 9, 15–16, 19, 45, 52–53, 71, 74–75, 82, 88, 90, 93, 95, 98, 113, 128, 130, 153, 164, 170–171, 173, 175, 183–184, 206
Thompson, James W., 239
Thorsteinsson, Runar M., 70, 98, 175
Thrall, Margaret, 84
Tofighi, Fatima, 137, 199
Tomson, Peter J., 127, 239
Tooth, Sydney, 7, 79, 180
Torjesen, Karen Jo, 226
Torrance, T. F., 32
Tov, Emanuel, 112
Trebilco, Paul, 186
Trench, Richard Chenevix, 116
Trivedi, Harish, 3

Ullucci, Daniel C., 11

Vaage, Leif E., 210
Valdez, Jason, 204
Van den Berghe, Pierre L., 156

van Henten, Jan Willem, 39–40
van Kooten, George H., 139, 148, 182, 240
Vander Stichele, Caroline, 210
VanderKam, James C., 112
Vermes, Geza, 57, 112, 217
Voltaire, 50, 76
von Soden, Hermann, 201
Vos, Geerhardus, 6–7

Wagner, J. Ross, 97, 176, 183
Walker, William O., 22
Wasserman, Emma, 68, 100, 165, 201, 203
Wasserman, Mira Beth, 147
Watson, Francis, 45, 54–55, 86, 95–96, 169
Weber, Ferdinand, 118
Weissenberg, Hanne von, 57
Weizsäcker, K. H., 89
Welborn, Larry, 86
Wells, Bruce, 128
Wells, Kyle B., 174
Wendt, Heidi, 84
Werblowsky, R. J. Zwi, 201
Westerholm, Stephen, 117, 193–194, 196, 226, 239
Wheeler-Reed, David, 127, 144
Wheelwright, John, 115
White, B. G., 19
White, Benjamin L., 21
White, L. Michael, 197
Wilckens, Ulrich, 122, 215
Wilhite, David E., 32
Wilk, Florian, 176
Wilken, Robert L., 6
Williams, A. Lukyn, 161
Williams, Bernard, 159
Williams, Demetrius K., 168
Williams, Logan, 194, 212, 238
Williams, Margaret H., 39
Williams, Sam K., 194
Wilson, Annalisa Phillips, 129, 165
Wilson, Stephen G., 61, 106
Wimbush, Vincent L., 210
Windischmann, F., 89
Windsor, Lionel J., 98, 175
Winninge, Mikael, 239
Winter, Sean F., 67
Wire, Antoinette Clark, 85

Wolfson, Harry Austryn, 113
Wollenberg, Rebecca Scharbach, 211–213
Wright, Benjamin G., 146
Wright, N. T., 8–9, 11, 51, 58, 66, 69, 137, 155, 162, 170, 172, 174, 176, 179
Wyschogrod, Michael, 49

Yee, Tet-Lim N., 140
Yinger, Kent L., 64, 114–115

Young, James O., 34
Young, Stephen L., 68–69, 158, 179

Zahn, Theodor, 202
Zellentin, Holger M., 60
Zetterholm, Karin Hedner, 67, 109
Zetterholm, Magnus, 9, 12, 29
Ziegler, Philip G., 198
Zuntz, Günther, 66

For EU product safety concerns, contact us at Calle de José Abascal, 56–1°, 28003 Madrid, Spain or eugpsr@cambridge.org.

www.ingramcontent.com/pod-product-compliance
Lightning Source LLC
LaVergne TN
LVHW041206250326
834689LV00002BA/35